Lecture Notes in Computer Science   9535

Commenced Publication in 1973
Founding and Former Series Editors:
Gerhard Goos, Juris Hartmanis, and Jan van Leeuwen

Editorial Board

More information about this series at http://www.springer.com/series/7407

Harald Atmanspacher · Thomas Filk
Emmanuel Pothos (Eds.)

Quantum Interaction

9th International Conference, QI 2015
Filzbach, Switzerland, July 15–17, 2015
Revised Selected Papers

 Springer

Editors
Harald Atmanspacher
ETH Zurich
Zurich
Switzerland

Thomas Filk
University of Freiburg
Freiburg
Germany

Emmanuel Pothos
City University London
London
UK

ISSN 0302-9743   ISSN 1611-3349 (electronic)
Lecture Notes in Computer Science
ISBN 978-3-319-28674-7   ISBN 978-3-319-28675-4   (eBook)
DOI 10.1007/978-3-319-28675-4

Library of Congress Control Number: 2015959920

LNCS Sublibrary: SL1 – Theoretical Computer Science and General Issues

Printed on acid-free paper

This Springer imprint is published by SpringerNature
The registered company is Springer International Publishing AG Switzerland

Preface

Since its inception in 2007, the conference series on Quantum Interaction is now a tradition in its own right. This year's ninth meeting within the series took place at the Conferene Center Lihn (Filzbach, Switzerland), the same exciting environment as the year before, close to Lake Walensee and the Glarner Alps, during July 15–17, 2015. It was co-hosted by Collegium Helveticum, an interdisciplinary research institute jointly operated by the University of Zurich and the Swiss Federal Institute of Technology (ETH) at Zurich, and by the International Society for Mind-Matter Research.

The title of the conference, Quantum Interaction, refers to the study of cognitive processes using mathematical tools that are inspired by quantum theory, e.g., non-commutative operations, Bell-type inequalities, contextuality, etc. In this sense quantum interaction is not to be understood in terms of interactions between particles or fields as in quantum physics. It is also not intended to address perception, cognition, and consciousness in general at the level of neuronal processes. Quantum interaction attempts to describe cognitive processes at the level at which they actually occur: psychology and cognitive science.

The Quantum Interaction conferences have provided a debating ground for foundational and applied issues and have developed into an emerging interdisciplinary area of science, combining research topics in mathematics, physics, psychology, economics, cognitive science, and computer science. The breadth reflected in this list of disciplines remains a challenge for a coherent framework in which all the different approaches find their systematic place.

The presentations at this year's Quantum Interaction conference covered seven thematic fields: (1) fundamental issues, (2) contextuality and correlations, (3) decision making, (4) complementarity, (5) social and cultural applications, (6) semantic representations, and (7) operators and operator-valued measures. Two distinguished keynote speakers, Alexei Grinbaum (Saclay Research Center, Gif-sur-Yvette) and Ioannis Antoniou (Aristotle University of Thessaloniki) added exciting novel research directions.

Grinbaum's contribution addresses the issue of correlations that apparently violate Bell-type inequalities and yet are of no conclusive quantum origin. The contributions by Dzhafarov and colleagues expand on this theme and suggest a quasi-classical correlation term (due to signaling) that needs to be subtracted from the measured correlations before evidence for nonlocal quantum correlations can be claimed. This development represents a truly novel step toward understanding quantum and post-quantum correlations in non-physical systems.

The work presented by Antoniou is based on decades of previous research on mixing and chaotic systems that started with Gustafson, Misra, and Prigogine in the 1970s. A key point in this approach is a time operator that does not commute with a Liouville operator generating the dynamics of such systems. In an appropriately defined innovation space, this time operator gives rise to an "eigentime" that can be related to the "age" of a system. In recent work, these topics have been extended to the study of networks.

The 22 papers included in this volume are based on the contributions to the conference. Each one of them was assessed by at least two reviewers and revised according to their comments. We are grateful to all members of the Program Committee for their hard work and timely delivery of reports. In an interdisciplinary area like this one, careful and accurate reviews are certainly not a matter of course.

We are grateful for the splendid hospitality we experienced at the Lihn and thank Hannes Hochuli and his staff for their sensitive cooperation in matters large and small, ensuring the success of the conference. Alfred Hofmann and Anna Kramer at Springer provided helpful advice for the smooth and speedy publication of the proceedings in the Springer series *Lecture Notes in Computer Science*. And, last but not least, we thank Gerd Folkers, director at Collegium Helveticum, for his invaluable support.

December 2015   Harald Atmanspacher
                                                              Thomas Filk
                                                         Emmanuel Pothos

Organization

Steering Committee

Peter Bruza	Queensland University of Technology, Brisbane, Australia
Trevor Cohen	University of Texas at Houston, USA
Bob Coecke	Oxford University, UK
Ariane Lambert-Mogiliansky	Paris School of Economics, France
Dominic Widdows	Microsoft Inc., Seattle, USA

General Chair

Harald Atmanspacher	Collegium Helveticum Zurich, Switzerland

Program Chairs

Thomas Filk	University of Freiburg, Germany
Emmanuel Pothos	City University London, UK

Program Committee

Harald Atmanspacher	Collegium Helveticum Zurich, Switzerland
Irina Basieva	Linnaeus University, Växjö, Sweden
Reinhard Blutner	University of Amsterdam, The Netherlands
Peter Bruza	Queensland University of Technology, Brisbane, Australia
Trevor Cohen	University of Texas at Houston, USA
Thomas Filk	University of Freiburg, Germany
Peter beim Graben	Humboldt University, Berlin, Germany
Emmanuel Haven	University of Leicester, UK
Andrei Khrennikov	Linnaeus University, Växjö, Sweden
Kirsty Kitto	Queensland University of Technology, Brisbane, Australia
Ariane Lambert-Mogiliansky	Paris School of Economics, France
Bill Lawless	Paine College, Augusta, USA
Massimo Melucci	University of Padova, Italy
Emmanuel Pothos	City University London, UK
Mcernoosh Sadrzadeh	Oxford University, UK
Sonja Smets	University of Amsterdam, The Netherlands

Sandro Sozzo	University of Leicester, UK
Jennifer Trueblood	Vanderbilt University, Nashville, USA
Giuseppe Vitiello	University of Salerno, Italy
Dominic Widdows	Microsoft Inc., Seattle, USA
James Yearsley	City University London, UK

Website

| Claudia Bergomi | University Hospital of Psychiatry, Bern, Switzerland |

Contents

Contextuality and Correlations

Quantum Correlations: Challenging the Tsirelson Bound

Alexei Grinbaum[(✉)]

CEA-Saclay/IRFU/LARSIM, 91191 Gif-sur-Yvette, France
alexei.grinbaum@cea.fr

Abstract. A detailed study of quantum correlations reveals that reconstructions based on physical principles often fail to reproduce the quantum bound in the general case of N-partite correlations. We read here an indication that the notion of system, implicitly assumed in the operational approaches, becomes problematic. Our approach addresses this issue using algebraic coding theory. If the observer is defined by a limit on string complexity, information dynamics leads to an emergent continuous model in the critical regime. Restricting it to a family of binary codes describing 'bipartite systems,' we find strong evidence of an upper bound on bipartite correlations equal to 2.82537, which is measurably lower than the Tsirelson bound.

1 Mathematics Guides Understanding

A large swath of new research in the foundations of quantum theory addresses the problem of correlations between distant parties. It had been known since the "second quantum revolution" started by John Bell [3] that the amount of correlations is a decisive quantity distinguishing between local (classical) and nonlocal physical theories. However, it was only noticed quite recently that the amount of correlations or, more broadly, quantum bounds in Bell inequalities are, by themselves, a formidable puzzle through which, once we are able to understand it better, we may get an entirely new understanding of quantum theory.

Quantum logical reconstructions have reached their peak when George Mackey and, later, Constantin Piron gave examples of mathematical derivations of the Hilbert space formalism from an orthomodular lattice with additional assumptions [18,26]. After a decline of two decades, operational reconstructions of quantum theory took over from quantum logic around the turn of the century. Finite-dimensional Hilbert spaces came into focus of these reconstructions as a result of the development of quantum information. To derive the Hilbert space, one posits several physical principles that are given a mathematical formulation with the operation framework [5,15,22]. Such reconstructions contain an important insight: an assumption of continuity is a necessary, but not a sufficient, ingredient of quantum mechanical axiomatic systems. Differently worded continuity assumptions exist in every reconstruction [16,32]: a prominent representative is the existence of a continuous reversible transformation between any

© Springer International Publishing Switzerland 2016
H. Atmanspacher et al. (Eds.): QI 2015, LNCS 9535, pp. 3–11, 2016.
DOI: 10.1007/978-3-319-28675-4_1

two pure states of the system [8]. On their own, however, these assumptions are insufficient for reconstructing quantum theory, as demonstrated by C^*-algebraic approaches [7]. Moreover, quantum theory has emerged from the reconstruction program [13], not only as a description of individual systems with continuous state spaces, but also requiring an extra axiom about how such systems compose [29]. This insight must be complemented with a quantitative bound on the amount of correlations given by the Bell inequalities and explored in postquantum models [2,30,31]. There exists a fundamental fact about nature: the amount of correlations between distant subsystems is limited by a non-classical bound, e.g., the Tsirelson bound for bipartite correlations [6]. All mathematical alternatives to the Hilbert space formalism must strive to predict its empirical value.

Reaching the Tsirelson bound of the CHSH inequality is not yes sufficient for a complete reconstruction of quantum mechanics. Various attempts to characterize this boundary have led, in particular, to the understanding that no bipartite principle on how two systems compose can fully characterize the quantum bound [12]. Further, many principles developed in the reconstruction program [4,11,17,25] were shown to be satisfied by a set of correlations which is larger than the quantum set [24]. This line of research, then, though stemming from the reconstructions, comes to invalidate most, if not all, of the desiderata on which the latter are built [23].

In our view, this points to a staggering evolution: the notion of system may not be an essential building block of quantum theory. Like other formerly unquestionable fundamental concepts in physics, a 'system' is now amenable to analysis and derivation. One is trying to imagine a quantum theory without systems. In Sect. 2 we introduce a framework based on the algebraic coding theory. It provides a general model of communication and deals mathematically with errors or ambiguity. The use of coding theory is enabled by the definition of observer in information-theoretic terms introduced in Sect. 3. It involves a limit on the complexity of strings, which (to use a common-language expression) the observer can 'store and handle'. Strings contain all descriptions of states allowed by quantum theory but also much more: they need not refer to systems or be interpretable in terms of preparations or measurements. Using the work of Manin and Marcolli, we show that symbolic dynamics on such strings leads to an emergent continuous model in the critical regime (Sect. 4). Restricting this model to a subfamily of 'quantum' binary codes describing 'bipartite systems' (Sect. 5), we find strong evidence of an upper bound on bipartite correlations equal to 2.82537. The difference between this number and the Tsirelson bound $2\sqrt{2}$ can be tested. The Hilbert space formalism, then, emerges from this mathematical approach as an effective description of a fundamental discrete theory of 'quantum' languages in the critical regime, somewhat similarly to the description of phase transitions by the effective Landau theory.

2   Codes

Communication implies that messages are encoded and transmitted in suitable codes using an alphabet shared between the parties involved in communication.

An alphabet is a finite set A of cardinality $q \geq 2$. A code is a subset $C \subset A^n$ consisting of some of the words of length $n \geq 1$. A language is an ensemble of codes of different lengths using the same alphabet. As an example, take binary codes of length n based on a two-letter alphabet, say, $\{0, 1\}$. Strings of zeros and ones of arbitrary length belong to a language formed by binary codes with different values of n.

In full generality, nothing can be stipulated about message semantics, material support of the encoding and decoding operations or their practical efficiency. One can observe, however, that decoding a message is less prone to error if the number of words in the code is small. On the other hand, reducing the number of code words requires the words to be longer. The number

$$R = \frac{\log_q \#C}{n} \tag{1}$$

is called the (transmission) rate of code C.

One can associate a fractal to any code in the following way [20,21]. Define a rarified interval $(0, 1)_q = [0, 1] \setminus \{m/q^n | m, n \in \mathbb{Z}\}$. Points $x = (x_1, \ldots, x_n) \in (0, 1)_q^n$ can be identified with $(\infty \times n)$ matrices whose k-th column is the q-ary decomposition of x_k. For a code C define $S_C \subset (0, 1)_q^n$ as the set of all matrices with rows in C. It is a Sierpinski fractal and its Hausdorff dimension is R. The closure of S_C inside the cube $[0, 1]^n$ includes the rational points with q-ary digits. This new fractal $\hat{S}_C$ is a metric space in the induced topology from $[0, 1]^n$. Now consider a family of codes C_r of $\#C_r = q^{k_r}$ words of length n_r, with rates:

$$\frac{k_r}{n_r} \nearrow R. \tag{2}$$

They define a fractal $S_R = \bigcup_r S_{C_r}$ of Hausdorff dimension $\dim_H(S_R) = R$.

3   Bounded Complexity

Any observer's memory is limited in size. While their material constitution may be radically different, different observers with the same memory size should demonstrate similar performance in handling information. This intuition serves as a motivation for the following information-theoretic definition of observer.

Definition. An observer is a subset of strings of bounded complexity, i.e., strings compressible below a certain threshold.

This limit can be viewed as the length of observer's memory. If a string has high complexity, it cannot describe an observer with a memory smaller that the minimal length required to store it; but it remains admissible for an observer with a larger memory.

The definition of observer requires a notion of string complexity independent of the observer's material organization. Kolmogorov complexity is a suitable candidate, for it strives to grasp complexity in a machine-independent way. For a set of strings that are code words of code C with rate R, the lower Kolmogorov complexity satisfies [20]:

$$\sup_{x \in \hat{S}_C} \kappa(x) = R. \tag{3}$$

For all words $x \in S_R$ in a language formed by codes C_r, the lower Kolmogorov complexity is bounded by $\kappa(x) \leq R$. Hence the closure $\hat{S}_R$ of the fractal S_R is a metric space that describes the handling of words of bounded Kolmogorov complexity. It is a 'minimal' geometric structure corresponding to the notion of observer.

4   Critical Language Dynamics

A change in the observer's information can be modeled via dynamical evolution on the fractal set S_R. In quantum theory, new information enters when a projective or a POVM measurement produce a new string in the observer's memory. Taking inspiration from Manin and Marcolli [20], we represent this process as a statistical mechanical system evolving on the set of all possible strings in codes C_r. A change in the observer's information corresponds to a change in the 'occupation numbers' λ_a of words $a \in \bigcup_r C_r$. The evolution of λ_a is described via Hamiltonian dynamics on the Fock space:

$$H_{stat}\epsilon_{a_1 \ldots a_m} = (\lambda_{a_1} + \ldots + \lambda_{a_m})\epsilon_{a_1 \ldots a_m}, \tag{4}$$

with the Keane 'ergodicity' condition:

$$\sum_{a \in \bigcup_r C_r} e^{-R\lambda_a} = 1, \tag{5}$$

where vectors $\epsilon_{a_1 \ldots a_m}$ belong to the Fock space representation $l^2(W(\bigcup_r C_r))$ of the set W of all words in the codes C_r. To be precise, the Fock space is a representation of the algebra defined below in (7); at this stage it is justified by the completeness of W, which by construction includes all possible observer information states. If the observer's information remains within W, then the Keane condition gives a meaning to the weights λ_a as normalized logarithms of inverse probabilities that a is stored in the observer's memory. This evolution has a partition function:

$$Z(\beta) = \cfrac{1}{1 - \sum\limits_{a \in \bigcup_r C_r} e^{-\beta\lambda_a}}. \tag{6}$$

Manin and Marcolli show that at the critical temperature (equivalently, string complexity) $\beta = R$, the behaviour of this system is given by a KMS state on an algebra respecting unitarity [20]. This algebra is built out of a geometric object, namely the fractal $\hat{S}_C$, as follows. Consider characteristic functions $\chi_{\hat{S}_C(w)}$, where $w = w_1 \ldots w_m$ runs over finite words composed of $w_i \in C$ and $\hat{S}_C(w)$ denotes the subset of infinite words $x \in \hat{S}_C$ that begin with w. These functions can be identified with the range projections

$$P_w = T_w T_w^* = T_{w_1} \ldots T_{w_m} T_{w_m}^* \ldots T_{w_1}^*. \tag{7}$$

At the low temperature $\beta > R$ there exists a unique type I_∞ KMS-state ϕ_R on the statistical system of codes, which is a Toeplitz-Cuntz algebra with time evolution:

$$\sigma_t(T_w) = q^{itn} T_w. \tag{8}$$

The partition function is:

$$Z_C(\beta) = (1 - q^{(R-\beta)n})^{-1}. \tag{9}$$

However, the isometries in the algebra do not add up to unity. Only at the critical temperature $\beta = R$, where a phase transition occurs for all codes C_r, is there a unique KMS state on the Cuntz algebra, i.e., an algebra such that, importantly for our argument, isometries add up to unity: $\sum_a T_a T_a^* = 1$.

Critical behavior of the original discrete linguistic model is described at $\beta = R$ by a field theory on the metric space $\hat{S}_R$, which obeys unitarity. By construction, this fractal also has scaling symmetry. This yields a field theory respecting scaling and unitarity. While there has been some discussion of models that are scale invariant but not conformal, we assume that, in agreement with Polyakov's general conjecture [28], this field theory is conformal. The field it describes is clearly an emergent phenomenon, for its underlying dynamics is given in terms of codes. However, within the conformal field theory this field, now a basic object, is to be considered fundamental. Due to the properties of continuity, unitarity and to the geometric character of its state space, the conformal model becomes a tentative candidate for a reconstruction of quantum theory.

5 Amount of Correlations

Since quaternionic quantum mechanics or, in some limited cases, real-number quantum mechanics can be represented in the Hilbert space [1], one should expect that continuity and unitarity alone do not single out quantum theory. In other words, the conformal model of Sect. 4 likely contains more than a description of 'quantum' languages. In this section, we do not seek to provide a necessary and sufficient condition that selects only code words generated by quantum theory. Rather, we pick out a particular example, namely a class of models corresponding to the critical regime of binary codes describing measurements on bipartite quantum systems in the usual 3-dimensional Euclidean space.

First we define an informational analog of 'bipartite.' In quantum theory, subsystems that are entangled can be materially different but they are described by the same number of entangled degrees of freedom. Their informational content is represented by strings of identical complexity. For example, measurements in a

CHSH-type experiment produce binary strings of results for a choice of $\sigma_x, \sigma_y, \sigma_z$ measurements. The no-signalling condition implies that the probability of 0 on Alice's side is independent of Bob's settings, and vice versa. Hence the strings resemble Bernoulli distributions with a Kolmogorov complexity equal to the binary entropy of the probability of 0, plus a correction due to the existence of non-zero mutual information between Alice's and Bob's outputs. Since both sides enter symmetrically in the CHSH inequality, this correction to Kolmogorov complexity is *a priori* the same on Alice's and Bob's sides. We use this argument to replace Eq. (4) with a class of Hamiltonians assumed to describe a 'bipartite system' in the framework of codes.

The Kolmogorov order is an arrangement of words $a_i \in \bigcup_r C_r$ in the increasing order of complexity [19]. It is not computable and it differs radically from any numbering of a_i based on the Hamming distance in the codes C_r. Words that are adjacent in the Kolmogorov order have similar complexity. We now select an Ising-type Hamiltonian:

$$H_2 = -\sum_{ij} a_i \times a_j, \tag{10}$$

as a dynamical model on the language that describes bipartite quantum systems. The sum is taken over N neighbors in the Kolmogorov order, i.e. all strings of identical complexity. The result of multiplication on binary words is a new word with letters isomorphic to multiplication results in a two-element group $\{\pm 1\}$. Hence, for a two-letter alphabet $\{a, b\}$,

$$a \times a = b \times b = b, \quad a \times b = b \times a = a. \tag{11}$$

A binary language with $N = 6$ using H_2 gives rises to information dynamics which is, on the one hand, equivalent to information dynamics of a bipartite quantum system and, on the other hand, equivalent to the dynamics of a 3-dim Ising model. This is because a class of Hamiltonians with $N = 6$ has the same number of terms as in three spatial dimensions, although the codes that belong to this class are uncomputable due to the properties of Kolmogorov complexity. Plainly, one cannot tell which binary codes give rise to the $N = 6$ situation nor should one expect that Hamiltonians H_{stat} and H_2 belong to the same universality class. However, the equivalence of (10) with a 3-dim Ising model suggests that, just like the Ising model itself, the Hamiltonian H_2 also exhibits critical behaviour described by a conformal field theory.

As it is usually the case in statistical mechanics, the critical regime can be studied without knowing the details of the dynamics. Correlations of order 2 in this regime are described by the lowest-dimensional even primary scalar $\epsilon = \sigma \times \sigma$ in the conformal field theory. This field is symmetric; hence it provides a good candidate to describe the symmetry of bipartite correlations in the CHSH inequality under the switch between Alice and Bob. Following the above intuition, we assume that it provides a description of 'bipartiteness' within the conformal model. The operator dimension of ϵ is

$$\Delta_\epsilon = 3 - \frac{1}{\nu}, \tag{12}$$

where ν is a well-known critical exponent describing the correlation length [9].

The 3-dim Ising equivalence has its limitations since the true metric space of code evolution is not flat space but the fractal $\hat{S}_C$. Still, it provides significant evidence that H_2 has a critical regime. Further, the exponential character of the mapping that links the fractal embedded in the unit cube with flat Euclidean space hints at the existence of a connection between the critical behaviours of the Ising model and the code. The correlation length in the fractal representation of a language describes a logarithmic distance in $\hat{S}_C$ from which words are brought in groups of equal complexity by the Kolmogorov reordering. If H_2 exhibits a critical behaviour similar to that of H_{stat}, then correlations in the critical regime at string complexity $\beta = R$ come from the entire fractal. The Ising analogy with the scaling of the correlator of the lowest primary even field suggests a power law for the amount of correlations on the words of equal complexity:

$$\langle \epsilon(a)\epsilon(0) \rangle \sim a^{-2\Delta_\epsilon}. \tag{13}$$

We conjecture that, due to the exponential mapping between spaces, the corresponding correlations in the fractal are limited by the logarithm of the RHS of (13). Their maximum strength $2\Delta_\epsilon$ can be computed based on the value $\nu = 0.62999(5)$ in [10]:

$$2\Delta_\epsilon = 2.82537(2). \tag{14}$$

An attempt to test the difference between this value and the Tsirelson bound is currently in progress [14,27].

6 Conclusion

Historically, quantum logical reconstructions of quantum theory drive home the importance of the assumptions of continuity and composition rule. These are two pillars of quantum theory. A detailed study of quantum correlations reveals, however, that reconstructions based on physical principles often fail to lead to the quantum bound in the general case of N-partite correlations. We take this seriously as an indication that the notion of system, implicitly assumed in the operational approaches, becomes problematic. Using a model based on codes, we suggest an approach free of the observer-system distinction. Although our model is highly speculative, we believe that it demonstrates the interest to explore quantum theory via novel mathematical formalisms.

References

1. Adler, S.: Quaternionic Quantum Mechanics and Quantum Fields. Oxford University Press, New York (1995)
2. Barrett, J.: Information processing in generalized probabilistic theories. Phys. Rev. A **75**, 032304 (2007)
3. Bell, J.: On the Einstein-Podolsky-Rosen paradox. Physica **1**, 195–200 (1964)
4. Brassard, G., Buhrman, H., Linden, N., Méthot, A.A., Tapp, A., Unger, F.: Limit on nonlocality in any world in which communication complexity is not trivial. Phys. Rev. Lett. **96**(25), 250401 (2006)

5. Chiribella, G., d'Ariano, G.M., Perinotti, P.: Informational derivation of quantum theory. Phys. Rev. A **84**, 012311 (2011)
6. Cirel'son, B.S.: Quantum generalizations of Bell's inequality. Lett. Math. Phys. **4**(2), 93–100 (1980)
7. Clifton, R., Bub, J., Halvorson, H.: Characterizing quantum theory in terms of information-theoretic constraints. Found. Phys. **33**(11), 1561–1591 (2003)
8. Dakić, B., Brukner, Č.: Quantum theory and beyond: is entanglement special? In: Halvorson, H. (ed.) Deep Beauty: Understanding the Quantum World through Mathematical Innovation, pp. 365–392. Cambridge University Press, Cambridge (2011)
9. El-Showk, S., et al.: Solving the 3D ising model with the conformal bootstrap. Phys. Rev. D **86**, 025022 (2012)
10. El-Showk, S., et al.: Solving the 3D ising model with the conformal bootstrap II. c-Minimization and precise critical exponents. J. Stat. Phys. **157**, 869–914 (2014)
11. Fritz, T., Sainz, A.B., Augusiak, R., Brask, J.B., Chaves, R., Leverrier, A., Acín, A.: Local orthogonality as a multipartite principle for quantum correlations. Nat. Commun. **4**, 2263 (2013)
12. Gallego, R., Würflinger, L.E., Acín, A., Navascués, M.: Quantum correlations require multipartite information principles. Phys. Rev. Lett. **107**, 210403 (2011)
13. Grinbaum, A.: Reconstruction of quantum theory. Brit. J. Philos. Sci. **58**, 387–408 (2007)
14. Grinbaum, A.: Quantum theory as a critical regime of language dynamics. Found. Phys. **45**, 1341–1350 (2015). http://dx.doi.org/10.1007/s10701-015-9937-y
15. Hardy, L.: Quantum theory from five reasonable axioms (2000). http://arxiv.org/abs/quant-ph/0101012
16. Landsman, N.: Mathematical Topics Between Classical and Quantum Mechanics. Spinger, New York (1998)
17. Linden, N., Popescu, S., Short, A.J., Winter, A.: Quantum nonlocality and beyond: limits from nonlocal computation. Phys. Rev. Lett. **99**(18), 180502 (2007). http://link.aps.org/doi/10.1103/PhysRevLett.99.180502
18. Mackey, G.: Quantum mechanics and Hilbert space. Am. Math. Mon. **64**, 45–57 (1957)
19. Manin, Y.: Complexity vs. energy: theory of computation and theoretical physics. J. Phys. Conf. Ser. **532**, 012018 (2014)
20. Manin, Y., Marcolli, M.: Errorcorrecting codes and phase transitions. Math. Comput. Sci. **5**, 155–179 (2011)
21. Manin, Y., Marcolli, M.: Kolmogorov complexity and the asymptotic bound for errorcorrecting codes. J. Differ. Geom. **97**(1), 91–108 (2014)
22. Masanes, L., Müller, M.: A derivation of quantum theory from physical requirements. New J. Phys. **13**, 063001 (2011)
23. Navascués, M., Guryanova, Y., Hoban, M.J., Acín, A.: Almost quantum correlations. Nat. Commun. **6**, 6288 (2015)
24. Navascués, M., Pironio, S., Acín, A.: A convergent hierarchy of semidefinite programs characterizing the set of quantum correlations. New J. Phys. **10**(7), 073013 (2008)
25. Pawlowski, M., Paterek, T., Kaszlikowski, D., Scarani, V., Winter, A., Zukowski, M.: Information causality as a physical principle. Nature **461**, 1101–1104 (2009)
26. Piron, C.: Axiomatique quantique. Helv. Phys. Acta **36**, 439–468 (1964)
27. Poh, H.S., Joshi, S.K., Ceré, A., Cabello, A., Kurtsiefer, C.: Approaching Tsirelson's bound in a photon pair experiment. Phys. Rev. Lett. **115**, 180408 (2015). http://arxiv.org/abs/1506.01865

28. Polyakov, A.M.: Conformal symmetry of critical fluctuations. JETP Lett. **12**, 381–383 (1970)
29. Popescu, S., Rohrlich, D.: Nonlocality as an axiom for quantum theory. Found. Phys. **24**, 379 (1994)
30. Popescu, S.: Nonlocality beyond quantum mechanics. Nat. Phys. **10**, 264–270 (2014)
31. Spekkens, R.: Evidence for the epistemic view of quantum states: a toy theory. Phys. Rev. A **75**, 032110 (2007)
32. Zieler, N.: Axioms for non-relativistic quantum mechanics. Pac. J. Math. **11**, 1151–1169 (1961)

Contextuality-by-Default: A Brief Overview of Ideas, Concepts, and Terminology

Ehtibar N. Dzhafarov[1]([✉]), Janne V. Kujala[2],
and Victor H. Cervantes[1]

[1] Purdue University, West Lafayette, USA
ehtibar@purdue.edu
[2] University of Jyväskylä, Jyväskylän yliopisto, Finland
jvk@iki.fi

Abstract. This paper is a brief overview of the concepts involved in measuring the degree of contextuality and detecting contextuality in systems of binary measurements of a finite number of objects. We discuss and clarify the main concepts and terminology of the theory called "contextuality-by-default," and then discuss generalizations of the theory to arbitrary systems of arbitrary random variables.

Keywords: Contextuality · Contextuality-by-default · Connection · Coupling · Cyclic system · Inconsistent connectedness · Measurements

1 Introduction

1.1 On the Name of the Theory

The name "contextuality-by-default" should not be understood as suggesting that any system of measurements is contextual, or contextual unless proven otherwise. The systems are contextual or noncontextual depending on certain criteria, to be described. The name of the theory reflects a philosophical position according to which every random variable's identity is inherently contextual, i.e., it depends on all conditions under which it is recorded, whether or not there is a way in which these conditions could affect the random variable physically. Thus, in the well-known EPR-Bell paradigm, Alice and Bob are separated by a space-like interval that prevents Bob's measurements from being affected by Alice's settings; nevertheless, Bob's measurements should be labeled by both his own setting and by Alice's setting; and as the latter changes with the former fixed, the identity of the random variable representing Bob's measurement changes "by default." One does not have to ask "why." Bob's measurements under two different settings by Alice have no probabilisitic relation to each other; they possess no joint distribution. Therefore one cannot even meaningfully ask the question of whether the two may be "always equal to each other." The questions one can ask meaningfully are all about what joint distributions can be *imposed* (in a well-defined sense) on the system in a way consistent with observations.

© Springer International Publishing Switzerland 2016
H. Atmanspacher et al. (Eds.): QI 2015, LNCS 9535, pp. 12–23, 2016.
DOI: 10.1007/978-3-319-28675-4_2

A system is contextual or noncontextual (or, as we say, has a noncontextual description) depending on the answers to these questions. Thus, the famous Kochen-Specker demonstration of contextuality is, from this point of view, a reductio ad absurdum proof that measurements of a spin in a fixed direction made under different conditions cannot be imposed a joint distribution upon, in which these measurements would be equal to each other with probability 1.

1.2   Notation

We use capital letters $A, B, \ldots, Q$ to denote sets of "objects" (properties, quantities) being measured, and the script letter $\mathscr{C}$ to denote a collection of such sets. We use capital letters R, S, and T to denote the measurements (random variables), and the Gothic letter $\mathfrak{R}$ to denote sets of random variables that do not possess a joint distribution.

2   Contextuality-by-Default at a Glance

The following is an overview of the main concepts and definitions of the contextuality-by-default theory. This is not done at a very high level of generality, in part in order not to be too abstract, and in part because the criterion and measure of contextuality have been developed in detail only for a broad subclass of finite sets of binary measurements. Thus, the notion of a context given below in terms of subsets of measured objects is limited, but it is intuitive, and a way to generalize it is clear (Sect. 5). The definition of maximally connected couplings is given for binary (± 1) measurements only, and reasonable generalizations here may not be unique. In Sect. 5 we discuss one, arguably most straightforward way of doing this.

2.1   Measurements Are Labeled Contextually

There is a set Q of "*objects*" we want to measure. For whatever reason, we cannot measure them "*all at once*" (the meaning of this is not necessarily chronological, as explained in Sect. 4). Instead we define a collection of subsets of Q,

$$\mathscr{C} = \{A \subset Q, B \subset Q, \ldots\}, \tag{1}$$

and measure the objects "*one subset at a time.*" We call these subsets of objects *contexts*. Different contexts may overlap. This definition has limited applicability, and we discuss a general definition in Sect. 5. For now we consider only finite sets Q (hence finite collections of finite contexts).

The *measurement outcome* of each object q (from the set Q) in each context C (from the collection $\mathscr{C}$) is a random variable, and we denote it R_q^C (with $q \in C \in \mathscr{C}$). This is called *contextual labeling* of the measurement outcomes. It ensures that the collection

$$\left\{R_q^A\right\}_{q \in A}, \left\{R_q^B\right\}_{q \in B}, \ldots \tag{2}$$

for all $A, B, \ldots$ comprising $\mathscr{C}$, are pairwise disjoint, as no two random variables taken from two different members of the collection have the same superscript (whether or not they have the same subscript).

2.2 Measurements in Different Contexts Are Stochastically Unrelated

We call $R^C = \left\{ R_q^C \right\}_{q \in C}$ for every $C \in \mathscr{C}$ a *bunch* (of random variables). The random variables within a bunch are *jointly distributed*, because of which we can consider each bunch as a single (multicomponent) random variable. If $q, q' \in C \in \mathscr{C}$, we can answer questions like "what is the correlation between R_q^C and $R_{q'}^C$?". However, if $q \in C$, $q' \in C'$, and $C \neq C'$, then we cannot answer such questions: R_q^C and $R_{q'}^{C'}$ belong to different bunches and do not have a joint distribution. We say that they are *stochastically unrelated*.

2.3 All Possible Couplings for all Measurements

Consider now the (necessarily disjoint) union of all bunches

$$\mathfrak{R} = \bigcup_{C \in \mathscr{C}} R^C = \bigcup_{C \in \mathscr{C}} \left\{ R_q^C \right\}_{q \in C}, \tag{3}$$

i.e., the set of all measurements contextually labeled. The use of the Gothic font is to emphasize that this set is *not* a multicomponent random variable: except within bunches, its components are not jointly distributed. We call $\mathfrak{R}$ a *system* (of measurements).

Now, we can be interested in whether and how one could *impose a joint distribution* on $\mathfrak{R}$. To impose a joint distribution on $\mathfrak{R}$ means to find a set of jointly distributed random variables $S = \left\{ S_q^C \right\}_{q \in C \in \mathscr{C}}$ such that, for every $C \in \mathscr{C}$,

$$S^C = \left\{ S_q^C \right\}_{q \in C} \sim \left\{ R_q^C \right\}_{q \in C} = R^C. \tag{4}$$

The symbol $\sim$ means "has the same distribution as." Note that

$$S = \left\{ S^C \right\}_{C \in \mathscr{C}} = \left\{ S_q^C \right\}_{q \in C \in \mathscr{C}} \tag{5}$$

is a single (multicomponent) random variable, and in probability theory S is called a *coupling* for (or of) $\mathfrak{R}$. Any subset of the components of S is its *marginal*, and S^C is the marginal of S whose components are labeled in the same way as are the components of the bunch R^C.

If no additional constraints are imposed, one can always find a coupling S for any union of bunches. For instance, one can always use an *independent coupling*: create a *copy* S^C of each bunch R^C (i.e., an identically labelled and identically distributed set of random variables), and join them so that they are stochastically independent. The set $S = \left\{ S^C \right\}_{C \in \mathscr{C}}$ is then jointly distributed. The existence of a coupling *per se* therefore is not informative.

2.4   Connections and their Couplings

Let us form, for every object q, a set of random variables

$$\mathfrak{R}_q = \left\{ R_q^C \right\}_{C \in \mathscr{C}}, \tag{6}$$

i.e., all random variables measuring the object q, across all contexts, We call this set, which is not a random variable, a *connection* (for q). Let us adopt the convention that if a context C does not contain q, then R_q^C is not defined and does not enter in $\mathfrak{R}_q$.

A system is called *consistently connected* if, for every $q \in Q$ and any two contexts C, C' containing q,

$$R_q^C \sim R_q^{C'}. \tag{7}$$

Otherwise a system is called (strictly) *inconsistently connected*. Without the adjective "strictly," inconsistent connectedness means that the equality above is not assumed, but it is then not excluded either: consistent connectedness is a special case of inconsistent connectedness.

One possible interpretation of strictly inconsistent connectedness is that the conditions under which a context is recorded may physically influence (in some cases one could say, "signal to") the measurements of the context members. Another possibility is that a choice of context may introduce biases in how the objects are measured and recorded.

2.5   Maximally Connected Couplings for Binary Measurements

Every coupling S for $\mathfrak{R}$ has a marginal $S_q = \left\{ S_q^C \right\}_{C \in \mathscr{C}}$ that forms a coupling for the connection $\mathfrak{R}_q$. We can also take $\mathfrak{R}_q$ for a given q in isolation, and consider all its couplings $T_q = \left\{ T_q^C \right\}_{C \in \mathscr{C}}$. Clearly, the set of all S_q extracted from all possible couplings S for $\mathfrak{R}$ is a subset of all possible couplings T_q for $\mathfrak{R}_q$.

Let us now confine the consideration to *binary measurements*: each random variable in the system has value $+1$ or -1. In Sect. 5 we will discuss possible generalizations.

A coupling T_q for a connection $\mathfrak{R}_q$ is called *maximal* if, given the expected values $\left\langle R_q^C \right\rangle$ for all C, the value of

$$\mathsf{eq}\,(T_q) = \Pr\left[T_q^C = 1 : C \in \mathscr{C} \right] + \Pr\left[T_q^C = -1 : C \in \mathscr{C} \right] \tag{8}$$

is the largest possible among all couplings for $\mathfrak{R}_q$ (again, R_q^C and T_q^C are not defined and are not considered if C does not contain q).

Let us denote

$$\max \mathsf{eq}\,(\mathfrak{R}_q) = \max_{\substack{\text{all possible} \\ \text{couplings } T_q \text{ for } \mathfrak{R}_q}} \mathsf{eq}\,(T_q). \tag{9}$$

It follows from a general theorem mentioned in Sect. 5 that this quantity is well-defined for all systems, i.e., that the supremum of $\mathsf{eq}\,(T_q)$ is attained in some coupling T_q. Clearly, for consistently connected systems $\max \mathsf{eq}\,(\mathfrak{R}_q) = 1$ (the measurements can be made "perfectly correlated"). For (strictly) inconsistently connected systems, $\max \mathsf{eq}\,(\mathfrak{R}_q)$ is always well-defined, and it is less than 1 for some q. It may even be zero: for ± 1 variables this happens when the $\mathfrak{R}_q$ contains two measurements R_q^A and R_q^B such that $\Pr\left[R_q^A = 1\right] = 1$ and $\Pr\left[R_q^B = 1\right] = 0$.

2.6   Definition of Contextuality

Consider again a coupling S for the entire system $\mathfrak{R}$, and for every $q \in Q$, extract from S the marginal S_q that forms a coupling for the connection $\mathfrak{R}_q$.

Central Concept. If, for every $q \in Q$,

$$\mathsf{eq}\,(S_q) = \max \mathsf{eq}\,(\mathfrak{R}_q),\qquad(10)$$

(i.e., if every marginal S_q in S is a maximal coupling for $\mathfrak{R}_q$) then the coupling S for $\mathfrak{R}$ is said to be *maximally connected*.

Intuitively, in this case the measurements can be imposed a joint distribution upon in which the measurements R_q^C of every object q in different contexts C are maximally "correlated," i.e., attain one and the same value with the maximal probability allowed by their observed individual distributions (expectations).

Main Definition. A system $\mathfrak{R}$ is said to be *contextual* if no coupling S of this system is maximally connected. Otherwise, a maximally connected coupling of the system (it need not be unique if it exists) is said to be this system's *noncontextual description* (or, as a terminological variant, *maximally noncontextual description*).

For consistently connected systems this definition is equivalent to the traditional understanding of (non)contextuality. According to the latter, a system has a noncontextual description if and only if there is a coupling for the measurements *labeled noncontextually*. The latter means that all random variables R_q^C within a connection are treated as being equal to each other with probability 1.

2.7   Measure and Criterion of Contextuality

If (and only if) a system $\mathfrak{R}$ is contextual, then for every coupling S there is at least one $q \in Q$ such that $\mathsf{eq}\,(S_q) < \max \mathsf{eq}\,(\mathfrak{R}_q)$. This is equivalent to saying that a system is contextual if and only if for every coupling S of it,

$$\sum_{q \in Q} \mathsf{eq}\,(S_q) < \sum_{q \in Q} \max \mathsf{eq}\,(\mathfrak{R}_q).\qquad(11)$$

Define

$$\max \mathsf{eq}\,(\mathfrak{R}) = \max_{\substack{\text{all couplings} \\ S \text{ for } \mathfrak{R}}} \left(\sum_{q \in Q} \mathsf{eq}\,(S_q)\right).\qquad(12)$$

In this definition we assume that this maximum exists, i.e., the supremum of the sum on the right is attained in some coupling S. (This is likely to be true for all systems with finite Q and binary measurements, but we only have a formal proof of this for the cyclic systems considered below.) Then (11) is equivalent to

$$\max \text{eq}\,(\mathfrak{R}) < \sum_{q \in Q} \max \text{eq}\,(\mathfrak{R}_q)\,, \tag{13}$$

which is a *criterion of contextuality* (necessary and sufficient condition for it). Moreover, it immediately leads to a natural *measure of contextuality*:

$$\text{cntx}\,(\mathfrak{R}) = \sum_{q \in Q} \max \text{eq}\,(\mathfrak{R}_q) - \max \text{eq}\,(\mathfrak{R})\,. \tag{14}$$

Written *in extenso* using (9) and (12),

$$\text{cntx}\,(\mathfrak{R}) = \sum_{q \in Q} \max_{\substack{\text{all possible} \\ \text{couplings}\, T_q \,\text{for}\, \mathfrak{R}_q}} \text{eq}\,(T_q) - \max_{\substack{\text{all couplings} \\ S \,\text{for}\, \mathfrak{R}}} \sum_{q \in Q} \text{eq}\,(S_q)\,, \tag{15}$$

where, one should recall, S_q is the marginal of S that forms a coupling for $\mathfrak{R}_q$. We can see that the minuend and subtrahend in the definition of $\text{cntx}\,(\mathfrak{R})$ differ in order of the operations max and $\sum_{q \in Q}$; and while in the minuend the choice of couplings T_q for $\mathfrak{R}_q$ is unconstrained, in the subtrahend the choice of couplings S_q for $\mathfrak{R}_q$ is constrained by the requirement that it is a marginal of the coupling for the entire system $\mathfrak{R}$.

3   The History of the Contextuality-by-Default Approach

A systematic realization of the idea of contextually labeling a system of measurements $\mathfrak{R}$, considering all possible couplings S for it, and characterizing it by the marginals S_q that form couplings for the connections $\mathfrak{R}_q$ of the system was developing through a series of publications [3–7]. The idea of maximally connected couplings as the central concept for contextuality in consistently connected systems was proposed in Refs. [2,8,11] and then generalized to inconsistently connected systems [9,10].

In the latter two references the measure of contextuality (14) and the criterion of contextuality (13) were defined and computed for simple QM systems (cyclic systems of rank 3 and 4, as defined below). Later we added to this list cyclic systems of rank 5, and formulated a conjecture for the measure and criterion formulas for cyclic systems of arbitrary rank [12].

In Refs. [12,18] the contextuality-by-default theory is presented in its current form. The conjecture formulated in Ref. [12] was proved in Ref. [19].

A cyclic system (with binary measurements) is defined as one involving n "objects" (n being called the *rank* of the system) measured two at a time,

$$(q_1, q_2)\,, (q_2, q_3)\,, \ldots, (q_{n-1}, q_n)\,, (q_n, q_1)\,. \tag{16}$$

For $i = 1, \ldots, n$, the pair $(q_i, q_{i \oplus 1})$ forms the context C_i ($\oplus$ standing for circular shift by 1). Each object q_i enters in precisely two consecutive contexts, $C_{i \ominus 1}$ and C_i. Denoting the measurement of q_i in context C_j by R_i^j, we have the system represented by bunches $R^i = (R_i^i, R_{i \oplus 1}^i)$ and connections $\mathfrak{R}_i = (R_i^{i \ominus 1}, R_i^i)$.

The formula for the measure of contextuality conjectured in Ref. [12] and proved in Ref. [19] is

$$\mathsf{cntx}\,(\mathfrak{R}) = \frac{1}{2} \max \begin{cases} \mathsf{s}_{\mathrm{odd}} \left(\langle \mathrm{R}_i^i \mathrm{R}_{i \oplus 1}^i \rangle : i = 1, \ldots, n \right) - \sum_{i=1}^n \left| \langle \mathrm{R}_i^i \rangle - \langle \mathrm{R}_i^{i \ominus 1} \rangle \right| - (n - 2) \\ 0 \end{cases}. \tag{17}$$

The function $\mathsf{s}_{\mathrm{odd}}$ is defined for an arbitrary set of argument $x_1, \ldots, x_k$ as

$$\mathsf{s}_{\mathrm{odd}}\,(x_1, \ldots, x_k) = \max\,(\pm x_1 \pm \ldots \pm x_k), \tag{18}$$

where the maximum is taken over all assignments of $+$ and $-$ signs with an odd number of $-$'s. The criterion of contextuality readily derived from (17) is: the system is contextual if ands only if

$$\mathsf{s}_{\mathrm{odd}} \left(\langle R_i^i R_{i \oplus 1}^i \rangle : i = 1, \ldots, n \right) > (n - 2) + \sum_{i=1}^n \left| \langle R_i^i \rangle - \langle R_i^{i \ominus 1} \rangle \right|. \tag{19}$$

For consistently connected systems, the sum on the right vanishes, and we can derive the traditional formulas for Legget-Garg ($n = 3$), EPR/Bell ($n = 4$), and Klyachko-Can-Binicioglu-Shumovsky-type (KCBS) systems ($n = 5$). But the formula also allows us to deal with the same experimental paradigm when they create inconsistently connected systems, due to signaling or contextual biases in experimental design (see Refs. [9, 10, 12, 18] for details).

The contextuality-by-default theory does have precursors in the literature. The idea that random variables in different contexts are stochastically unrelated was prominently considered in Refs. [15–17]. Probabilities of the eq-type with the contextual labeling of random variables, as defined in (8), were introduced in Refs. [20, 21, 23, 25]. The distinguishing feature of the contextuality-by-default theory is the notion of a maximally connected coupling, which in turn is based on the idea of comparing maximal couplings for the connections taken in isolation and those extracted as marginals from the couplings of the entire system. Contextuality-by-default is a more systematic and more general theory of contextuality than those proposed previously, also more readily applicable to experimental data [1, 18].

4   Conceptual and Terminological Clarifications

4.1   Contextuality and Quantum Mechanics (QM)

The notion of (non)contextuality has its origins in logic [22], but since the publication of Ref. [14] it has been widely considered a QM notion. QM indeed provides the only known to us theoretically justified examples of contextual systems. (Non)contextuality per se, however, is a purely probabilisitic concept, squarely within the classical, Kolmogorovian probability theory (that includes the notion of stochastic unrelatedness and that of couplings) [7,8,11]. When contextuality is present in a QM system, QM is relevant to answering the question of exactly how the noncontextuality conditions in the system are violated, but it is not relevant to the question of what these conditions are.

4.2   Contexts and QM Observables

In particular, the "objects" being measured need not be QM observables. They may very well be questions asked in a poll of public opinion, and the binary measurements then may be Yes/No answers to these questions. It is especially important not to confuse being "measured together" in the definition of a context with being represented by compatible (commutative) observables. Thus, in the theory of contextuality in cyclic systems, $n = 4$ is exemplified by the EPR-Bell paradigm, with Alice's "objects" (spins) being q_1, q_3 and Bob's q_2, q_4. In each of the contexts $(q_1, q_2), \ldots, (q_4, q_1)$, the two objects are compatible in the trivial sense: any observable in Alice's Hilbert space H_A is compatible with any observable in Bob's Hilbert space H_B because the joint space is the tensor product $H_A \otimes H_B$. The case $n = 5$ is exemplified by the KCBS paradigm, where the spins $q_1, \ldots, q_5$ are represented by observables in three-dimensional Hilbert space. In each of the five contexts $(q_1, q_2), \ldots, (q_5, q_1)$ the observables are compatible in the narrow QM sense: they are commuting Hermitian operators. The case $n = 3$ is exemplified by the Leggett-Garg paradigm, where three measurements are made at three distinct time moments, two measurements at a time. The QM representations of the observables in each of the contexts $(q_1, q_2), (q_2, q_3), (q_3, q_1)$ are generally incompatible (noncommuting) operators. In spite of the profound differences in the QM structure of these three cyclic systems, their contextually analysis is precisely the same mathematically, given by (17) and (19).

4.3   The Meaning of Being Measured "together"

It should be clear from the discussion of the Leggett-Garg paradigm that "measuring objects one context at a time" does not necessarily have the meaning of chronological simultaneity. Rather one should think of measurements being grouped and recorded in accordance with some fixed coupling scheme: if q and q' belong to the same context C, there is an empirical procedure by which observations of R_q^C are paired with observations of R_q^C. Thus, if the objects being measured are tests taken by students, and the measurements are their test scores, the tests are grouped into contexts by the student who takes them, however they are distributed in time. The grouping of (potential) observations is in essence what couplings discussed in Sects. 2.3 and 2.4 do for a set of stochastically unrelated random variables, except that these couplings do not provide a uniquely (empirically) defined joint distribution. Rather the probabilistic couplings imposed on different bunches are part of a purely mathematical procedure that generally yields an infinity of different joint distributions.

4.4   The Meaning of a Noncontextual Description

In the traditional approach to (non)contextuality, where the measurements are labeled by objects but not by contexts, one can define a noncontextual description as simply a coupling imposed on the system. For instance, in the Leggett-Garg paradigm the noncontextual labeling yields three random variables, R_1, R_2, R_3, with $(R_1, R_2), (R_2, R_3), (R_3, R_1)$ jointly observed. A noncontextual description here is any three-component random variable $S = (S_1, S_2, S_3)$ with $(S_1, S_2) \sim (R_1, R_2)$, $(S_2, S_3) \sim (R_2, R_3)$, and $(S_3, S_1) \sim (R_3, R_1)$. The system is contextual if no such description exists.

The situation is different with contextually labeled measurements. For the Leggett-Garg paradigm we now have six variables grouped into three stochastically unrelated contexts, $\left(R_1^1, R_2^1\right), \left(R_2^2, R_3^2\right), \left(R_3^3, R_1^3\right)$. As explained in Sect. 2.3, such a system always has a coupling, in this case a sextuple S with $\left(S_1^1, S_2^1\right) \sim \left(R_1^1, R_2^1\right)$, $\left(S_2^2, S_3^2\right) \sim \left(R_2^2, R_3^2\right)$, and $\left(S_3^3, S_1^3\right) \sim \left(R_3^3, R_1^3\right)$. One can call any of these couplings a noncontextual description of the system. To characterize (non)contextuality then one can use the term "maximally noncontextual description" for any maximally connected coupling [18]. Alternatively, one can confine the term "noncontextual description" of a system only to maximally connected couplings for it. With this terminology the definition of a contextual system in our theory is the same as in the traditional approach: a system is contextual if it does not have a noncontextual description. The choice between the two terminological variants will be ultimately determined by whether couplings other than maximally connected ones will be found a useful role to play.

5   Instead of a Conclusion: Generalizations

5.1   Beyond Objects and Subsets

Defining a context as a subset of objects measured together [12, 18] is less general than defining it by conditions under which certain objects are measured [2, 9, 10]. For instance, by the first of these definitions $\{q_1, q_2\}$ for a given pair of objects is a single context, while the second definition allows one to speak of the same pair of objects q_1, q_2 forming several different contexts. Thus, if q_1, q_2 are two tests, they can be given in one order or the other, (q_1, q_2) or (q_2, q_1). In fact, in all our previous discussion of cyclic systems we used the notation for ordered pairs, $(q_i, q_{i\oplus 1})$ rather than $\{q_i, q_{i\oplus 1}\}$. This is inconsequential for cyclic systems of rank $n \geq 3$. For $n = 2$, however, the difference between (q_1, q_2) and (q_2, q_1) is critical if $n = 2$ is to be a nontrivial system (with the distributions of the two bunches not identical). It can be shown that the system can be nontrivial, and $n = 2$ is a legitimate value for (17) and (19).

Being formal and mathematically rigorous here makes things simpler. A context is merely a label (say, superscript) at a random variable with the convention that identically superscripted variables are "bunched together," i.e., they are jointly distributed. An object is merely another label (in our notation, a subscript) that makes all the elements of a bunch different and indicates which elements from different bunches should be put together to form a connection. So if there are six random variables grouped into three distinct bunches $\left(R_1^1, R_2^1\right)$, $\left(R_1^2, R_2^2\right)$, and $\left(R_1^3, R_2^3\right)$ and into two connections $\left(R_1^1, R_1^2, R_1^3\right)$ and $\left(R_2^1, R_2^2, R_2^3\right)$, we can (but do not have to) interpret this as three different contexts involving the same two objects. From mathematical (and perhaps also philosophical) point of view, measurements grouped into bunches and connections are more fundamental than objects being measured within contexts.

5.2   Beyond Binary Measurements

How could the definition of a maximally connected coupling be generalized to arbitrary random variables? A straightforward way to do this is to extend definition (8) for a coupling T_q of a connection $\mathfrak{R}_q$ as

$$\mathsf{eq}\left(T_q\right) = \Pr\left[T_q^C = T_q^{C'} \text{ for any two } C, C' \in \mathscr{C}\right]. \tag{20}$$

This is an approach adopted in [2, 12, 18]. It is based on the following mathematical considerations, derived from the discussion of maximal couplings in Thorisson's monograph [24] (Sect. 7 of Chap. 3).

Given two sigma-additive measures μ and ν on the same sigma algebra, let us write $\mu \leq \nu$ if $\mu(E) \leq \nu(E)$ for every measurable set E. Let μ_q^C be the probability measure associated with R_q^C. Let X_q and $\varSigma_q$ be the set of values and sigma algebra associated with R_q^C (they are assumed the same for all C, because otherwise one should not consider R_q^C measurements of one and the same object). For every object q, define μ_q as the largest sigma-additive measure such that $\mu_q \leq \mu_q^C$ for all contexts C. The measure μ_q is the largest in the sense that $\mu_q' \leq \mu_q$ for any other measure μ_q' such that $\mu_q \leq \mu_q^C$ for all contexts C. A theorem proved in Ref. [24] (Theorem 7.1) guarantees the existence and uniqueness of μ_q, for any set of probability measures $\left\{\mu_q^C\right\}_{C \in \mathscr{C}}$, whatever the indexing set $\mathscr{C}$. That is, μ_q is uniquely defined for any connection $\mathfrak{R}_q$. Note that μ_q is not generally a probability measure, so $\mu_q(X_q)$ can be any number in $[0, 1]$. Let us denote

$$\max \mathsf{eq}\left(\mathfrak{R}_q\right) = \mu_q\left(X_q\right). \tag{21}$$

For ± 1-measurements R_q^C this definition specializes to (8)–(9).

Consider now a coupling T_q for $\mathfrak{R}_q$. It is defined on the product sigma-algebra $\bigotimes_{\mathscr{C}} \varSigma_q$ on the product set $\prod_{\mathscr{C}} X_q$. An event $E_q \in \bigotimes_{\mathscr{C}} \varSigma_q$ is called a *coupling event* if $S_q \in E_q$ implies $T_q^C = T_q^{C'}$ for any two $C, C' \in \mathscr{C}$ (assuming, as always, that both C and C' involve q). It follows from Theorem 7.2 in Ref. [24] that

$$\Pr\left[T_q \in E_q\right] \leq \max \mathsf{eq}\left(\mathfrak{R}_q\right), \tag{22}$$

for any q and any choice of E_q. Now, it is natural to define a *maximal coupling* for $\mathfrak{R}_q$ as a coupling T_q for which E_q can be chosen so that

$$\Pr\left[T_q \in E_q\right] = \max \mathsf{eq}\left(\mathfrak{R}_q\right). \tag{23}$$

Theorem 7.3 in Ref. [24] says that such a maximal coupling always exists. Note that E_q in a maximal coupling can always be thought of as the largest measurable subset of the diagonal of the set $\prod_{\mathscr{C}} X_q$.

Having established this generalized notion of a maximal coupling, the theory of contextuality can now be generalized in a straightforward fashion. Consider a coupling S for the entire system $\mathfrak{R}$. The definition of a *maximally connected coupling* remains unchanged: every marginal S_q of a maximally connected coupling S is a maximal coupling for the corresponding connection $\mathfrak{R}_q$. Our Main Definition could remain unchanged too: a system $\mathfrak{R}$ is *contextual* if and only if no coupling S of this system is maximally connected. This can be equivalently presented as follows. For any set P of probability values, let $f(P)$ be a bounded smooth nonnegative function strictly increasing in all components of P. Thus, for finite systems of random variables f can be chosen as a sum or average, as in (11). Define

$$\max \mathsf{eq}\,(\mathfrak{R}) = \max_{\substack{\text{all couplings} \\ S \text{ for } \mathfrak{R}}} f\left(\Pr\left[S_q \in E_q\right] : q \in Q\right), \tag{24}$$

and, if this value exists,

$$\mathsf{cntx}\,(\mathfrak{R}) = f\left(\max \mathsf{eq}\,(\mathfrak{R}_q) : q \in Q\right) - \max \mathsf{eq}\,(\mathfrak{R}). \tag{25}$$

The system is defined as contextual if and only if $\mathsf{cntx}\,(\mathfrak{R}) > 0$. We do not know whether $\max \mathsf{eq}\,(\mathfrak{R})$ exists for all possible systems of random variables. If it does not, however, the definition can be extended by replacing max with sup.

This generalization has to be further explored to determine whether it is a good generalization, i.e., whether it provides valuable insights, leads to interesting mathematical developments, and does not yield non-interpretable results when applied to specific systems of measurements.

Acknowledgments. This research has been supported by NSF grant SES-1155956 and AFOSR grant FA9550-14-1-0318.

References

1. Bacciagaluppi, G.: Leggett-Garg inequalities, pilot waves and contextuality. Int. J. Quantum Found. **1**, 1–17 (2015)
2. de Barros, J.A., Dzhafarov, E.N., Kujala, J.V., Oas, G.: Measuring observable quantum contextuality (2014). arXiv:1406.3088
3. Dzhafarov, E.N., Kujala, J.V.: All-possible-couplings approach to measuring probabilistic context. PLoS One **8**(5), e61712 (2013). doi:10.1371/journal.pone.0061712
4. Dzhafarov, E.N., Kujala, J.V.: Order-distance and other metric-like functions on jointly distributed random variables. Proc. Amer. Math. Soc. **141**, 3291–3301 (2013)
5. Dzhafarov, E.N., Kujala, J.V.: No-forcing and no-matching theorems for classical probability applied to quantum mechanics. Found. Phys. **44**, 248–265 (2014)

6. Dzhafarov, E.N., Kujala, J.V.: Embedding quantum into classical: contextualization vs conditionalization. PLoS One **9**(3), e92818 (2014). doi:10.1371/journal.pone.0092818
7. Dzhafarov, E.N., Kujala, J.V.: A qualified Kolmogorovian account of probabilistic contextuality. In: Atmanspacher, H., Haven, E., Kitto, K., Raine, D. (eds.) QI 2013. LNCS, vol. 8369, pp. 201–212. Springer, Heidelberg (2014)
8. Dzhafarov, E.N., Kujala, J.V.: Contextuality is about identity of random variables. Physica Scripta T **163**, 014009 (2014)
9. Dzhafarov, E.N., Kujala, J.V.: Probabilistic contextuality in EPR/Bohm-type systems with signaling allowed (2014). arXiv:1406.0243
10. Dzhafarov, E.N., Kujala, J.V.: Generalizing Bell-type and Leggett-Garg-type inequalities to systems with signaling (2014). arXiv:1407.2886
11. Dzhafarov, E.N., Kujala, J.V.: Random variables recorded under mutually exclusive conditions: contextuality-by-default. Advances in Cognitive Neurodynamics IV, pp. 405–410 (2015)
12. Dzhafarov, E.N., Kujala, J.V., Larsson, J.-A.: Contextualityin three types of quantum-mechanical systems. Foundations of Physics (2105). doi:10.1007/s10701-015-9882-9
13. Dzhafarov, E.N., Kujala, J.V.: Probability, random variables, and selectivity. In: Batchelder, W., et al. (eds.) The New Handbook of Mathematical Psychology. Cambridge University Press (2015) (to be published)
14. Kochen, S., Specker, E.P.: The problem of hidden variables in quantum mechanics. J. Math. Mech. **17**, 59–87 (1967)
15. Khrennikov, A.: The principle of supplementarity: a contextual probabilistic viewpoint to complementarity, the interference of probabilities, and the incompatibility of variables in quantum mechanics. Found. Phys. **35**, 1655–1693 (2005)
16. Khrennikov, A.: Bell-Boole inequality: nonlocality or probabilistic incompatibility of random variables? Entropy **10**, 19–32 (2008)
17. Khrennikov, A.: Contextual Approach to Quantum Formalism. Springer, Berlin (2009)
18. Kujala, J.V., Dzhafarov, E.N., Larsson, J.-Å.: Necessary, sufficient conditions for maximal contextuality in a broad class of quantum mechanical systems (2015). arXiv:1412.4724
19. Kujala, J.V., Dzhafarov, E.N.: Proof of a conjecture on contextuality in cyclic systems with binary variables (2015). arXiv:1503.02181
20. Larsson, J.-Å.: A Kochen-specker inequality. Europhys. Lett. **58**(6), 799–805 (2002)
21. Simon, C., Brukner, Č., Zeilinger, A.: Hidden-variable theorems for real experiments. Phys. Rev. Lett. **86**(20), 4427–4430 (2001)
22. Specker, E.P.: Die Logik Nicht Gleichzeitig Entscheidbarer Aussagen. Dialectica **14**, 239–246 (1960). (English translation by M.P. Seevinck available as arXiv:1103.4537.)
23. Svozil, K.: How much contextuality? Nat. Comput. **11**, 261–265 (2012)
24. Thorisson, H.: Coupling, Stationarity, and Regeneration. Springer, New York (2000)
25. Winter, A.: What does an experimental test of quantum contextuality prove or disprove? J. Phys. A Math. Theor. **47**(42), 42403 (2014)

Contextuality and the Weak Axiom
in the Theory of Choice

William Zeng[1] and Philipp Zahn[2]([⊠])

[1] Department of Computer Science, University of Oxford, Oxford, UK
`william.zeng@cs.ox.ac.uk`
[2] Department of Economics, University of Mannheim, Mannheim, Germany
`philipp.m.zahn@gmail.com`

Abstract. Recent work on the logical structure of non-locality has constructed scenarios where observations of multi-partite systems cannot be adequately described by compositions of non-signaling subsystems. In this paper we apply these frameworks to economics. First we construct a empirical model of choice, where choices are understood as observable outcomes in a certain sense. An analysis of contextuality within this framework allows us to characterize which scenarios allow for the possible construction of an adequate global choice rule. In essence, we mathematically characterize when it makes sense to consider the choices of a group as composed of individual choices. We then map out the logical space of some relevant empirical principles, relating properties of these *contextual choice scenarios* to no-signalling theories and to the weak axiom of revealed preference.

Keywords: Contextuality · Choice theory · Weak axiom of choice · No-signalling

1 Introduction

In this paper we uncover a connection between observed choices in economics and empirical models in quantum physics. In particular, we show the precise relationships between the weak axiom, a consistency property often imposed in choice theory, and contextuality and no-signalling conditions on measurements in the foundations of quantum physics.

The framework we use is borrowed from work in the foundations of quantum mechanics where a general logical theory of contextuality has been developed in recent years. Our work applies the empirical models and the framework of contextuality beyond quantum physics or computer science. In this sense, we are furthering the work of Abramsky et al. [1–4,12] by showing that observed economic choices can be seen as one instantiation of an abstract contextual semantics.

Our paper is related to two strands of work. On the one hand there is a growing literature that considers the consequences of quantum-resources for economic theory. This interaction between quantum foundations and the foundations of economics, where agents can make use of quantum resources, has led to results in quantum games [7], decision theory [6], voting systems [5], and other areas.

© Springer International Publishing Switzerland 2016
H. Atmanspacher et al. (Eds.): QI 2015, LNCS 9535, pp. 24–35, 2016.
DOI: 10.1007/978-3-319-28675-4_3

On the other hand there is a well developed literature that combines classical decision theory with elements from quantum mechanics to address various empirical puzzles in a unified theoretical framework [8]. Quantum theory is used, for instance, to model ambiguity and fundamental uncertainty. In [14], for example, players' preferences are allowed to be indeterminate before they make a decision. Moreover, various authors have translated probabilistic choice models into a quantum setting to account for empirical violations of classical choice theory. For instance, [15] provides a quantum probability framework that accounts for violations of the sure-thing principle in experiments. Order effects of measurements on behavior and attitudes also have been addressed, for example, in [17]. The utility of quantum mechanics (and often its contextual nature) in addressing these specific issues, helps motivate our move to study contextuality in general, rather than just as a part of a quantum mechanical model.

While we share the idea of using elements from quantum motivated settings for classical decision theory, the focus in our paper is different. We consider only the observed choices of agents from particular empirical scenarios. This means that we do not provide an internal model of the agent. This focus is similar to the perspective taken by [9], but, in contrast to their focus on measurement induced effects, our main investigation is to specify under which conditions it is possible to construct a sensible measurement at all, via an adequate global (context-independent) choice rule from local choices. Note also that while the presentation of our framework focuses on individual agents, it can easily be extended to groups of agents via the connection between decision theory and voting theory [16].

The paper is structured as follows: We first describe the mathematical framework of contextuality using empirical models. Next, we define choice scenarios and show how observed choices fit into this setting. In Sects. 4 and 5 we state the general definitions and theorems that characterize the relationship between contextual semantics and choice scenarios. We show that, while choice scenarios that do not obey the weak axiom can be either contextual or non-contextual, choice scenarios that do not obey the weak axiom must be contextual. We also show that the weak axiom is strictly weaker than the no-signalling condition. Moreover, we show that under sufficient overlap of budgets, made precise in the paper, the weak axiom and no-signalling are equivalent. Section 6 briefly indicates how our setting can be extended to include probabilistic choices and mentions how they can be characterized by the logical Bell inequalities of [2]. We conclude with a discussion that interprets these results in economic terms.

2   Mathematical Framework of Contextuality

In [2], the authors generalize a notion of contextuality from the quantum mechanical setting into an abstractly logical one that can be applied to many empirical scenarios.

Definition 1. *An* **empirical scenario** *is given by*

1. *a set of measurements X*
2. *a set O of possible outcomes for the measurements*
3. *subsets $U \subseteq X$ that represent possible* measurement contexts
4. *$\mathcal{U}$, a subset of the powerset of X that defines the set of all possible measurement contexts. We will call this the* set of feasible experiments.

Example 2. As a simple example, we consider an empirical scenario given by two systems A and B. We further posit that on each system we have a choice of two different measurements, each of which has outcomes either 0 or 1, i.e. $O = \{0, 1\}$. These systems could, for example, be two coins and we could either check if a coin is heads or weigh it to check if it is heavier than 1 gram. This means our empirical scenario consists of four boolean variables, $X = \{a, b, a', b'\}$ where:

a is 1 iff the first coin is heads.
a' is 1 iff the first coin weighs over a gram.
b is 1 iff the second coin is heads.
b' is 1 iff the second coin weighs over a gram.

As our scenario only allows us to choose one of the two measurements on the coin at a time, an example of a measurement context is $U = \{a', b'\}$, corresponding to weighing both coins. The complete set of feasible experiments is given by these two element subsets of X:

$$\mathcal{U} = \{\{a, b\}, \{a, b'\}, \{a', b\}, \{a', b'\}\}.$$

Joint outcomes for experiments are then given by functions from measurement contexts to the set of outcomes. In our example, an example function

$$\{a \mapsto 1, b \mapsto 1\}$$

represents measuring both coins to be heads.

Definition 3. *Given an empirical scenario where $O = \{0, 1\}$, a* **binary empirical model** *is a map $C : \mathcal{U} \to \mathcal{P}(\mathcal{P}(X))$ such that*

$$U \mapsto C(U),$$

where $C(U)$ is a set of subsets of measurement context U that could have outcome 1.[1]

Example 4. Consider our coin scenario, but where the first coin is a double-sided heads coin. We can specify the binary empirical model C explicitly:

$$\{a, b\} \mapsto \{a, \{a, b\}\}$$
$$\{a', b\} \mapsto \{\phi, a', b, \{a', b\}\}$$
$$\{a, b'\} \mapsto \{a, \{a, b'\}\}$$
$$\{a', b'\} \mapsto \{\phi, a', b', \{a', b'\}\}$$

---

[1] In other literature, $C(U)$ is referred to as the *support* of the measurement context U under the model C.

We can more easily represent the empirical model with a table like the following:

	(0,0)	(1,0)	(0,1)	(1,1)
(a,b)	0	1	0	1
(a',b)	1	1	1	1
(a,b')	0	1	0	1
(a',b')	1	1	1	1

In this table, the choice of row denotes a measurement context. Each column then represents a particular outcome. For example, the left-most column corresponds to an outcome of 0 for both systems. The column to its right corresponds to an outcome of 1 for the first system and an outcome of 0 for the second. This would mean that $\{a\} \in C(U)$. The value of each cell in the table is defined by the following rule: 1 if the set of measurements with outcome 1 is contained in $C(U)$ and zero otherwise. In our example the double-headed first coin means that it is impossible for us to get a 0 outcome for the first coin when we check its side. This gives the zeros on the first and third columns.

2.1   Contextuality

It is important to note that we do not have completely free choice in choosing the empirical model as some empirical models lead to contradictions. We reproduce one such example from [2] that is based on the Hardy paradox about possible outcomes for certain quantum mechanical systems.[2]

Example 5. In this example we again have two systems, measurements $X = \{a, b, a', b'\}$, and outcomes $O = \{0,1\}$. Consider the binary empirical model given by the following table:

	(0,0)	(1,0)	(0,1)	(1,1)
(a,b)	1	1	1	1
(a',b)	0	1	1	1
(a,b')	0	1	1	1
(a',b')	1	1	1	0

The model specified by this table is logically inconsistent by the following reasoning. Interpret outcome 0 as false and outcome 1 as true and consider the following formulas:

$$a \wedge b, \qquad \neg(a \wedge b'), \qquad \neg(a' \wedge b), \qquad a' \vee b'.$$

According to the empirical model these should all be possible (true). However, it is impossible to find individual assignments of a, b, a', b' to be true or false that manifest this [2]. This observation forces us to conclude that the given empirical model cannot be constructed by a composition of systems with defined values for a, b, a', and b'. This empirical model is *contextual.*

In short, should we encounter a system that fits a contextual model, then we know that its behavior is not modelled by the composition of a series of separate

---

[2] The Greenberger-Horne-Zeilinger states [10].

subsystems. Likewise, we know that a composition of individual systems will never generate contextual behavior.

3 Choice

This section applies the above empirical framework to an economic choice setting over a set of alternatives X. An agent has to choose from menus of alternatives which comprise subsets of all possible alternatives.

Definition 6. *A **choice scenario** is defined as the following:*

1. *A set of alternatives X.*
2. *A set $O = \{0, 1\}$. 1 indicates that an element $x \in X$ is possibly chosen.*
3. *Subsets $U \subseteq X$ that represent possible menus an agent can choose from.*
4. *A set $\mathcal{U}$ of menus that represents the set of feasible menus an agent can face.*
5. *A global choice rule $C : \mathcal{U} \to \mathcal{P}(\mathcal{P}(X))$ such that $U \mapsto C(U)$. This means that $C(U)$ is the set of subsets of elements in a given menu U that are possibly chosen, i.e. whose outcome is 1.*

The set of alternatives X can represent various types of choice problems. It could be a set of consumer goods, a list of political candidates, a set of survey questions, etc. The crucial point here is that it may be impossible to get a complete answer to the whole set X given only answers to particular menus one at a time. There may be various reasons for this impossibility and we will illustrate with some examples.

When only partial information can be gathered, the key question is: Can we infer from the local choices what an agent would choose if he or she faced the complete set of alternatives? Under which conditions is it impossible to aggregate local choices in a coherent way?

Example 7. Consider the following setting. A retailer offers wine at two periods in time. Availability of wines or other concerns may naturally dictate which menus he can offer at a given time. Let the alternatives be given by

$$X = \{Riesling14, PinotBlanc14, Riesling13, PinotBlanc13\}.$$

We will use the shorthand labels a, a', b, b' for the wines respectively so that

a is 1 iff Riesling13 is chosen.
a' is 1 iff Pinot Blanc13 is chosen.
b is 1 iff Riesling14 is chosen.
b' is 1 iff Pinot Blanc14 is chosen.

In such a choice scenario, choices could be observed to follow a contextual rule as in Example 5. The contradiction in this scenario is precisely the same one in the physical measurement setting.

Another example would be to consider two waiters who are taking orders, one takes orders for food, and the other takes orders for beverages such that $X = \{beef, cake, wine, coffee\}$.

What is the economic meaning of a global choice rule? Its simplest interpretation is that if it were possible to let an agent choose from the global menu, where all alternatives are available at the same time, the global choice rule determines what the agent will choose. In the following section we make precise when one can aggregate local choices into global ones.

Note that the impossibility of aggregating choices coherently depends on the analyst's definition of the set of alternatives. In the example above, a redefinition of the goods would have cleared the contradictions. However, this presupposes an understanding of the situation and background knowledge which, though obvious in these examples, is not necessarily available to the analyst in general. Consider another example where a coherent aggregation is obviously impossible.

Example 8 (due to Luce and Raiffa [11]). Suppose an agent is going to a restaurant twice. The set of meals is $Salmon, Steak, FrogLegs, FriedSnails$. The first time he faces the following menu $Salmon, Steak$ and chooses $Salmon$. But the next time, facing the menu $Salmon, Steak, FrogLegs$, he chooses $Steak$.

In contrast to the examples before, the reasons why a global choice rule does not exist is less obvious. For instance, it could mean that crucial information is missing which would explain the agent's choices, or it could be the case that the agent is choosing in an incoherent way: potentially his choices are affected by the context itself.[3] All of these choice examples and any others can be brought under the unified heading of empirical scenarios.

Theorem 9. *Every choice scenario defines a unique empirical scenario with binary empirical model and vice versa.*

Proof. This is clear by inspecting the definitions. The following table provides a glossary of sorts:

Choices	Measurements
alternatives	measurements
choice or non-choice	outcomes
menus	measurement contexts
all feasible menus	all feasible experiments
global choice rule	binary measurement model

4   Generalized Choice Contextuality

Having illustrated by example the connection between empirical scenarios and choice settings, we can leverage this correspondence more generally. We begin

---

[3] There are many alternative explanations. See also [9] on the possibility that the measurement itself is changing the agent's preferences.

with some definitions of contextuality from the quantum foundations literature [2].

A restriction of a function $s : X \to \{0,1\}$ to $U \subseteq X$ will be written $s|X$. The support of $s|X$ are all the elements that are mapped to 1 by it, as in the following example. Take $X = \{a,b,c,d\}$ and $s = \{a \mapsto 1, b \mapsto 1, c \mapsto 0, d \mapsto 0\}$. Consider the restriction to $U = \{a,b,d\}$. We obtain $s|U = \{a \mapsto 1, b \mapsto 1, d \mapsto 0\}$ and the support of $s|U$ is $\{a,b\}$.

Definition 10. *Given an empirical scenario $(X, O, \mathcal{U})$ and a binary empirical model C, a* **global section** *is an assignment $s : X \to O$ such that for all $U \in \mathcal{U}$ the support of $s|U$ is in $C(U)$.*

In physical terms, this says that a global section[4] gives a specific outcome to every measurement that can be used to represent any particular measurement context. In other words, the binary empirical model can be reproduced from restrictions of the global section.

In the choice setting, a global section means that we are able to assign a choice or non-choice to each alternative in such a way as to reproduce the choices that are made when restricted to any particular menu. In this sense, the existence of such a global section determines whether or not our choices depend on the menu with which they are presented. The following makes this intuition more precise:

Definition 11 (Adapted from [1]). *A binary empirical model is* **possibilistically noncontextual** *if for every element $\eta \in C(U)$ for some U, there is a global section s' such that η is in the support of $s'|U$.*

When Definition 11 does not hold, the model is *contextual*.

The correspondence between empirical models and choice scenarios from Theorem 9 motivates the construction of the following definition:

Definition 12 (Contextual Choice Scenarios). *A choice scenario is* **noncontextual** *if and only if for every element $\eta \in C(U)$ for some U, there is a global section s' such that η is in the support of $s'|U$. Otherwise the choice scenario is* **contextual**.

As a way of interpreting contextuality in economic terms, we can imagine noncontextual choice scenarios as those where we would make the same choices if we were presented every alternative at once in a single menu.

Definition 13 (Strongly Contextual Choice Scenarios). *A choice scenario is* **strongly contextual** *if there exists no global section.*

Scenarios that are strongly contextual[5] do not even have some sub-part that can be modeled as choices made independent of context.

---

[4] As noted in [2], the terminology global section arises because these binary empirical models can be given the structure of a presheaf. More details on this approach can be found in [1].

[5] The notion of strong contextuality in contextual semantics comes from [1].

5 Choice Scenarios and the Theory of Choice

So far, we have interpreted the measurement of choices as a purely empirical approach without any reference to a specific economic theory. In this section, we will link this empirical approach to the theory of choice. To this end, we need the notion of *budgets*. Economic agents have wealth constraints such that not all alternatives may be affordable given a certain wealth level. Changing income, or changing prices of goods, may alter the set of alternatives that are available. In the following, we will give menus an alternative interpretation: they represent the budget; thus they represent the alternatives that are affordable for a given agent.[6]

When menus and budgets coincide, choice scenarios will always allow us to capture the observed behavior of agents acting according to the usual economic choice structures [13, p.9]. In fact, choice scenarios are more general than the usual choice structures, as the following is clear by definition:

Proposition 14. *A choice structure is a choice scenario where $|C(U)| = 1$ for all U.*

5.1 The Weak Axiom and Contextuality

A central question in the theory of choice is how behavior changes over different budgets. As a rationality requirement, consistency of choices is imposed via the weak axiom of revealed preferences. In our choice scenario setting, this has the following form:

Definition 15. *A choice scenario obeys the weak axiom if for every pair of budgets A, B, with elements $x, y \in A \cap B$ such that $x \in C(A)$ and $y \in C(B)$ then*

$$x \in C(B).$$

For a simple example where the weak axiom is violated reconsider Example 8. As Salmon is preferred over Steak in the first menu, it should also be chosen in the larger menu $Salmon, Steak, FrogLegs$.

In the following, we investigate the relationship between contextual choice scenarios and ones whose choice rules obey the weak axiom (Fig. 1).

Theorem 16. *Choice scenarios that do not obey the weak axiom are contextual if the set of budgets is closed under intersection.*

Proof. As our scenario does not obey the weak axiom, we know that there exists a pair of budgets A, B, with elements $x, y \in A \cap B$ such that $x \in C(A)$ and $y \in C(B)$, but x is not in $C(B)$. We will use this to demonstrate that there exists no global section that can adequately assign a value to x.

---

[6] Obviously, one could also consider a blend of the two views: (i) what is presented in a menu and (ii) what is affordable? We focus on the extreme case for simplicity.

Suppose there were such a section $s : X \to O$. As $x \in C(A)$ but not in $C(B)$, we would require x to be in the support of $s|A$ but not in the support of $s|B$. As budgets are closed under intersection, we reach a contradiction when trying to assign x to the support of $s|A \cap B$. As we cannot construct a global section that satisfies the definition of possibilistic noncontextuality, the choice scenario must be contextual.

Theorem 17. *Choice scenarios that obey the weak axiom can be either contextual or non-contextual.*

Proof. We show this with two examples. In the first, let budget $A = \{a, b\}$ and budget $B = \{a, c\}$. Choose a global section $s : \{a, b, c\} \to \{0, 1\}$ that sends only a to 1. A choice rule that has $C(A) = C(B) = \{a\}$ obeys the weak axiom and is non-contextual. As the second example, let $A = \{a, b\}$ and $B = \{b, c\}$. Again, choose a global section $s : \{a, b, c\} \to \{0, 1\}$ that sends only a to 1. A choice rule that has $C(A) = \{a\}$ and $C(B) = \{b\}$ obeys the weak axiom and is contextual.

In some sense, this decoupling of the weak axiom and contextuality results from the fact that the weak axiom only conditions the behavior of the choice rule for elements that are in $C(U)$, i.e. elements that are chosen. Contextuality, on the other hand, requires a consistency over contexts where elements are not chosen as well, i.e. if an element is not chosen in some context, then it must also be not chosen in other contexts.

5.2   The Weak Axiom and No-Signalling

The weak axiom can also be related to the no-signalling condition for empirical models, whose definition from [1] we adapt to our setting. For a budget $A \in \mathcal{U}$, let $f_A : A \to \{0, 1\}$ be the choice function that sends an element to 1 when it is chosen - i.e. is in some element of $C(A)$ - and sends an element to 0 when it is not.

Definition 18. *A choice scenario $(X, \mathcal{U}, C)$ is non-signalling if and only if for any two budgets $A, B \in \mathcal{U}$:*

$$f_A|(A \cap B) = f_B|(A \cap B),$$

i.e. all the choice functions have to agree when restricted to their intersections.

In our framework, no-signalling choices are those where the choice or non-choice of an alternative must be consistent across all the budgets in which that alternative appears. It is perhaps not surprising then that such a strong global consistency condition obeys the weak axiom, as is shown in the following theorem:

Theorem 19. *Non-signalling choice scenarios obey the weak axiom.*

Proof. Using this notion of choice functions for budgets, the weak axiom states that if $f_A(x) = 1$ and $f_B(y) = 1$ then $f_B(x) = 1$. By the symmetry of the definition, it is easy to see that $f_A(y) = 1$ necessarily as well. If $f_A(x) = 1$ and $f_B(y) = 1$, then no-signalling implies the same.

Indeed, the no-signalling requirement is actually stronger then that required for the weak axiom (Fig. 1). There do exist choice scenarios where agents act rationally, but not exactly consistently over all budgets.

Theorem 20. *The weak axiom is strictly weaker than no-signalling.*

Proof. Consider the following example for $x, y \in A \cap B$. Let $f_A(x) = 1$ and $f_A(y) = f_B(x) = f_B(y) = 0$.

As in the previous discussion of the weak axiom and contextuality, the economic condition is weaker than the physically influenced one because non-choices are not required to be consistent. One can freely not choose an alternative in one budget, but then choose it in another if there is no preferable option. In an empirical scenario though, the observed outcome of "not-chosen" needs to be considered in consistency conditions.

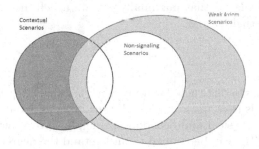

Fig. 1. The overlapping space of scenarios, summarizing the results of Sect. 5. Scenarios in the red region are specified in Theorem 21. Scenarios in the blue region are charecterized by Theorem 16.

Still, we can give a clear picture of when the two are equivalent.

Theorem 21. *The weak axiom is equivalent to no-signalling if a choice scenario has the following property for all budgets A and B:*

$$\text{there exists not necc. distinct } x, y \in A \cap B \text{ s.t. } x \in C(A) \text{ and } y \in C(B). \tag{1}$$

Proof. We show this by contradiction. Consider a choice scenario that obeys the weak axiom and property (1) but that is not no-signalling. A signalling choice scenario has some $z \in A \cap B$ such that $f_A(z) \neq f_B(z)$. Without loss of generality we can take $f_A(z) = 1$ and $f_B(z) = 0$. By property (1), we can always find some $y \in A \cap B$ such that $f_B(y) = 1$, yet the weak axiom states that if $f_A(z) = 1$ and $f_B(y) = 1$ then $f_B(z) = 1$ causing a contradiction.

In economic terms this property (1) states that an agent, when presented with two budgets that have overlapping alternatives, must, in each budget, choose at least one alternative from the overlapping ones.

Results from this section are summarized in Fig. 1, showing how contextual, non-signalling, and weak axiom scenarios are interrelated.

6   Probabilistic Choices

Our setting naturally generalizes to probabilistic choice scenarios. Here the outcome set is $O = [0, 1]$, where 1 indicates that an element $x \in X$ is always chosen, and the choice rule C is replaced with probability distributions $d_U : X \to O$ for each context.

Every probabilistic choice scenario can be reduced to an underlying choice scenario by taking $C(U)$ as the support of d_U. In this way we are able to label probabilistic choice scenarios contextual or strongly contextual according to the property of this underlying choice scenario.

In these probabilistic settings, we can use a single *logical bell inequality* to test for contextuality [2]. Further, these inequalities provide a metric for understanding the degree to which a scenario is contextual from how close a scenario is to the bound. Scenarios that maximally violate a bell inequality are exactly the strongly contextual ones [2].

7   Discussion

In this paper, we have constructed a framework for analyzing the contextuality of choices using tools from quantum foundations, mapping out the logical space of some important physical and economic principles. We show that a series of logical Bell inequalities can be applied to understand the degree of contextuality of choice scenarios. In economic terms, these results are of particular interest for the following reasons:

The observation of contextual choices can imply the non-existence of consistent internal models of choice. To the extent that we believe individual agents not to be purely motivated by individual preferences, measures of contextuality can act as measurements of collusion as they categorically represent behaviors that cannot be generated from fixed individual choices.

To the extent that we doubt agents are well modelled by individual preferences, contextual frameworks provide a setting to investigate more general alternatives without sacrificing rigor and specificity. The foundations of quantum computation, that are well suited to deal with contextualities, provide a rich toolbox for economics to address these problems.

Even if the phenomena of contextuality is, at present, rarely observed it is still relevant because we know that it is possible to physically implement it with quantum systems. One could program quantum computers to make contextual choices and, by so doing, allow for more behaviors than can be modelled classically if it proves advantageous.

Acknowledgements. The authors thank Samson Abramsky for suggesting investigation of the no-signalling condition. Zeng gratefully acknowledges the support of The Rhodes Trust and Zahn gratefully acknowledges financial support by the Deutsche Forschungsgemeinschaft (DFG) through SFB 884 "Political Economy of Reforms".

References

1. Abramsky, S., Brandenburger, A.: The sheaf-theoretic structure of non-locality and contextuality. New J. Phys. **13**(11), 113036 (2011)
2. Abramsky, S., Hardy, L.: Logical bell inequalities. Phys. Rev. A **85**(6), 062114 (2012)
3. Abramsky, S.: Contextual semantics: from quantum mechanics to logic, databases, constraints, and complexity. Bulletin of EATCS 2(113) (2014)
4. Abramsky, S., Mansfield, S., Barbosa, R.S.: The cohomology of non-locality and contextuality. In: 2011 Proceedings of Quantum Physics and Logic, Electronic Proceedings in Theoretical Computer Science (EPTCS), pp. 1–14 (2011)
5. Bao, N., Halpern, N.Y.: Quantum voting and violation of arrow's impossibility theorem. arXiv preprint arXiv:1501.00458 (2015)
6. Brandenburger, A., La Mura, P.: Quantum decision theory. arXiv preprint arXiv:1107.0237 (2011)
7. Brunner, N., Linden, N.: Connection between bell nonlocality and Bayesian game theory. Nature communications 4 (2013)
8. Busemeyer, J.R., Bruza, P.D.: Quantum Models of Cognition and Decision. Cambridge University Press, Cambridge (2012)
9. Danilov, V., Lambert-Mogiliansky, A.: Measurable systems and behavioral sciences. Math. Soc. Sci. **55**(3), 315–340 (2008)
10. Greenberger, D.M., Horne, M.A., Zeilinger, A.: Going beyond Bells theorem. In: Kafatos, M. (ed.) Bells theorem, quantum theory and conceptions of the universe. Fundamental Theories of Physics, vol. 37, pp. 69–72. Springer, Netherlands (1989)
11. Luce, R., Raiffa, H.: Games and Decisions: Introduction and Critical Survey. Dover books on advanced mathematics. Dover books on advanced mathematics. Dover Publications, New York (1957)
12. Mansfield, S.: The mathematical structure of non-locality and contextuality. D.Phil. thesis, Oxford University (2013)
13. Mas-Colell, A., Whinston, M.D., Green, J.: Microeconomic Theory. Oxford University Press, New York (1995)
14. Mogiliansky, A.L., Zamir, S., Zwirn, H.: Type indeterminacy: A Model for the KT(Kahneman-Tversky)-Man. J. Math. Psychol. **53**(5), 349–361 (2009). special Issue: Quantum Cognition
15. Pothos, E.M., Busemeyer, J.R.: A quantum probability explanation for violations of 'rational' decision theory. In: Proceedings of the Biological sciences / The Royal Society, vol. 276(1665), pp. 2171–2178 (2009)
16. Saari, D.G.: The profile structure for Luce's choice axiom. J. Math. Psychol. **49**(3), 226–253 (2005)
17. Wang, Z., Busemeyer, J.R.: A quantum question order model supported by empirical tests of an a priori and precise prediction. Top. Cogn. Sci. **5**(4), 689–710 (2013)

Measuring Observable Quantum Contextuality

Jose Acacio de Barros[1]([✉]), Ehtibar N. Dzhafarov[2], Janne V. Kujala[3],
and Gary Oas[4]

[1] San Francisco State University, San Francisco, USA
barros@sfsu.edu
[2] Purdue University, West Lafayette, USA
ehtibar@purdue.edu
[3] University of Jyväskylä, Jyväskylä, Finland
jvk@iki.fi
[4] Stanford University, Stanford, USA
oas@stanford.edu

Abstract. Contextuality is a central property in comparative analysis of classical, quantum, and supercorrelated systems. We examine and compare two well-motivated approaches to contextuality. One approach ("contextuality-by-default") is based on the idea that one and the same physical property measured under different conditions (contexts) is represented by different random variables. The other approach is based on the idea that while a physical property is represented by a single random variable irrespective of its context, the joint distributions of the random variables describing the system can involve negative (quasi-)probabilities. We show that in the Leggett-Garg and EPR-Bell systems, the two measures essentially coincide.

1 Introduction

Contextuality is a key feature of quantum systems, as no noncontextual hidden-variable theory exists that is consistent with quantum theory. This feature has been at the core of recent research in quantum information, such as attempts to identify the underlying principles for the quantum boundary. Despite its importance, there seem to be no universally accepted measure of contextuality (see, e.g., the different approaches in Refs. [6, 10, 12–17, 20, 22, 26, 27, 29, 37]). Here, we consider and compare two measures inspired by the idea that contextuality means the impossibility of finding a joint probability distribution (jpd) for different sets of random variables with some elements in common. One measure (denoted below by $\Delta_{\min}$) is based on extended sets of context-indexed random variables; its precursors can be found in Refs. [10, 11, 14, 29, 33, 37, 38] and in its current form it is presented in Refs. [12, 15–18, 27, 28]. The other measure (denoted below by $\Gamma_{\min}$) is based on negative (quasi-)probabilities dating back to Dirac, and recently explored in connection to contextuality in Refs. [1, 7–9, 31, 35].

As an example of contextuality, let there be three properties of a system, P, Q, and R, whose measurement outcomes are represented by the random

© Springer International Publishing Switzerland 2016
H. Atmanspacher et al. (Eds.): QI 2015, LNCS 9535, pp. 36–47, 2016.
DOI: 10.1007/978-3-319-28675-4_4

variables $\mathbf{P}$, $\mathbf{Q}$, and $\mathbf{R}^1$. Assume we can never observe P, Q, and R simultaneously, but only in pairwise combinations, $(\mathbf{P}, \mathbf{Q})$, $(\mathbf{P}, \mathbf{R})$, or $(\mathbf{Q}, \mathbf{R})$. We may think of each pair as recorded under a different experimental condition providing a context. The system exhibits contextuality if one cannot find a jpd of $(\mathbf{P}, \mathbf{Q}, \mathbf{R})$ that agrees with the observed distributions of $(\mathbf{P}, \mathbf{Q})$, $(\mathbf{P}, \mathbf{R})$, and $(\mathbf{Q}, \mathbf{R})$ as its marginals. The two approaches to be considered in this paper deal with this situation differently. The negative probabilities (NP) approach relaxes the notion of a jpd by allowing some (unobservable) joint probabilities for $(\mathbf{P}, \mathbf{Q}, \mathbf{R})$ to be negative. The "contextuality-by-default" (CbD) approach treats random variables recorded under different conditions as different "by default", so that, e.g., property P in the context of experiment $(\mathbf{P}, \mathbf{Q})$ is represented by some random variable $\mathbf{P}_A$, and in the context $(\mathbf{P}, \mathbf{R})$ by another random variable, $\mathbf{P}_B$. Denoting the three contexts by A, B, C, this yields three pairs of contextually labeled random variables, $(\mathbf{P}_A, \mathbf{Q}_A)$, $(\mathbf{P}_B, \mathbf{R}_B)$, and $(\mathbf{Q}_C, \mathbf{R}_C)$, and in the CbD approach the joint distribution imposed on them allows, say, $\mathbf{P}_A$ and $\mathbf{P}_B$ to be unequal with some probability.

Here we compare the NP and CdB approaches applied to the simplest contextual case possible, with three pairwise correlated random variables, and to the standard EPR-Bell experiment. We show that for such examples the two measures of contextuality coincide (although they differ for more complex systems). The details of proofs and computations used in the main text are presented in Appendix.

2   Negative Probabilities (NP)

Using our above example, with $\mathbf{P}$, $\mathbf{Q}$, $\mathbf{R}$ observed in pairs, in the NP approach one ascribes to the vector $(\mathbf{P}, \mathbf{Q}, \mathbf{R})$ a joint quasi-distribution by means of assigning to each possible combination $w = (p, q, r)$ a real number $\mu(w)$ (possibly negative), such that

$$\begin{aligned}
\sum_r \mu(w) &= \Pr[\mathbf{P} = p, \mathbf{Q} = q], \\
\sum_q \mu(w) &= \Pr[\mathbf{P} = p, \mathbf{R} = r], \\
\sum_p \mu(w) &= \Pr[\mathbf{Q} = q, \mathbf{R} = r].
\end{aligned} \tag{1}$$

Such μ exists if and only if the no-signaling condition (built into EPR paradigms with spacelike separation) is satisfied [2,3,31], i.e., the distribution of, say, $\mathbf{P}$ is the same in $(\mathbf{P}, \mathbf{Q})$ and in $(\mathbf{P}, \mathbf{R})$.^{2} The numbers $\mu(w)$ can then be interpreted as quasi-probabilities of events $\{w\}$, with the quasi-probability of any other event (subset of w values) being computed by additivity, inducing thereby a signed measure [21] on the set of all events. The quasi-probability of the entire set of w will then be necessarily equal to unity, because, e.g.,

---

[1] This example has the same structure as the Leggett-Garg system [30]. A special version of it was examined by Suppes and Zanotti [36], and also by Specker [34].

[2] No-signaling condition is a fundamental limitation of any approach with noncontextually labeled random variables, including NP.

$$1 = \sum_{p,q} \Pr\left[\mathbf{P} = p, \mathbf{Q} = q\right] = \sum_{w} \mu\left(w\right). \tag{2}$$

The function μ is generally not unique. In our approach [7,8] we restrict the class of possible μ to those as close as possible to a proper jpd by requiring that the L1 norm of the probability distribution, defined by $M = \sum_{w} |\mu\left(w\right)|$, be minimized. This ensures that if the class of all possible μ satisfying (1) contains proper probability distributions, the chosen μ will have to be one of them. Since in this case $|\mu\left(w\right)| = \mu\left(w\right)$ for all w, the minimum of M is 1. If (and only if) no proper probability distribution exists, then the minimum of M exceeds 1. As a result, the smallest possible value $\Gamma_{\min}$ of $M - 1$ can be taken as a measure of contextuality.

3   Contextuality-by-Default (CbD)

A more direct approach to contextuality [10–18,27,28] is to posit that the identity of a random variable is determined by all systematically recorded conditions under which it is observed. Thus, in $(\mathbf{P}_A, \mathbf{Q}_A)$, $(\mathbf{P}_B, \mathbf{R}_B)$, and $(\mathbf{Q}_C, \mathbf{R}_C)$ of our example, any random variable in any of the pairs is *a priori* different from and stochastically unrelated to any random variable in any other pair [12,14], but a jpd can always be imposed on the six random variables. In other words, one can always assign probability masses λ to $v = (p_A, p_B, q_A, q_C, r_B, r_C)$ in such a way that

$$\begin{aligned}
\textstyle\sum_{p_B, q_C, r_B, r_C} \lambda\left(v\right) &= \Pr\left[\mathbf{P}_A = p_A, \mathbf{Q}_A = q_A\right], \\
\textstyle\sum_{p_A, q_A, q_C, r_C} \lambda\left(v\right) &= \Pr\left[\mathbf{P}_B = p_B, \mathbf{R}_B = r_B\right], \\
\textstyle\sum_{p_A, p_B, q_A, r_B} \lambda\left(v\right) &= \Pr\left[\mathbf{Q}_C = q_C, \mathbf{R}_C = r_C\right].
\end{aligned} \tag{3}$$

The noncontextuality hypothesis for $\mathbf{P}_A, \mathbf{Q}_A, \mathbf{R}_B$ and $\mathbf{P}_B, \mathbf{Q}_C, \mathbf{R}_C$ is that among these jpds λ we can find at least one for which $\Pr\left[\mathbf{P}_A \neq \mathbf{P}_B\right] = \Pr\left[\mathbf{Q}_A \neq \mathbf{Q}_C\right] = \Pr\left[\mathbf{R}_B \neq \mathbf{R}_C\right] = 0$, which is equivalent to $\Delta = \Pr\left[\mathbf{P}_A \neq \mathbf{P}_B\right] + \Pr\left[\mathbf{Q}_A \neq \mathbf{Q}_C\right] + \Pr\left[\mathbf{R}_B \neq \mathbf{R}_C\right] = 0$. Such a jpd need not exist, and then the smallest possible value $\Delta_{\min}$ of Δ for which a jpd of $(\mathbf{P}_A, \mathbf{P}_B, \mathbf{Q}_A, \mathbf{Q}_C, \mathbf{R}_B, \mathbf{R}_C)$ exists can be taken as a measure of contextuality.[3]

The CdB approach has its precursors in the literature: various aspects of the contextual indexation of random variables and probabilities of the kind shown are considered in Refs. [10,14,23–25,29,33,37,38]. The principal difference, however, is in the use of minimization of Δ under the assumption that a jpd exists. This is a well-defined mathematical problem, solvable in principle for any set of distributions observed empirically. We will now compare and interrelate the two approaches, NP and CbD, by applying them to the Leggett-Garg and the EPR-Bell setups.

---

[3] This formulation is predicated on no-signaling, which we assume throughout this paper. CbD has been generalized to situations when this condition is violated [4,15–18,27,28].

4 Leggett-Garg

Let us consider Leggett and Garg's ± 1-valued random variables, $\mathbf{Q}_1$, $\mathbf{Q}_2$, and $\mathbf{Q}_3$ [30]. Applying the NP approach, we seek signed probabilities μ for $(\mathbf{Q}_1, \mathbf{Q}_2, \mathbf{Q}_3)$ that are consistent with the observed correlations $\langle \mathbf{Q}_i \mathbf{Q}_j \rangle$ and individual expectations $\langle \mathbf{Q}_i \rangle$, with the smallest possible value of the L1 norm $M \equiv \sum_w |\mu(w)|$, where w denotes all possible combinations of values (q_1, q_2, q_3) for $(\mathbf{Q}_1, \mathbf{Q}_2, \mathbf{Q}_3)$. Here, we use the standard notation $\langle \cdot \rangle$ for the expectation operator. This problem can be easily solved, as we only have 2^3 atomic elements w: $(1,1,1)$, $(1,1,-1)$, ... , $(-1,-1,-1)$. Thus, for $\mathbf{Q}_1$, $\mathbf{Q}_2$, and $\mathbf{Q}_3$, the minimal L1 norm $1 + \Gamma_{\min}$ satisfies

$$\Gamma_{\min} = \max \left\{ 0, -\frac{1}{2} + \frac{1}{2} S_{LG} \right\}, \tag{4}$$

where S_{LG} is defined as

$$S_{LG} \equiv \max_{\#^- = 1,3} \{ \pm \langle \mathbf{Q}_1 \mathbf{Q}_2 \rangle \pm \langle \mathbf{Q}_1 \mathbf{Q}_3 \rangle \pm \langle \mathbf{Q}_2 \mathbf{Q}_3 \rangle \}, \tag{5}$$

where each $\pm$ in the expression should be replaced with $+$ or $-$, and $\#^-$ indicates the possible numbers of minuses. Notice that $S_{LG} \leq 1$, which is equivalent to $\Gamma_{\min} = 0$, is a necessary and sufficient condition for the existence of a proper jpd.

Turning now to the CbD approach, we create a set of six random variables

$$\mathbf{Q}_{1,2}, \mathbf{Q}_{1,3}, \mathbf{Q}_{2,1}, \mathbf{Q}_{2,3}, \mathbf{Q}_{3,1}, \mathbf{Q}_{3,2}, \tag{6}$$

each indexed by the measurement conditions under which it is recorded: for any two random variables recorded at moments t_i and t_j, with $i < j$, the $\mathbf{Q}_{i,j}$ designates the earlier variable and $\mathbf{Q}_{j,i}$ the later one. We have thus three pairs of variables with known jpds:

$$(\mathbf{Q}_{1,2}, \mathbf{Q}_{2,1}), (\mathbf{Q}_{1,3}, \mathbf{Q}_{3,1}), (\mathbf{Q}_{2,3}, \mathbf{Q}_{3,2}). \tag{7}$$

A jpd can always be constructed for these pairs (e.g., they can always be connected as stochastically independent pairs), but we seek a jpd with the smallest value $\Delta_{\min}$ of

$$\Delta = \Pr[\mathbf{Q}_{1,2} \neq \mathbf{Q}_{1,3}] + \Pr[\mathbf{Q}_{2,1} \neq \mathbf{Q}_{2,3}] + \Pr[\mathbf{Q}_{3,1} \neq \mathbf{Q}_{3,2}]. \tag{8}$$

A classical joint exists for $\mathbf{Q}_1$, $\mathbf{Q}_2$, and $\mathbf{Q}_3$ (no contextuality) if and only if a joint exists for (7) with $\Delta = 0$. The more we depart from the classical joint, the larger the minimum value $\Delta_{\min}$. Thus, $\Delta_{\min}$ can serve as a measure of contextuality.

Requiring a jpd consistent with (7) means to assign a probability to each of the 2^6 possible values of these random variables,

$$\mathbf{Q}_{1,2} = \pm 1, \mathbf{Q}_{1,3} = \pm 1, \ldots, \mathbf{Q}_{3,2} = \pm 1, \tag{9}$$

constrained by being nonnegative and summing to the observed probabilities. For instance, the probabilities assigned to all combinations with $\mathbf{Q}_{1,2} = 1$ and $\mathbf{Q}_{2,1} = -1$ should sum to the observed $\Pr[\mathbf{Q}_{1,2} = 1, \mathbf{Q}_{2,1} = -1]$. A computer-assisted Fourier-Motzkin elimination algorithm gives the following analytic expression for the minimum value of Δ consistent with the observable pairs (7):

$$\Delta_{\min} = \max\left\{0, -\frac{1}{2} + \frac{1}{2}S_{LG}\right\}. \tag{10}$$

This is a special case of the result in Ref. [16, 17, 27].

Comparing the general expressions (4) for $\Gamma_{\min}$ and (10) for $\Delta_{\min}$ we see that the two simply coincide:

$$\Delta_{\min} = \Gamma_{\min}. \tag{11}$$

5   EPR-Bell

We now turn to the EPR-Bell case where Alice and Bob have each two distinct settings, 1 and 2, corresponding to four observable random variables $\mathbf{A}_1$, $\mathbf{A}_2$, $\mathbf{B}_1$, and $\mathbf{B}_2$. This notation implicitly contains the assumption that the identity of Alice's measurements as random variables does not depend on Bob's settings, and vice versa. It is well known [19] that under the no-signaling conditions the existence of the jpd is equivalent to the CHSH inequalities being satisfied. Applying the NP approach, the minimal L1 norm of the probability distribution is given by [31]

$$\Gamma_{\min} = \max\left\{0, \frac{1}{2}S_{CHSH} - 1\right\}, \tag{12}$$

where

$$S_{CHSH} = \max_{\#^- = 1,3}\{\pm\langle\mathbf{A}_{1,1}\mathbf{B}_{1,1}\rangle \pm \langle\mathbf{A}_{1,2}\mathbf{B}_{1,2}\rangle \pm \langle\mathbf{A}_{2,1}\mathbf{B}_{2,1}\rangle \pm \langle\mathbf{A}_{2,2}\mathbf{B}_{2,2}\rangle\}. \tag{13}$$

Here $\Gamma_{\min} = 0$ corresponds to the CHSH inequalities, and $\Gamma_{\min} > 0$ to contextuality.

Turning now to the CbD approach, we have four pairs of random variables,

$$(\mathbf{A}_{1,1}, \mathbf{B}_{1,1}), (\mathbf{A}_{1,2}, \mathbf{B}_{1,2}), (\mathbf{A}_{2,1}, \mathbf{B}_{2,1}), (\mathbf{A}_{2,2}, \mathbf{B}_{2,2}). \tag{14}$$

Here, $\mathbf{A}_{i,j}$ denotes Alice's measurement under her setting $i = 1, 2$ when Bob's setting is $j = 1, 2$, and analogously for $\mathbf{B}_{i,j}$. We seek a jpd with the smallest value $\Delta_{\min}$ of

$$\Pr[\mathbf{A}_{1,1} \neq \mathbf{A}_{1,2}] + \Pr[\mathbf{A}_{2,1} \neq \mathbf{A}_{2,2}] + \Pr[\mathbf{B}_{1,1} \neq \mathbf{B}_{2,1}] + \Pr[\mathbf{B}_{1,2} \neq \mathbf{B}_{2,2}]. \tag{15}$$

No contextuality means $\Delta_{\min} = 0$. A computer assisted Fourier-Motzkin elimination algorithm yields (this is a special case of the result in Ref. [16, 17, 27])

$$\Delta_{\min} = \max\left\{0, \frac{1}{2}S_{CHSH} - 1\right\}. \tag{16}$$

We have the same simple coincidence the two measures as in the case of the Leggett-Garg systems,

$$\Delta_{\min} = \Gamma_{\min}. \tag{17}$$

6   Final Remarks

We have discussed two ways to measure contextuality. The direct approach, named Contextuality-by-Default (CbD), assigns to each random variable an index related to their context. If a system is noncontextual, a jpd can be imposed on the random variables so that any two of them representing the same property in different contexts always have the same values. If the system is contextual, the minimum value of Δ in (10)–(16) across all possible jpds has the interpretation of how close a variable can be in two different contexts: the larger the value the greater contextuality, zero representing a necessary and sufficient condition for no contextuality.

The other approach maintains the original set of random variables, but requires negative (quasi-)probabilities. This leads to nonmonotonicity (i.e., a set of outcomes can have a smaller probability than some of its proper subsets), which is a characteristic of quantum interference. The departure from a proper probability distribution is measured by $\Gamma_{\min}$ in the minimum L1 norm $1 + \Gamma_{\min}$. Similar to the CbD approach, we use here a minimization principle that gives the closest probability distribution to an ideal (but impossible) jpd. The value of $\Gamma_{\min}$ has the interpretation of how contextual the system is: a necessary and sufficient condition for no contextuality is $\Gamma_{\min} = 0$, and the larger the value of $\Gamma_{\min}$, the more contextual the system is.

As we have seen, in the case of EPR-Bell and Leggett-Garg systems the two approaches lead to simple coincidence, $\Delta_{\min} = \Gamma_{\min}$. The two measures, $\Gamma_{\min}$ and $\Delta_{\min}$, can be computed for any given system, and they do not coincide for more complex systems. Thus, for a bi-partite system with three settings for Alice and for Bob our computations show that $\Gamma_{\min}$ has a value of 1 for all Popescu-Rohrlich (PR) boxes [5,32], whereas for some PR boxes $\Delta_{\min} = 2$ and for others $\Delta_{\min} = 1$. Still more complex systems exhibit still richer patterns of values for $\Gamma_{\min}$ and $\Delta_{\min}$.

Of the two measures of contextuality, $\Gamma_{\min}$ is computationally much simpler, as it involves fewer random variables and a simpler set of conditions (no non-negativity constraints). However, CbD has the advantage of being more general than NP, as it can include cases where no NP distributions exist due to violations of the no-signaling condition [15,17,27].

Acknowledgments. This work was supported by NSF grant SES-1155956, AFOSR grant FA9550-14-1-0318, and A. von Humboldt Foundation. The authors are grateful to Samson Abramsky, Guido Bacciagaluppi, Andrei Khrennikov, Jan-Åke Larsson, and Patrick Suppes for helpful discussions.

A   Proofs of Statements

In this appendix, we describe how the analytic results of the main text were obtained for each of the expressions (4), (10), (12), and (16) of the main text.

A.1   EPR-Bell: Contextuality-by-Default

Following the computations of Dzhafarov and Kujala [10, TextS3], or the more general formulation in Ref. [16], it can be shown that the observable distributions with probabilities given by the matrices

	$B_{1,1}=+1$	$B_{1,1}=-1$	
$A_{1,1}=+1$	$p_{1,1}$	$a_1 - p_{1,1}$	a_1
$A_{1,1}=-1$	$b_1 - p_{1,1}$	$1 - a_1 - b_1 + p_{1,1}$	$1 - a_1$
	b_1	$1 - b_1$	

	$B_{1,2}=+1$	$B_{1,2}=-1$	
$A_{1,2}=+1$	$p_{1,2}$	$a_1 - p_{1,2}$	a_1
$A_{1,2}=-1$	$b_2 - p_{1,2}$	$1 - a_1 - b_2 + p_{1,2}$	$1 - a_1$
	b_2	$1 - b_2$	

	$B_{2,1}=+1$	$B_{2,1}=-1$	
$A_{2,1}=+1$	$p_{2,1}$	$a_2 - p_{2,1}$	a_2
$A_{2,1}=-1$	$b_1 - p_{2,1}$	$1 - a_2 - b_1 + p_{2,1}$	$1 - a_2$
	b_1	$1 - b_1$	

	$B_{2,2}=+1$	$B_{2,2}=-1$	
$A_{2,2}=+1$	$p_{2,2}$	$a_2 - p_{2,2}$	a_2
$A_{2,2}=-1$	$b_2 - p_{2,2}$	$1 - a_2 - b_2 + p_{2,2}$	$1 - a_2$
	b_2	$1 - b_2$	

$$(18)$$

are compatible with the connections

	$A_{1,2}=+1$	$A_{1,2}=-1$	
$A_{1,1}=+1$	$a_1 - \alpha_1$	α_1	a_1
$A_{1,1}=-1$	α_1	$1 - a_1 - \alpha_1$	$1 - a_1$
	a_1	$1 - a_1$	

	$B_{2,1}=+1$	$B_{2,1}=-1$	
$B_{1,1}=+1$	$b_1 - \beta_1$	β_1	b_1
$B_{1,1}=-1$	β_1	$1 - b_1 - \beta_1$	$1 - b_1$
	b_1	$1 - b_1$	

	$A_{2,2}=+1$	$A_{2,2}=-1$	
$A_{2,1}=+1$	$a_2 - \alpha_2$	α_2	a_2
$A_{2,1}=-1$	α_2	$1 - a_2 - \alpha_2$	$1 - a_2$
	a_2	$1 - a_2$	

	$B_{2,2}=+1$	$B_{2,2}=-1$	
$B_{1,2}=+1$	$b_2 - \beta_2$	β_2	b_2
$B_{1,2}=-1$	β_2	$1 - b_2 - \beta_2$	$1 - b_2$
	b_2	$1 - b_2$	

$$(19)$$

if and only if

$$s_u(\langle \mathbf{A}_{1,1}\mathbf{B}_{1,1}\rangle, \langle \mathbf{A}_{1,2}\mathbf{B}_{1,2}\rangle, \langle \mathbf{A}_{2,1}\mathbf{B}_{2,1}\rangle, \langle \mathbf{A}_{2,2}\mathbf{B}_{2,2}\rangle)$$
$$\leq 6 - s_{1-u}(\langle \mathbf{A}_{1,1}\mathbf{A}_{1,2}\rangle, \langle \mathbf{A}_{2,1}\mathbf{A}_{2,2}\rangle, \langle \mathbf{B}_{1,1}\mathbf{B}_{2,1}\rangle, \langle \mathbf{B}_{1,2}\mathbf{B}_{2,2}\rangle), \qquad (20)$$

where u stands for 0 or 1, and

$$s_0(x_1, \ldots, x_n) = \max\{\pm x_1 \pm \cdots \pm x_n : \text{even} \ \# \ \text{of} \ -'s\},$$
$$s_1(x_1, \ldots, x_n) = \max\{\pm x_1 \pm \cdots \pm x_n : \text{odd} \ \# \ \text{of} \ -'s\}.$$

Here we use the parameterization by the 12 expectation variables defined as (with $i, j \in \{1, 2\}$)

$$\langle \mathbf{A}_{i,j}\mathbf{B}_{i,j}\rangle = (4p_{ij} - 1) - (2a_i - 1) - (2b_j - 1), \qquad (21)$$

$$\langle \mathbf{A}_{i,1}\mathbf{A}_{i,2}\rangle = 1 - 4\alpha_i = 1 - 2\Pr[\mathbf{A}_{i,1} \neq \mathbf{A}_{i,2}], \qquad (22)$$

$$\langle \mathbf{B}_{1,j}\mathbf{B}_{2,j}\rangle = 1 - 4\beta_j = 1 - 2\Pr[\mathbf{B}_{1,j} \neq \mathbf{B}_{2,j}], \qquad (23)$$

$$\langle \mathbf{A}_i\rangle = 2a_i - 1, \quad \langle \mathbf{B}_j\rangle = 2b_j - 1. \qquad (24)$$

Writing the inequality (20) in terms of these expectations rather than in terms of probabilities is the most economic way of presenting the 128 non-trivial inequalities of the system, as the marginal probabilities a_1, a_2, b_1, b_2 (or expectations $\langle \mathbf{A}_1 \rangle, \langle \mathbf{A}_2 \rangle, \langle \mathbf{B}_1 \rangle, \langle \mathbf{B}_2 \rangle$) vanish in this form. However, it should be noted that in addition to these 128 inequalities, the form of the observed distributions and connections itself imposes further 28 trivial constraints on the 12 expectation variables of the system: the probabilities within each 2×2 matrix in (18) and (19) should be nonnegative and sum to one. 16 of these trivial constraints pertain to the observed distributions and 12 to the connections. In terms of the expectations, these trivial constraints correspond to

$$-1 + |\langle \mathbf{A} \rangle + \langle \mathbf{B} \rangle | \leq \langle \mathbf{AB} \rangle \leq 1 - |\langle \mathbf{A} \rangle - \langle \mathbf{B} \rangle |, \tag{25}$$

for given marginals for each pair $(\mathbf{A}, \mathbf{B})$ of random variables in (21)–(23). This expands to four inequalities for each of the observed distributions and to three inequalities for each of the connections (the two upper bounds in (25) coincide when $\langle \mathbf{A} \rangle = \langle \mathbf{B} \rangle$). Although these trivial constraints can usually be assumed implicitly, it is important to keep them explicitly in the system for the next step.

Adding the equation

$$\Delta = \Pr\left[\mathbf{A}_{1,1} \neq \mathbf{A}_{1,2}\right] + \Pr\left[\mathbf{A}_{2,1} \neq \mathbf{A}_{2,2}\right] + \Pr\left[\mathbf{B}_{1,1} \neq \mathbf{B}_{2,1}\right] + \Pr\left[\mathbf{B}_{1,2} \neq \mathbf{B}_{2,2}\right]$$

$$= 2 - \frac{1}{2}\left(\langle \mathbf{A}_{1,1}\mathbf{A}_{1,2} \rangle + \langle \mathbf{A}_{2,1}\mathbf{A}_{2,2} \rangle + \langle \mathbf{B}_{1,1}\mathbf{B}_{2,1} \rangle + \langle \mathbf{B}_{1,2}\mathbf{B}_{2,2} \rangle \right)$$

to the system and then eliminating the connection correlations $\langle \mathbf{A}_{1,1}\mathbf{A}_{1,2} \rangle$, $\langle \mathbf{A}_{2,1}\mathbf{A}_{2,2} \rangle$, $\langle \mathbf{B}_{1,1}\mathbf{B}_{2,1} \rangle$, $\langle \mathbf{B}_{1,2}\mathbf{B}_{2,2} \rangle$ from the system using the Fourier–Motzkin elimination algorithm, we obtain the system

$$-1 + \frac{1}{2}S_{CHSH} \leq \Delta \leq 4 - \left[-1 + \frac{1}{2}S_{CHSH} \right], \tag{26}$$

$$0 \leq \Delta \leq 4 - \left(|\langle \mathbf{A}_1 \rangle| + |\langle \mathbf{A}_2 \rangle| + |\langle \mathbf{B}_1 \rangle| + |\langle \mathbf{B}_2 \rangle| \right), \tag{27}$$

where we denote

$$S_{CHSH} = s_1\left(\langle \mathbf{A}_{1,1}\mathbf{B}_{1,1} \rangle, \langle \mathbf{A}_{1,2}\mathbf{B}_{1,2} \rangle, \langle \mathbf{A}_{2,1}\mathbf{B}_{2,1} \rangle, \langle \mathbf{A}_{2,2}\mathbf{B}_{2,2} \rangle \right) \tag{28}$$

as in the main text. This means that Δ is compatible with the given observed probabilities if and only if the above inequalities are satisfied. Since the set of possible values of Δ constrained by (26) and (27) is known to be nonempty, it follows that the minimum value of Δ is always given by

$$\Delta_{\min} = \max\left\{ 0, \frac{1}{2}S_{CHSH} - 1 \right\}.$$

A.2 EPR-Bell: Negative Probabilities

The analogous result for the negative probabilities approach is that the observable distributions (18) are obtained as the marginals of some negative probability joint of $\mathbf{A}_1 = \mathbf{A}_{1,1} = \mathbf{A}_{1,2}$, $\mathbf{A}_2 = \mathbf{A}_{2,1} = \mathbf{A}_{2,2}$, $\mathbf{B}_1 = \mathbf{B}_{1,1} = \mathbf{B}_{2,1}$, and $\mathbf{B}_2 = \mathbf{B}_{1,2} = \mathbf{B}_{2,2}$ given by

$$\Pr\left[\mathbf{A}_1 = a_1', \mathbf{A}_2 = a_2', \mathbf{B}_1 = b_1', \mathbf{B}_2 = b_2'\right] = p^+(a_1', a_2', b_1', b_2') - p^-(a_1', a_2', b_1', b_2'),$$

$a_1', a_2', b_1', b_2' \in \{1, -1\}$, for some nonnegative functions p^+ and p^- having a total probability mass value

$$M = \sum_{a_1', a_2', b_1', b_2'} p^+(a_1', a_2', b_1', b_2') + p^-(a_1', a_2', b_1', b_2')$$

if and only if $M \geq 1 + \Gamma_{\min}$, where

$$\Gamma_{\min} = \max\left\{0, \frac{1}{2}S_{CHSH} - 1\right\}.$$

The computations are similar to those of the CbD approach, but there are two general differences. First, in the CbD approach, the convex range of the possible observed and connection expectations (21)–(24) over the convex polytope of all possible joints is obtained by looking at these expectations at the 2^8 vertices defining the polytope of all joints and then applying a computer algorithm to find the set of inequalities delineating the extreme values of the expectations at these vertices. However, in the negative probabilities approach, the joint is represented by the 2^4 differences of the positive and negative components of the distribution and so, although these $2 \cdot 2^4$ components are nonnegative as in the CbD approach, they do not need to sum to one. Hence, the joint is represented by a convex cone rather than a bounded polytope. Still, a convex cone is a special case of a general polytope and can be handled by the same algorithms that we have used in the CbD approach.

Second, we do not need to apply the Fourier–Motzkin elimination algorithm here as we have defined M directly by the representation of the joint so there are no extra variables we would need to eliminate. This difference, however, is not really a difference between the two approaches, as we could have done the same in the CbD approach as well: we could have defined Δ directly based on the joint of all eight variables without explicitly defining the connection correlations (22)–(23), and then we would have obtained the result directly from the half-space representation, as we do in the negative probabilities approach.

A.3   Leggett–Garg: Contextuality-by-Default

The results for Leggett–Garg $\mathbf{Q}_1, \mathbf{Q}_2, \mathbf{Q}_3$ can be obtained in the same way as for the EPR-Bell systems. In the CbD approach, the observed correlations $\langle \mathbf{Q}_{1,2}\mathbf{Q}_{2,1}\rangle$, $\langle \mathbf{Q}_{1,3}\mathbf{Q}_{3,1}\rangle$, $\langle \mathbf{Q}_{2,3}\mathbf{Q}_{3,2}\rangle$, $\langle \mathbf{Q}_1\rangle = \langle \mathbf{Q}_{1,2}\rangle = \langle \mathbf{Q}_{1,3}\rangle$, $\langle \mathbf{Q}_2\rangle = \langle \mathbf{Q}_{2,1}\rangle = \langle \mathbf{Q}_{3,2}\rangle$, $\langle \mathbf{Q}_3\rangle = \langle \mathbf{Q}_{3,1}\rangle = \langle \mathbf{Q}_{3,2}\rangle$ are consistent with the connection correlations $\langle \mathbf{Q}_{1,2}\mathbf{Q}_{1,3}\rangle$, $\langle \mathbf{Q}_{2,1}\mathbf{Q}_{2,3}\rangle$, $\langle \mathbf{Q}_{3,1}\mathbf{Q}_{3,2}\rangle$ if and only if these connection correlations are realizable with the given marginals (i.e., each correlation $\langle \mathbf{AB}\rangle$ has to satisfy $-1 + |\langle \mathbf{A}\rangle + \langle \mathbf{B}\rangle| \leq \langle \mathbf{AB}\rangle \leq 1 - |\langle \mathbf{A}\rangle - \langle \mathbf{B}\rangle|$ as discussed in the EPR-Bell case above) and satisfy

$$s_u\left(\langle \mathbf{Q}_{1,2}\mathbf{Q}_{2,1}\rangle, \langle \mathbf{Q}_{1,3}\mathbf{Q}_{3,1}\rangle, \langle \mathbf{Q}_{2,3}\mathbf{Q}_{3,2}\rangle\right) \\ + s_{1-u}\left(\langle \mathbf{Q}_{1,2}\mathbf{Q}_{1,3}\rangle, \langle \mathbf{Q}_{2,1}\mathbf{Q}_{2,3}\rangle, \langle \mathbf{Q}_{3,1}\mathbf{Q}_{3,2}\rangle\right) \leq 4, \tag{29}$$

These two inequalities (with u standing for 0 or 1) expand to 32 linear inequalities and there are 21 trivial constraints.

Denoting

$$\Delta = \Pr\left[\mathbf{Q}_{1,2} \neq \mathbf{Q}_{1,3}\right] + \Pr\left[\mathbf{Q}_{2,1} \neq \mathbf{Q}_{2,3}\right] + \Pr\left[\mathbf{Q}_{3,1} \neq \mathbf{Q}_{3,2}\right]$$

$$= \frac{3}{2} - \frac{1}{2}\left(\langle\mathbf{Q}_{1,2}\mathbf{Q}_{1,3}\rangle + \langle\mathbf{Q}_{2,1}\mathbf{Q}_{2,3}\rangle + \langle\mathbf{Q}_{3,1}\mathbf{Q}_{3,2}\rangle\right)$$

and eliminating the connection correlations from the system using the Fourier–Motzkin algorithm, we obtain the system

$$-\frac{1}{2} + \frac{1}{2}S_{LG} \leq \Delta \leq 3 - \left[-\frac{1}{2} + \frac{1}{2}S_{LG}^0\right], \tag{30}$$

$$0 \leq \Delta \leq 3 - |\langle\mathbf{Q}_1\rangle| - |\langle\mathbf{Q}_2\rangle| - |\langle\mathbf{Q}_3\rangle|, \tag{31}$$

where we denote

$$S_{LG} = s_1\left(\langle\mathbf{Q}_{1,2}\mathbf{Q}_{2,1}\rangle, \langle\mathbf{Q}_{1,3}\mathbf{Q}_{3,1}\rangle, \langle\mathbf{Q}_{2,3}\mathbf{Q}_{3,2}\rangle\right),$$

$$S_{LG}^0 = s_0\left(\langle\mathbf{Q}_{1,2}\mathbf{Q}_{2,1}\rangle, \langle\mathbf{Q}_{1,3}\mathbf{Q}_{3,1}\rangle, \langle\mathbf{Q}_{2,3}\mathbf{Q}_{3,2}\rangle\right).$$

That is, Δ is consistent with the observed probabilities if and only if the above inequalities are satisfied. It follows that the minimum value of Δ is given by

$$\Delta_{\min} = \max\left\{0, \frac{1}{2}S_{LG} - \frac{1}{2}\right\}.$$

A.4   Leggett–Garg: Negative Probabilities

With the same additional comments as in the negative probability calculations for the EPR-Bell case, our calculations show that the observable probabilities $\Pr\left[\mathbf{Q}_{12} = q_1, \mathbf{Q}_{21} = q_2\right]$, $\Pr\left[\mathbf{Q}_{13} = q_1, \mathbf{Q}_{31} = q_3\right]$, $\Pr\left[\mathbf{Q}_{23} = q_2, \mathbf{Q}_{32} = q_3\right]$, $q_1, q_2, q_3 \in \{0, 1\}$, can be obtained as the marginals of a negative probability jpd of $\mathbf{Q}_1 = \mathbf{Q}_{1,2} = \mathbf{Q}_{1,3}$, $\mathbf{Q}_2 = \mathbf{Q}_{2,1} = \mathbf{Q}_{3,2}$, and $\mathbf{Q}_3 = \mathbf{Q}_{3,1} = \mathbf{Q}_{3,2}$ with the total probability mass of M if and only if $M \geq 1 + \Gamma_{\min}$, where

$$\Gamma_{\min} = \max\left\{0, \frac{1}{2}S_{LG} - \frac{1}{2}\right\}.$$

References

1. Abramsky, S., Brandenburger, A.: The sheaf-theoretic structure of non-locality and contextuality. New J. Phys. **13**, 113036 (2011)
2. Abramsky, S., Brandenburger, A.: An operational interpretation of negative probabilities and no-signalling models. In: van Breugel, F., Kashefi, E., Palamidessi, C., Rutten, J. (eds.) Horizons of the Mind. LNCS, vol. 8464, pp. 59–75. Springer, Heidelberg (2014)

3. Al-Safi, S., Short, A.: Simulating all nonsignaling correlations via classical or quantum theory with negative probabilities. Phys. Rev. Lett. **111**, 170403 (2013)
4. Bacciagaluppi, G.: Leggett-Garg inequalities, pilot waves and contextuality. Int. J. Quant. Found. **1**(1), 1–17 (2015)
5. Brunner, N., Scarani, V., Gisin, N.: Bell-type inequalities for non-local resources. J. Math. Phys. **47**, 112101 (2006)
6. Chaves, R., Fritz, T.: Entropic approach to local realism and noncontextuality. Phys. Rev. A **85**, 032113 (2012)
7. de Barros, J.A.: Decision making for inconsistent expert judgments using negative probabilities. In: Atmanspacher, H., Haven, E., Kitto, K., Raine, D. (eds.) QI 2013. LNCS, vol. 8369, pp. 257–269. Springer, Heidelberg (2014)
8. de Barros, J.A., Oas, G., Suppes, P.: Negative probabilities and counterfactual reasoning on the double-slit experiment. In: Beziau, J.-Y., Krause, D., Arenhart, J.B. (eds.) Conceptual Clarification: Tributes to Patrick Suppes. College Publications, London (2015). (1992–2014)
9. de Barros, J.A., Oas, G.: Negative probabilities and counter-factual reasoning in quantum cognition. Phys. Scripta **T163**, 014008 (2014)
10. Dzhafarov, E., Kujala, J.: All-possible-couplings approach to measuring probabilistic context. Plos One **8**, e61712 (2013)
11. Dzhafarov, E., Kujala, J.: Embedding quantum into classical: contextualization vs conditionalization. Plos One **9**, e92818 (2014)
12. Dzhafarov, E., Kujala, J.: Contextualityis about identity of random variables. Phys. Scripta **T163**, 014009 (2014)
13. Dzhafarov, E., Kujala, J.: Random variables recorded under mutually exclusive conditions: contextuality-by-default. In: Liljenström, H. (Ed.) Advances in Cognitive Neurodynamics IV, pp. 405–410 (2015)
14. Dzhafarov, E.N., Kujala, J.V.: A qualified kolmogorovian account of probabilistic contextuality. In: Atmanspacher, H., Haven, E., Kitto, K., Raine, D. (eds.) QI 2013. LNCS, vol. 8369, pp. 201–212. Springer, Heidelberg (2014)
15. Dzhafarov, E., Kujala, J.: probabilistic contextuality in EPR/Bohm-type systems with signaling allowed. arXiv:1406.0243 [quant-ph, q-bio] (2014)
16. Dzhafarov, E., Kujala, J.: Generalizing Bell-type and Leggett-Garg-type inequalities to systems with signaling. arXiv:1407.2886 [quant-ph] (2014)
17. Dzhafarov, E., Kujala, J., Larsson, J.-Å.: Contextuality in three types of quantum mechanical systems. Found. Phys. **45**, 762–782 (2014). doi:10.1007/s10701-015-9882-9
18. Dzhafarov, E., Kujala, J., Larsson, J.-Å.: Contextuality-by-default: a brief overview of ideas, concepts, and terminology. arXiv:1504.00530 [quant-ph] (2015)
19. Fine, A.: Hidden variables, joint probability, and the Bell inequalities. Phys. Rev. Lett. **48**, 291 (1982)
20. Grudka, A., Horodecki, K., Horodecki, M., Horodecki, P., Horodecki, R., Joshi, P., Kłobus, W., Wójcik, A.: Quantifying contextuality. Phys. Rev. Lett. **112**, 120401 (2014)
21. Halmos, P.: Measure Theory. Springer-Verlag, New York (1974)
22. Kleinmann, M., Gühne, O., Portillo, J., Larsson, J.-Å., Cabello, A.: Memory cost of quantum contextuality. New J. Phys. **13**, 113011 (2011)
23. Khrennikov, A.: The principle of supplementarity: a contextual probabilistic viewpoint to complementarity, the interference of probabilities, and the incompatibility of variables in quantum mechanics. Found. Phys. **35**, 1655–1693 (2005)
24. Khrennikov, A.: Bell-Boole inequality: nonlocality or probabilistic incompatibility of random variables? Entropy **10**, 19–32 (2008)

25. Khrennikov, A.: Contextual Approach to Quantum Formalism. Springer, Berlin (2009)
26. Kurzyński, P., Ramanathan, R., Kaszlikowski, D.: Entropic test of quantum contextuality. Phys. Rev. Lett. **109**, 020404 (2012)
27. Kujala, J., Dzhafarov, E., Larsson, J.Å.: Necessary and sufficient conditions for maximal noncontextuality in a broad class of quantum mechanical systems. Phys. Rev. Lett. (in press)
28. Kujala, J., Dzhafarov, E.: Proof of a conjecture on contextuality in cyclic systems with binary variables. arXiv:1503.02181 [quant-ph] (2015)
29. Larsson, J.-Å.: A Kochen-Specker inequality. EPL (Eur. Lett.) **58**, 799–805 (2002)
30. Leggett, A., Garg, A.: Quantum mechanics versus macroscopic realism: is the flux there when nobody looks? Phys. Rev. Lett. **54**, 857 (1985)
31. Oas, G., de Barros, J.A., Carvalhaes, C.: Exploring non-signalling polytopes with negative probability. Phys. Scripta **T163**, 014034 (2014)
32. Popescu, S., Rohrlich, D.: Nonlocality as an axiom. Found. Phys. **24**, 379 (1994)
33. Simon, C., Brukner, Č., Zeilinger, A.: Hidden-variable theorems for real experiments. Phys. Rev. Lett. **86**(20), 4427–4430 (2001)
34. Specker, E.P.: The logic of propositions which are not simultaneously decidable. In: Hooker, C.A. (ed.) The Logico-Algebraic Approach to Quantum Mechanics. The University of Western Ontario Series in Philosophy of Science, vol. 5a, pp. 135–140. Springer, Netherlands (1975)
35. Spekkens, R.W.: Negativity and contextuality are equivalent notions of nonclassicality. Phys. Rev. Lett. **101**, 020401 (2008)
36. Suppes, P., Zanotti, M.: When are probabilistic explanations possible? Synthese **48**, 191 (1981)
37. Svozil, K.: How much contextuality? Nat. Comput. **11**, 261 (2012)
38. Winter, A.: What does an experimental test of quantum contextuality prove or disprove? J. Phys. A: Math. Theor. **47**, 424031 (2014)

Fundamentals

Age and Time Operator
of Evolutionary Processes

Ioannis Antoniou[1(✉)], Ilias Gialampoukidis[1,2], and E. Ioannidis[1]

[1] School of Mathematics, Aristotle University of Thessaloniki,
54124 Thessaloniki, Greece
iantonio@math.auth.gr
[2] Information Technologies Institute,
Centre for Research and Technology Hellas,
Thermi, 57001 Thessaloniki, Greece

Abstract. The Time Operator and Internal Age are intrinsic features of Entropy producing Innovation Processes. The innovation spaces at each stage are the eigenspaces of the Time Operator. The internal Age is the average innovation time, analogous to lifetime computation. Time Operators were originally introduced for Quantum Systems and highly unstable Dynamical Systems. The goal of this work is to present recent extensions of Time Operator theory to regular Markov Chains and Networks in a unified way and to illustrate the Non-Commutativity of Net Operations like Selection and Filtering in the context of Knowledge Networks.

Keywords: Time operator · Internal age · Chaos · Bernoulli processes · Markov chains · Networks

1 Introduction

Aristotle related Time to the numerical assessment of the observation of change by the following statements: (1) We are not aware of the becoming of time, unless changes are registered in our mind [Arist. Physics Δ 218 β] and (2) Time is the number of motion with respect to before and after. [Arist. Physics Δ 219 β]. Following this key remark, time has no sense, if no events are observable and Time should be comprehended from the estimation of the rate of change according to the (temporal-causal) order of events. Time is the Awareness of Registered (Simulated-Observed) Succession of Events. Further progress was not possible without two key discoveries, namely: (1) the experimental possibility to measure the local (in space) rates of change with high resolution, realized with the mechanical clocks and (2) the mathematical possibility to formulate, compute and predict from theoretical rate laws, realized with calculus. Both discoveries took place in the 17th century and initiated a new era of investigation of Temporality. The observed processes and/or theoretical models of processes were distinguished by the different rate laws. This is the well-known triumph of Dynamics [1]. Determinism prevailed as the dominant view [1, 2]. Even the Gods of Planets preferred astronomers and mathematicians, than astrologers to reveal themselves. Neptune and Pluto were actually revealed themselves to mathematicians [3] and then

© Springer International Publishing Switzerland 2016
H. Atmanspacher et al. (Eds.): QI 2015, LNCS 9535, pp. 51–75, 2016.
DOI: 10.1007/978-3-319-28675-4_5

astrologers ascribed their features. Regular motions, like the periodic orbits of Pendula or Planetary motions were both observed and predicted. This regular view of temporality conditioned only by the rates of change, was challenged by two discoveries: First, the Thermodynamic Principle of Entropy increase of Irreversible Processes [4] and Second the discovery of Chaos in the Three Body Problem by Poincaré [5, 6]. On one hand, the Irreversible Entropy increase contradicts the Reversible character of Dynamics and on the other hand Chaos introduces intrinsic limits to computability-determinability of the mathematically deterministic Dynamics [7, 8]. It is a remarkable fact that the two challenges somehow resolve each other. Irreversibility is a property of chaotic systems characterized by the rate of Entropy production. In other words entropy increases in deterministic Systems producing information or innovation and these systems are precisely the chaotic ones. We arrive therefore at a new non-local manifestation of temporality, namely the rate of Innovation production estimated by the Entropy Production of the System. Systems with the same Entropy production are effectively equivalent [9, 10]. As we cannot detect chaos by observing the rate laws only, we cannot appreciate the innovation processes without actually observing the possible scenaria. Entropy production is also the key feature of Processes far from Equilibrium [7, 11]. The useful conclusion is that understanding Time is not possible by observing the evolution laws only. We have to take into account the novelties introduced or emerging in the durations we observe. As this is not possible in the frame of the dummy variable model of Time, the non-local concept of Time as an Operator was formulated in a natural way for Entropy Producing Reversible Systems both classical and quantum mechanical by Misra, Prigogine and Courbage [12–15]. The presence of Time Operators allows the representation of the unstable dynamics as Entropy increasing Irreversible Markov processes, thus resolving the problem of Irreversibility in a natural way.

The idea to represent time as an operator goes back to Pauli who remarked that although the Time-Energy uncertainty relation is analogous to the Position-Momentum uncertainty relation, there is no self-adjoint Time Operator $\mathbb{T}$ canonically conjugate to the Energy Operator H (Hamiltonian) of a quantum system as is the case with the Position-Momentum operators [16, 17]. Time Operators, however, can be defined for density matrices describing ensembles in Quantum Statistical Mechanics. Quantum Systems admitting Time Operators include irreversible processes like resonance scattering, decay, radiation transition and Quantum measurement [16, 18–21]. In fact, the presence of Time Operators is a manifestation of the Complementarity between the Dynamic and Thermodynamic descriptions [22–25]. Time Operator theory was further extended to describe the statistical properties of relativistic systems [26–30], non-invertible Entropy producing dynamical systems [31–36], Diffusion [37], Wavelets [38–40], providing new representation of non-equilibrium processes and the innovation of non-predictable stationary stochastic processes [41, 42]. The Time Operator of Markov chains has been constructed [43, 44] as an extension of the Time Operator of Bernoulli Processes [43, 45, 46]. Following this construction it was possible to construct Time operators for evolving Networks [43, 47] by considering their evolution as link observations.

The eigenspaces of the Time operator incorporate the innovations introduced in the successive durations. From the Time Operator we can compute the internal Age

Age(X_t) of the process X_t at each clock time t, as averaging with respect to the innovation probabilities. Therefore, the Time Operator is a natural model of the so-called Bergson's Time [42, 48]. Defining the ontology of time in terms of events, incorporated in the concept of Time Operator, justifies Bergson's views expressed during the Conference of the Société Française de Philosophie in 1922. Einstein's distinction of "the time of physicists" from "the time of philosophers" [49] is understood now as the distinction between the clock time as a dummy variable and the Internal time as an operator constructed from the successive innovations associated to the observed events. Entropy production and Time Operators [50, 51] are key concepts to comprehend and to estimate the present Complexity of our Networked Society, thus shaping the modern Ontology of Time. After defining the Time operator (Sect. 2) and the Age (Sect. 3) we present three examples (Sects. 4, 5 and 6). After discussing Network Evolution (Sect. 7) we present the Aging of three Networks (Sects. 8, 9 and 10) and the Non-Commutativity of the Net Operations Selection and Filtering by computing the knowledge attainment curves (Sect. 11).

2   Time Operator of Processes

The Time Operator of a Process $X(t)$ is a Self-Adjoint Operator on the space $\mathcal{H}$ of fluctuations $(X(t) \quad X_{equilibrium})$ with eigenvalues the clock times t and corresponding eigenspaces the successive innovations. The clock time t is the registration time of what we observe or model theoretically. Without loss of generality we consider the simplest case t = 0,1,2,3,.... The fluctuations are assumed to be square integrable, so that the correlations are finite. This justifies the fact that the space of fluctuations $\mathcal{H}$ is a Hilbert Space with the correlation scalar product.

The Time Operator is constructed as follows: At each stage t the observation of $X(t)$ defines a partition of the sample space Y into cells of indistinguishable states corresponding to the observed values of $X(t)$. This idea of partitioning the elementary events into cells of events indistinguishable by observations goes back to Kolmogorov [51]. At the next stage $t+1$ the observation defines another partition of the sample space Y. Therefore, the knowledge obtained after all successive observations up to time t is the common refinement of the corresponding partitions. In the same way we construct the successive innovations of observations. The innovation during each interval [t, t + 1] is simply the difference of our best prediction from the observation. (Fig. 1).

We denote by $\mathbb{E}_t$ the conditional expectation projecting onto the fluctuations $\mathcal{H}$ observed up to time t. The sequence of conditional expectation projections: $\mathbb{E}_t, t = 0, 1, \ldots$ is a resolution of the identity in $\mathcal{H}$, i.e.: $\mathbb{E}_0 = O, \mathbb{E}_\infty = I$ and $\mathbb{E}_{t_1} \leq \mathbb{E}_{t_2}, t_1 < t_2$. We have omitted the mathematical and technical details, as they are presented elsewhere [12–15, 18–21, 26–47] and they are not necessary within the scope of this work.

Definition 1. *The self-adjoint operator with spectral projections the conditional expectations $\mathbb{E}_t$ on the space of fluctuations $\mathcal{H}$ is called the Time Operator of the stochastic process $X(t), t = 1, 2, \ldots$:*

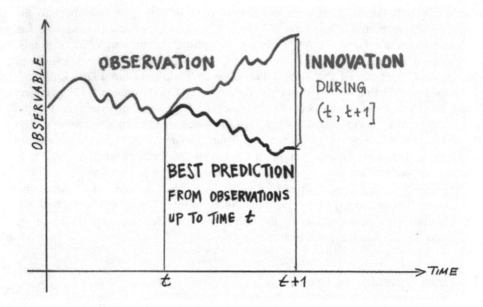

Fig. 1. Observation versus best prediction

$$\mathbb{T} = \sum_{t=1}^{\infty} t(\mathbb{E}_t \ominus \mathbb{E}_{t-1})$$

$\mathbb{E}_t \ominus \mathbb{E}_{t-1}$ *are the projections onto the spaces of Innovations* $\mathcal{N}_t$ *at each stage* $t = 1, 2, \ldots$

The Time Operator is constructed from the Conditional Expectations $\mathbb{E}_t$ of the observed process and the Age is computed as a function of the clock time t. Regular Systems like Oscillators or Planetary Motions produce no Innovation, therefore they have null Time Operator, their Internal Time is just the Clock Time. On the other hand, Unstable Chaotic Systems producing Entropy are qualified by non-trivial Time Operators and are called Intrinsically Irreversible, because they admit Lyapunov Functionals [7, 12, 15, 28], evolving Irreversibly.

A Lyapunov Functional satisfies the conditions:

LF1. $\mathcal{V}(y) \geq 0$, for all y
LF2.   The equation $\mathcal{V}(y) = 0$ has the unique solution y = 0: $\mathcal{V}(y) = 0 \Longleftrightarrow y = 0$
LF3. $\mathcal{V}$ vanishes as t $\rightarrow \infty$: $\lim_{t \to \infty} \mathcal{V}(y_t) = 0 = \mathcal{V}(0)$
LF4. $\mathcal{V}$ is monotonically decreasing: $\mathcal{V}(y_{t_2}) \leq \mathcal{V}(y_{t_1})$, if $t_2 > t_1$.

Each Lyapunov functional defines a corresponding Entropy:

$$\mathcal{S}[\rho(t)] = -k\mathcal{V}(\rho(t) - \rho_{eq}) + \mathcal{S}_{eq}$$

ρ_{eq} is the Equilibrium probability distribution. The Entropy $\mathcal{S}$ is increasing monotonically towards the equilibrium value $\mathcal{S}_{eq}$ for Intrinsically Irreversible Systems or equivalently for Systems satisfying the Second Thermodynamic Principle.

Constructions of Time Operators are summarized in the following Table:

Systems	Model	Reference
Maps	Baker transformation	[7, 13]
	Bernoulli Systems	[14]
	Renyi map	[31, 32]
	Cusp map	[33, 34]
	Dilations of Exact Systems	[35, 36]
Flows	Relativistic Fields	[26–29]
	Cosmological Models	[30]
	Diffusion	[37]
Quantum Mechanical		[15, 16, 18–21]
Processes	Wavelets	[38–40]
	Stochastic Processes	[41, 42]
	Bernoulli Processes	[43, 45, 46]
	Markov chains	[43, 44]
	Network Evolution	[43, 47]

3 Age of Processes

The internal Age of the random variable Z is obtained from the Time Operator as the average time with respect to the innovation probabilities $p_t, t = 1, 2, \ldots$:

$$Age(Z) = \sum_t t p_t = \frac{<Z - <Z>, \mathbb{T}(Z - <Z>)>}{\|Z - <Z>\|^2}$$

$$p_t = \text{Prob}\{Z \in \mathcal{N}_t\} = \frac{\|\mathbb{P}_t Z\|^2}{\|Z - E[Z] 1_\Omega\|^2} = \frac{\text{Var}[\mathbb{P}_t Z]}{\text{Var}[Z]}$$

The Aging of canonical processes (Kolmogorov and Bernoulli Systems) has been shown [7, 12–14] to keep step with the clock time t:

$$Age(t) = Age(0) + t$$

In general, however, the Age formula is non-linear, as in the case of cosmological models [30]:

$$Age(t) = Age(0) + t - \eta(t)$$

The nonlinear function $\eta(t)$ is the deviation of the Age formula from the canonical linear model. General analytical formulas for the internal Age are hard to obtain because there are no general formulas for the conditional expectations $\mathbb{E}_t$.

For regular (irreversible) Markov chains [53] non-canonical Age formulas are found, where the correction $\eta(t)$ depends on a decaying exponential term [43, 44]:

$$Age(t) = Age(0) + t - \left(\alpha + \beta \cdot |\gamma|^t\right), \ \beta > 0$$

The parameter γ is the second eigenvalue of the stochastic matrix of the Markov process [52] conditioning the approach to equilibrium. The internal Age also determines the mixing time of Markov chains [44]. Mixing time estimations are useful in Non-Equilibrium Statistical Physics, in Web Analysis and Network Dynamics, Computer Science and Statistics. More specifically, the mixing time of a Markov chain determines the running time of Monte Carlo simulations, the time needed for a randomized algorithm to find a solution so as to quantify the computational cost, the average navigation time within a website [58–60], the average travel time within a road network [61], the time needed for Google's Page Rank algorithm to compute the pageranks and find the right webpage [62] and the time of validity of specific Markov models, such as the Markov switching between growth and recession of the US GNP [63]. The internal Age is applicable to all the above Markov models. However, the internal Age can also be estimated directly from real data, as illustrated for specific financial applications [43, 44]. For the Athens Stock Market the internal Age was found to take lower values in periods of low uncertainty and greater values in periods of high uncertainty, such as the Greek National Elections of June 2012. This explicit calculation confirms the intuition underlying the Age concept. Age is increasing when innovations appear, therefore predictability is low. The non-canonical Age formula of Markov Processes indicates that Aging is linked with the associated Entropy [50].

Different non-canonical Aging formulas were found when considering evolving networks [45], namely:

For Erdős-Rényi random graphs [54, 55] where the size may change but the order (number of nodes) remains constant in time t, $N(t) = N$, we found [47] canonical Aging:

$$Age(t) = \frac{t+1}{2}$$

The canonical age formula is not unexpected because Erdős-Rényi graphs are in fact Bernoulli processes. However, for Scale-free Networks with simple linear growth and preferential attachment [56, 57], we found [47] more complicated Aging formulas:

$$Age(t) = \frac{ct^2}{2} + \frac{c}{4}\left(\frac{1}{2}N(0)\left(\ln^2 N(t) - \ln^2 N(0)\right) - \ln\frac{N(t)^{N(t)}}{N(0)^{N(0)}} + t\right)$$

Where: $c = \frac{2}{2t - \ln^2 N(t) + \ln^2 N(0)}$

Several Age formulas found in Models or in Observations of real processes are summarized in the following Table [43]:

Process	Age formula	Reference
Kolmogorov Systems	$Age(t) = Age(0) + t$	[7, 12, 13]
Cosmological model	$Age(t) = Age(X_0) + \int_{t_0}^{t} \frac{A}{R(s)\sqrt{a^2 + R^2(s)}} ds$	[30]
Bernoulli Process	$Age(t) = t$	[14, 43]
Random Walk	$Age(t) = \frac{t+1}{2}$	[14, 43]
Markov Chains	$Age(t) = t - \alpha - \beta\|\gamma\|^t$ γ is the second eigenvalue of the stochastic matrix	[43, 44]
US GNP	$Age(t) = t - 0.8062 + 1.2123\|\gamma_{GNP}\|^t$	[43, 44]
Dow Jones	$Age(t) = t - 0.0001 + 0.0112\|\gamma_{DJ}\|^t$	[43, 44]
Mixing Process	$Age(t) = Age(X_0) + t + \mathcal{V}(\rho(t) - \rho_{eq})\theta(t^{\mathcal{V}}_{mix} - t)$ $\mathcal{V}$ the Lyapunov function selected to observe the evolution $t^{\mathcal{V}}_{mix}$ the Mixing Time associated with the Lyapunov function	[43, 44]
Network Evolution	$Age(t) = \sum_{\tau=1}^{t} \tau \frac{\sum_{\kappa,\lambda=1}^{N} w_{\kappa\lambda}(\tau)(1-w_{\kappa\lambda}(\tau))}{\sum_{\tau=1}^{t}\sum_{\kappa,\lambda=1}^{N} w_{\kappa\lambda}(\tau)(1-w_{\kappa\lambda}(\tau))} w_{\kappa\lambda}(\tau)$ the weight of the link $\kappa \to \lambda$ at time τ	[43, 47]
Bernoulli Nets (loopless)	$Age(t) = \sum_{\tau=1}^{t} \tau \frac{N(\tau)(N(\tau)-1)}{\sum_{\tau=1}^{t} N(\tau)(N(\tau)-1)}$ $N(\tau)$ the order (number of nodes) at time τ	[43, 47]
Bernoulli Nets (with loops)	$Age(t) = \sum_{\tau=1}^{t} \tau \frac{(N(\tau))^2}{\sum_{\tau=1}^{t}(N(\tau))^2}$	[43, 47]
Markov Nets	$Age(t) = \sum_{\tau=1}^{t} \tau \frac{\sum_{\kappa=1}^{N} \mathcal{I}_2(w_\kappa(\tau))}{\sum_{\tau=1}^{t}\sum_{\kappa=1}^{N} \mathcal{I}_2(w_\kappa(\tau))}$ $\mathcal{I}_2(w_\kappa(\tau)) = 1 - \sum_{\lambda=1}^{N} w_{\kappa\lambda}^2$ the quadratic entropy of the probability distribution for the transitions from node κ at time τ	[43, 47]
Nets Linearly Growing	$Age(t) = \sum_{\tau=1}^{t} \tau \frac{\mathcal{I}_2(w_t)}{\sum_{\tau=1}^{t} \mathcal{I}_2(w_\tau)}$	[43, 47]
Preferential Attachment	$Age(t) = \frac{\eta t^2}{2} + \frac{\eta}{4}\left(\frac{1}{2}N(0)\left(\ln^2 N(t) - \ln^2 N(0)\right) - \ln\frac{N(t)^{N(t)}}{N(0)^{N(0)}} + t\right)$ $\eta = \frac{2}{2t - \ln^2 N(t) + \ln^2 N(0)}$	[43, 47]

4 Aging of the Baker Map

The Baker Map is defined on the unit square $[0,1) \times [0,1)$ by the baker's operation:

$$S = \begin{cases} \left(2x, \frac{y}{2}\right) & 0 \leq x < \frac{1}{2}, \quad 0 \leq y \leq 1 \\ \left(2x - 1, \frac{y+1}{2}\right) & \frac{1}{2} \leq x < 1, \quad 0 \leq y \leq 1 \end{cases}$$

The action of the Baker Map is illustrated in Fig. 2.

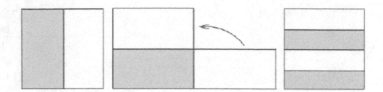

Fig. 2. Baker's transformation

Baker Map is the simplest chaotic invertible System producing one bit per iteration. The mixing of the information on the unit square is so strong that it is useful for cryptography, Fig. 3 [64].

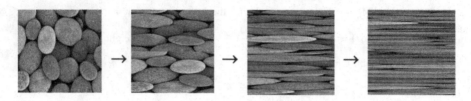

Fig. 3. Mixing by Baker's transformation

The Age of the Baker's Map is canonical (keeps step with clock time), Fig. 4.

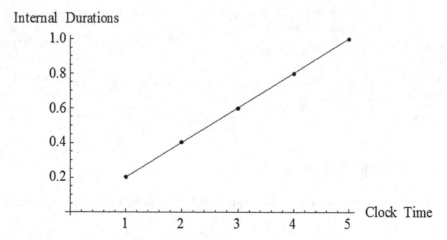

Fig. 4. Canonical aging of Baker's transformation

5   The Greek Elections in June 2012 as Innovations

See (Fig. 5).

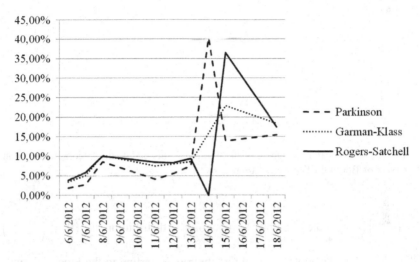

Fig. 5. The innovation probabilities during elections in June 2012 for the Parkinson, Garman-Klass and Rogers-Satchell estimators [45]

6   Aging of Markov Chains

The evolution of Age for 2-state Markov Chains is [44], Fig. 6:

$$Age(t) = Age(0) + t + \beta \cdot |\gamma|^t$$

$\gamma = 1 - w_{01} - w_{10}$, $|\gamma| < 1$, is the second largest eigenvalue of the stochastic matrix:

$$W = \begin{pmatrix} w_{00} & w_{01} \\ w_{10} & w_{11} \end{pmatrix}$$

The Age is related to the Mixing Time by the Formula:

$$Age(t) = Age(0) + t + \mathcal{V}(\rho(t) - \rho_{eq})\theta(t_{mix}^{\gamma} - t)$$

where $\theta(x)$ is the Heaviside function:

$$\theta(x) = \begin{cases} 1 & if \ x > 0 \\ 0 & if \ x \leq 0 \end{cases}$$

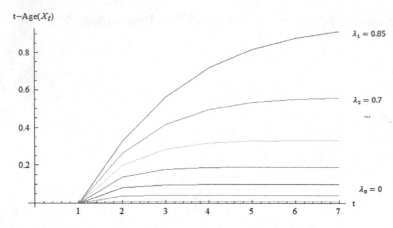

Fig. 6. The non-canonical Time Operator of Markov chains eventually becomes the canonical Time Operator of Bernoulli Processes: $Age(X_t) = t + \alpha$

$\rho = \begin{pmatrix} \rho_0 \\ \rho_1 \end{pmatrix}$ is the initial probability distribution $\rho(t) = \begin{pmatrix} \rho_{eq,0} \\ \rho_{eq,1} \end{pmatrix} +$

$\gamma^t \begin{pmatrix} \rho_0 - \rho_{eq,0} \\ -\rho_0 + \rho_{eq,0} \end{pmatrix}$ is the evolved initial distribution according to the Stochastic matrix:

$W = \begin{pmatrix} w_{00} & w_{01} \\ w_{10} & w_{11} \end{pmatrix}$ with Equilibrium distribution: $\rho_{eq} = \begin{pmatrix} \rho_{eq,0} \\ \rho_{eq,1} \end{pmatrix} t_{mix}^{\mathcal{V}}$ is the Mixing

Time associated with the Lyapunov function $\mathcal{V}$ selected to observe the evolution.

After the mixing time, Markov chains become indistinguishable from Bernoulli processes and the Age formula becomes indistinguishable from the canonical Age formula.

7 Networks Evolution

Networks represent the Relations between Entities as Links between the Nodes representing the Entities. Every System is represented as Network, but a specific Network may represent distinct homologous Systems. Networks are distinguished as Transport Nets (of Matter, Energy, Cost, Duration) and Communication Nets (of Information, Opinion, Knowledge, Trust, Emotions). Transport results in local diminishing (we lose our time or our money when we offer time or money), but there is no local diminishing in Communication Nets due to traffic (we do not lose our knowledge or our emotions when we offer knowledge or emotions). If no sources or sinks are present, Transport is characterized by global preservation within the Network, while Communication results in increase due to traffic. Complex networks are not decomposable to simpler independent components [7].

Present day Graph and Network theory is the synthesis of several lines of research, including Algebraic Topology, Complex Systems and Chaos, Chemistry and Statistical Physics, Electric Circuits and Communication Networks, Transport Networks, Social Dynamics [65]. This unique synthesis was catalyzed by the effort to investigate the structure and emergence of the World Wide Web as a Graph. The small worldness [66, 67] and the scale-invariance [56, 57] features, although known before, were the missing link for the understanding of interdepended systems. These results initiated an explosion of innovative activity in complex systems and networks which spread to almost all scientific fields, like Systems Biology and Systems Medicine, Socio-Economic Dynamics and of course, Communication and Knowledge networks [68–73].

The network evolution is described by the evolution of the elements of the weight matrix $w(t) = \{w_{\kappa\lambda}(t)\}, \kappa, \lambda = 1, 2, \ldots, N(t)$, where $N = N(t)$ is the number of existing nodes at time t. The weights $w_{\kappa\lambda}(t)$ describe the probability to have a link from node κ to node λ, Fig. 7. In other words, the weight matrix is a transition probability matrix.

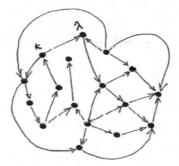

Fig. 7. The network links at time t

Although weighted graphs model the features of the links-channels, in order to study the features of the nodes, like the number of visitors in a website, or the activation of a neuron or the electric potential, we need a further extension of weighted graphs. Thus we arrive at the concept of the network, originally introduced in the context of electrical circuits. The networks are graphs with weights $w_{\kappa\lambda}$ and activation functions ψ_κ on the Nodes $= 1, 2, 3, \ldots$. The activations ψ_κ are Real or Symbolic Variables on the nodes, depending on the specific model. The network state at time t is the time dependent vector:

$$\begin{pmatrix} \psi(t) \\ w(t) \end{pmatrix} = \begin{pmatrix} \psi_\kappa(t) \\ w_{\kappa\lambda}(t) \end{pmatrix}$$

Trees, like those used by Newton to comprehend and represent Aristotle's Organon, Fig. 8, as a Semantic Network seem to be the first specific graph considered.

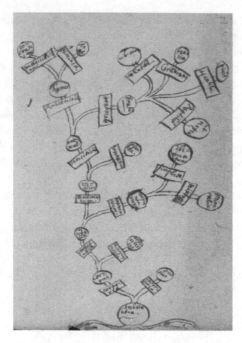

Fig. 8. Isaac Newton's notes on the Organon of Aristotle, Trinity College, 32TU http://cudl.lib. cam.ac.uk/view/MS-ADD-03996/5U32T.

Euler showed in 1736 that there is no path crossing all 7 bridges of Konigsberg exactly once [74]. Graph theory emerged after Euler proved (1752) the polyhedral formula:

$$V - E + F = 2$$

Where: V is the number of vertices, E the number of edges and F the number of faces of the polyhedron. The analysis of chemical compounds motivated Cayley to introduce the concept tree in 1875. Sylvester, three years later introduced the graph concept. However it was Kirchhooff's analysis of electric circuits in 1847, which inspired Poincare [75] to define the incidence structures and Algebraic Topology as the fundamental mathematical background underlying graphs and networks [76, 77]. At the same time Poincare discovered that the famous three body problem is analytically non-integrable [5, 6] and introduced the concept of Dynamical Systems [5] in order to provide a common language for Dynamics and Thermodynamics. Chaos as a mechanism of Complexity, and Dynamical Systems Theory were the first steps towards the modeling of Network Dynamics.

Network Dynamics is formulated in the Dynamical Systems language either as Differential equations (continuous time):

$$\frac{dy(t)}{dt} = \Phi(y(t))$$

$$\frac{d}{dt}\begin{pmatrix}\psi(t)\\w(t)\end{pmatrix}=\Phi\begin{pmatrix}\psi(t)\\w(t)\end{pmatrix}$$

$$\frac{d}{dt}\begin{pmatrix}\psi_1(t)\\\psi_2(t)\\\vdots\\w_{\kappa\lambda}(t)\end{pmatrix}=\begin{pmatrix}\Phi_1\big(\psi_1(t),\psi_2(t),\ldots,w_{\alpha\beta}(t)\big)\\\Phi_2\big(\psi_1(t),\psi_2(t),\ldots,w_{\alpha\beta}(t)\big)\\\vdots\\\Phi_{\kappa\lambda}\big(\psi_1(t),\psi_2(t),\ldots,w_{\alpha\beta}(t)\big)\end{pmatrix}$$

or as difference Equations (discrete time):

$$y(t+1)=S(y(t))$$

$$\begin{pmatrix}\psi(t+1)\\w(t+1)\end{pmatrix}=S\begin{pmatrix}\psi(t)\\\psi(t)\end{pmatrix}=\begin{pmatrix}\psi(t)\\\psi(t)\end{pmatrix}+\Phi\begin{pmatrix}\psi(t)\\\psi(t)\end{pmatrix}$$

$$\begin{pmatrix}\psi_1(t+1)\\\psi_2(t+1)\\\vdots\\w_{\kappa\lambda}(t+1)\end{pmatrix}=\begin{pmatrix}S_1\big(\psi_1(t),\psi_2(t),\ldots,w_{\alpha\beta}(t)\big)\\S_2\big(\psi_1(t),\psi_2(t),\ldots,w_{\alpha\beta}(t)\big)\\\vdots\\S_{\kappa\lambda}\big(\psi_1(t),\psi_2(t),\ldots,w_{\alpha\beta}(t)\big)\end{pmatrix}$$
$$=\begin{pmatrix}\psi_1(t)+\Phi_1\big(\psi_1(t),\psi_2(t),\ldots,w_{\alpha\beta}(t)\big)\\\psi_2(t)+\Phi_2\big(\psi_1(t),\psi_2(t),\ldots,w_{\alpha\beta}(t)\big)\\\vdots\\w_{\kappa\lambda}(t)+\Phi_{\kappa\lambda}\big(\psi_1(t),\psi_2(t),\ldots,w_{\alpha\beta}(t)\big)\end{pmatrix}$$

The Weight Dynamics:

$$w_{\kappa\lambda}(t+1)=S_{\kappa\lambda}\big(\psi_1(t),\psi_2(t),\ldots,w_{\alpha\beta}(t)\big)=w_{\kappa\lambda}(t)+\Phi_{\kappa\lambda}\big(\psi_1(t),\psi_2(t),\ldots,w_{\alpha\beta}(t)\big)$$

is also known as Learning Rule in the context of Neural Networks [78], where the first neighbors are only influential.

Further analysis of Networks came in another parallel direction, from Social Psychology and Systems Psychology. Jacob Moreno introduced Social Networks Analysis and Sociometry in 1934 [79]. The graph in Fig. 9 is the first explicit social network.

The development of social network analysis [80] focused on three main problems:

(a) the identification of influential entities (nodes or groups of nodes) and their roles in the network, resulting only from the topology of interrelations. In order to analyze quantitatively the roles from the position in the network, the so-called Centrality indicators have been introduced [68, 81]. The main Centrality index is the number k of links of the node. It is quite remarkable that the degree distribution $\rho(k)$ (percentage of nodes with degree k = 0, 1, 2,...,N), defines many structural properties and functionalities of the graph, Fig. 10.
(b) the identification of local and global patterns, like Communities or Modules [82]. Community or module detection is essentially the application of statistical cluster analysis to graphs.

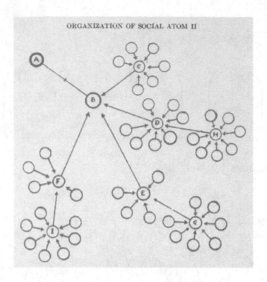

Fig. 9. Social Networks [79]

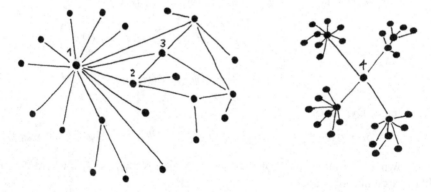

Fig. 10. Centralities

(c) the dynamical mechanisms underlying the formation of structures [71, 83].

Centrality	Role of Node or Group with High Centrality	Node
Degree Centrality	Hub	1
Betweenness Centrality	Intermediary, Broker, Liaison Officer	2
Closeness Centrality	Interconnected, Communicator	3
Eigenvector Centrality	Regulator, Strategic Player, Leader	4, B in Moreno's graph, Fig. 8

8 Aging of Web Navigation

Estimations of the transitions among 17 webpages within a website are described by the 17×17 transition probability matrix W [59]. The Markov evolution is absorbing, thus decreasing uncertainty by reaching maturity i.e. the observer knows eventually the "Exit" location with probability one, Fig. 11. As a result the innovation probability decreases, Fig. 12 and eventually there is no aging, Fig. 13.

9 Aging of Populations

The Moran process [84] has served as a model of the evolution of a population of finite constant size. The weights $w_{\kappa\lambda}(t)$ are the probabilities that individual κ will replace individual λ after t steps:

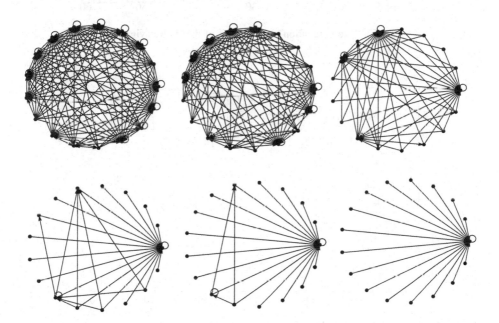

Fig. 11. The graph of probable transitions at times $t = 10$ (up, left), 20, 30, 40, 50 and 60 (down, right)

$$w(t) = w^t, w = \begin{pmatrix} 0 & a & 1-a & 0 & 0 \\ 0 & 0 & b & 1-b & 0 \\ c & 0 & 0 & 0 & 1-c \\ 0 & 1 & 0 & 0 & 0 \\ 0 & 0 & 0 & 1 & 0 \end{pmatrix}$$

The graph of transitions of the Moran process is illustrated I Fig. 14.

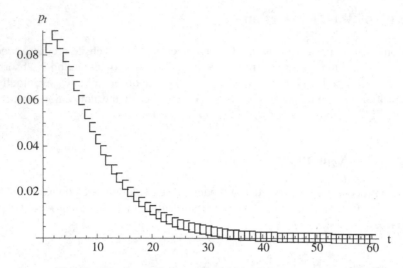

Fig. 12. The innovation probabilities of the Web navigation

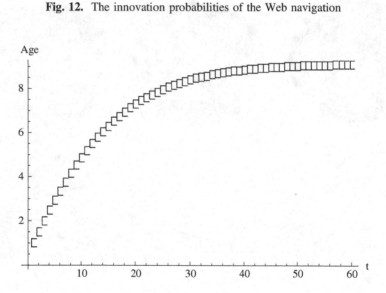

Fig. 13. The internal Age of the Web navigation example up to $t = 60$. The average innovation time is less than 10 steps. Then the system is absorbed to the final "Exit" state.

Contrary to the absorbing Markov chain modeling Web navigation, the observer of a Moran Evolution never knows the final state of the system with probability one, i.e. the observation of the transition graph is intrinsically unpredictable at all stages. Unpredictability is rapidly increasing during the first (four) steps and then slowly increasing with clock time t, Figures 15, 16, 17 and 18.

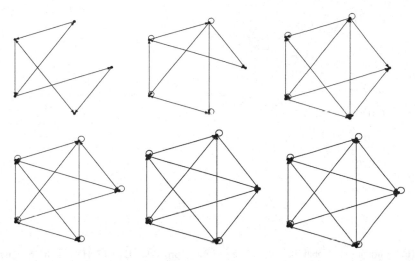

Fig. 14. The graph of probable transitions at times $t = 1$ (up, left), 2, 3, 4, 5 and 6 (down, right)

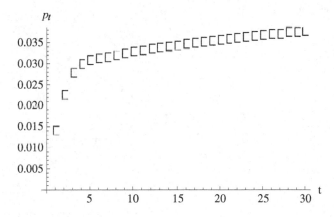

Fig. 15. Innovation probabilities of the Moran process, Eq. (7.41), with parameters $a = 0.3, b = 0.4, c = 0.2$.

10 Aging of Scale-Free Networks

The evolution of the Barabási and Albert [56, 57] scale-free networks involves both growth and preferential attachment, generating loopless and undirected networks at all stages.

The growth mechanism is the simplest linear growth. In order to illustrate the mechanism without computational complications we discuss only the case where at each stage the newly added node λ is linked to only one pre-existing node κ. The number of nodes at stage t is:

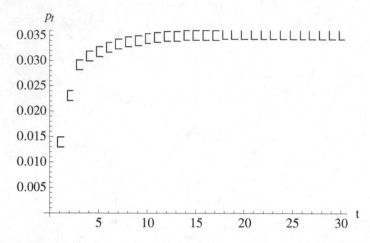

Fig. 16. Innovation probabilities of the Moran process, Eq. (7.41), with parameters $a = 0.5, b = 0.5, c = 0.5$.

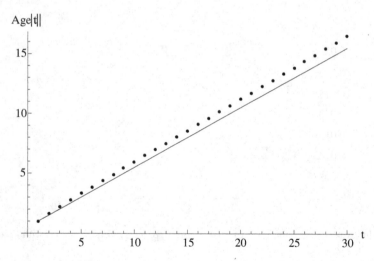

Fig. 17. Internal Age of the Moran process graph, Eq. (7.41), with parameters $a = 0.3, b = 0.4, c = 0.2$. The solid line indicates the Age of the corresponding Bernoulli graph.

$$N(t) = N(0) + t, \quad t = 1, 2, \ldots$$

According to the preferential attachment model, the probability for linking of each newly added node denoted here as $N(\tau)$ is proportional to the number of links (degree) of each existing node κ. The innovation probabilities at each stage $\tau = 1, 2, \ldots,$ t(specified by the clock time) and the internal Age are:

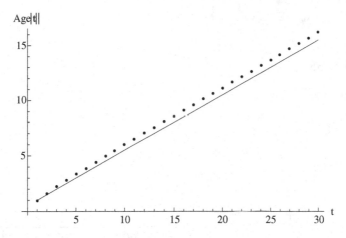

Fig. 18. Internal Age of the Moran process graph, Eq. (7.41), with parameters $a = 0.5, b = 0.5, c = 0.5$. The line indicates the Age of the corresponding Bernoulli graph.

$$p_\tau = \eta \left(1 - \frac{\ln N(\tau)}{4N(\tau)} \right) \quad \tau \in [0, t]$$

$$Age(t) = \frac{\eta t^2}{2} + \frac{\eta}{4} \left(\frac{1}{2} N(0) \left(\ln^2 N(t) - \ln^2 N(0) \right) - \ln \frac{N(t)^{N(t)}}{N(0)^{N(0)}} + t \right)$$

where

$$\eta = \frac{2}{2t - ln^2 N(t) + ln^2 N(0)} \quad (7.53)$$

The distribution of innovations and the internal Age at time t associated with the Barabasi-Albert evolution model are computed and presented in Figs. 19 and 20.

The Barabasi-Albert network evolves with a rapidly increasing innovation (uncertainty) during the first 1/5 (here 2000 steps) of the clock time duration $\tau \in [0, t]$. Afterwards, evolution becomes more certain because nodes with high degree (hubs) have emerged, so it is expected that the new link will be added at the hubs with higher probability, i.e. more certainly.

11   Non-Commutativity of Knowledge Networks Operations

Knowledge networks involve agents with knowledge levels $\psi_\kappa(t)$. The knowledge levels are scalar variables, taking values within the interval $[0, 1]$, so that agents with higher knowledge are effectively more knowledgeable than agents with lower knowledge. The links of the network are the communication channels between the agents through which knowledge is transferred. Each link $\lambda \to \kappa$ is characterized by the

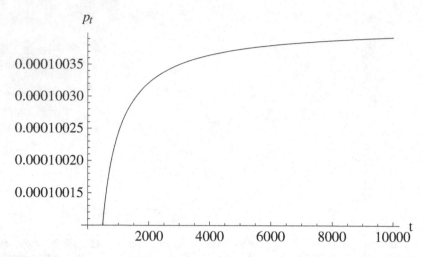

Fig. 19. The distribution of innovations associated with the Barabasi-Albert evolution model at time $T = 10000$.

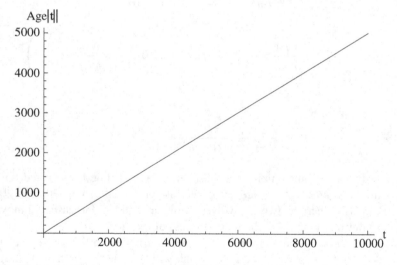

Fig. 20. The internal Age associated with the Barabasi-Albert evolution model at time $T = 10000$.

corresponding weight $w_{\lambda\kappa}$, which incorporates the channel efficiency and takes values within the interval $[0, 1]$. The weights $w_{\lambda\kappa}$ estimate the efficiency of knowledge transfer through the communication channel $\lambda \rightarrow \kappa$ from agent λ to agent κ. The in-neighbors of each agent κ are the agents who have direct access to agent κ.

The selection of the in-neighbor agent for the knowledge upgrade of each agent, at every time t, is specified by the value of the selection (decision) function of each agent κ: $\mathfrak{D}_\kappa(t) : \{1, 2, \ldots, N\} \times \mathbb{T} \rightarrow \{1, 2, \ldots, N\}$. For example, $\mathfrak{D}_\kappa(t) = \lambda$ means that agent λ was selected by agent κ at time t. The selection of the in-neighbor agent λ by agent κ may depend on the knowledge transfer efficiency $w_{\lambda\kappa}$ or/and the knowledge level $\psi_\lambda(t)$ of agent λ, at time t. The weighted diffusion equation [85] provides the simplest description of the knowledge transfer process:

$$\psi_\kappa(t+1) - \psi_\kappa(t) = \sum_{\lambda=1}^{N} \Phi_{\lambda\kappa}(t)$$

where $\Phi_{\lambda\kappa}(t)$ is the knowledge transfer of agent λ to agent κ at time t, given by the formula:

$$\Phi_{\lambda\kappa}(t) = \mathfrak{D}_\kappa^\Omega(t) = \lambda \cdot \psi_\lambda(t) > \psi_\kappa(t) \cdot w_{\lambda\kappa}(t) \cdot (\psi_\lambda(t) - \psi_\kappa(t))$$

Q is the Iverson bracket [86] which converts Boolean values to numbers $0, 1$:

$$Q = \begin{cases} 1 & \text{if } Q \text{ is True} \\ 0 & \text{if } Q \text{ is False} \end{cases}$$

The specific bracket $\psi_\lambda(t) > \psi_\kappa(t)$, guarantees that knowledge transfer may take place if only if $\psi_\lambda(t) > \psi_\kappa(t)$.

The selection of the neighbor for knowledge transfer depends on the awareness of each receiving agent. For example, knowledge aware agents restrict their selection to agents with higher knowledge, thus filtering their neighbours, before selecting. The question we address here is whether Filtering before Selection gives the same result with selection before filtering. In other words whether the operations Filtering and Selection Commute. The result is demonstrated by the so-called Knowledge Attainment Curves indicating the percentage of agents attaining a certain knowledge level, Fig. 21 [87, 88]. It is remarkable that: (1) Filtering before Selection improves

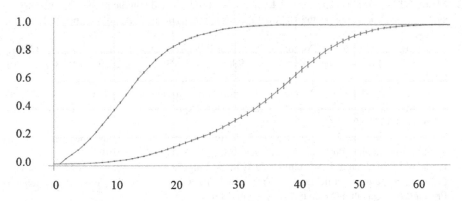

Fig. 21. Knowledge Attainment Curve in an organizational network of size 46 of a "Consulting Company" [87]. The horizontal axis marks the time steps and the vertical axis the knowledge attained. The blue curve describes knowledge evolution by selecting after filtering and the black curve describes knowledge evolution by filtering before selecting.

Knowledge Attainment and that (2) Filtering and Selection are Non-Commutative, indicating a Non-Boolean Logic at the network level.

Acknowledgements. The present work has benefitted from the highly interactive and at the same time relaxed atmosphere which emerged during the Quantum Interaction Conference. Special thanks to H. Atmanspacher and T. Filk who catalyzed the event, for fruitful discussions and for supporting our contribution. We acknowledge the Aristotle University of Thessaloniki and especially the Research Committee for supporting one of us (IG) and the Faculty of Sciences.

References

1. Dugas, R.: A History of Mechanics, Griffon, Switzerland. Dover Republication, New York (1988)
2. Laplace, P.: Essai Philosophique sur les Probabilités, Transl. by F. Truscott and F. Emory, Dover, New York (1951)
3. Littmann, M.: Planets Beyond: Discovering the Outer Solar System. Wiley, New York (1988)
4. Clausius, R.: The Mechanical Theory of Heat. McMillan, London (1879)
5. Poincaré, H.: Les Methodes Nouvelles de la Mécanique Céleste Vols 1-3, Gauthier-Villars, Paris; English Translation, American Inst. Physics, New York (1993)
6. Barrow-Green, J.: Poincaré and the three body problem. American Mathematical Society and London Mathematical Society (1997)
7. Prigogine, I.: From Being to Becoming. Freeman, New York (1980)
8. Lighthill, J.: The recently recognized failure of predictability in Newtonian dynamics. Proc. Roy. Soc. London **A407**, 35–50 (1986)
9. Kolmogorov, A.N.: Entropy per unit time as a metric invariant of Automorphisms. Dokl. Akad. Nauk SSSR **124**, 754–755 (1959)
10. Cornfeld, I., Fomin, S., Ya, Sinai: Ergodic Theory. Springer-Verlag, Berlin (1982)
11. Kondepudi, D., Prigogine, I.: Modern Thermodynamics: From Heat Engines to Dissipative Structures. Wiley, New York (1998)
12. Misra, B.: Nonequilibrium Entropy, Lyapounov variables, and ergodic properties of classical systems. In: Proceedings of the National Academy of Sciences USA, vol. 75, pp. 1627–1631 (1978)
13. Misra, B., Prigogine, I., Courbage, M.: From deterministic dynamics to probabilistic descriptions. Phy. A: Stat. Mech. Appl. **98**(1), 1–26 (1979). doi:10.1016/0378-4371(79) 90163-8
14. Courbage, M., Misra, B.: On the equivalence between Bernoulli dynamical systems and stochastic Markov processes. Phy. A: Stat. Mech. Appl. **104**(3), 359–377 (1980). doi:10. 1016/0378-4371(80)90001-1
15. Misra, B., Prigogine, I., Courbage, M.: Lyapunov variable: entropy and measurements in quantum mechanics. Proc. Nat. Acad. Sci. USA **76**, 4768–4772 (1979)
16. Pauli, W.: Prinzipien der Quantentheorie 1. In: S. Flugge (ed.) Encyclopedia of Physics, vol. 5, Springer-Verlag, Berlin. English Translation: P. Achuthan and K. Venkatesan, General Principles of Quantum Mechanics. Springer, Berlin (1980)
17. Putnam, C.R.: Commutation Properties of Hilbert Space Operators and Related Topics. Springer-Verlag, Berlin (1967)

18. Courbage, M.: On necessary and sufficient conditions for the existence of time and entropy operators in quantum mechanics. Lett. Math. Phy. **4**(6), 425–432 (1980). doi:10.1007/BF00943427
19. Lockhart, C.M., Misra, B.: Irreversibility and measurement in quantum mechanics. Phy. A: Stat. Mech. Appl. **136**(1), 47–76 (1986). doi:10.1016/0378-4371(86)90042-7
20. Antoniou, I., Suchanecki, Z., Laura, R., Tasaki, S.: Intrinsic irreversibility of quantum systems with diagonal singularity. Phy. A: Stat. Mech. Appl. **241**(3), 737–772 (1997)
21. Courbage, M., Fathi, S.: Decay probability distribution of quantum-mechanical unstable systems and time operator. Phy. A: Stat. Mech. Appl. **387**(10), 2205–2224 (2008)
22. Rosenfeld, L.: Questions of irreversibility and ergodicity. In: Caldirola, P. (eds.) Proceedings of the International School of Physics "Enrico Fermi", Course XIv, pp. 1–20. Academic Press, New York (1960)
23. George, C., Prigogine, I., Rosenfeld, L.: The macroscopic level of quantum mechanics. Kon. Danske Videns. Sels. Mat-fys. Meddelelsev **38**(12), 1–44 (1973)
24. Atmanspacher, H.: Propositional lattice for the logic of temporal predictions. In: Antoniou, I., Lambert, F. (eds.) Solitons and Chaos, pp. 58–70. Springer, Berlin (1991)
25. Luzzi, R., Ramos, J.G., Vasconcellos, A.R.: Rosenfeld-prigogine's complementarity of description in the context of informational statistical thermodynamics. Phys. Rev. E **57**, 244–251 (1998)
26. Antoniou, I.: Internal Time and Irreversibility of Relativistic Dynamical Systems, Ph.D. thesis, University of Brussels (1988)
27. Antoniou, I., Misra, B.: Non-unitary transformations of conservative to dissipative evolutions. J. Phys. A. Math. Gen. **24**, 2723–2729 (1991)
28. Antoniou, I.: Information and dynamical systems. In: Atmanspacher, H., Scheingraber, H. (eds.) Information Dynamics, pp. 221–236. Plenum, New York (1991)
29. Antoniou, I., Misra, B.: Relativistic internal time operator. Int. J. Theor. Phy. **31**, 119–136 (1992)
30. Lockhart, C. M., Misra, B., Prigogine, I.: Geodesic instability and internal time in relativistic cosmology. Phy. Rev. D **25**(4), 921 (1982). doi:10.1103/PhysRevD.25.921
31. Antoniou, I., Sadovnichii, V., Shkarin, S.: Time operators and shift representation of dynamical systems. Physica **A299**, 299–313 (1999)
32. Antoniou, I., Suchanecki, Z.: Non-uniform time operator Chaos Wavelets Interval. Chaos Solitons Fractals **11**, 423–435 (2000)
33. Antoniou, I.: The time operator of the cusp map. Chaos Solitons Fractals **12**, 1619–1627 (2001)
34. Antoniou, I., Shkarin, S.A.: Resonances and time operator for the cusp map. Chaos Solitons Fractals **17**, 445–448 (2003)
35. Antoniou, I., Gustafson, K., Suchanecki, Z.: On the inverse problem of statistical physics: from irreversible semigroups to chaotic dynamics. Physica A **252**, 345–361 (1998)
36. Antoniou, I., Suchanecki, Z.: Time Operators Associated to Dilations of Markov Processes. In: Iannelli, M., Lumer, G. (eds.) Evolution Equations: Applications to Physics, Industry, Life Sciences Economics. Progress in Nonlinear Differential Equations and their Applications, vol. 55, pp. 13–23. Birkhauser Verlag, Basel (2003)
37. Antoniou, I., Prigogine, I., Sadovnichii, V., Shkarin, S.: Time operator for diffusion. Chaos Solitons Fractals **11**, 465–477 (2000)
38. Antoniou, I., Gustafson, K.: Haar's wavelets and differential equations. J. Diff. Equ. **34**, 829–832 (1998)
39. Antoniou, I., Gustafson, K.: Wavelets and stochastic processes. Math. Comput. Simul. **49**, 81–104 (1999)

40. Antoniou, I., Gustafson, K.: The time operator of wavelets. Chaos, Solitons Fractals **11**, 443–452 (2000)
41. Antoniou, I., Suchanecki, Z.: Internal time and innovation. In: Buccheri, R., et al. (eds.) The Nature of Time: Geometry, Physics and Perception. Kluwer, Netherlands (2003)
42. Antoniou, I., Christidis, T.: Bergson's time and the time operator. Mind Matter **8**(2), 185–202 (2010)
43. Gialampoukidis, I.: The time operator and age of evolutionary processes, Ph.D. thesis, School of Mathematics, Aristotle University of Thessaloniki (2014)
44. Gialampoukidis, I., Gustafson, K., Antoniou, I.: Time operator of Markov chains and mixing times. Applications to financial data. Phy. A: Stat. Mech. Appl. **415**, 141–155 (2014)
45. Gialampoukidis, I., Gustafson, K., Antoniou, I.: Financial time operator for random walk markets. Chaos Solitons Fractals **57**, 62–72 (2013). doi:10.1016/j.chaos.2013.08.010
46. Gustafson, K., Antoniou, I.: Financial time operator and the complexity of time. Mind Matter **11**(1), 83–100 (2013)
47. Gialampoukidis, I., Antoniou, I.: Age, innovations and time operator of networks. Physica A **432**, 140–155 (2015)
48. Wiener, N.: Cybernetics or Control and Communication in the Animal and the Machine. MIT Press, Cambridge (1948)
49. Bergson, H.: Société Française de Philosophie Conference Proceedings, Bulletin de la Société française de Philosophie, vol. 22(3), pp. 102–113 (1922)
50. Gialampoukidis, I., Antoniou, I.: Entropy, age and time operator. Entropy **17**, 407–424 (2015). doi:10.3390/e17010407
51. Atmanspacher, H.: Dynamical entropy in dynamical systems. In: Atmanspacher, H., Ruhnau, E. (eds.) Time, Temporality, Now, Experiencing Time and Concepts of Time in an Interdisciplinary Perspective, pp. 327–346. Springer, Heidelberg (1997)
52. Kolmogorov, A.N.: Foundations of the Theory of Probability, 2nd English edn. Chelsea, New York (1956)
53. Kemeny, J.G., Snell, J.L.: Finite Markov Chains, D. Van Nostrand (1960)
54. Erdős, P., Rényi, A.: On the evolution of random graphs. Publ. Math. Inst. Hung. Acad. Sci. **5**, 17–61 (1960)
55. Bollobás, B.: Random Graphs. Springer, New York (1998)
56. Barabási, A.L., Albert, R.: Emergence of scaling in random networks. Science **286**(5439), 509–512 (1999). doi:10.1126/science.286.5439.509
57. Albert, R., Barabási, A.L.: Statistical mechanics of complex networks. Rev. Modern Phys. **74**(1), 47 (2002). doi:10.1103/RevModPhys.74.47
58. Levene, M., Loizou, G.: Kemeny's constant and the random surfer. Am. Math. Monthly **109**, 741–745 (2002)
59. Jenamani, M., Mohapatra, P.K., Ghose, S.: A stochastic model of e-customer behavior. Electron. Commer. Res. Appl. **2**(1), 81–94 (2003). doi:10.1016/S1567-4223(03)00010-3
60. Kirkland, S.: Fastest expected time to mixing for a Markov chain on a directed graph. Linear Algebra Appl. **433**(11), 1988–1996 (2010)
61. Crisostomi, E., Kirkland, S., Shorten, R.: A Google-like model of road network dynamics and its application to regulation and control. Int. J. Control **84**(3), 633–651 (2011)
62. Brin, S., Page, L.: The anatomy of a large-scale hypertextual Web search engine. Comput. Netw. ISDN Syst. **30**(1), 107–117 (1998)
63. Hamilton, J.D.: A new approach to the economic analysis of nonstationary time series and the business cycle. Econometrica: J. Econometric Soc. **57**, 357–384 (1989)
64. Makris, G., Antoniou, I.: Cryptography with chaos. Chaotic Model. Simul. (CMSIM) **1**, 169–178 (2013)

65. Meyers, A. (ed.): Encyclopedia of Complexity and Systems Science. Springer, New York (2009)
66. Watts, J., Strogatz, S.: Collective dynamics of small-world networks. Nature **393**, 440–442 (1998)
67. Strogatz, S.: Sync: The Emerging Science of Spontaneous Order. Hyperion, New York (2003)
68. Newman, M.: Networks: An Introduction. Oxford University Press, Oxford (2010)
69. Caldarelli, G., Vespignani, A.: Large Scale Structure and Dynamics of Complex Networks: From Information Technology to Finance and Natural Science. World Scientific, Singapore (2007)
70. Barrat, A., Barthelemy, M., Vespignani, A.: Dynamical Processes on Complex Networks. Cambridge University Press, Cambridge (2008)
71. Jackson, M.: Social and Economic Networks. Princeton University Press, New Jersey (2008)
72. Lewis, T.G.: Network Science: Theory and Applications. Wiley, Hoboken (2010)
73. Estrada, E.: The Structure of Complex Networks. Oxford University Press, New York (2010)
74. Euler, L.: Solutio problematic ad Geometriam situs pertinentis. Comm. Academiae Petropolitanae, **8**, 128–140 (1736)
75. Poincaré, H.: Analysis situs. J. de l'École Polytechnique ser **2**(1), 1–123 (1895)
76. Lefschetz, S.: Applications of Algebraic Topology: Graphs and Networks. Springer, Berlin (1975)
77. Biggs, N., Lloyd, E., Wilson, R.: Graph Theory 1736–1936. Clarendon Press, Oxford (1977)
78. Heykin, S.: Neural Networks: A Comprehensive Foundation. Pearson Prentice Hall, New Jersey (1999)
79. Moreno, J.L.: Who Shall Survive? A New Approach to the Problem of Human Interrelations, 3d edn. Nervous and Mental Disease Publishing Co., Washington, D.C. (1978)
80. Freeman, L.: The Development of Social Network Analysis: A Study in the Sociology of Science. Empirical Press, Vancouver (2004)
81. Wasserman, S., Faust, K.: Social Network Analysis: Methods and Applications. Cambridge University Press, New York (1994)
82. Newman, M.: Communities, modules and large-scale structure in networks. Nature Phy. **8**, 25–31 (2012)
83. Edmonds, B., Meyer, R. (eds.): Simulating Social Complexity: A Handbook. Springer, Berlin (2013)
84. Lieberman, E., Hauert, C., Nowak, M.A.: Evolutionary dynamics on graphs. Nature **433** (7023), 312–316 (2005)
85. Krol, D., Fay, D., Gabryś, B.: Propagation Phenomena in Real World Networks. Springer, New York (2015)
86. Knuth, D.: Two notes on notation. Am. Math. Monthly **99**(5), 403–422 (1992)
87. Cross, R., Parker, A.: The Hidden Power of Social Networks. Harvard Business Press, Boston (2004)
88. Ioannidis, E., Antoniou, I.: Knowledge Networks Dynamics. Hellenic Mathematical Society Congress (to appear)

Can Bohmian Quantum Information Help us to Understand Consciousness?

Paavo Pylkkänen[1,2(✉)]

[1] Department of Philosophy, History, Culture and Art Studies,
The Academy of Finland Center of Excellence in the Philosophy of the
Social Sciences (TINT), P.O. Box 24, 00014 University of Helsinki, Finland
paavo.pylkkanen@helsinki.fi
[2] Department of Cognitive Neuroscience and Philosophy,
School of Biosciences, University of Skövde,
P.O. Box 408, 541 28 Skövde, Sweden

1 Introduction

A key idea in the field of "quantum interaction" or "quantum cognition" is that certain principles and mathematical tools of quantum theory (such as quantum probability, entanglement, non-commutativity, non-Boolean logic and complementarity) provide a good way of modeling many significant cognitive phenomena (such as decision processes, ambiguous perception, meaning in natural languages, probability judgments, order effects and memory; see Wang *et al.* 2013). However, when we look at research in philosophy of mind during recent decades, it is clear that *conscious experience* has been the most important topic (see e.g. Chalmers ed. 2002; Lycan and Prinz eds. 2008). Even in the field of cognitive neuroscience consciousness has become a very important area of study (see e.g. Baars *et al.* eds. 2003). Might the principles and mathematical tools of quantum theory be also useful when trying to understand the character of conscious experience and its place in nature?

Note that many of the proposals in the area of "quantum mind" were not originally designed to deal specifically with the question of consciousness (i.e. with questions such as "What is it that makes a non-conscious mental state conscious?"). For example, Penrose's (1989) well-known proposal about orchestrated and objective quantum collapse (ORCH-OR) in neural microtubules was originally proposed to account for the presumably non-computational physical aspect of human *intelligence*, rather than conscious phenomenal experience *per se*. Yet, given that explaining the relationship of conscious experience to the physical domain is widely considered to be a truly hard problem (Chalmers 1996), it seems relevant and valid to consider whether our best theories of matter, such as quantum theory, might play a role in tackling it (cf. Atmanspacher 2015).

In this paper I will explore whether David Bohm's proposal about *quantum theoretical active information,* and the mind-matter scheme he developed on the basis of it, can help us to explain consciousness (Bohm and Hiley 1987, 1993; Bohm 1989, 1990; Pylkkänen 2007). Here it is important to acknowledge that other researchers in philosophy of mind and consciousness studies have also made use of the concept of

© Springer International Publishing Switzerland 2016
H. Atmanspacher et al. (Eds.): QI 2015, LNCS 9535, pp. 76–87, 2016.
DOI: 10.1007/978-3-319-28675-4_6

information in their theories of mind and consciousness. For example, Dretske (1981) and Barwise and Seligman (1997) have explored the possibility that information in the sense of factual semantic contents (i.e. information as meaningful data that represents facts correctly or incorrectly) can be grounded in environmental information (i.e. information as mere correlation, e.g. the way tree rings carry information about age). For Dretske this was an important part of his attempts to give a naturalistic account of sensory experiences, qualia and consciousness. During recent years the notion of information has been used to explain consciousness most notably by David Chalmers (1996), as well as by Giulio Tononi and his co-workers (Tononi and Koch 2014; Oizumi, Albantakis and Tononi 2014). The strategy of this paper will be to first describe Bohm's mind-matter scheme, and then to briefly consider Chalmers' and Tononi *et al.*'s ideas in the light of this scheme.

2 Bohm's Mind-Matter Scheme Based on Quantum Theoretical Active Information

To understand the significance of Bohm's interpretation of quantum theory, which underlies his mind-matter scheme, it is necessary to briefly consider the development of physics in the 20th century. When quantum theory was emerging, people were trying to make sense of puzzling features such as wave-particle duality and a little later, entanglement. In particular they were attempting to develop ontological models of quantum systems such as electrons. In the 1920s de Broglie came up with the idea of an electron being a particle guided by a pilot wave, while Schrodinger was trying to describe the electron as some kind of a physical field. These models had some difficulties, though in retrospect we can see that at least de Broglie's ideas could have been developed further (see Bacciagaluppi and Valentini 2009). What happened however was that the so-called "Copenhagen interpretation" won the day in the 1920s. There are actually many different versions of this interpretation, but it is typical of them that they emphasize epistemology – in the sense our ability to predict the results of measurement, rather than ontology – in the sense of a model of what quantum reality may be like also when we are not making measurements. As a result, physicists were not able to offer a new notion of objective physical reality, which philosophers could then use when discussing ontological issues, such as the mind-matter relation.

It is here that Bohm comes in. In the early 1950s, after discussions with Einstein in Princeton, he independently rediscovered de Broglie's theory and formulated it in a more coherent way, providing a first consistent realistic model of quantum systems (Bohm 1952). Bohm's interpretation was initially resisted, but is today more and more widely acknowledged as one of the key possible interpretations of quantum theory. Later on further ontological models were proposed, for example Everett's 1957 "many worlds" interpretation and Ghirardi, Rimini and Weber's 1986 objective collapse theory, and currently the nature of quantum reality is intensively debated within the philosophy of physics community (see Ney and Albert eds. 2013).

We do not know which ontological interpretation (if any) is correct, but each may reveal something significant about the nature of physical reality at a very fundamental level.

One should note that there are by now also different versions of the Bohm theory. Much attention has in recent years been given to a minimalist version known as "Bohmian mechanics" (see Goldstein 2013; Dürr *et al.* 2013). Bohm himself developed since the mid-1970s, with Basil Hiley, a philosophically more radical version they called the "ontological interpretation", culminating in their 1993 book *The Undivided Universe*. While there has been a tendency in the Bohmian mechanics camp (see also Bacciagaluppi and Valentini 2009) to downplay the significance of Bohm and Hiley's approach, a more balanced examination suggests that both approaches have their value (see Holland 2011).

Let us now briefly consider the Bohm theory in some more detail. It assumes that every particle has a well-defined position and momentum and is accompanied by a field ψ which satisfies the Schrödinger equation (Eq. 1) .

$$i\hbar \frac{\partial \varphi}{\partial t} = -\frac{\hbar^2}{2m} \nabla^2 \varphi + V(r)\varphi. \tag{1}$$

If we make a polar substitution (Eq. 2)

$$\varphi(r, t) = R(r, t) \exp[iS(r, t)/\hbar] \tag{2}$$

and then separate out the real and imaginary parts, we find two equations, firstly (Eq. 3)

$$\frac{\partial S}{\partial t} + \frac{1}{2m}(\nabla S)^2 + V + Q = 0 \tag{3}$$

where (Eq. 4)

$$Q = -\frac{\hbar^2}{2m} \frac{\nabla^2 R}{R} \tag{4}$$

is known as *the quantum potential*.

The second equation (Eq. 5)

$$\frac{\partial P}{\partial t} + \nabla.(P\frac{\nabla S}{m}) = 0 \tag{5}$$

is a probability conservation equation. We also identify (Eq. 6)

$$p = \nabla S \tag{6}$$

This is known as the guidance condition, from which the trajectory of the particle can be calculated. Figures 1 and 2 provide well-known visualizations for the two-slit experiment.

How, then, might Bohm's theory be relevant to the mind-matter relation? It postulates that an electron is a particle, always accompanied by a new type of field, which guides its behaviour - thus the name "pilot wave theory" which is sometimes used. Jack Sarfatti has described the Bohmian electron imaginatively by saying that it consists of a

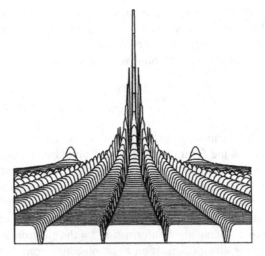

Fig. 1. Quantum potential for two Gaussian slits

Fig. 2. Trajectories for two Gaussian slits

"thought-like" pilot wave, guiding a "rock-like" particle. This metaphor suggests that matter at the quantum level is fundamentally different from the sort of mechanical matter of classical physics that is presupposed in philosophy of mind by typical materialists. If even the basic elements that constitute us have "thought-like" and "rock-like" aspects, then it is perhaps not so surprising that a very complex aggregate of such elements (such as a human being) has a body, accompanied by a mind that guides it.

But, one might think, this is merely a vague metaphor. Now, Bohm himself realized in the early 1980s that the pilot wave might be more literally "thought-like" in a very interesting sense. He considered the mathematical expression of the so-called quantum potential, which describes the way the pilot wave field affects the particle (Eq. 4):

$$Q = -\frac{\hbar^2}{2m}\frac{\nabla^2 R}{R}$$

He realized that the quantum potential, and thus the effect of the wave upon the particle, only depends on the form or shape of the field, not on its size or amplitude R (mathematically, the quantum potential depends only on the second spatial derivative of the amplitude R of the field; h-bar is a constant and m is the mass of the particle). He went on to suggest that the quantum wave field is literally putting form into, or in-forming the particle, rather than pushing and pulling it mechanically.

Note that we are here talking about information for the electron, not information for us – we are thus thinking about information as an objective commodity that exists out there in the world, independently of us, and guides physical processes. The form of the quantum wave reflects the form of the environment of the particle – for example the presence of slits in the two-slit experiment. Subtle differences in the environment of the particle are then reflected in its behaviour – which is exactly what we observe in, say, the two-slit experiment or the Aharonov-Bohm effect. What happens with the electron is somewhat analogous to a ship on autopilot, guided by radar waves that carry information about the environment of the ship. The radar waves are not pushing and pulling the ship, but rather in-forming the much greater energy of the ship.

Bohm generalized this into a notion of "active information" – which applies in situations where a form with small energy enters and informs a larger energy. We see this not only with various artificial devices, but also in the way the form of the DNA molecule informs biological processes, and even in the way forms act in human subjective experience (for example, seeing the form of a shadow in a dark night and interpreting it as "danger" may give rise to a powerful psycho-somatic reaction). Indeed, Bohm (1989, 1990) sketched how the active information approach could be developed into a theory of mind and matter.

He suggested that we understand mental states as involving a hierarchy of levels of active information. We not merely think about objects in the external world, but we can also become aware of our thinking. He suggested that such meta-level awareness typically involves a higher level of thought. This higher level gathers information about the lower level. But because its essential nature is active information, it not merely makes a passive representation of the lower level. Rather, the higher level also acts to organize the lower level, a bit analogously to the way the active information in the pilot wave acts to organize the movement of the particle. And of course, we can become aware of this higher level of thought from a yet higher level, and so on.

How does then mind, understood as a hierarchy of levels of active information, connect with matter in the Bohmian scheme? First of all, Bohm suggested that it is natural to extend the quantum ontology. So just as there is a pilot wave that guides the particle, there can be a super-pilot wave that guides the 1st order pilot wave, and so on. He claimed that such an extension is "natural" from the mathematical point of view;

Bohm and Hiley briefly discuss such extensions in the context of quantum field (rather than particle) theory (1993: 378–381; 385). Now it seems that we have two hierarchies, one for mind and another for matter. Bohm's next step was to postulate that these are the same hierarchy, so that there is only one hierarchy. This then allows, at least in principle, for a new way of understanding how mind can affect the body. Information at a given level of active information in the mind can act downwards, all the way to the active information in the pilot waves of particles in, say, the synapses or neural microtubules, and this influence can then be amplified to signals in motor cortex, leading to a physical movement of the body.

The above proposal differs strongly from the usual theories in cognitive neuroscience. Most neuroscientists ignore quantum considerations, and seek the "neural correlates of consciousness" in some macroscopic neural phenomena, which can presumably be understood in terms of classical physics. Yet Bohm is proposing that mind, understood as a hierarchy of levels of active information, is implemented in (or perhaps identical with) a hierarchy of quantum fields. However, these fields are not separate from the macroscopic neural processes. On the contrary the role of the former is in the end to guide the latter and to gather information about them.

Of course, it is a tremendous challenge to work out an empirically testable theory along the Bohmian lines, but these ideas provide a scheme for such an endeavour. For example, Hiley and Pylkkänen (2005) discuss the prospects of applying the Bohm scheme to Beck and Eccles's quantum model of synaptic exocytosis (for an account of the latter, see Atmanspacher 2015). While this may be a small step forward, problems remain. For instance, Henry Stapp (private communication) has pointed out that the sort of interference of the mind upon the laws of quantum mechanics that the Bohmian mind-matter scheme involves can lead to problems with special relativity. This is a challenge that future research along Bohmian lines needs to face (see also Maleeh and Amani 2012).

While the possibility of non-negligible quantum effects in the brain is often dismissed as implausible, there are interesting recent advances in quantum biology (see e.g. Ball 2011). And it is already part of mainstream neuroscience that the retina acts to amplify the effects of individual photons. Also, researchers such as Roger Penrose and Stuart Hameroff have discussed in great detail how quantum effects might play a role in neural processes via quantum coherence and collapse in neural microtubules (for recent advances with this approach, see Craddock et al. 2014) Connecting the Hameroff-Penrose work with the Bohm scheme is one potentially fruitful line for future research.

Note that Bohm introduced a new category, namely information to the debate. Is information physical or mental? He suggested that it is simultaneously both physical and mental, or has these two as its aspects. This sort of view is called a double-aspect theory in philosophy of mind. The traditional worry with double-aspect views is that it is left into a mystery what the underlying thing, which has the aspects, is. The hypothesis that information is the fundamental, underlying feature of reality can be seen as a way to alleviate this worry.

3   Consciousness in the Quantum Theoretical Active Information Scheme

It is well known that a major problem with both the identity theory and functionalism in philosophy of mind is that they leave out conscious experience, instead of explaining it. How might conscious experience fit into the active information scheme? While Bohm saw nature as a dynamic process where information plays a key dynamic role, he assumed that "99.9 %" of the activity of information is not conscious (Weber 1987). Thus, for example, he thought it obvious that the particles of physics are not conscious. But how can one then approach the hard problem of consciousness in this scheme? In other words, why is there sometimes conscious experience associated with the activity of information (as seems obvious at least with humans and higher animals)? Why doesn't all the activity of information in humans proceed "in the dark", as it seems to do in physical and biological processes in general? Bohm himself did not say much about the hard problem of consciousness (he died a little before the hard problem was made the center of attention by David Chalmers in 1994). However, I think that the most natural context to explore this issue is some version of a higher order (HO) theory of consciousness. A simple possibility would be to postulate that what makes a given mental state (or level of information or mental activity) conscious is that there exists a higher level of (typically) unconscious information, which has the content that one is in the first order mental state or activity (cf. Rosenthal 1997; Gennaro 2012).

Note also that David Chalmers (1996) famously suggested that we tackle the hard problem of consciousness with a double-aspect theory of information. The idea is that information is a fundamental feature of the world, which always has both a phenomenal and a physical aspect. Now, we could take this idea to the Bohm scheme and postulate that active information, too, has phenomenal properties. This then raises the question about what we should think about the active information in the pilot wave of an electron. Does it, too, have phenomenal properties in some sense? Bohm went as far as to say that electrons have a "primitive mind-like quality", but by "mind" he was here referring to the "activity of form", rather than conscious phenomenal experience in any full sense.

I think that it is reasonable to combine Chalmers's hypothesis to active information, but we need to restrict the hypothesis. For example, we could say that certain kind of active information (for example, a holistic active information that is analogous to quantum active information) has the potentiality for phenomenal properties, but this potentiality is actualized only in suitable circumstances (for example, when a given level of active information is the intentional target of a higher level of active information). Of course, this also opens up the possibility for genuine artificial consciousness. If we could implement quantum-like holistic active information in an artificial system and set of up a suitable higher-order relationship of levels in the system, phenomenal properties should actualize themselves, according to this hypothesis.

One advantage is that while Chalmers' double-aspect theory suffers from epiphenomenalism, Bohm's scheme, when modified, opens up the possibility of a genuine causal efficacy of phenomenal properties on the physical domain (see Pylkkänen 2007:

244–6; Pylkkänen (forthcoming).) Also, Chalmers thinks it an interesting possibility that some sort of activity is required for experience, and that static information (e.g. information in a thermostat in a constant state) thus is not likely to have experience associated with it (1996: 298). If we say that phenomenal properties are always properties of some kind of Bohmian active information, we could do justice to the intuition that activity is required for experience.

Bohm and Hiley emphasize that active information is quite different from Shannon information. The latter provides quantitative measure of information that represents the way in which the state of a system is *uncertain to us*, in the sense that we can only specify probabilities of various states. In contrast, active information is not essentially related to *our* knowledge or lack of it. At the quantum level Bohm and Hiley refer to information that is relevant to determining the movement of the electron itself, i.e. information *for* the electron. Information is here seen as an "objective commodity" (cf. Dretske 1981). Bateson characterized information as "a difference that makes a difference". Bohm felt this is too broad, as strictly speaking every difference makes a difference. To restrict it, he proposed that information is a difference of form that makes a difference of content.

4 Tononi *et al.*'s Integrated Information Theory of Consciousness

Much attention in consciousness studies has in recent years been given to Giulio Tononi and co-workers' Integrated Information Theory (IIT) of consciousness, as it promises to offer a principled account of what experience is and what type of physical systems can have it (for recent reviews, see Tononi and Koch 2014; Oizumi, Albantakis and Tononi 2014). Tononi *et al.*'s strategy is to start by identifying the essential properties of consciousness and then ask what kinds of physical mechanisms could possibly account for them. This has resulted in a mathematical theory of consciousness that is not restricted to neural explanation. According to many, IIT takes consciousness theorizing into a new level.

Tononi *et al.* think it self-evident that consciousness exists and is compositionally structured, differentiated, unified and singular. These five features (which they call EXISTENCE, COMPOSITION, INFORMATION, INTEGRATION, EXCLUSION) are the *phenomenological axioms* of their theory. They then make a number of *postulates* to account for these axioms or features. Finally, they propose some *identities*. Let us first consider the five axioms and the postulates that account for them in turn.

EXISTENCE. To account for the existence of consciousness (from its own intrinsic perspective) they propose that there has to be a system of mechanisms with a cause-effect power upon itself (i.e. intrinsically, independent of extrinsic causes and effects).

COMPOSITION. To account for the compositional structure of consciousness (i.e. that each experience is composed of many phenomenological distinctions/has multiple aspects), it must be possible to compose elementary mechanisms into higher-order mechanisms which have irreducible causes and effects.

INFORMATION. To account for the fact that consciousness is differentiated (i.e. that each experience has a specific set of phenomenological distinctions/differs in its particular way from others), a system of mechanisms must specify a differentiated conceptual structure via a process of in-forming. Through its cause-effect power, a system of mechanisms in a state gives rise to a form or "informs" a conceptual structure in the space of possibilities. A concept is how each mechanism within the system specifies the probability of past-future states of the system (cause-effect repertoire). A conceptual structure then is the set of concepts specified by the mechanisms of the system in various combinations.

INTEGRATION. To account for the irreducible unity of consciousness (i.e. that each experience is strongly irreducible to non-interdependent components), there has to be integrated information, in the sense that the conceptual structure specified by the system is irreducible to that specified by non-interdependent sub-systems. The presence of integration (characterized by big phi or Φ) means that a partitioning of a system of mechanisms would destroy several cause-effect repertoires and change others.

EXCLUSION. Finally, to account for the singularity of consciousness in content and spatio-temporal grain (i.e. that there is no superposition of multiple experiences), the system of mechanisms must be such that there is no superposition of conceptual structures over elements and spatio-temporal grain.

In this framework Tononi and Koch define a *complex* as the system of mechanisms that generates a maximally irreducible conceptual structure or a *quale*.

The central identity of IIT then states that a conscious experience is *identical* to a maximally irreducible conceptual structure: "..the quale completely specifies both its quality (the set of concepts in the quale is the content of consciousness) and its quantity (the value of irreducibility Φ_{max} of the quale is the level of consciousness") (Tononi and Koch 2014).

5 Integrated Information Theory of Consciousness and the Bohmian Mind-Matter Scheme: A Brief Comparison

It is not a straightforward task to compare and contrast Tononi's IIT with Bohm's mind-matter scheme. For one thing, Tononi's theory is a fairly well developed mathematical theory, with a number of new concepts, making it somewhat difficult to understand. In contrast, Bohm's approach remains a scheme. There have been some developments related to it (see e.g. Smith 2003), but quite a bit more is needed before it can be seen as a full alternative to IIT. So in this preliminary attempt to compare these frameworks, I will just draw attention to some points of mutual relevance, which can then act as a basis for further development.

Both Tononi and Bohm use the concept of information in a way different than it is used in communication theory. For Tononi, information refers to how a system of mechanisms in a state, through its cause-effect power, gives rise to a form ("informs" a conceptual structure) in the space of possibilities. For Bohm active information refers to situations when a form (carrying a little energy) enters and literally in-forms a larger energy. This is an interesting similarity between the schemes, although there are subtle differences.

Both Tononi and Bohm build upon Bateson's idea of information as a "difference that makes a difference". For Tononi the key point is that to generate information, a mechanism must make a difference in the sense that it constrains the states of a system that can be its possible causes and effects. Neurons and logic gates made of transistors qualify as such information generators. When it comes to consciousness, Tononi notes that for conscious experience to be able to exist from its own intrinsic experience, the system of mechanisms that generates such information and experience must have cause-effect power within itself (i.e. intrinsically, independent of extrinsic causes and effects).

Bohm, too starts from Bateson's notion that information is a difference that makes a difference. But, Bohm notes, every difference makes a difference. Bateson's notion thus has to be constrained. Bohm does this by saying that information is a *difference of form* that makes a *difference of content* (Bohm 1989). To make this notion better suitable for explaining consciousness I suggest that we say that information underlying consciousness is a difference that makes a difference of (at least potentially) conscious phenomenal or intentional content.

Finally, let us consider the idea that consciousness requires integrated information (in the sense that the conceptual structure or *quale* specified by the system is irreducible to that specified by non-interdependent sub-systems). Now, there is an interesting sense in which Bohmian quantum theoretical active information can be understood as integrated information. We can see this by considering the N-body system in the Bohm theory, where, first of all, the behavior of each particle may depend nonlocally on all the others, no matter how far away they may be. Nonlocality is an important new feature of the quantum theory, but Bohm used to emphasize that there is yet another feature that is even more radical. For in the Bohm theory there can be a nonlocal connection between particles that depends on the quantum state of the whole, in a way that cannot be expressed in terms of the relationships of the particles alone (see Bohm and Hiley 1987: 332). This quantum state of the whole, described by the many-body wave function, evolves in time according to the Schrödinger equation, which led Bohm and Hiley to write:

> Something with this sort of independent dynamical significance that refers to the whole system and that is not reducible to a property of the parts and their inter-relationships is thus playing a key role in the theory. ... this is the most fundamental new ontological feature implied by quantum theory. (Bohm and Hiley 1987, 332)

Recall that according to Bohm and Hiley this state of the whole has to be understood as active information. I think it is a promising hypothesis that this provides a prototype model for the sort of "integrated information" that we also encounter, in much more complex form, in conscious experience. In future research my aim is to work out a view of consciousness, where Bohmian quantum-like integrated information is a key concept characterizing the holistic features of conscious experience. With the help of some version of a higher-order theory of consciousness (e.g. Gennaro 2012) it is hoped that one is able to provide an account of what it is that makes non-conscious mental states (understood as integrated active information) conscious. (For an attempt to apply a higher order theory of consciousness to the Hameroff-Penrose scheme, see Hameroff, Gennaro and Pylkkänen 2014.)

Acknowledgments. Sections 2 and 3 of this article contain text that has been adapted from a longer article by the author (Pylkkänen, P. (forthcoming)).

References

Atmanspacher, H.: Quantum approaches to consciousness. In: Zalta, E.N. (ed.) The Stanford Encyclopedia of Philosophy (2015). http://plato.stanford.edu/archives/sum2015/entries/qt-consciousness/

Baars, B.J., Banks, W.B., Newman, J.B. (eds.): Essential Sources in the Scientific Study of Consciousness. MIT Press, Cambridge (2003)

Bacciagaluppi, G., Valentini, A.: Quantum Theory at a Crossroads: Reconsidering the 1927 Solvay Conference. Cambridge University Press, Cambridge (2009)

Ball, P.: The dawn of quantum biology. Nature **474**, 272–274 (2011)

Barwise, J., Seligman, J.: Information Flow: The Logic of Distributed Systems. Cambridge University Press, Cambridge (1997)

Bohm, D.: A suggested interpretation of the quantum theory in terms of "hidden" variables I and II. Phys. Rev. **85** (2), 166–179 and 180-193 (1952)

Bohm, D.: Meaning and information. In: Pylkkänen, P. (ed.) The Search for Meaning. Crucible, Wellingborough (1989)

Bohm, D.: A new theory of the relationship of mind and matter. Philos. Psychol. **3**, 271–286 (1990)

Bohm, David, Hiley, B.J.: An ontological basis for quantum theory I: non-relativistic particle systems. Phys. Rep. **144**(6), 323–348 (1987)

Bohm, D., Hiley, B.J.: The Undivided Universe: An Ontological Interpretation of Quantum Theory. Routledge, London (1993)

Chalmers, D.: The Conscious Mind: In Search of a Fundamental Theory. Oxford University Press, Oxford (1996)

Chalmers, D. (ed.): Philosophy of Mind: Classical and Contemporary Readings. Oxford University Press, Oxford (2002)

Craddock, T.J.A., Friesen, D., Mane, J., Hameroff, S., Tuszynski, J.A.: The feasibility of coherent energy transfer in microtubules. J. R. Soc. Interface **11**, 20140677 (2014). http://dx.doi.org/10.1098/rsif.2014.0677

Dretske, F.: Knowledge and the Flow of Information. MIT Press, Cambridge (1981)

Dürr, D., Goldstein, S., Zanghi, N.: Quantum Physics Without Quantum Philosophy. Springer, Berlin (2013)

Gennaro, R.: The Consciousness Paradox. MIT Press, Cambridge (2012)

Goldstein, S.: Bohmian mechanics. In: Zalta, E.N. (ed.) The Stanford Encyclopedia of Philosophy (2005). http://plato.stanford.edu/archives/spr2013/entries/qm-bohm/

Hiley, B.J., Pylkkänen, P.: Can mind affect matter via active information? Mind Matter 3(2), 7–26 (2005). http://www.mindmatter.de/resources/pdf/hileywww.pdf

Hameroff, S., Gennaro, R., Pylkkänen, P.: HOT to DOT: a 'deeper-order thought' theory of consciousness. In: Brain, Mind and Cosmos. Trident (2014)

Holland, P.: A quantum of history. Contemp. Phys. 52, 355 (2011)

Lycan, W.G., Prinz, J.J.: Mind and Cognition: An Anthology, 3rd edn. Blackwell, Oxford (2008)

Maleeh, R., Amani, P.: Bohm's theory of the relationship of mind and matter revisited. Neuroquantology 10, 150–163 (2012)

Ney, A., Albert, D. (eds.): The Wave Function: Essays on the Metaphysics of Quantum Mechanics. Oxford University Press, Oxford (2013)

Oizumi, M., Albantakis, L., Tononi, G.: From the phenomenology to the mechanisms of consciousness: integrated information theory 3.0. PLoS Comput. Biol. 10(5), e1003588 (2014)

Penrose, R.: The Emperor's New Mind. Oxford University Press, Oxford (1989)

Pylkkänen, P.: Mind Matter and the Implicate Order. Springer Frontiers Collection, Berlin and New York (2007)

Pylkkänen, P.: Is there room in quantum ontology for a genuine causal role of consciousness? In: Khrennikov, A., Haven, E. (eds.) The Palgrave Handbook of Quantum Models in Social Science. Palgrave Macmillan (forthcoming)

Rosenthal, D.M.: A theory of consciousness. In: Block, N., Flanagan, O., Guüzeldere, G. (eds.) The Nature of Consciousness. MIT Press, Cambridge (1997)

Smith, Q.: Why cognitive scientists cannot ignore quantum mechanics? In: Smith, Q., Jokic, A. (eds.) Consciousness: New Philosophical Perspectives. Oxford University Press, Oxford (2003)

Tononi, G., Koch, C.: Consciousness: Here, There but not Everywhere (2014). arXiv:1405.7089v1

Wang, Z., Busemeyer, J.R., Atmanspacher, H., Pothos, E.M.: The potential of using quantum theory to build models of cognition. Topics Cogn. Sci. 5, 672–688 (2013)

Weber, R.: Meaning as being in the implicate order philosophy of David Bohm: a conversation. In: Hiley, B.J., Peat, F.D. (eds.) Quantum Implications: Essays in honour of David Bohm. Routledge, London (1987)

Non-Classical Probabilities
from Pilot Wave Models

Thomas Filk[1,2(✉)]

[1] Institute of Physics, Albrecht-Ludwigs University Freiburg,
Freiburg im Breisgau, Germany
[2] Parmenides Foundation for the Study of Thinking, Munich, Germany
thomas.filk@physik.uni-freiburg.de

Abstract. A class of models is defined which are in the broadest sense generalizations of the deBroglie-Bohm pilot wave model of quantum mechanics. It is shown that essentially any type of probability assignment – including, of course, quantum probability – can be obtained from this type of models. Therefore, pilot-wave models are one possible explanation for the occurrence of non-classical probabilities in systems which are not considered as fundamentally quantum but which show strong resemblances to quantum systems.

1 Introduction

Ever since the pioneering work of Aerts et al. [1,22], there have been many reports of experimental results, in particular in the cognitive sciences, which indicate that models based on a quantum formalism are better predictors for observed phenomena than classical approaches (see e.g. [12,13,29,34]). Most of these models represent states (e.g. mental states) as rays in a vector space, and the probabilities for transitions from one mental state to another (for instance as the result of a particular response to a question) are obtained by squaring vector products. This way of calculating probabilities has sometimes been coined quantum probability.

Despite many attempts over the past years, the major question remains: Why should a formalism which was tailored to fit the phenomena of the quantum world be applicable in a context in which one would not expect that proper quantum effects are relevant. Apart from attempts to interpret cognitive phenomena as real quantum effects (e.g. [9,25,33]), some authors have argued that it is the similarity of fundamental concepts in both fields (e.g., the similarity of categorial apparatus [20] or the task of remaining coherent in a complex environment [3], to give two examples) which also require similar mathematical structures. However, why a Hilbert space model is suited for this type of task remains an open issue.

T. Filk — Financial support has been provided by the European Research Council under the European Communitys Seventh Framework Programme (FP7/20072013)/ ERC grant agreement no [294332], EvoEvo project.

H. Atmanspacher et al. (Eds.): QI 2015, LNCS 9535, pp. 88–100, 2016.
DOI: 10.1007/978-3-319-28675-4_7

Other approaches try to generalize the concept of "observation" or "measurement" to situations in which an observation (or measurement) is (almost) always an interference with or even an intrusion into the observed system, leading to a changed state of this system (e.g. [6,7]). In this case the axioms required for a proper interpretation of "measurement" lead, under mild conditions, to the formalism of quantum theory. Again other approaches have revealed that under certain conditions classical systems can exhibit quantum-like behavior (see, e.g., [8,24]). For an overview of "quantum approaches to consciousness" as well as further examples of applications see also [5,14,30].

At the QI2012 conference, the author presented Bohmian mechanics as a model with a classical ontology (of course, such a statement requires a definition of "classical ontology" and has been put into question; for two opinions, see, e.g., [17,21]) but which phenomenologically is equivalent to quantum theory proper [19]. The idea is that a system with two entities – a guiding field and a guided quantity – can easily give rise to non-classical probabilities for events which refer to the guided quantity alone. Note that "non-classical probability" does not necessarily imply "quantum probability". There are many more possibilities of how the probability of a subevent, the union of events or the intersection of events can be related to the probabilities for the events alone.

In the present article, these ideas will be developed further while putting more emphasis on the notion of "event". In particular, Bohmian mechanics is just a special case of this generalized class of models, for which the guiding entity does not have to fulfill Schrödinger's equation (however, it usually fulfills *some* differential field equation, which may or may not be linear) and the guided entity is not necessarily a particle. Furthermore, the probability for finding the guided entity in an experiment in a particular state (or location) may not be given by the absolute square of the guiding entity but by more general relations. This generality of pilot wave models may lead to probability assignments which are neither classical (Kolmogorovian) nor quantum probabilities.

The next section defines the general class of models, which I will call pilot wave models and of which Bohmian mechanics is a special example. In Sect. 3, I will give two examples to which the formalisms of quantum theory and quantum probability have been applied: the double-slit experiment in quantum theory and "the pet fish effect", a famous example for a conjunction fallacy in psychology. The aim of this section is an analysis of the concept of "event" in these circumstances. In Sect. 3.5, I will also explain in more detail how pilot wave models can lead to non-standard forms of probability. Finally, in Sect. 4, I will use the principle of pilot wave models as a framework for the dynamics of mental states, which could explain the occurrence of quantum probabilities in cognititive systems. A brief summary and outlook concludes the article.

2   Pilot Wave Models

In this section, I define a general framework for pilot-wave models. Even though Bohmian mechanics is a prominent example, not many attempts have been made to generalize this concept beyond its possible application to quantum theory. I first explain the general idea behind Bohmian mechanics and pilot-wave models. Then I will define pilot-wave models in a general (however, not the most general) framework, and finally I will comment on possible generalizations.

2.1 Bohmian Mechanics and the General Ideas

Essentially, Bohmian mechanics [10] (see [15,27] for more recent accounts) is a theory of two entities: a guiding field (or pilot-wave) $\psi(x,t)$, which obeys Schrödinger's equation, *and* a particle, which is described by its position $x(t)$. The dynamics of the particle can be expressed as a first-order equation

$$m\dot{x}(t) = \nabla S(x,t), \tag{1}$$

where S is the phase of the complex-valued field $\psi(x,t)$,

$$\psi(x,t) = |\psi(x,t)| \exp(\frac{\mathrm{i}}{\hbar}S(x,t)) \tag{2}$$

and m the mass of the particle. If ψ describes an ensemble of systems and the spatial distribution for a particular moment t is given by $|\psi(x,t)|^2$, this dynamics guarantees that it will remain that way for all t. All observed effects in this theory agree with the usual predictions of quantum theory. Like the Schrödinger field, the guiding field "lives" on configuration space, i.e. for n particles (each in $\mathbb{R}^3$) it is a field on $\mathbb{R}^{3n}$.

Bohmian mechanics is a deterministic theory: Not only the field $\psi(x,t)$ obeys a deterministic equation (the Schrödinger equation) but also the particle (Eq. 1). However, in order to reproduce all quantum effects, it is sufficient that the dynamics of the particle is such that it's probability of being measured at a position x is proportional to $|\psi(x)|^2$. Therefore, one may replace Eq. 1 by any (possibly stochastic) equation which guarantees this property.

The pilot wave models to be defined in the next section will essentially extend these features: there will be a guiding quantity defined as a field on a configurations space and there will be a guided quantity. However, this guided quantity does not have to be a particle but can also be a sub-structure of the field. While the dynamics of the guiding field can be quite arbitrary (in particular, it does not have to follow from a Schrödinger equation), the dynamics of the guided quantity will depend on the guided quantity. This implies, that the probability of measuring the guided quantity in a particular state depends on the guiding field, and as the guiding field is in most cases a non-local quantity, this conveys non-local ("holistic") features to the guided quantity. The resulting probability of finding the guided quantity in a particular state does not have to be a quantum probability.

2.2 Definition of Pilot Wave Models

We begin with a configuration space G. This can be three-dimensional real space $\mathbb{R}^3$ or the real line $\mathbb{R}$, but it can also be an abstract space of concepts (like a conceptual space, see [23]), meanings, alternative decisions, or the space of nodes of a graph (like, e.g., the network of neurons in a brain).

On this configuration space we consider a dynamical system consisting of two quantities:

1. A field $\psi(x, t)$ (where $x \in G$ and t refers to time) which will be used as a pilot wave. ψ can be non-local, i.e., non-vanishing almost everywhere on G. In most cases, ψ is either complex-valued or real-valued: $\psi(t) : G \longrightarrow \mathbb{C}(\mathbb{R})$. ψ may also have several components. Note that independent of the structure of G the set of fields form a vector space, i.e. we can take the sum of two fields or multiply them with real or complex numbers.
2. A second entity $p(x, t)$ which usually will be more localized, i.e. $p(x, t)$ will be different from zero only on a small subset of G (which, of course, can vary with time). Very often this will be only one point, in which case we often write $x(t)$.

The idea of a pilot wave model is that the dynamics of $p(x, t)$ (or $x(t)$) depends on the field ψ and hence is guided by ψ, while on the other hand the dynamics of ψ does not necessarily depend on $p(x, t)$. The probability of finding ("measuring") p in a particular location or region of G depends on the value of ψ. As the dynamics of the local entity p depends on the global entity ψ, the local entity may exhibit holistic features. Note, however, that in general there will be no equivalent to the quantum potential.

Independent of the details of the dynamics of ψ and p the probability of finding p in some particular configuration depends on ψ or, even stronger, may be expressed by a functional of ψ. In general, this functional will explicitly depend on time. If it does not depend on time (like in quantum theory where it is simply given by $|\psi|^2$), special consistency conditions between the dynamics of p and the dynamics of ψ have to hold.

ψ may have several components or, in other words, $p(t)$ may depend on several guiding quantities. The dynamical equations of these fields as well as the dependence of p on these components may be different for each component.

2.3   Some Examples

In biology we find numerous examples for the general structure defined above. Essentially in all cases where $\psi(x)$ describes the distribution of nutrition or environmental conditions on which living organisms depend (temperature, humidity, chemical components etc.) and where p (or $x(t)$) describes the location of an organism we find the general structure of pilot wave models:

1. Amongst other conditions and for various reasons, migratory birds prefer a particular average temperature of the air, which is (one of) the reasons why they tend to move closer to the equator in winter and further away from the equator in summer. Therefore, the probability of finding these birds in particular locations depends on the (global) temperature field and varies through the year.

2. Some bacteria use chemotaxis to find food (e.g. sugar) or avoid poisonous environments. They use a combination of directed and random motion in order to propagate to a region with a larger concentration of sugar (or a smaller concentration of poison). The probability of finding a bacterium in a particular location depends on the concentration of sugar or poison in the solution they live in, and this concentration may be subject to it's own dynamics.
3. Some predators depend crucially on a particular prey. Therefore, the probability of finding such a predator in a particular location depends on the distribution of the population of this prey, and this may vary with time (season, daytime, climate, etc.).
4. Apart from the concentration of reagents, chemical reactions may depend on several conditions like temperature, pressure, concentration of catalysts, etc. The probabilities for the occurrence of the products of the reactions depend on several "guiding fields". (In the context of quantum probability, a similar example has been discussed in [4]).

Finally, I want to discuss an example from physics, where the equations of the guiding quantity are known and where the probability distribution of the particles is given by a stochastic influence and differs from quantum probability. The Chladni patterns of sand or salt, placed on a metallic plate which is stimulated to vibrations (e.g. by a violin bow), denote the nodes of the vibrational patterns. The non-local guiding quantity $\psi(x)$ corresponds to the vibrational pattern of the plate and the guided quantities are the "particles" of sand. Even if only one grain of sand is placed on the plate, the probability $w(x)$ of finding this grain in a location x will be concentrated around the node lines of the vibrational pattern. The guiding quantity $\psi(x)$ satisfies a linear field equation similar to the free, time-independend Schrödinger equation, and the probability $w(x)$ will be given approximately by a Gaussian distribution

$$w(x) \propto \exp\left(-\alpha|\psi(x)^2|\right) \tag{3}$$

with some constant α depending on the details of the system but large enough for the distribution to be located narrowly around the zeros of $|\psi(x)|^2$. This is in contrast to quantum theory, where $w(x) = |\psi(x)|^2$. I will come back to this example in the next section.

In all these examples (and it is easy to extend the list) we have direct access to the "field" which influences the probability of finding the "guided object" in a particular place. Therefore, we do not consider the sometimes complicated probability function of observing the guided quantity in particular states as nonclassical. However, without direct access to this guiding quantity and no concrete model of it's dynamics this probability might look "non-Kolmogorovian". In particular, we may find non-local coherencies which will be difficult to explain by local interactions between the guided quantities alone.

3   Events

In this section, I will first consider two situations to which the formalism of quantum probabilities has been applied. The first will be the famous double-slit experiment in quantum physics, the second will be the guppy effect – a well-known example for a conjunction fallacy in psychology. I consider these models in more detail because I want to emphasize the notion of "event" in this context, which is slightly different from it's usual mathematical notion. The example of Chladni patterns discussed in the last section will be a third example; here the non-Kolmogorovian nature of "probability" is obvious. Finally, I will make more general comments on the notions of event and probability in pilot wave models.

3.1   The Double-Slit Experiment

The double-slit experiment is well-known in quantum physics (for an extensive discussion see, e.g., [18]), therefore, I will restrict myself to the features relevant for the notion of quantum probability.

The experimental set-up is as follows: A beam of collimated electrons (or neutrons, or photons, or any other "particle") is directed onto a screen with two very narrow slits. A few of these electrons will pass through the slits and hit a second screen in a certain distance behind the first one where they can be detected. There are two important observations: (1) whenever one of the particles (photon, electron, ...) hits the second screen, it's energy is transferred to the screen locally, i.e. it leaves a localized dot, which often is taken as evidence for the particle-nature of the system. (2) If both slits are open, one observes statistically an interference pattern of dots (the distribution of the single-particle signals shows interference fringes), while if only one slit is open, one observes a broad distribution.

The quantum mechanical description requires the electrons to be treated as waves which pass through the two slits of the first screen. These waves superimpose behind the first screen and exhibit an interference pattern at the second screen. The probability for a particle to hit the second screen is proportional to the absolute square of the total wave:

$$|\psi(x)|^2 = \frac{1}{2}|\psi_1(x) + \psi_2(x)|^2 \tag{4}$$

$$= \frac{1}{2}\Big(|\psi_1(x)|^2 + |\psi_2(x)|^2 + \psi_1(x)\psi_2(x)^* + \psi_1(x)^*\psi_2(x)\Big). \tag{5}$$

The mixed terms on the right hand side give rise to the interference pattern. In particular, it is possible that at certain locations x the sum of the two single-slit probabilities is "cancelled" by the interference terms, but it is also possible that at other locations the total probability is twice as large as the sum of the probabilities from the single-slit situation. This formula (adding amplitudes and calculating the probabilities from the absolute square of the sum) is often referred to as "quantum probability".

Why is it sometimes argued that classical probability doesn't work? Of course, this experiment doesn't violate Kolmogorovian probability *per se*, but in applying Kolmogorovian probabliity to this situation, we tend to make certain assumptions which then lead to apparent paradoxa. The probability $p(x)$ for finding a particle at point x depends on the circumstances, so we should specify the conditions. Let $p(x; E)$ be the probability of finding a particle at point x, given situation E. Now let E_1 be the situation in which only slit 1 is open (slit 2 closed) and vice versa for E_2. Furthermore we define E_{12} to be the situation for which slit 1 and 2 are open. For each of these cases we can calculate $p(x, E_i)$ ($i = 1, 2, 12$). There is absolutely no reason why the probabilities in these three situations should be related.

The paradox appears if we assume that the probability for situation E_{12} is related to the probabilities for E_1 and E_2 in the form of an OR: If both slits are open, the particle can only pass through slit 1 OR through slit 2 (these two events are considered as mutually exclusive) *and* in both cases the probabilities are the same as if the other slit were closed. So we make essentially two assumptions: (1) we are dealing with a particle, so that the first assumption is true (it can only pass through *one* of the slits – this assumption is violated if we replace "particle" by "wave", as in standard quantum theory), and (2) the probability for a particle to hit the second screen at a particular location after it has passed, say, slit 1 is independent of whether slit 2 is open or not. This assumption is violated in Bohmian mechanics, where indeed we are dealing with particles which can pass through one of the slits only, but for which the guidance field (and, therfore, the trajectory of the particle) depends on whether the second slit is open or not.

Considered from this point of view, the miracle is not, why $p(x; E_{12}) \neq p(x; E_1) + p(x; E_2)$, but why we obtain the correct probability by assigning amplitudes $\psi_i(x)|$ to the events E_i, obtain the amplitude for event E_{12} as a simple OR-superposition of these two amplitudes, and get the correct result from the absolute square of the superimposed amplitude. The Bohmian interpretation of the quantum mechanical wave function ψ being a guidance field which obeys a linear field equation (such that superpositions of solutions are again solutions) and which influences the trajectory of the particles seems to be an intuitive explanation.

3.2   The Guppy Effect

The guppy effect has first been described by Osherson and Smith [32] and refers to a conjunction fallacy in psychology. Several groups have described this effect in the context of a quantum formalism (see, e.g., [2]).

In a simplified version we can describe the guppy effect as follows: Many people consider a guppy to be a prototypical example for a pet fish, however it is considered to be much less prototypical for the concepts of either pet or fish. If we apply (fuzzy) set theory, why should a guppy be more typical for the conjunction "pet fish" than for "pet" or "fish" alone? It is true that pet fishes are a subset of fishes as well as a subset of pets. However, there is no reason that we can assign a probability $w(f)$ to a statement like "a guppy is a prototype for a fish" (measured, e.g., by the number of people who would consider this statement as correct) and a probability $w(p)$ to the statement "a guppy is a prototype for a pet" and then obtain the probability that "a guppy is a prototype for a pet fish" as the product of these probabilities. If this could be done, the joint probability would indeed have be smaller than the minimum of $w(f)$ and $w(p)$.

Again, probability theory is not violated, it only seems to be violated if we apply (fuzzy) set theory in a too simplistic way. As described in the previous section, quantum probability is one possibility to account for such effects, as the probability for a "conjunction" can be larger than the sum of the probabilities of the single cases.

3.3 Chladni Patterns

Chladni patterns are an instructive example where "classical probability" can fail and even quantum probability fails, despite the fact that the field equations for the vibrational patterns are linear. Let $\psi(y_i; x)$ be particular vibrational pattern under the condition, that the point y_i on the boundary of the metallic plate is fixated. We denote this "event" as E_i. It is known that in general (unless the two points y_i have "commensurable" coordinates) the two patterns will be different. Now define $\psi(y_1, y_2; x)$ to be one of the patterns which appear if *both* points y_1 and y_2 are kept fixed. This pattern will in general not only be different from the other two, but it is not even given by the linear superposition of the other two patterns (and the probabilities of finding the grains of sand on the plate are, of course, also completely different).

If we forget about the guiding quantity, i.e. the vibrations of the metallic plate, and look only at the grains of sand and the probability of finding such a grain of sand on a metallic plate, it seems plausible that the events are related (maybe not as OR but rather as AND, in which case the probability for the situation E_{12} would be the product of the single probablities for E_i). Obviously, this is not the case and the exact probabilities depend crucially on the commensurability features of the coordinates of y_1 and y_2.

3.4 Events in Pilot Wave Models

In the context of the double-slit scenario we have seen that the notion of event is used in two different contexts:

– The event of "measuring" or detecting a particle hitting the second screen at a particular location x. The probability density for this event is given by $p(x) = |\psi(x)|^2$.
– The "event" E_i which rather corresponds to a context for the first type of events.

As remarked above, in the double-slit experiment we find points x for which

$$p(x; E_{12}) < p(x; E_1) + p(x; E_2), \tag{6}$$

and other points for which

$$p(x; E_{12}) > p(x; E_1) + p(x; E_2), \tag{7}$$

which is difficult to explain in terms of classical probability theory if we assume $E_{12} = E_1 \cup E_2$ (for $E_1 \cap E_2 = \emptyset$), i.e. events E_{12} is of the form of an OR relationship between the distinct events E_1 and E_2 (as one might expect for an ordinary particle).

In pilot wave models we can stick to the notion of a particle, however, this particle is guided by the non-local quantity ψ so that it's behavior depends on the global context. The guiding field ψ depends on the context E_i (i.e., we have $\psi(x; E_i)$), and in many cases where the contexts can be related by an OR or an AND condition, the guiding fields may either add up or get multiplied. However, the probability of finding the guided quantity may depend non-trivially on the guiding field and, therefore, differs from the classical probability relations.

3.5   Probabilities from Pilot-Wave Models

As already mentioned, in pilot wave models the probability for finding the guided quantity (to which we have direct observational access) in a particular state depends on properties of the guiding field as well as the dynamics of the guided quantity. This probability does not necessarily have to be the absolute square of the guiding field like in Bohmian mechanics. The examples given in Sect. 2.3 indicate other possibilities:

1. The probability for finding migratory birds in a certain region of the earth may be proportional to a function $f(T(x) - T_0)$, where f describes a distribution peaked around 0 (e.g. a Gaussian or Lorentzian) and T_0 denotes the prefered temperature.
2. For bacteria finding their nutrition by chemotaxis, the concentration $c(x)$ of, say, glucose may be relevant. Actually, in some cases the bacteria detect the gradient of the concentration and move into the direction of increasing concentration. The probability of finding such bacteria in a solution is (in first order approximation) proportional to this concentration.
3. An interesting model is provided by the predator-prey scenario. There exist many models in population dynamics which describe the concentration of predators and prey as a function of time. The Lotka-Volterra equations constitute a famous classical model. If we had no access to the concentration of prey, the concentration of the predators alone would suggest an extremely complicated and maybe non-classical description. Note that due to the mutual dependence of the populations of prey and predator, the equations are coupled and there is no clear-cut distinction between guided and guiding quantity. Nevertheless, if we had no observational access to one of the populations, the dynamics of the other would look "non-classical".

   Most of these population dynamics models emphasize the time dependence, but extended by diffusion terms (like, e.g., in Turing's reaction diffusion system [36]), such models can also describe the spatial distribution of populations. In many cases even interference-type patterns occur.

The pilot wave models introduced here have a distinguished base space which is the configuration space G. In Bohmian mechanics, $x(t)$ is the position of the particle at time t, while all other properties (momentum, energy, etc.) are related to the wave function and are not properties of the particle: The quantum mechanical momentum as measured by the momentum operator is not the "classical" momentum of the particle (which would be $m\dot{x}$) but a property of the wave function (as is also obvious from deBroglie's relation $p = h/\lambda$, where λ is the wave length of the wave function and h Planck's constant), and for energy eigenstates the wave functions can be chosen as real valued, i.e. they do not have a phase and, therefore, according to Eq. 1, we obtain $\dot{x} = 0$ – the particles are at rest.

This let to some criticism against Bohmian mechanics as a model for quantum mechanics, because quantum mechanics has no distinguished base space. In particular, the quantum mechanical symmetry between position base and momentum base is lost. (However, in relativistic mechanics, this symmetry is lost anyhow: Spacetime has a causal structure and we require a locality condition for interactions, while, e.g., particles with hugely different momenta – non-locality in momentum space – are allowed to interact. Note, however, that we are refering not the the spacetime reference frames in SRT, but to the bases in the Hilbert space of quantum mechanics.) Therefore, in pilot wave models all probabilities are calculated with respect to wave functions (pilot waves) defined over the distinguished set G.

In quantum theory the transition from a state $|1\rangle$, defined by a wave function $\psi_1(x) = \langle x|1\rangle$, to a second state $|2\rangle$, defined by a wave function $\psi_2(x) = \langle x|2\rangle$, is given by the absolute square of the scalar product:

$$p(1 \to 2) = |\langle 2|1\rangle|^2 = \left| \int \psi_2(x)^* \psi_1(x) \, \mathrm{d}x \right|^2 . \tag{8}$$

The scalar plays a special role in the vector space formalism of quantum theory and makes the vector space into a Hilbert space. It is linear in both of its arguments. In a more general formalism, the probablity for a transition from $|1\rangle$ to $|2\rangle$ might be given by a more complex functional of the two wave functions. This raises the question, to which extend the linearity condition of the vector product has been tested in cognitive experiments. General pilot wave models as introduced in this article allow the probabilities to depend in a more general form on the pilot waves.

4 A Pilot Wave Model for Mental States

This section will be quite speculative and the proposed mechanism (first published in [19]) may rather be considered as a general principle and not as an explicit model for the observed occurrence of quantum-like probabilities in cognitive systems. Furthermore, I should remark that the general idea of Bohmian mechanics has been applied to mental models already by Bohm himself, however with a completely different interpretation, assignment, and context (see, e.g., [11,35]).

In this model I will assume that the guiding quantity $\psi(x,t)$ is closely related to the general neuronal activity in the brain. The quantity x may refer to single neurons, in which case $\psi(x)$ is some measure for the neuronal activity of this neuron, or x may denote an idealized location in the brain in the sense of a field theory, where x refers to a point and $\psi(x)$ to the averaged activity in a small volume around x. On the other hand, the guided quantity $p(t)$ should be a particular neuronal activity which can be considered as the "neuronal correlate of mental states", and again I am not very precise whether this refers to the neuronal correlate of "attention", "intentionality", "consciousness" etc. What is measured in cognitive or psychological experiments is the mental correlate of $p(t)$. Note that $p(t)$ does not necessarily refer to a single neuron (even though it could) but rather to an activity of a subnetwork of the total network or even a subactivity.

Furthermore, it seems plausible that the dynamics of the particular neuronal activity $p(t)$ is "guided" by the general neuronal activity $\psi(x,t)$. It may even be possible, that the dynamics of $p(t)$ has an influence onto the dynamics of $\psi(x,t)$. This may be called a "top-down" effect, while the "guiding" – the influence of $\psi(x,t)$ onto the dynamics of $p(t)$ – can be interpreted as a "bottom-up" effect. It is also very likely, that the probability of finding the mental correlate of $p(t)$ in regions, where the general neuronal activity $\psi(x,t)$ is large.

In standard models of neuronal activity there are two ways that activities can cancel each other: (1) there are excitatory and inhibitory activities, such that an increased inhibitory activity can down-regulate an increased excitatory activity, and (2) there is an average activity due to noise or the background activity of the network, and deviations from this averaged activity (in both directions, increased and decreased) may carry "information". This possibility of activity cancellation activities may lead to interference effects.

Some neural network models (like, e.g., the Hopfield models [28], or, more general, attractor networks [16]) have the property, that the transition probability from an internal state 1 to a second internal state 2 depends on the overlap of the network activity for state 1 with an external input (a "question" to the system), corresponding to the internal state 2 (e.g., the input might be a noisy or slightly damaged version of state 2). This resembles formula (8). The general idea of associative memory as proposed by Hebb [26] is based on the overlap of an induced activity pattern of a cell assembly with an imprinted pattern which was generated by past experience. Therefore, such types of networks share certain features with the quantum formalism and are good candidates for the occurrence of quantum-like properties in classical systems.

5   Summary

Pilot wave models are examples for classical physical systems which can exhibit non-classical probabilistic features. In particular, quantum probabilities can occur in such models which are generalizations of Bohmian mechanics. Pilot wave models are based on a simple principle: a guiding (non-local) field, which in many cases cannot be observed directly, and a guided (more localized) quantity which is observed in experiments. It is suggested that various types of attractor networks (simulating associative memory) may also exhibit quantum-like features.

The examples given in this article, like the chemotaxis of bacteria in their search for nutrition or Cladni patterns, indicate that non-classical probabilities are not necessarily quantum probabilities. Therefore, it might be interesting to re-evaluate those cognitive experiments, to which quantum probabilities have been successfully applied, whether other non-classical probabilities can be ruled out.

References

1. Aerts, D., Aerts, S.: Applications of quantum statistics in psychological studies of decision processes. Found. Sci. **1**, 85–97 (1994)
2. Aerts, D., Broekaert, J., Gabora, L., Veloz, T.: The guppy effect as interference. In: Busemeyer, J.R., Dubois, F., Lambert-Mogiliansky, A., Melucci, M. (eds.) QI 2012. LNCS, vol. 7620, pp. 36–47. Springer, Heidelberg (2012)
3. Aerts, D., Sozzo, S.: What is quantum? unifying its micro-physical and structural appearance. In: Atmanspacher, H., Bergomi, C., Filk, T., Kitto, K. (eds.) QI 2014. LNCS, vol. 8951, pp. 12–23. Springer, Heidelberg (2015)
4. Asano, M., Basieva, I., Khrennikov, A., Ohya, M., Tanaka, Y., Yamato, I.: A quantum-like model of *Escherichia coli*'s metabolism based on adaptive dynamics. In: Busemeyer, J.R., Dubois, F., Lambert-Mogiliansky, A., Melucci, M. (eds.) QI 2012. LNCS, vol. 7620, pp. 60–67. Springer, Heidelberg (2012)
5. Atmanspacher, H.: Quantum approaches to consciousness. In: Zalta, E.N. (ed.) Stanford Encyclopedia of Philosophy. Stanford University, Stanford (2011). http://plato.stanford.edu/entries/qt-consciousness/
6. Atmanspacher, H., Römer, H., Walach, H.: Weak quantum theory: complementarity and entanglement in physics and beyond. Found. Phys. **32**, 379–406 (2002)
7. Atmanspacher, H., Filk, T., Römer, H.: Weak quantum theory: formal framework and selected applications. In: Adenier, G., Khrennikov, A., Nieuwenhuizen, T. (eds.) Quantum Theory: Reconsideration of Foundations - 3, pp. 34–46. American Institut of Physics, New York (2006)
8. Atmanspacher, H., beim Graben, P., Filk, T.: Epistemic entanglement due to non-generating partitions of classical dynamical systems. Int. J. Theor. Phys. **52**, 723–734 (2013)
9. Beck, F., Eccles, J.: Quantum aspects of brain activity and the role of consciousness. Proc. Natl. Acad. Sci. U.S.A. **89**, 11357–11361 (1992)
10. Bohm, D.: A suggested interpretation of the quantum theory in terms of "Hidden" variables I & II. Phys. Rev. **85**(166–179), 180–193 (1952)
11. Bohm, D., Hiley, B.: The Undivided Universe: An Ontological Interpretation of Quantum Theory. Routledge, London (1993)
12. Bruza, P., Kitto, K., Nelson, D., McEvoy, C.L.: Is there something quantum-like about the human mental lexicon? J. Math. Psychol. **53**, 362–377 (2007)
13. Busemeyer, J., Wang, Z., Townsend, J.T.: Quantum dynamics of human decision making. J. Math. Psychol. **50**, 220–241 (2006)
14. Busemeyer, J., Bruza, P.: Quantum Models of Cognition and Decision. Cambridge University Press, Cambridge (2012)

15. Dürr, D., Teufel, S.: Bohmian Mechanics: The Physics and Mathematics of Quantum Theory. Springer, Heidelberg (2012)
16. Eliasmith, C.: Attractor network. Scholarpedia 2(10), 1380 (2007)
17. Essfeld, M., Lazarovici, D., Dürr, D.: The ontology of quantum physics. Br. J. Philos. Sci. 65, 773–796 (2014)
18. Feynman, R., Leighton, R., Sands, M.: The Feynman Lectures on Physics, vol. 3. Addison-Wesley, New York (1965)
19. Filk, T.: Quantum-like behavior of classical systems. In: Busemeyer, J.R., Dubois, F., Lambert-Mogiliansky, A., Melucci, M. (eds.) QI 2012. LNCS, vol. 7620, pp. 196–206. Springer, Heidelberg (2012)
20. Filk, T., von Müller, A.: Quantum physics and consciousness: the quest for a common conceptual foundation. Mind Matter 7, 59–80 (2009)
21. Filk, T.: It is the theory which decides what we can observe (Einstein). In: Oktober, E., Dzhafarov, S.J. (eds.) Proceedings of the Winers Memorial Lectures 2014, Purde, 31. Oktober-3 - November 3, 2014 (to appear)
22. Gabora, L., Aerts, D.: Contextualizing concepts using a mathematical generalization of the quantum formalism. J. Exp. Theory Artif. Intell. 14, 327–358 (2002)
23. Gärdenfors, P.: Conceptual Spaces. Bradford Books, MIT Press, Bradford (2000)
24. beim Graben, P., Atmanspacher, H.: Complementarity in classical dynamical systems. Found. Phys. 36, 291–306 (2006)
25. Hameroff, S., Penrose, R.: Orchestrated reduction of quantum coherence in brain-microtubules: a model for consciousness. In: Hameroff, S., Kahzniak, A., Scott, A. (eds.) Toward a Science of Consciousness, pp. 507–540. MIT Press, Cambridge (1996)
26. Hebb, D.O.: The Organization of Behavior. Wiley, New York (1949)
27. Holland, P.R.: The Quantum Theory of Motion: An Account of the DeBroglie-Bohm Causal Interpretation of Quantum Mechanics. Cambridge University Press, Cambridge (1993)
28. Hopfield, J.J.: Neural networks and physical systems with emergent collective computational properties. Proc. Nat. Acad. Sci. (USA) 79, 2554–2558 (1982)
29. Khrennikov, A.: Classical and quantum mechanics on information spaces with applications to cognitive, psychological, social and anomalous phenomena. Found. Phys. 29, 1065–1098 (1999)
30. Khrennikov, A.: Ubiquitous Quantum Structure: From Psychology to Finances. Springer, Heidelberg (2010)
31. Lambert-Mogliansky, D.: Verallgemeinerte Messungen
32. Osherson, D.N., Smith, E.E.: On the adequacy of prototype theory as a theory of concepts. Cognition 9, 35–58 (1981)
33. Penrose, R., Hameroff, S.: Consciousness in the universe: neuroscience, quantum space-time geometry and orch OR theory. J. Cosmol. 14, 1–17 (2011)
34. Pothos, E., Busemeyer, J.: A quantum probability model explanation for violations of rational decision theory. Proc. R. Soc. B 276, 2171–2178 (2009)
35. Pylkkänen, P.: Mind, Matter and the Implicate Order. Springer, New York and Berlin (2007)
36. Turing, A.: The chemical basis of morphogenesis. Philos. Trans. R. Soc. London Ser. B. 237(641), 37–72 (1952)

Why Linear? An Illustration Using a Geometric Model of Quantum Interaction

Paul Baird[✉]

Laboratoire de Mathématiques de Bretagne Atlantique,
Université de Bretagne Occidentale, Brest, France
paul.baird@univ-brest.fr

Abstract. Quantum mechanics is a linear theory. This is a strange fact. Why should nature be so convenient? Perhaps linearity is simply a consequence of small perturbations against a relatively uniform background. This can be formalized within the mathematical notions of *weak solution* and *linearization*. The true picture is unlikely to be so and some more appropriate framework may be required to deal with theories where this uniformity is lost, such as for example quantum gravity. A geometric model of quantum interaction provides a useful illustration. In this case the equations are quadratic, but both their weak form and linearization leads to a striking analogue of the Schrödinger equation.

1 Introduction

The formalism of quantum mechanics (QM) proceeds as follows. To a physical system one associates a separable Hilbert space over the complex numbers. States of the system correspond to rays in this space. An observable corresponds to a Hermitian operator whose eigenvalues are the only possible quantities that may be observed. Once an observation is made, the system collapses onto the corresponding eigenstate via a projection operator. Changes of state (not involving observation) are given by unitary transformations, which, when applied in a continuous setting lead to the (time dependent) Schrödinger equation. It is remarkable that nature should proceed in this way. Or is there perhaps a deeper underlying phenomenon, by which non-linear laws are perceived to be linear by dint of the contextual nature of the process? We generally make observations with respect to a relatively stable macroscopic background. But then the entire process consisting of the measuring apparatus, the environment both near and far and the system to be measured, may well not obey this convenient law.

The mathematics of partial differential equations exploits the notion of *linearization*. This is particularly useful for showing local existence, the Einstein equations being an important example in general realtivity. If φ is a function of several variables and $P(\varphi) = 0$ is a partial differential equation, where P is some operator that involves higher order derivatives; then one may calculate the

---

P. Baird—The author would like to thank the referees whose comments have improved this paper.

H. Atmanspacher et al. (Eds.): QI 2015, LNCS 9535, pp. 101–112, 2016.
DOI: 10.1007/978-3-319-28675-4_8

expression $\frac{d}{d\epsilon}P(\varphi + \epsilon\psi)|_{\epsilon=0}$ to obtain a linear equation in ψ whose coefficients depend on φ. From a physical point of view, it is natural to consider φ as a fixed background with ψ a local perturbation and as such we would expect a local expression of the law $P \equiv 0$ to be given by some linear approximation.

An alternative approach is to study the weak form of the equations, whereby, using a suitable Hilbert space, we couple $P(\varphi)$ with some arbitray function ξ to form the inner product $\langle P(\varphi), \xi \rangle$, where derivatives are shifted across onto ξ. By choosing ξ appropriately, as we show below, one may also be led to a linear equation.

Quantum interaction describes macroscopic phenomema through quantum models, so we should be prepared to encompass non-linear laws into the theory, while retaining the essential quantum features of choice (uncertainty of measurement) and state collapse. Linear approximations should then arise when the process is occuring within a stable "flat" environement, such as our own ingrained concept of space. The term *flat* here should be interpreted as the vanishing of some intrinsic curvature. In the combinatorial setting of the model we discuss below, notions of curvature are developed in [5].

The author proposes a model of quantum interaction based on our perception of 3D objects. An approximation of an object is given by a combinatorial graph and its possible perceived states by a complex valued function on the vertices which satisfies a quadratic difference equation. This equation contains a real-valued parameter which we view as its spectrum: only certain values of the parameter allow for a non-trivial solution. Depending on the graph, these values may be discrete or continuous. For a given element of the spectrum, there is a linear freedom in the solution, so we may apply some normalization. A similar formalism to quantum mechanics can now be applied. Until an observation is made, the graph is not in any state; once an observation is made (correlation between systems takes place), it collapses into a geometric state. However, the quadratic nature of the equations means linear superposition of solutions is generally forbidden. In this article, we deduce a weak form of the equations, as well as apply linearization, to obtain a linear version on some fixed background. The resulting equation is remarkably similar to the Schrödinger equation.

2   A Geometric Model

The geometric model has been discussed in detail in a number of references, see [1–4], so we give an abridged version here. Our impression from the illustration below is of a framework in Euclidean 3-space. We see a tetrahedron attached to a cube by a rigid bar, rather than just lines on a piece of paper.

In fact there are potentially four apparent configurations depending upon whether the edges that cross are perceived to be above or below each other, with a consistency requirement for the two pairs of crossing edges of the cube. Our eyes may rove across the picture and flip between the different 3D–realizations, although it is quite hard to simultaneously concentrate on both the tetrahedron and the cube. Once we have fixed on a configuration, it is likely to persist until we make a significant mental effort to change it. However, let us remind ourselves that the physical reality consists of a collection of vertices joined by edges drawn on a flat piece of paper. So how do we get from the drawing to a 3D-realization?

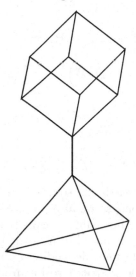

Let $\Gamma = (V, E)$ be a finite simple graph which may or may not be connected, with vertex set V and edge set E. Simple means there are no loops or multiple edges. For vertices x and y, we use the notation $x \sim y$ to indicate that x and y are joined by an edge and we let $n(x)$ denote the degree of vertex x, that is, the number of edges incident with x.

The Laplacian of a function $\varphi : V \to \mathbf{C}$ is defined by the mean-value property:

$$\Delta\varphi(x) := \frac{1}{n(x)} \sum_{y \sim x} (\varphi(x) - \varphi(y))$$

where $n(x)$ is the degree of vertex $x \in V$ (the number of edges incident with x). Although this appears to be a first order operator, formally, as we explain in Sect. 3, it arises as the negative of the coderivative of the derivative, which is its usual definition in smooth geometry.

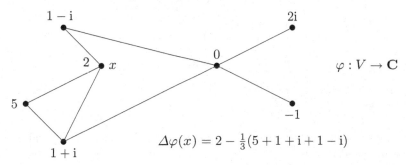

The symmetric square of the derivative of φ is defined by (cf. Sect. 3):

$$(\nabla\varphi)^2(x) := \frac{1}{n(x)} \sum_{y \sim x} \left(\varphi(y) - \varphi(x)\right)^2.$$

Given a real-valued function $\gamma : V \to \mathbf{R}$, consider the equation

$$\frac{\gamma(x)}{n(x)} \left(\sum_{y \sim x} \left(\varphi(y) - \varphi(x)\right) \right)^2 = \sum_{y \sim x} \left(\varphi(x) - \varphi(y)\right)^2, \tag{1}$$

at each vertex $x \in V$, where $\varphi : V \to \mathbf{C}$ is a complex-valued function. In more economical form, this can be expressed as

$$\gamma(x)(\Delta\varphi(x))^2 = (\nabla\varphi)^2(x).$$

Clearly $\varphi = $ constant is a particular solution which we call trivial. Any real-valued φ will also give solutions, so we also impose the requirement that $\gamma < 1$, which, by the Cauchy-Schwarz inequality, means that any non-constant solution φ cannot be real on any vertex and all of its neighbours. The equation may or may not admit non-trivial solutions, depending on the function γ.

By a *framework* in Euclidean space, we mean a graph that is realized as a subset of Euclidean space with edges straight line segments joining the vertices. The framework is called *invariant* if, for a particular γ, it satisfies (1) with φ the restriction to the vertices of some orthogonal projection to the complex plane *independently of any similarity transformation of the framework*.

The underlying framework of a regular polytope is always invariant. For example, the restriction of any orthogonal projection φ to the underlying frameworks of the convex regular polytopes in Euclidean 3-space as well as the 4D 600-cell satisfies (1) with γ constant as given in the following table:

Polytope	γ
Tetrahedron	$3/4$
Cube	0
Octahedron	$1/2$
Icosahedron	$\dfrac{2 - \sqrt{5}}{3 - \sqrt{5}} < 0$
Dodecahedron	$\dfrac{3(1 - \sqrt{5})}{2(3 - \sqrt{5})} < 0$
600-cell	$\dfrac{5(1 - 2\sqrt{5})}{3} < 0$

There are many other examples of invariant frameworks [3]. The figure depicted above also satisfies (1) invariantly provided the bar joining the tetrahedron with the cube extends through the centre of mass of each of these objects.

It is important to note that the invariance property means that however we scale, translate, rotate or reflect the framework (a similarity transformation), it still satisfies (1) with γ unchanged. Scale invariance and translation invariance corresponds to the freedom $\varphi \mapsto \lambda\varphi + \mu$ ($\lambda, \mu \in \mathbf{C}$) of a solution to (1), whereas reflection invariance corresponds to the freedom of taking the complex conjugate: $\varphi \mapsto \overline{\varphi}$. Rotation invariance, when it occurs, is more subtle and requires an algebraic analysis of the equations.

For an invariant framework, the geometry is inherent in the underlying combinatorial structure and the function γ and does not depend on any embedding in Euclidean space. To see this, one should be able to reconstruct the framework from the given information, which is always locally possible provided $\gamma < 1$ [3]. A global reconstruction requires additional information such as an edge colouring of the underlying graph, see [5].

For a given graph, we would like to know what are the admissible functions $\gamma : V \to \mathbf{R}$ for which (1) has a solution. Define the *geometric spectrum* of Γ to be the collection of equivalence classes of such functions:

$$\Sigma = \{\gamma : V \to [-\infty, 1) \subset \mathbf{R} : \exists \, \mathrm{non-const} \; \varphi : V \to \mathbf{C} \text{ satisfying } (1)\},$$

where two functions are identified when they determine a common solution φ and agree on the compliment of the set $\{x \in V : \Delta\varphi(x) = (\nabla\varphi)^2(x) = 0\}$. We allow γ to take on the value $-\infty$ at points where the Laplacian vanishes. It is our contention that the geometric spectrum provides an analogue of the spectrum of a Hermitian operator and that the corresponding family of solutions to (1) together with their liftings into Euclidean 3-space (*geometric states*), an analogue of eigenstate in QM.

This point of view is put forward in the article [4] from QI-2014, where striking similarities are noted between the geometric states of the Necker cube and a spin 1/2 particle, particularly in respect of decoherence.

In [1,2], a model is proposed in which graphs can interact by falling into compatible geometric states to form a new state. This would seem to mirror the way in which perception translates physical data into "meaningful" images: our brain-system correlates with a configuration of lines on a piece of paper to produce compatible 3D-geometric states. However, to date, no reasonable model has been constructed to describe evolution of a geometric model, in a similar way to which unitary evolution models change in QM. We take the first steps here by first deriving the weak form of the Eq. (1) and then by applying the technique of linearization in a discrete setting. This requires a novel approach involving *symmetric* complex calculus, rather than the usual *Hermitian* forms used in QM. However, Hermitian forms still come into play when solutions are normalized.

Background is an essential factor in how we perceive objects as optical illusions demonstrate. The parallel lines below appear to bend apart due to the suggestion of a spherical background.

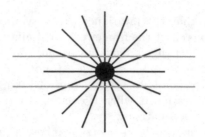

We propose that this is a phenomenon that can be formalized within the mathematical framework below[1]. Specifically, in order to interpret our geometric model, we introduce a fixed background with which the geometric state interacts. This can now be introduced into the equations via either *the weak form* or *linearization*. Both approaches lead to a linear Schrödinger-type equation that may now provide a reasonable framework of quantum interaction for the geometric model.

3   The Linearized and Weak Forms of the Equations

Let $\Gamma = (V, E)$ be a finite simple graph with vertex set V and edge set E, where elements e of E are expressed as unordered couples $e = xy$ for $x, y \in V$. For $x \in V$ define the *tangent space to Γ at x* to be the set of oriented edges with base point x together with an element $\vec{0}$: $T_x\Gamma = \{\overrightarrow{xy} : y \sim x\} \cup \{\vec{0}\}$. Define the *tangent bundle to Γ* to be the union: $T\Gamma = \cup_{x\in V}T_x\Gamma$. Then a 1-*form* on Γ is a map $\omega : T\Gamma \to \mathbf{C}$ such that $\omega(\overrightarrow{xy}) = -\omega(\overrightarrow{yx})$ and $\omega(\vec{0}) = 0$. To a function $\varphi : V \to \mathbf{C}$, we can naturally associate a 1-form, the *derivate* $\mathrm{d}\varphi$, by $\mathrm{d}\varphi(\overrightarrow{xy}) = \varphi(y) - \varphi(x)$.

For two 1-forms ω, η, define their *pointwise symmetric product at $x \in V$* by

$$\langle \omega, \eta \rangle_x = \sum_{y \sim x} \omega(\overrightarrow{xy})\eta(\overrightarrow{xy}),$$

and their *(global) symmetric product* by

$$(\omega, \eta) = \sum_{e \in E} \omega(e)\eta(e) = \frac{1}{2} \sum_{x \in V} \sum_{y \sim x} \omega(\overrightarrow{xy})\eta(\overrightarrow{xy}).$$

Note that in the first sum the 1-forms act on unoriented edges so that only their product is well-defined; the factor of one half occurs in the second sum, since there, unoriented edges are counted twice.

For functions $\varphi, \psi : V \to \mathbf{C}$, define their *(global) symmetric product* by

$$(\varphi, \psi) = \sum_{x \in V} n(x)\varphi(x)\psi(x),$$

---

[1] Another viable explanation for these kinds of optical illusions could be contextual emergence, see for example [7].

where $n(x)$ is the degree of vertex x.

The above definitions are the complex symmetric analogues of standard L^2 products that arise in functional analytic theory on a graph; in the latter situation they are replaced by Hermitian products rather than symmetric products [8].

Given a function $\xi : V \to \mathbf{C}$ and a 1-form $\omega : T\Gamma \to \mathbf{C}$, we can define a new 1-form $\xi\omega$ by

$$(\xi\omega)(\overrightarrow{xy}) = \frac{1}{2}(\xi(x) + \xi(y))\omega(\overrightarrow{xy}).$$

Then it is easily checked that

$$d(\varphi\psi) = \varphi d\psi + \psi d\varphi.$$

Given a 1-form ω, define its *co-deriviative* $d^*\omega$ to be the function which at each vertex $x \in V$ is given by

$$d^*\omega(x) = -\frac{1}{n(x)} \sum_{y \sim x} \omega(\overrightarrow{xy}).$$

Then for a function $\varphi : V \to \mathbf{C}$,

$$d^*d\varphi = -\frac{1}{n(x)} \sum_{y \sim x} d\varphi(\overrightarrow{xy}) = \frac{1}{n(x)} \sum_{y \sim x} (\varphi(y) - \varphi(x)) = -\Delta\varphi.$$

Lemma 1. *Let $\varphi, \psi : V \to \mathbf{C}$ be functions and $\omega : T\Gamma \to \mathbf{C}$ a 1-form. Then the following formulae hold:*

(i) $(d\varphi, \omega) = (\varphi, d^*\omega)$;
(ii) $(\Delta\varphi, \psi) = -(d\varphi, d\psi)$;
(iii) $(\Delta\varphi, \psi) = (\varphi, \Delta\psi)$;
(iv) $d^*(\varphi\omega)(x) = \varphi(x)d^*\omega(x) - \frac{1}{2n(x)}\langle d\varphi, \omega\rangle_x$ *for each $x \in V$.*

Proof. To prove (i), we notice that for $x \sim y$, the sum

$$(d\varphi, \omega) = \frac{1}{2} \sum_{x \in V} \sum_{y \sim x} (\varphi(y) - \varphi(x))\omega(\overrightarrow{xy})$$

contributes $(\varphi(y) - \varphi(x))\omega(\overrightarrow{xy}) = -\varphi(x)\omega(\overrightarrow{xy}) - \varphi(y)\omega(\overrightarrow{yx})$ (the term being symmetric in x and y), which equates to the corresponding terms in the sum

$$(\varphi, d^*\omega) = -\sum_{x \in V} \varphi(x) \sum_{y \sim x} \omega(\overrightarrow{xy}).$$

The identity (ii) now follows from the fact that $d^*d\varphi = -\Delta\varphi$. Identity (iii) follows from (ii), by symmetry. Finally

$$d^*(\varphi\omega)(x) = -\frac{1}{n(x)} \sum_{y \sim x} (\varphi\omega)(\overrightarrow{xy})$$

$$= -\frac{1}{2n(x)} \sum_{y \sim x} (\varphi(x) + \varphi(y))\omega(\overrightarrow{xy})$$

$$= \varphi(x)\mathrm{d}^*\omega(x) - \frac{1}{2n(x)} \sum_{y \sim x} (\varphi(y) - \varphi(x))\omega(\overrightarrow{xy})$$

$$= \varphi(x)\mathrm{d}^*\omega(x) - \frac{1}{2n(x)} \langle \mathrm{d}\varphi, \omega \rangle_x,$$

which gives (iv).

With the above notation and formulae established, we can give a weak form of Eq. (1).

Proposition 1. *The Eq. (1) holds if and only if*

$$(\Delta\varphi, \xi\gamma\Delta\varphi) - 2(\mathrm{d}\varphi, n\xi\mathrm{d}\varphi) = 0, \tag{2}$$

for any function $\xi : V \to \mathbf{C}$.

Proof. Let $\xi : V \to \mathbf{C}$. Then if (1) holds, we have:

$$\sum_{x \in V} n(x)\xi(x) \left(\gamma(x)(\Delta\varphi(x))^2 - \mathrm{d}\varphi(x)^2 \right) = 0,$$

equivalently

$$(\Delta\varphi, \xi\gamma\Delta\varphi) - (\mathrm{d}\varphi^2, \xi) = 0,$$

where we recall that $\mathrm{d}\varphi^2(x) = \sum_{y \sim x} (\varphi(y) - \varphi(x))^2 = \langle \mathrm{d}\varphi, \mathrm{d}\varphi \rangle_x$. But we claim that $(\mathrm{d}\varphi^2, \xi) = 2(\mathrm{d}\varphi, \xi\mathrm{d}\varphi)$. Indeed,

$$(\mathrm{d}\varphi^2, \xi) = \sum_{x \in V} n(x)\xi(x) \left(\sum_{y \sim x} (\varphi(y) - \varphi(x))^2 \right),$$

which, for each $x \sim y$, contributes the term $(n(x)\xi(x) + n(y)\xi(y))(\varphi(y) - \varphi(x))^2$. But precisely this term occurs within

$$2(\mathrm{d}\varphi, n\xi\mathrm{d}\varphi) = \frac{1}{2} \sum_{x \in V} \sum_{y \sim x} (n(x)\xi(x) + n(y)\xi(y))(\varphi(y) - \varphi(x))^2.$$

(on noting the symmetry of the expression to be summed on the right-hand side).

Conversely, if we fix a vertex $x \in V$ and consider the function $\xi : V \to \mathbf{C}$ given by $\xi(x) = 1$ and $\xi(y) = 0$ for all $y \neq x$, then, recalling the factor of $1/2$ in the inner product of forms, (2) gives $\gamma(x)\Delta\varphi(x)^2 - \mathrm{d}\varphi^2(x) = 0$, so that (1) holds.

On taking the function ξ to be identically equal to 1, we obtain the following consequence.

Corollary 1. *Let* $\varphi : V \to \mathbf{C}$ *be a solution to Eq. (1) with* γ *constant. Then*

$$\left(\gamma\Delta(\Delta\varphi) + 2n\Delta\varphi + \frac{1}{n}\langle \mathrm{d}n, \mathrm{d}\varphi \rangle, \varphi \right) = 0.$$

4   The Schrödinger Equation

Corollary 1 suggests heuristic arguments as to why we might consider a pair (Γ, φ) consisting of a connected graph endowed with a solution φ to (1) with γ constant as an analogue of a quantum particle with mass inversely proportional to $|\gamma|$; in the case when $\gamma = 0$, we view the pair as representing a massless particle[2].

In the first instance, we do not admit any fixed background with respect to which we can define parameters of equations: the particle creates its own background, which is reflected in the form $(\mathcal{P}(\varphi), \varphi)$, where $\mathcal{P}$ is some (discrete) differential operator. Furthermore, in a geometric realization of a solution to (1) as an invariant framework in Euclidean space, the function φ is taken to be an orthogonal projection to the complex plane. Thus if we now fix the background with which φ interacts as say a fine mesh in Euclidean space with vertices placed on a regular lattice, then this in no way affects φ: the right-hand term of $(\mathcal{P}(\varphi), \varphi)$ it is still orthogonal projection, now defined on the vertices of the mesh, where the inner product should now be taken by summing over the vertices of the mesh that approximate the geometric realization of the original graph.

Let us therefore take the left-hand side of the inner product of Corollary 1 as a measure of change in our geometric model of quantum interaction. To do this, suppose that the centre of mass of the framework is located at the origin in Euclidean 3-space and that, as in quantum mechanics, a solution φ to (1) is normalized so as to have norm 1 with respect to some appropriate Hermitian inner product, so that, for example:

$$||\varphi|| := \left(\sum_{x \in V} |\varphi(x)|^2 \right)^{1/2} = 1.$$

Now define a discrete step by step evolution $\{\varphi_t\}$ $(t = 0, 1, 2, \ldots)$ by the equation

$$\frac{\partial \varphi_t}{\partial t} := \varphi_{t+1} - \varphi_t = \gamma \Delta(\Delta \varphi_t) + 2n \Delta \varphi_t + \frac{1}{n} \langle dn, d\varphi_t \rangle, \qquad \varphi_0 = \varphi. \quad (3)$$

This should be compared with the time-dependent Schrödinger equation on a smooth fixed background with potential U [13]:

$$i\hbar \frac{\partial \psi}{\partial t} = -\frac{\hbar^2}{2m} \Delta \psi + U \psi.$$

for some function $\psi(x, t)$ which represents the probability density of finding a particle at position x. When ψ is identified with $\Delta \varphi$ the similarity is striking. It should be noted that at least for the regular polytopes, as the number of vertices increases and the polytope increasingly approximates a smooth object, the parameter γ becomes negative, reinforcing the idea that if we pursue the particle analogy, γ be inversely proportional to the mass.

---

[2] This latter case is precisely the model proposed in [6] to describe massless particles via twistor theoretic methods in a combinatorial setting.

The relation of the step by step process (3) to solutions to (1) needs to be further explored, however, we may investigate how the equation behaves for the regular polytopes. In fact, remarkably, provided the centre of mass is located at the origin in Euclidean space, we find that $\Delta\varphi = c\varphi$ for some constant c depending on the polytope. In particular, if we normalize at each step so that $\|\varphi_t\| = 1$, then, since n is also constant, so is φ_t and the solution remains invariant. Thus the regular polytopes are stable solutions to (3). Linearization leads to a remarkably similar result.

In order to define the linearized equation, we consider a family $\{\varphi_t\}$ of functions such that $\varphi_0 = \varphi$ solves (1) with γ independent of t. On writing $\xi(x) = \frac{\partial\varphi(x)}{\partial t}|_{t=0}$, we obtain the equation linear in both ξ and φ:

$$\gamma(x)\Delta\varphi(x)\Delta\xi(x) = \langle \mathrm{d}\varphi(x), \mathrm{d}\xi(x)\rangle_x. \tag{4}$$

Note that $\xi = \lambda\varphi + \mu$ solves the linearized equation ($\lambda, \mu \in \mathbf{C}$ constant), reflecting the normalisation freedom $\varphi \mapsto \lambda\varphi + \mu$. If we multiply (4) by $n(x)$ and sum over $x \in V$, we obtain

$$0 = (\gamma\Delta\varphi, \Delta\xi) - \sum_{v\in V} n(x)\langle \mathrm{d}\varphi(x), \mathrm{d}\xi(x)\rangle_x.$$

It is not immediately obvious how to deal with the latter term of this equation. However, if we suppose that $n(x)$ is constant and apply Lemma 1, we obtain

$$(\Delta(\gamma\Delta\varphi), \xi) - 2n(\mathrm{d}\varphi, \mathrm{d}\xi) = (\Delta(\gamma\Delta\varphi), \xi) - 2n(\mathrm{d}^*\mathrm{d}\varphi, \xi)$$
$$= (\Delta(\gamma\Delta\varphi) + 2n\Delta\varphi, \xi) = 0.$$

In particular, taking ξ to be 1 at a given vertex x and zero elsewhere, we deduce that at each $x \in V$, we have

$$\Delta(\gamma\Delta\varphi) + 2n\Delta\varphi = 0.$$

But, with both $\gamma(x)$ and $n(x)$ constant, this is precisely the time-independent version of (3).

5   Quantum Interaction

In order to pursue a quantum formalism, we can introduce a normalized linear superposition of states of the type $\lambda X + \mu Y$, where both X and Y are the lifts into Euclidean space of geometric states of (1). If we take standard projection $(x, y, z) \mapsto x + iy$ from Euclidean space to the complex plane. Then the two corresponding states of the Necker cube have z coordinate differing by a sign on the relevant vertices. Factoring out an overall phase factor, we can suppose the coefficients of x and y are 1 to obtain the expression $(x, y, e^{i\theta}z)$ as a representation of the possible superpositions at a particular vertex–see [4] for a more thorough account. Only when $e^{i\theta} = \pm 1$ do we obtain an invariant framework corresponding to the geometric state.

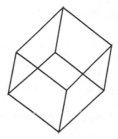

Indeed, it would seem impossible to visualize an arbitrary superposition, but only the two invariant realizations, which provides a convincing argument for a quantum model of geometric interaction. Change of a system should now come about by some unitary-type transformation governed by the equations of the last section.

In deriving this model, the author has in mind a process of *reconstruction* of the geometric world from basic information-theoretic principles, as has been pursued in the domain of quantum mechanics by L. Hardy and A. Grinbaum [11,12]. As a first step, we need to create a graph. Given a set V of vertices, we can associate to each unordered couple $\{x, y\}$ in V ($x \neq y$) a bit of information $q(x, y)$ which takes the value 0 or 1 with a certain probability. A basic state now corresponds to a graph, where we connect x and y with an edge whenever $q(x, y)$ takes the value 1. Geometric states, may be considered as potential information implicit in the graph [1,4]. Change of the system only makes sense relative to some other system, for example, a background state as introduced in the last section. The realization of geometric states and their potential step by step evolution could then be a driver of change of the underlying combinatori al structure.

Geometric information is only one kind of information implicit in a basic combinatorial system and the realization of other types of information could also drive change. The underlying principle we evoke is the way demands and responses in economic, linguistic, evolutionary and other systems drive change. These ideas are speculative and require further investigation to provide a workable theory.

References

1. Baird, P.: Information, universality and consciousness: a relational perspective. Mind Matter **11**(1), 21–44 (2013)
2. Baird, P.: Emergence of geometry in a combinatorial universe. J. Geom. Phys. **74**, 185–195 (2013)
3. Baird, P.: An invariance property for frameworks in Euclidean space. Linear Algebra Appl. **440**, 243–265 (2014)
4. Baird, P.: Feedback loops: a fundamental ingredient of information processing. In: Atmanspacher, H., Bergomi, C., Filk, T., Kitto, K. (eds.) QI 2014. LNCS, vol. 8951, pp. 24–38. Springer, Heidelberg (2015)
5. Baird, P.: The geometric spectrum of a graph and associated curvatures. In: Najman, L., Romon, P. (eds.) Discrete Curvature, p. 25

6. Baird, P., Wehbe, M.: Twistor theory on a finite graph. Commun. Math. Phys. **304**, 499–511 (2011)
7. Bishop, R.C., Atmanspacher, H.: Contextual emergence in the description of properties. Found. Phys. **36**(12), 1753–1777 (2006)
8. Chung, F.R.K.: Spectral Graph Theory. CBMS Regional Conference Series in Mathematics, vol. 92. American Mathematical Society, Providence, Rhode Island (1997)
9. Eastwood, M.G., Penrose, R.: Drawing with complex numbers. Math. Intelligencer **22**, 8–13 (2000)
10. Gauss, C.F.: Werke. Zweiter Band, Königlichen Gesellschaft der Wissenschaften, Göttingen (1876)
11. Grinbaum, A.: Reconstruction of quantum theory. Br. J. Philos. Sci. **58**(3), 387–408 (2007). http://philsci-archive.pitt.edu/2703/1/reconstruction2.pdf
12. Hardy, L.: Quantum theory from five reasonable axioms (2001). quantph/00101012
13. Le Bellac, M.: Quantum Physics. Cambridge University Press, New York (2006)

On Incompatible Descriptions of Systems Across Scales of Granularity

Harald Atmanspacher[1,2]([✉]) and Peter beim Graben[1,2]

[1] Collegium Helveticum, University and ETH Zürich, Zürich, Switzerland
[2] Institute of Linguistics, Humboldt University Berlin, Berlin, Germany
atmanspacher@collegium.ethz.ch

Abstract. The scientific description of any system depends on the target properties of that description. A detailed, fine-grained account of all individual constituents of a system differs from that of properties at larger scales of granularity, up to the system as a whole. All these level-specific descriptions can be compatible or incompatible with one another. This contribution addresses a particular pair of descriptions of complex dynamical systems: their Liouville dynamics, treating each constituent separately in a conventional state space, and their information dynamics, based on partitions of that state space. The relation between them can be formulated as a commutation relation, in which the commutator quantifies the degree of their incompatibility.

Keywords: Commutation relation · Compatibility · Descriptive levels · Deterministic chaos · Dynamical entropy · Information flow · Liouville dynamics · Partition

1 Introduction

The notion of incompatible properties and descriptions became popular in the early years of quantum physics, when Bohr imported the notion of complementarity from psychology into physics (Bohr 1928, Holton 1970). The standard examples in quantum physics refer to properties of physical systems which do not commute, such as position and momentum. If they are maximally incompatible in the sense that they have no eigenstate in common, they are said to be complementary. This complementarity is *horizontal* in the sense that it refers to observables at the same descriptive level.

It has been shown by beim Graben and Atmanspacher (2006) that complementarity may also exist for classical dynamical systems, where non-commuting properties in the sense of quantum physics do not exist. Nevertheless, non-commuting descriptions may arise for state-space partitions at different scales accounted for by different degrees of granularity. Typically, such partitions define different levels of description, so that the resulting complementarity can be considered *vertical*. A special case of this situation is a commutation relation between the standard Liouville description and an information theoretical description first proposed by Atmanspacher and Scheingraber (1987).

© Springer International Publishing Switzerland 2016
H. Atmanspacher et al. (Eds.): QI 2015, LNCS 9535, pp. 113–125, 2016.
DOI: 10.1007/978-3-319-28675-4_9

There is a close parallel of this idea with Bohr's (1932) speculation that one might find not only horizontal complementarities between quantum physical properties (at the same descriptive level) but also vertical complementarities across descriptive levels, such as between mechanical and thermodynamical descriptions. In fact, work by Prigogine and collaborators (see Prigogine 1980) in the 1970 s and later, introducing a time operator for dynamical systems, was guided precisely by this idea.

This contribution embeds the result by Atmanspacher and Scheingraber (1987) within the broader framework of relations between descriptions on different scales of granularity, with different partitions. For that purpose, we start with some general remarks on partitions and dynamics in Sects. 2, 3, and 4. Then we recapitulate the conditions under which coarse-grained descriptions are compatible or incompatible in Sect. 5. In Sect. 6 we present the commutation relation between Liouville dynamics and information dynamics, with a refined discussion of some of its implications. Section 7 concludes the article and adds some remarks on its general relevance.

2   Observables and Partitions

A classical dynamical system is characterized by the fact that all observables are compatible with each other. However, in general this holds only for a so-called *ontic description* (Atmanspacher 2000) where the state of a system is idealized by a point x in state space X. Classical observables are real-valued functions $f : X \to \mathbb{R}$, such that $a = f(x)$ is the value of observable f in state x.

A family of observables $f = \{f_i : X \to \mathbb{R} | 1 \leq i \leq n\}$ spans one of many possible *observation spaces* $Y = f(X)$ (Birkhoff and von Neumann 1936). Only if all functions f_i spanning the observation space Y are injective, their preimages contain exactly one point $x = f_i^{-1}(a_i)$ for all i, and can be called *ontic observables*. By contrast, *epistemic descriptions* acquire significance if at least one observable is not injective. They refer to the knowledge that can be obtained about an ontic state (Atmanspacher 2000) from representing a measurement result as a point in observation space.

Figure 1 displays a situation in which an observable f is not injective, such that different states $x \neq y \in A \subset X$ lead to the same measurement result

$$f(x) \ = \ f(y). \tag{1}$$

In this case, the states x and y are *epistemically* indistinguishable by means of the observable f Measuring f cannot tell us whether the system is in state x or y. The two states are *epistemically equivalent* with respect to f (beim Graben and Atmanspacher 2006).

In this way, the observable f induces an equivalence relation "$\sim_f$" on the state space X: $x \sim_f y$ if $f(x) = f(y)$. The resulting equivalence classes of ontic states partition the state space into mutually exclusive and jointly exhaustive subsets $A_1, A_2, \ldots$ such that $A_i \cap A_j = \emptyset$ for all $i \neq j$ and $\bigcup_i A_i = X$. These subsets can be identified with the *epistemic states* that are induced by

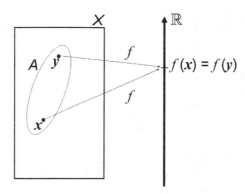

Fig. 1. States x, y in a state space X of a classical system (left) and the real numbers as the range of a classical observable $f : X \to \mathbb{R}$ (right). Epistemically equivalent states $x, y \in X$ belong to the same equivalence class $A \subset X$.

the observable f. More generally, we refer to subsets $S \subset X$ in state space as to epistemic states.[1] The collection $\mathcal{F} = \{A_1, A_2, \dots\}$ of epistemic states is a then state space *partition*.

We call f an *epistemic observable* if the partition $\mathcal{F}$ is not the *identity partition* $\mathcal{I}$ where every cell A_k is a singleton set containing exactly one element $A_k = \{x_k\}$ (Shalizi and Moore 2003). In this limiting case, f is injective and becomes an ontic observable. In the opposite limit, there is only one cell covering the entire state space X, and epistemic observables are constant over X: $f(x) = \text{const}$ for all $x \in X$. In this case, all states are epistemically equivalent with one another and belong to the (same) equivalence class X of the *trivial partition* $\mathcal{T}$.

Most interesting for our purposes are finite partitions $\mathcal{F} = \{A_1, A_2, \dots A_n\}$ (where $n \in N$ is finite) which are neither trivial nor identity. Figure 2(a,b) display two such finite partitions $\mathcal{F}$ and $\mathcal{G}$ from which a *product partition* $\mathcal{P} = \mathcal{F} \vee \mathcal{G}$ as in Fig. 2(c) can be constructed. It contains all possible intersections of sets in $\mathcal{F}$ with sets in $\mathcal{G}$:

$$\mathcal{P} = \mathcal{F} \vee \mathcal{G} = \{A_i \cap B_j | A_i \in \mathcal{F}, B_j \in \mathcal{G}\}. \tag{2}$$

The product partition $\mathcal{P}$ is a *refinement* of both partitions $\mathcal{F}$ and $\mathcal{G}$. The refinement relation introduces a partial ordering relation "$\prec$" among partitions. If $\mathcal{G}$ is a refinement of $\mathcal{F}$, $\mathcal{G} \prec \mathcal{F}$, then there is a "factor partition" $\mathcal{H}$ such that $\mathcal{G} = \mathcal{F} \vee \mathcal{H}$. If neither $\mathcal{G}$ is a refinement of $\mathcal{F}$ nor *vice versa* (and $\mathcal{G} \neq \mathcal{F}$), the partitions $\mathcal{G}$ and $\mathcal{F}$ are called *incomparable* (Shalizi and Moore 2003).

---

[1] Epistemic states are actually defined as distributions over measurable sets from a σ-algebra in measure theory (beim Graben and Atmanspacher 2006). For a simplified exposition, which captures the very basic ideas, set-theoretical concepts are sufficient (cf. beim Graben and Atmanspacher 2009).

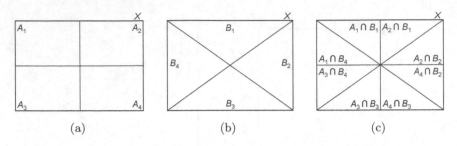

Fig. 2. Examples for finite partitions of the state space X: (a) "rectangular" partition $\mathcal{F} = \{A_1, A_2, A_3, A_4\}$, (b) "triangular" partition $\mathcal{G} = \{B_1, B_2, B_3, B_4\}$, (c) product partition $\mathcal{F} \vee \mathcal{G}$.

3   Dynamics and Extended Measurements

A dynamical system evolves as a function of parameter time t. In other words, any present state (e.g. an initial condition) in state space, $\boldsymbol{x}_0 \in X$, gives rise to future states $\boldsymbol{x}_t \in X$. This evolution is described by a flow map $\Phi^t : X \to X$. In the simple case of a deterministic dynamics in discrete time, Φ maps any state $\boldsymbol{x}_t$ onto its successor $\boldsymbol{x}_{t+1}$. Iterating the map Φ yields a *trajectory*

$$\boldsymbol{x}_{t+1} = \Phi^{t+1}(\boldsymbol{x}_0) = \Phi(\Phi^t(\boldsymbol{x}_0)) = \Phi(\boldsymbol{x}_t) \tag{3}$$

for integer positive times $t \in \mathbb{N}$. Likewise, the inverse map Φ^{-1} can be iterated if the dynamics is invertible: $\boldsymbol{x}_{-(t+1)} = \Phi^{-(t+1)}(\boldsymbol{x}_0) = \Phi^{-1}(\Phi^{-t}(\boldsymbol{x}_0)) = \Phi^{-1}(\boldsymbol{x}_{-t})$, again for integer positive times $t \in \mathbb{N}$. In this way, the dynamics of an invertible discrete-time system is described by the one-parameter group of integer numbers $t \in \mathbb{Z}$.

In Sect. 2 we have described *instantaneous* measurements by the action of an observable $f : X \to \mathbb{R}$ on an ontic state $\boldsymbol{x}$. Now we are able to describe *extended measurements*[2] by combining the action of an observable f with the dynamics Φ. Let the system be in state $\boldsymbol{x}_0 \in X$ at time $t = 0$. Measuring $f(\boldsymbol{x}_0)$ tells us to which class of epistemically equivalent states in the partition $\mathcal{F}$, associated with f, the state $\boldsymbol{x}_0$ belongs. Suppose that this is the cell $A_{i_0} \in \mathcal{F}$. Suppose further that measuring f in the subsequent state $\boldsymbol{x}_1 = \Phi(\boldsymbol{x}_0) \in X$ reveals that $\boldsymbol{x}_1$ is contained in another cell $A_{i_1} \in \mathcal{F}$.

An alternative way to describe this situation is to say that the initial state $\boldsymbol{x}_0 = \Phi^{-1}(\boldsymbol{x}_1)$ belongs to the pre-image $\Phi^{-1}(A_{i_1})$ of A_{i_1}. The information about $\boldsymbol{x}_0$ that is gained by measuring $f(\boldsymbol{x}_1)$ is then that the initial state $\boldsymbol{x}_0$ was contained in the intersection $A_{i_0} \cap \Phi^{-1}(A_{i_1})$. Continuing the observation of the system over one more instant in time yields that the initial state $\boldsymbol{x}_0$ belonged to the set $A_{i_0} \cap \Phi^{-1}(A_{i_1}) \cap \Phi^{-2}(A_{i_2})$ if the third measurement result was $\boldsymbol{x}_2 = \Phi^2(\boldsymbol{x}_0) \in A_{i_2}$.

---

[2] The notion of an extended measurement refers to a series of measurements extending over time t.

A systematic investigation of extended measurements can now be based on the definition of the pre-image of a partition,

$$\Phi^{-1}(\mathcal{F}) \;=\; \{\Phi^{-1}(A_i) | A_i \in \mathcal{F}\}, \tag{4}$$

which consists of all pre-images of the cells A_i of the partition $\mathcal{F}$. Then, an extended measurement over two successive time steps is defined by the product partition $\mathcal{F} \vee \Phi^{-1}(\mathcal{F})$, containing all intersections of cells of the original partition $\mathcal{F}$ with cells of its pre-image $\Phi^{-1}(\mathcal{F})$. The result of the measurement of f over two time steps is $x_0 \in A_{i_0} \cap \Phi^{-1}(A_{i_1}) \subset \mathcal{F} \vee \Phi^{-1}(\mathcal{F})$. This product partition is called the *dynamic refinement* of $\mathcal{F}$.

Most information about the state of a system can be gained by an ideal, "ever-lasting" extended measurement that began in the infinite past and will terminate in the infinite future. This leads to the *finest dynamic refinement*

$$\mathbf{R}\mathcal{F} \;=\; \bigvee_{t=-\infty}^{\infty} \Phi^t(\mathcal{F}), \tag{5}$$

expressed by the action of the "finest-refinement operator" $\mathbf{R}$ upon a partition $\mathcal{F}$. It would be desirable that such an ever-lasting measurement yields complete information about the initial condition x_0 in state space. This is achieved if the refinement (5) yields the identity partition,

$$\mathbf{R}\mathcal{F} = \mathcal{I}. \tag{6}$$

A partition $\mathcal{F}$ obeying (6) is called *generating*. Generating partitions are structurally stable in the sense that they are robust under the dynamics. In other words, points on bondaries of cells are typically mapped onto points on boundaries of cells. In this way the epistemic states defined by the cells do not change over time — which would be the case for non-generating partitions.

Given the ideal finest refinement $\mathbf{R}\mathcal{F} = \mathcal{P}$ of a (generating or non-generating) partition $\mathcal{F}$ induced by an epistemic observable f, we are able to regain a description of extended measurements of arbitrary finite duration by joining subsets of $\mathcal{P}$ which are visited by the system's trajectory. Supplementing the "join" operation by the other Boolean set operations over $\mathcal{P}$ leads to a *partition algebra* $A(\mathcal{P})$ of $\mathcal{P}$. Then, every set in $A(\mathcal{P})$ is an epistemic state measurable by f.

4   Generating Partitions and Chaotic Behavior

The concept of a generating partition is of utmost significance in the ergodic theory of dynamical systems (Cornfeld et al. 1982) and in the field of symbolic dynamics (Lind and Marcus 1995). It is tightly related to the *dynamical entropy* of a system with respect to both its dynamics $\Phi : X \to X$ and a partition $\mathcal{P}$ (Cornfeld et al. 1982):

$$H(\Phi, \mathcal{P}) = \lim_{n \to \infty} \frac{1}{n} H(\mathcal{P} \vee \Phi^{-1}(\mathcal{P}) \vee \dots \vee \Phi^{-n}(\mathcal{P})) \tag{7}$$

In words, this is the limit of the entropy of the product of partitions of increasing dynamical refinement.

A special case of a dynamical entropy of the system with dynamics Φ is the *Kolmogorov-Sinai entropy* (Kolmogorov 1958, Sinai 1959)

$$H_{KS} = \sup_{\mathcal{P}} H(\Phi, \mathcal{P}). \tag{8}$$

This supremum over all partitions $\mathcal{P}$ is assumed if $\mathcal{P}$ is a *generating partition*, otherwise $H(\Phi, \mathcal{P}) < H_{KS}$. (Every Markov partition is generating , but not *vice versa.*) $\mathcal{P}_g$ minimizes correlations among partition cells A_i, so that they are *stable* under Φ and only correlations due to Φ itself contribute to $H(\Phi, \mathcal{P}_g)$. Boundaries of A_i are (approximately) mapped onto one another. Spurious correlations due to blurring cells are excluded, so that the dynamical entropy takes on its supremum.

The Kolomogorov-Sinai entropy is a key property of *chaotic systems* whose behavior depends sensitively on initial conditions. This dependence is due to an intrinsic instability that is formally reflected by the existence of positive Lyapunov exponents. The KS-entropy of a system is an operationally accessible quantity (Grassberger and Procaccia 1983). A positive (finite) KS-entropy is a necessary and sufficient condition for chaos in conservative as well as in dissipative systems (with a finite number of degrees of freedom). Chaos in this sense covers the range between totally unpredictable random processes, such as white noise ($H_{KS} \to \infty$) and regular (e.g., periodic, etc.) processes with $H_{KS} = 0$.

The KS-entropy is essentially given by the sum of positive Ljapounov exponents of the system, which characterize its stability (in linear approximation). Alternatively, it can be interpreted as the information flow rate in dynamical systems (Goldstein 1981). This is evident by replacing the notion of a perturbation in a stability analysis by the notion of a corresponding uncertainty. A good approximation of the resulting flow of Shannon information M is given by

$$M(t) = M(0) - H_{KS}\, t, \tag{9}$$

under the condition that the Shannon information is based on the generating partition of the state space. The generating partition is defined by the dynamics of a system, whereas the concept of an uncertainty usually refers to a partition due to an experimental resolution or other external conditions. Also, the linearity of the information flow in (9) is a consequence of the linear, hence local, stability analysis on which its derivation is based. Therefore, interpreting the KS-entropy as an information flow rate refers to a (shifted) average of local information flow rates.

The temporal decrease of $M(t)$ for $H_{KS} > 0$ describes how an external observer loses information about the actual state of a system as time passes by. The inverse of H_{KS} estimates the time interval τ for which the behavior of the system can still be predicted reasonably well from its deterministic equations. (If the partition for the Shannon information is not generating, this leads to an underestimation of H_{KS} and a corresponding overestimation of τ.)

The concept of a generating partition in the ergodic theory of deterministic systems is related to the concept of a *Markov chain* in the theory of stochastic systems. Every deterministic system of first order gives rise to a Markov chain which is generally neither ergodic nor irreducible. Such Markov chains can be obtained by so-called *Markov partitions* that exist for expanding or hyperbolic dynamical systems (Sinai 1968, Bowen 1970, Ruelle 1989). For non-hyperbolic systems no corresponding existence theorem is available, and the construction can be even more tedious than for hyperbolic systems (Viana *et al.* 2003). For instance, both Markov and generating partitions for nonlinear systems are generally non-homogeneous. In contrast to Fig. 2, their cells are typically of different size and form.

Note that every Markov partition is generating, but the converse is not necessarily true (Crutchfield and Packard 1983). For the construction of "optimal" partitions from empirical data it is often more convenient to approximate them by Markov partitions (Froyland 2001; see also Deuflhard and Weber 2005, Gaveau and Schulman 2005). See Allefeld *et al.* (2009) for a concrete example of how a Markov partition can be constructed from empirical data.

Since the cells of a generating partition are dynamically stable, they can be used to define dynamically stable symbolic states, whose sequence provides a *symbolic dynamics* Γ (Lind and Marcus 1995). This dynamics is a *faithful representation* of the underlying dynamics only for generating partitions. The technical term "faithful" expresses that the underlying dynamics Φ and the properly constructed symbolic dynamis Γ are *topologically equivalent*.

5   Compatibility and Incompatibility of Partitions

If a partition $\mathcal{F}$ is not generating, its finest refinement is not the identity partition. In this case, the refinement operator yields a partition $\mathcal{P} = \mathbf{R}\mathcal{F}$ with some residual coarse grain. Moreover, the cells of a non-generating partition are not stable under the dynamics Φ, so that they become dynamically ill-defined — a disaster for any attempt to formulate a robust coarse-grained (epistemic) description (Bollt *et al.* 2001, Atmanspacher and beim Graben 2007).

Let $P \in \mathcal{P}$ be an epistemic state of the finest refinement of $\mathcal{F}$. Because $\mathcal{F}$ is induced by an observable f whose epistemic equivalence classes are the cells of $\mathcal{F}$, all cells of $\mathcal{P}$ can be accessed by extended measurements of f. However, as $\mathcal{P}$ is not the identity partition $\mathcal{I}$, the singleton sets $\{x\}$ representing ontic states in X are not accessible by measuring f. An arbitrary epistemic state $S \subset X$ is called *epistemically accessible with respect to* f (beim Graben and Atmanspacher 2006) if S belongs to the partition algebra $A(\mathcal{P})$ produced by the finest refinement of $\mathcal{F}$.

Measuring the observable f in all ontic states $x \in P$ belonging to an epistemic state $P \in \mathcal{P}$ always yields the same result $a = f(x)$ since f is by construction constant over P. Therefore, the variance of $f(x)$ across P (with respect to some probability measure) vanishes such that f is dispersion-free in the epistemic state P. In other words, P is an eigenstate of f. One can now easily construct another observable g that is not dispersion-free in P such that P is not a common eigenstate of f and g. As a consequence, the observables f and g are incompatible as they do not share all (epistemically accessible) eigenstates. Beim Graben and Atmanspacher (2006) referred to this construction as an *epistemic quantization* of a classical dynamical system.

In an ontic description of a classical system, ontic states are common eigenstates of all observables. Therefore, classical observables associated with ontic states are always compatible. By contrast, if the ontic states are not epistemically accessible by extended measurements, the smallest epistemically accessible states are cells in the finest refinement of a partition $\mathcal{F}$ induced by an epistemic observable f. These epistemic states are not eigenstates of every observable, such that observables associated with them are incompatible. As in quantum theory, two observables f and g are complementary if they do not have any (epistemically accessible) eigenstate in common, i.e. if they are maximally incompatible (Raggio and Rieckers 1983). Beim Graben *et al.* (2013) demonstrated the incompatibility of position and momentum of a classical harmonic oscillator subjected to time-discretization and spatial coarse-graining.

Nevertheless, even in an epistemic description, classical observables f and g can be compatible with one another. This is the case if all ontic states $x \in X$ are epistemically accessible with respect to both f and g. The necessary and sufficient condition for this is that the partitions $\mathcal{F}, \mathcal{G}$ be generating (Eq. 6). This leads to a generalization of the concepts of compatibility and complementarity: Two partitions $\mathcal{F}, \mathcal{G}$ are called compatible if and only if they are both generating: $\mathbf{R}\,\mathcal{F} = \mathbf{R}\,\mathcal{G} = \mathcal{I}$. They are incompatible if $\mathbf{R}\,\mathcal{F} \neq \mathbf{R}\,\mathcal{G}$, which is always the case if at least one partition is not generating. They are complementary if their finest refinements are disjoint: $\mathbf{R}\,\mathcal{F} \cap \mathbf{R}\,\mathcal{G} = \emptyset$.

6   Non-Commutativity Across Descriptive Levels

In the early 1930s, Koopman (1931) suggested how to describe classical systems and their evolution within a Hilbert space formalism equivalent to that used in quantum theory. Koopman's approach is applicable as a method providing an exact (not approximate!) linear representation of the evolution of nonlinear dynamical systems (see, e.g., Lasota and Mackey 1985). The temporal evolution of a probability distribution $\rho(p, q)$ (or, more generally, $\rho(x_1, ..., x_d)$) in a canonical phase space X is then given by the Liouville equation

$$i\frac{\partial \rho}{\partial t} = L\rho \tag{10}$$

where

$$L = \sum \left(i\frac{\partial H}{\partial q}\frac{\partial}{\partial p} - i\frac{\partial H}{\partial p}\frac{\partial}{\partial q} \right) \tag{11}$$

is the (Hermitian) Liouville operator and the Hamilton function H is an energy observable. The primary meaning of L in this context is that of a generator of the temporal evolution of ρ according to

$$\rho(t) = \exp(-iLt)\,\rho(0). \tag{12}$$

However, since $L\rho$ can be expressed by the classical Poisson bracket $\{H, \rho\}$,

$$L\rho = i\{H, \rho\}, \tag{13}$$

the Liouville operator also represents a difference of energies, or an energy bandwidth (Banwell and Primas 1963).

Using the Liouville operator instead of the Hamilton operator as a generator of the dynamical evolution provides a promising shift in perspective on the notorious problem of a time operator (first stated by Pauli (1933), cf. the discussion by Atmanspacher (1994)). Such a time operator T can be defined as a shift operator according to

$$U_t^* T U_t = T + t \cdot \mathbb{1}, \tag{14}$$

where U_t is the unitary evolution in Hilbert space that in Koopman's formalism replaces the evolution Φ^t in phase space, $U_t \rho(x) = \rho(\Phi^t(x))$. A positive KS-entropy, i.e., a chaotic flow, is a sufficient condition for the existence of a time operator T for which Misra (1978) derived the formal relation[3]

$$i[L, T] = \mathbb{1}, \tag{15}$$

expressing that L (energy bandwidth) and T (time) do not commute.

Another approach toward an understanding of L has been proposed (Atmanspacher and Scheingraber 1987) by considering the information flow in the system according to Sect. 4. Using the linear approximation given by Eq. (9) one can define an information operator M by

$$U_t^* M U_t = M - H_{KS} t \cdot \mathbb{1}, \tag{16}$$

which does not commute with L if and only if $H_{KS} > 0$:

$$i[L, M] = H_{KS} \cdot \mathbb{1}. \tag{17}$$

This means that L and M do not commute if and only if the sufficient condition of $H_{KS} > 0$ for the existence of a time operator is satisfied. This result is significant in a number of respects:

– the KS-entropy H_{KS} as the commutator of (17) is an *empirically accessible* quantity that can be estimated from any given time series. By contrast, the unity operator in $i[L, T] = \mathbb{1}$ does not connect to a concretely observable commutator.
– M is not a conventional observable but can be characterized as a *meta-observable* (or "super-operator"; see Primas 1963). It refers to the dynamics of information about conventional observables rather than to those observables themselves.

---

[3] $H_{KS} > 0$ is only sufficient because time operators T also exist for mixing systems. Precise conditions under which T exists have been first formulated by Misra (1978), shortly after two pioneering papers by Tjøstheim (1976) and Gustafson and Misra (1976). For a later account see Suchanecki and Antoniou (2003).

- The KS-entropy specifies the change of this information in linear approximation. As a *statistical* quantity it reflects an "average" *local* flow of information as a *global* invariant of a system.
- Since H_{KS} is explicitly system- and parameter-dependent, the *degree of noncommutativity* of L and M is not universal but contextual. This situation is at variance with quantum mechanics with $\hbar$ as a universal commutator.
- The time operator T suggests an *internal time* ("age") which can be related to the predictability interval H_{KS}^{-1} if it is operationalized in terms of parameter time t. See also Antoniou (this volume) and Gialampoukidis and Antoniou (2015) for time operators of networks.
- The fact that T does not commute with L (Eq. 15) indicates temporal Bell inequalities and, as a consequence, *temporal nonlocality*. This has been explored by Atmanspacher and Amann (1999), see also Atmanspacher et al. (2011).

The partition, say $\mathcal{F}$, for the Liouville description of a system is based on a coarse-graining that is required for the definition of a probability measure for the epistemic states ρ and their dynamics. As a rule, this partition is not chosen to be generating. The partition, say $\mathcal{G}$, underlying the definition of the information flow typically yields a distinctly coarser topology, depending on which details are considered relevant and irrelevant for the information dynamics.

For reasons of consistency with the definition of H_{KS} (Eqs. 7 and 8), the partition $\mathcal{G}$ should be generating. However, practically speaking this would mean that the measurements used to determine H_{KS} should be "generating" themselves – which would require that measurement resolution is dynamically adapted to the nonlinear behavior of the system observed. Due to this difficulty, H_{KS} will typically be underestimated by a dynamical entropy based on a non-generating partition.

As a consequence, either both $\mathcal{F}$ and $\mathcal{G}$ are not generating or (in case of hard-to-achieve "generating measurements") at least $\mathcal{F}$ is not generating. In both cases, the descriptions by L and M are incompatible because they are based on incompatible partitions. While the degree of their incompatibility remains unspecified at this general level of discussion, the explicit types of dynamics L and M allow us to express their incompatibility by the concrete commuation relation (17).

This relation highlights an additional incompatible feature between L and M. The Liouville dynamics is known to be volume-preserving due to Liouville's theorem, i.e. the state space volume associated with a state ρ is constant under the dynamics (although the shape of that volume may drastically change). This is equivalent with the condition that the sum of all Ljapounov exponents of the system vanishes. The Liouville evolution L is time-reversal invariant.

For the definition of information flow, the situation is different because the contracting manifolds (negative Ljapounov exponents) become irrelevant as soon as the corresponding uncertainties decrease below the size of the volume element defined by the measurement resolution. Then, only the positive Ljapounov exponents (summing up to H_{KS}) of the expanding manifolds determine the information dynamics. This entails that time-reversal symmetry is broken if $H_{KS} > 0$: the information flow M is temporally directed.

7 Conclusion

Descriptions of systems based on different scales of granularity (different coarse-grainings) are at the heart of any hierarchical (or heterarchical) framework for scientific descriptions in science. In many disciplines this is expressed by the difference between micro-and macro-descriptions. Usually, macro-states of a system are related to ensembles of its micro-states (partitions, or coarse grains) which are chosen to disregard micro-state distinctions that are declared irrelevant at the macro-level considered. A well-known example is the relation between mechanical micro-states and thermodynamic macro-states.

The choice of the partition defining macro-states by ensembles of micro-states is crucial for the micro-macro connection. Depending on what partitions are used, micro- and macro-descriptions may be compatible or incompatible with one another. A rigorous criterion for compatible descriptions is that the partitions yielding the coarse grains are compatible. This raises serious issues for nonlinear systems, where compatibility can only be guaranteed if their descriptions are based on generating (or Markov) partitions. If the chosen partitions are not generating, the resulting descriptions are incompatible.

We showed that such an incompatibility can be expressed explicitly for two important classes of dynamics: the Liouville dynamics of a system and its information flow. They entail a commutaton relation whose commutator is the Kolmogorov-Sinai entropy H_{KS}. The time scale given by its inverse H_{KS}^{-1} quantifies the predictability horizon of the system, beyond which predictions become so inaccurate that they are meaningless. Strictly non-chaotic (e.g. strictly periodic) systems are infinitely predictable, $H_{KS} = 0$, so that their descriptions are compatible at any scale of granularity. In the general case of $H_{KS} > 0$ predictability is limited, and the value of H_{KS} determines the extent to which the descriptions are incompatible.

This incompatibility is vertical in the sense that it refers to relations across levels of description. This is at variance with the horizontal meaning of incompatibility at the same level of description, as applied in quantum physics and in many examples which have been explored in cognitive science recently (see, e.g., Busemeyer and Bruza 2012).

References

Allefeld, C., Atmanspacher, H., Wackermann, J.: Identifying emergent states from neural dynamics. Chaos **19**, 015102 (2009)

Atmanspacher, H.: Is the ontic/epistemic distinctionsufficient to represent quantum systems exhaustively? In: Laurikainen, K.V., Montonen, C., Sunnarborg, K. (eds.) Symposium on the Foundations of Modern Physics 1994, pp. 15–32. Editions Frontières, Gif-sur-Yvette (1994)

Atmanspacher, H.: Ontic and epistemic descriptions of chaotic systems. In: Dubois, D. (ed.) Computing Anticipatory Systems, pp. 465–478. Springer, Berlin (2000)

Atmanspacher, H., Amann, A.: Positive operator valued measures and projection valued measures of non-commutative time operators. Int. J. Theor. Phys. **37**, 629–650 (1999)

Atmanspacher, H., beim Graben, P.: Contextual emergence of mental states from neurodynamics. Chaos Complex. Lett. **2**, 151–168 (2007)

Atmanspacher, H., beim Graben, P., Filk, T.: Can classical epistemic states be entangled? In: Song, D., Melucci, M., Frommholz, I., Zhang, P., Wang, L., Arafat, S. (eds.) QI 2011. LNCS, vol. 7052, pp. 105–115. Springer, Heidelberg (2011)

Atmanspacher, H., Scheingraber, H.: A fundamental link between system theory and statistical mechanics. Found. Phys. **17**, 939–963 (1987)

Banwell, C.N., Primas, H.: On the analysis of high-resolution nuclear magnetic resonance spectra. I. methods of calculating NMR spectra. Mol. Phys. **6**, 225–256 (1963)

beim Graben, P., Atmanspacher, H.: Complementarity in classical dynamical systems. Found. Phys. **36**, 291–306 (2006)

beim Graben, P., Atmanspacher, H.: Extending the philosophical significance of the idea of complementarity. In: Atmanspacher, H., Primas, H. (eds.) Recasting Reality, pp. 99–113. Springer, Berlin (2009)

beim Graben, P., Filk, T., Atmanspacher, H.: Epistemic entanglement due to non-generating partitions of classical dynamical systems. Int. J. Theoret. Phys. **52**, 723–734 (2013)

Birkhoff, G., von Neumann, J.: The logic of quantum mechanics. Ann. Math. **37**, 823–843 (1936)

Bohr, N.: The quantum postulate and the recent development of atomic theory. Nature **121**, 580–590 (1928)

Bohr, N.: Chemistry and the quantum theory of atomic constitution. J. Chem. Soc. Lond. **134**, 349–384 (1932)

Bollt, E.M., Stanford, T., Lai, Y.C., Zyczkowski, K.: What symbolic dynamics do we get with a misplaced partition? On the validity of threshold crossings analysis of chaotic time-series. Physica D **154**, 259–286 (2001)

Bowen, R.: Markov partitions for axiom A diffeomorphisms. Am. J. Math. **92**, 725–747 (1970)

Busemeyer, J.R., Bruza, P.D.: Quantum Models of Cognition and Decision. Cambridge University Press, Cambridge (2012)

Cornfeld, I.P., Fomin, S.V., Sinai, Y.G.: Ergodic Theory, Chap. 10.6. Springer, Berlin (1982)

Crutchfield, J.P., Packard, N.H.: Symbolic dynamics of noisy chaos. Physica D **7**, 201–223 (1983)

Deuflhard, P., Weber, M.: Robust Perron cluster analysis in conformation dynamics. Linear Algebra Appl. **398**, 161–184 (2005)

Froyland, G.: Extracting dynamical behavior via Markov models. In: Mees, A.I. (ed.) Nonlinear Dynamics and Statistics, pp. 281–312. Birkhäuser, Boston (2001)

Gaveau, B., Schulman, L.S.: Dynamical Distance: Coarse grains, pattern recognition, and network analysis. Bulletin des Sciences Mathématiques **129**, 631–642 (2005)

Gialampoukidis, I., Antoniou, I.: Entropy, age and time operator. Entropy **17**, 407–424 (2015)

Goldstein, S.: Entropy increase in dynamical systems. Isr. J. Math. **38**, 241–256 (1981)

Grassberger, P., Procaccia, I.: Estimation of the Kolmogorov entropy from a chaotic signal. Phys. Rev. A **28**, 2591–2593 (1983)

Gustafson, K., Misra, B.: Canonical commutation relations of quantum mechanics and stochastic regularity. Lett. Math. Phys. **1**, 275–280 (1976)

Holton, G.: The roots of complementarity. Daedalus **99**, 1015–1055 (1970)

Kolmogorov, A.N.: A new metric invariant of transitive systems and automorphisms of Lebesgue spaces. Dokl. Akad. Nauk SSSR **119**, 861–864 (1958)

Koopman, B.: Hamiltonian systems and transformations in Hilbert space. Proc. Natl. Acad. Sci. USA **17**, 315–318 (1931)

Lasota and Mackey: Probabilistic Properties of Deterministic Systems. Cambridge University Press, Cambridge (1985)

Lind, D., Marcus, B.: An Introduction to Symbolic Dynamics and Coding. Cambridge University Press, Cambridge (1995)

Misra, B.: Nonequilibrium entropy, Lyapounov variables, and ergodic properties of classical systems. Proc. Natl. Acad. Sci. USA **75**, 1627–1631 (1978)

Pauli, W.: Die allgemeinen Prinzipien der Wellenmechanik. In: Geiger, H., Scheel, K. (eds.) Handbuch der Physik, vol. 24, pp. 88–272, p. 140. Springer, Berlin (1933). Reprinted in Flügge, S. (ed.) Encyclopedia of Physics, vol. V, Part 1, pp. 1–168, p. 60. Springer, Berlin (1958)

Prigogine, I.: From Being to Becoming. Freeman, San Francisco (1980)

Primas, H.: Generalized perturbation theory in operator form. Rev. Mod. Phys. **35**, 710–712 (1963)

Raggio, G.A., Rieckers, A.: Coherence and incompatibility in W*-algebraic quantum theory. Int. J. Theor. Phys. **22**, 267–291 (1983)

Ruelle, D.: The thermodynamic formalism for expanding maps. Commun. Math. Phys. **125**, 239–262 (1989)

Shalizi, C.R., Moore, C.: What is a macrostate? Subjective observations and objective dynamics (2003). http://xxx.lanl.gov/pdf/cond-mat/0303625

Sinai, Y.G.: On the concept of entropy of a dynamical system. Dokl. Akad. Nauk SSSR **124**, 768–771 (1959)

Sinai, Y.G.: Markov partitions and C-diffeomorphisms. Funct. Anal. Appl. **2**, 61–82 (1968)

Suchanecki, Z., Antoniou, I.: Time operators, innovations and approximations. Chaos Solitons Fractals **17**, 337–342 (2003)

Tjøstheim, D.: A commutation relation for widesense stationary processes. SIAM J. Appl. Math. **30**, 115–122 (1976)

Viana, R.L., Pinto, S.E., Barbosa, J.R.R., Grebogi, C.: Pseudo-deterministic chaotic systems. Int. J. Bifurcat. Chaos **13**, 3235–3253 (2003)

Applications in Decision Making

The Relation Between Acausality and Interference in Quantum-Like Bayesian Networks

Catarina Moreira[✉] and Andreas Wichert

Instituto Superior Técnico, INESC-ID, Av. Professor Cavaco Silva,
2744-016 Porto Salvo, Portugal
{catarina.p.moreira,andreas.wichert}@ist.utl.pt

Abstract. We analyse a quantum-like Bayesian Network that puts together cause/effect relationships and semantic similarities between events. These semantic similarities constitute acausal connections according to the Synchronicity principle and provide new relationships to quantum like probabilistic graphical models. As a consequence, beliefs (or any other event) can be represented in vector spaces, in which quantum parameters are determined by the similarities that these vectors share between them. Events attached by a semantic meaning do not need to have an explanation in terms of cause and effect.

Keywords: Quantum cognition · Quantum-like Bayesian Networks · Synchronicity principle

1 Introduction

Current decision-making systems face high levels of uncertainty resulting from data, which is either missing or untrustworthy. These systems usually turn to probability theory as a mathematical framework to deal with uncertainty. One problem, however, is that it is hard for these systems to make reliable predictions in situations where the laws of probability are being violated. These situations happen quite frequently in systems which try to model human decisions (Tversky and Kahnenman 1974; Tversky and Kahneman 1983; Tversky and Shafir 1992).

Uncertainty in decision problems arises, because of limitations in our ability to observe the world and in limitations in our ability to model it (Koller and Friedman 2009). If we could have access to all observations of the world and extract all the information it contained, then one could have access to the full joint probability distribution describing the relation between every possible random variable. This knowledge would eliminate uncertainty and would enable any prediction. This information, however, is not available and not possible to

This work was supported by national funds through Fundação para a Ciência e Tecnologia (FCT) with reference UID/CEC/50021/2013 and through the PhD grant SFRH/BD/92391/2013.

H. Atmanspacher et al. (Eds.): QI 2015, LNCS 9535, pp. 129–141, 2016.
DOI: 10.1007/978-3-319-28675-4_10

obtain as a full, leading to uncertainty. A formal framework capable of representing multiple outcomes and their likelihoods under uncertainty is probability theory (Murphy 2012).

In an attempt to explain the decisions that people make under risk, cognitive scientists started to search for other mathematical frameworks that could also deal with uncertainty. Recent literature suggests that quantum probability can accommodate these violations and improve the probabilistic inferences of such systems (Aerts 1995; Busemeyer et al. 2006; Bordley 1998).

Quantum cognition is a research field that aims at using the mathematical principles of quantum mechanics to model cognitive systems for human decision making (Busemeyer 2015; Busemeyer and Wang 2014; Aerts 2014). Given that Bayesian probability theory is very rigid in the sense that it poses many constraints and assumptions (single trajectory principle, obeys set theory, etc.), it becomes too limited to provide simple models that can capture human judgments and decisions, since people are constantly violating the laws of logic and probability theory (Tversky and Kahnenman 1974; Tversky and Kahneman 1983; Tversky and Shafir 1992). Recent literature suggests that quantum probability can be used as a mathematical alternative to the classical theory and can accommodate these violations (Mura 2009; Lambert-Mogiliansky et al. 2009; Aerts et al. 2011). It has been showed that quantum models provide significant advantages towards classical models (Busemeyer et al. 2015, 2012).

In this work, we explore the implications of causal relationships in quantum-like probabilistic graphical models and also the implications of semantic similarities between quantum events (Moreira and Wichert 2015). These semantic similarities provide new relationships to the graphical models and enables the computation of quantum parameters through vector similarities.

This work is organised as follows. In Sects. 2 and 3, we address two types of relationships, respectively: cause/effect and acausal relationships. In Sect. 4, we describe a quantum-like Bayesian Network that takes advantages of both cause/effect relationships and semantic similarities (acausal events). In Sect. 5, we show and analyse the applications of the proposed model in current decision problems. Finally, in Sect. 6, we conclude with some final remarks regarding the application of quantum-like Bayesian Networks to decision problems.

2 What is Causation

Most events are reduced to the principle of causality, which is the connection of phenomena where the cause gives rise to some effect. This is the philosophical principle that underlies our conception of natural law (Jung and Pauli 2012).

Under the principle of causality, some event A can have more than one cause, in which none of them alone is sufficient to produce A. Causality is usually: (1) transitive, if some event A is a cause of B and B is a cause of C, then A is also a cause of C; (2) irreflexible, an event A cannot cause itself; and (3) antisymmetric, if A is a cause of B, then B is not a cause of A (Spirtes et al. 2000).

The essence of causality is the generation and determination of one phenomenon by another. Causality enables the representation of our knowledge regarding a given context through *experience*. By experience, we mean that the observation of the relationships between events enables the detection of irrelevancies in the domain. This will lead to the construction of causal models with minimised relationships between events (Pearl 1988). Bayesian Networks are examples of such models.

Under the principle of causality, two events that are not causally connected should not produce any effects. When some acausal events occur by producing an effect, it is called a coincidence. Carl Jung, believed that nothing happens by chance and, consequently, all events had to be connected between each other, not in a causal setting, but rather in a meaningful way. Under this point of view, Jung proposed the Synchronicity principle (Jung and Pauli 2012).

3 Acausal Connectionist Principle

The Synchronicity principle may occur as a single event of a chain of related events and can be defined by a significant coincidence which appears between a mental state and an event occurring in the external world (Martin et al. 2009). Jung believed that two acausal events did not occur by chance, but rather by a shared meaning. Therefore, in order to experience a synchronised event, one needs to extract the meaning of its symbols for the interpretation of the synchronicity. So, the Synchronicity principle can be seen as a correlation between two acausal events which are connected through meaning (Jung and Pauli 2012).

Jung defended that the connection between a mental state and matter is due to the energy emerged from the emotional state associated to the synchronicity event (Jung and Pauli 2012). This metaphysical assertion was based on the fact that it is the person's interpretation that defines the meaning of a synchronous event. This implies a strong relation between the extraction of the semantic meaning of events and how one interprets it. If there is no semantic extraction, then there is no meaningful interpretation of the event, and consequently, there is no synchronicity (Lindorff 2004).

It is important to mention that the Synchronicity principle is a concept that does not question or compete with the notion of causality. Instead, it maintains that just as events may be connected by a causal line, they may also be connected by meaning. A grouping of events attached by meaning do not need to have an explanation in terms of cause and effect.

In this work, we explore the consequences of the synchronicity principle applied to quantum states with high levels of uncertainty as a way to provide additional information to quantum-like probabilistic graphical models, which mainly contain cause/effect relationships. Although the principles of probability are well established, such that synchronicity might be seen as the occurrence of coincidences, in the quantum mechanics realm, given the high levels of uncertainty that describe the quantum states, the coincidences or improbable occurrences happen quite often.

4   Quantum-Like Bayesian Networks: Combining Causal and Acausal Principles for Quantum Cognition

The reason why we are turning to Bayesian Networks is because they are inspired in human cognition (Griffiths et al. 2008). It is easier for a person to combine pieces of evidence and to reason about them, instead of calculating all possible events and their respective beliefs. In the same way, Bayesian Networks also provide this link between human cognition and rational inductive inference. Instead of representing the full joint distribution, Bayesian Networks represent the decision problem in small modules that can be combined to perform inferences. Only the probabilities which are actually needed to perform the inferences are computed.

4.1   Classical Bayesian Networks

A classical Bayesian Network is a directed acyclic graph structure. Each node represents a different random variable from a specific domain and each edge represents a direct influence from the source node to the target node. The graph also represents independence relationships between random variables and is followed by a conditional probability table which specifies the probability distribution of the current node given its parents (Koller and Friedman 2009).

A Bayesian Network represents a full joint probability distribution through conditional independence statements in order to answer queries about the domain. The full joint distribution (Russel and Norvig 2010) of a Bayesian Network, where X is the list of variables, is given by Eq. 1.

$$Pr_c(X_1, \ldots, X_n) = \prod_{i=1}^{n} Pr(X_i | Parents(X_i)) \tag{1}$$

In order to answer queries, the network enables the combination of the relevant entries of the full joint probability distribution. This process consists in the computation of the marginal probability distribution of the network. Let e be the list of observed variables and let Y be the remaining unobserved variables in the network. For some query X, the inference is given by Eq. 2.

$$Pr_c(X|e) = \alpha \left[\sum_{y \in Y} Pr_c(X, e, y) \right] \text{ Where } \alpha = \frac{1}{\sum_{x \in X} Pr_c(X = x, e)} \tag{2}$$

The summation is over all possible y, i.e., all possible combinations of values of the unobserved variables y. The α parameter, corresponds to the normalisation factor for the distribution $Pr(X|e)$ (Russel and Norvig 2010). This normalisation factor comes from some assumptions that are made in Bayes rule.

4.2   From Classical Bayesian Networks to Quantum-Like Networks

Suppose that we have a Bayesian Network with three random variables with the following structure: $B \leftarrow A \rightarrow C$. In order to determine the probability of node B, we would need to make the following computation based on Eq. 2.

$$
\begin{aligned}
Pr(B = t) = {} & Pr(A = t)Pr(B = t|A = t)Pr(C = t|A = t) \\
& + Pr(A = t)Pr(B = t|A = t)Pr(C = f|A = t) \\
& + Pr(A = f)Pr(B = t|A = f)Pr(C = t|A = f) \\
& + Pr(A = f)Pr(B = t|A = f)Pr(C = f|A = f)
\end{aligned}
\tag{3}
$$

A classical probability can be converted into a quantum probability amplitude in the following way. Suppose that events $A_1, \ldots, A_N$ form a set of mutually disjoint events, such that their union is all in the sample space, Ω, for any other event B. The classical law of total probability can be formulated like in Eq. 4.

$$
Pr(B) = \sum_{i=1}^{N} Pr(A_i)Pr(B|A_i) \qquad \text{where: } \sum_{i=1}^{N} Pr(A_i) = 1
\tag{4}
$$

The quantum law of total probability can be derived through Eq. 4 by applying Born's rule (Caves et al. 2002; Nielsen and Chuang 2000):

$$
Pr(B) = \left| \sum_{j=1}^{N} e^{i\theta_j} \psi_{A_j} \psi_{B|A_j} \right|^2 \qquad \text{where: } \sum_{j=1}^{N} \left| e^{i\theta_j} \psi_{A_j} \right|^2 = 1
\tag{5}
$$

Returning to our example, in order to convert the real probabilities in Eq. 3 into quantum amplitudes, one needs to apply Born's rule. In Eq. 6, the term $\psi_1 e^{\theta_1}$ corresponds to the quantum probability amplitude of the term $Pr(A = t)Pr(B = t|A = t)Pr(C = t|A = t)$; the term $\psi_2 e^{\theta_2}$ corresponds to the quantum probability amplitude of the term $Pr(A = t)Pr(B = t|A = t)Pr(C = f|A = t)$ and so on.

$$
Pr(B = t) = \left| \psi_1 e^{\theta_1} + \psi_2 e^{\theta_2} + \psi_3 e^{\theta_3} + \psi_4 e^{\theta_4} \right|^2
\tag{6}
$$

Expanding Eq. 6,

$$
\begin{aligned}
Pr(B = t) = {} & \left| \psi_1 e^{\theta_1} \right|^2 + \left| \psi_2 e^{\theta_2} \right|^2 + \left| \psi_3 e^{\theta_3} \right|^2 + \left| \psi_4 e^{\theta_4} \right|^2 + \left| \psi_1 e^{\theta_1} \right| \left| \psi_2 e^{\theta_2} \right| \\
& + \left| \psi_2 e^{\theta_2} \right| \left| \psi_1 e^{\theta_1} \right| + \left| \psi_1 e^{\theta_1} \right| \left| \psi_3 e^{\theta_3} \right| + \left| \psi_3 e^{\theta_3} \right| \left| \psi_1 e^{\theta_1} \right| + \left| \psi_1 e^{\theta_1} \right| \left| \psi_4 e^{\theta_4} \right| \\
& + \left| \psi_4 e^{\theta_4} \right| \left| \psi_1 e^{\theta_1} \right| + \left| \psi_2 e^{\theta_2} \right| \left| \psi_3 e^{\theta_3} \right| + \left| \psi_3 e^{\theta_3} \right| \left| \psi_2 e^{\theta_2} \right| + \left| \psi_2 e^{\theta_2} \right| \left| \psi_4 e^{\theta_4} \right| \\
& + \left| \psi_4 e^{\theta_4} \right| \left| \psi_2 e^{\theta_2} \right| + \left| \psi_3 e^{\theta_3} \right| \left| \psi_4 e^{\theta_4} \right| + \left| \psi_4 e^{\theta_4} \right| \left| \psi_3 e^{\theta_3} \right|
\end{aligned}
\tag{7}
$$

Knowing that, $2\cos(\theta_1 - \theta_2) = e^{i\theta_1 - i\theta_2} + e^{i\theta_2 - i\theta_1}$, then Eq. 8 becomes:

$$
\begin{aligned}
Pr(B = t) = {} & \sum_{i}^{N} |\psi_i|^2 + 2|\psi_1||\psi_2|\cos(\theta_1 - \theta_2) + 2|\psi_1||\psi_3|\cos(\theta_1 - \theta_3) \\
& + 2|\psi_1||\psi_4|\cos(\theta_1 - \theta_4) + 2|\psi_2||\psi_3|\cos(\theta_2 - \theta_3) + \cdots + 2|\psi_3||\psi_4|\cos(\theta_3 - \theta_4)
\end{aligned}
\tag{8}
$$

Equation 8 can be rewritten as:

$$Pr(B = t) = \sum_i^N |\psi_i|^2 + 2 \sum_{i=1}^{N-1} \sum_{j=i+1}^{N} |\psi_i| |\psi_j| \cos(\theta_i - \theta_j) \tag{9}$$

4.3   Quantum-Like Bayesian Network

A quantum-like Bayesian Network can be defined in the same way as a classical Bayesian Network with the difference that real probability numbers are replaced by quantum probability amplitudes (Tucci 1995; Leifer and Poulin 2008).

The quantum counterpart of the full joint probability distribution corresponds to the application of Born's rule to Eq. 1. This results in Eq. 10, where QPr corresponds to a quantum amplitude.

$$Pr_q(X_1, \ldots, X_n) = \left| \prod_{i=1}^{n} QPr(X_i | Parents(X_i)) \right|^2 \tag{10}$$

When performing probabilistic inferences in Bayesian Networks, the probability amplitude of each assignment of the network is propagated and influences the probabilities of the remaining nodes. In order to perform inferences on the network, one needs to apply Born's rule to the classical marginal probability distribution, just like in was presented in Eq. 9. If we rewrite this equation with the notation presented in Eq. 3, then the quantum counterpart of the classical marginalization formula for inferences in Bayesian Networks becomes:

$$Pr_q(X|e) = \alpha \sum_{i=1}^{|Y|} \left| \prod_x^N QPr(X_x | Parents(X_x), e, y = i) \right|^2 + 2 \cdot Interference \tag{11}$$

$$Interference =$$

$$\sum_{i=1}^{|Y|-1} \sum_{j=i+1}^{|Y|} \left| \prod_x^N QPr(X_x | Parents(X_x), e, y = i) \right| \cdot$$

$$\left| \prod_x^N QPr(X_x | Parents(X_x), e, y = j) \right| \cdot \cos(\theta_i - \theta_j)$$

In classical Bayesian inference, normalisation of the inference scores is necessary due to the independence assumptions made in Bayes rule. In quantum-like inferences, we need to normalize the final scores, not only because of the asme independence assumptions, but also because of the quantum interference term. If the conditional probability tables of the proposed quantum-like Bayesian Network were double stochastic, then this normalization would not be necessary. But, since in the proposed model we do not have this constraint, then a normalization is required after the computation of the probabilistic inference.

Following Eq. 11, when $\cos(\theta_i - \theta_j)$ equals zero, then it is straightforward that quantum probability theory converges to its classical counterpart, because the interference term will be zero.

For non-zero values, Eq. 11 will produce interference effects that can affect destructively the classical probability (when the interference term in smaller than zero) or constructively (when it is bigger than zero). Additionally, Eq. 11 will lead to a large amount of θ parameters when the number of events increases. For N binary random variables, we will end up with 2^N parameters.

4.4   Semantic Networks: Incorporating Acausal Connections

A semantic network is often used for knowledge representation. It corresponds to a directed or undirected graph in which nodes represent concepts and edges reflect semantic relations. The extraction of the semantic network from the original Bayesian Network is a necessary step in order to find variables that are only connected in a meaningful way (and not necessarily connected by cause/effect relationships), just like it is stated in the Synchronicity principle.

Consider the Bayesian Network in Fig. 1 (Russel and Norvig 2010; Pearl 1988). In order to extract its semantic meaning, we need to take into account the context of the network. Suppose that you have a new burglar alarm installed at home. It can detect burglary, but also sometimes responds to earthquakes. John and Mary are two neighbours, who promised to call you when they hear the alarm. John always calls when he hears the alarm, but sometimes confuses telephone ringing with the alarm and calls too. Mary likes loud music and sometimes misses the alarm.

From this description, we extracted the semantic network, illustrated in Fig. 2, which represents the meaningful connections between concepts. The following knowledge was extracted. It is well known that catastrophes cause panic among people and, consequently, increase crime rates, more specifically burglaries. So, a new pair of synchronised variables between *Earthquake* and *Burglar* emerges. Moreover, *John* and *Mary* derive both from the same concept *person*, so, these two nodes will also be synchronised. These synchronised variables mean

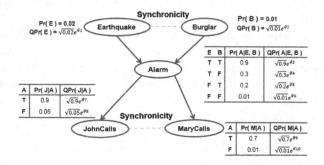

Fig. 1. Example of a Quantum-Like Bayesian Network (Russel and Norvig 2010). QPr represents quantum amplitudes. Pr corresponds to the real classical probabilities.

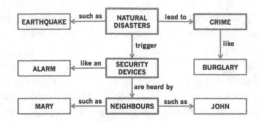

Fig. 2. Semantic network representation of the network in Fig. 1.

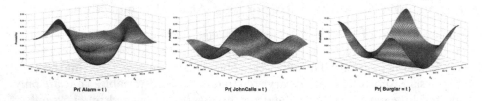

Fig. 3. Variation of the probability values of the Bayesian Network in Fig. 1 for different quantum parameters (Moreira and Wichert 2014).

that, although there is no explicit causal connection between these nodes in the Bayesian Network, they can become correlated through their meaning.

4.5 Setting Quantum Parameters According to the Synchronicity Principle

In Sect. 4.3, it was presented that Eq. 11 generates an exponential number of quantum θ parameters according to the number of unknown variables. If nothing is told about how to assign these quantum parameters, then we end up with an interval of possible probabilities. For instance, Fig. 3 shows that, the probabilities for the different random variables of the Quantum-Like bayesian Network from Moreira and Wichert (2014) can range from an interval of possible probability values. This means that one needs some kind of heuristic function that is able to assign these quantum parameters automatically. We define the Synchronicity heuristic in a similar way to Jung's principle: two variables are said to be synchronised, if they share a meaningful connection between them. This meaningful connection can be obtained through a semantic network representation of the variables in question. This will enable the emergence of new meaningful connections that would be inexistent when considering only cause/effect relationships. The quantum parameters are then tuned in such a way that the angle formed by these two variables, in a Hilbert space, is the smallest possible, this way forcing acausal events to be correlated.

For the case of binary variables, the Synchronicity heuristic is associated with a set of two variables, which can be in one of four possible states. The Hilbert space is partitioned according to these four states, as exemplified in Fig. 4. The angles formed by the combination of these four possible states are detailed in the table also in Fig. 4 (Moreira and Wichert 2015). In the right extreme of the Hilbert space represented in Fig. 4, we encoded it as the occurrence of a pair of synchronised variables. So, when two synchronised variables occur, the smallest angle that these vectors make between each other corresponds to $\theta = 0$. The most dissimilar vector corresponds to the situation where two synchronised variables do not occur. So, we set θ to be the largest angle possible, that is π.

Assignments of Variables		Angle
var_1 occurs	var_2 occurs	$\theta = 0$
var_1 occurs	var_2 not occurs	$\theta = \pi/4$
var_1 not occurs	var_2 occurs	$\theta = 3\pi/4$
var_1 not occurs	var_2 not occurs	$\theta = \pi$

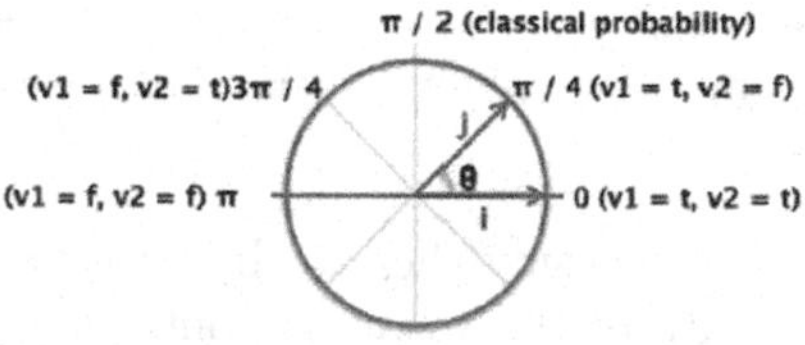

Fig. 4. Encoding of the Synchronized variables with their respective angles (left). Two synchronized events forming an angle of $\pi/4$ between them (right).

The other situations correspond to the scenarios where one synchronised variable occurs and the other one does not. In Fig. 4, the parameter θ is chosen according to the smallest angle that these two vectors, i and j, make between each other, that is $\pi/4$. We are choosing the smallest angle, because we want to correlate these two acausal events by forcing the occurrence of *coincidences* between them, just like described in the Synchronicity principle. The axis corresponding to $\pi/2$ and $3\pi/2$ were ignored, because they correspond to classical probabilities ($\cos(\pi/2) = \cos(3\pi/2) = 0$). We are taking steps of $\pi/4$ inspired by the quantum law of interference proposed by Yukalov and Sornette (2011), in which the authors suggest to replace the quantum interference term by $1/4$.

5 Example of Application

We queried each variable of the network in Fig. 1 without providing any observation. We performed the following queries: $Pr(JonhCalls = true)$, $Pr(MaryCalls = true)$, $Pr(Alarm = true)$, $Pr(Burglar = true)$ and $Pr(Earthquake = true)$. We then extracted both classical and quantum inferences and represented the results in the graph in Fig. 5.

Figure 5, shows that, when nothing is known about the state of the world, quantum probabilities tend to increase and overcome their classical counterpart. In quantum theory, when nothing is observed, all nodes of the Bayesian Network are in a superposition state. For each possible configuration in this superposition state, a probability amplitude is associated to it. During the superposition state, the amplitudes of the probabilities of the nodes of the Bayesian Network start to be modified due to the interference effects. If one looks at the nodes as waves crossing the network from different locations, these waves can crash between

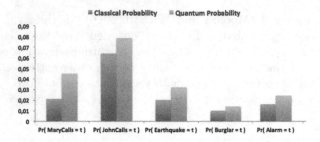

Fig. 5. Results for various queries comparing probabilistic inferences using classical and quantum probability when no evidences are observed: maximum uncertainty.

each other, causing them to be either destroyed or to be merged together. This interference of the waves is controlled through the Synchronicity principle by linking acausal events.

When one starts to provide information to the Bayesian Network, then the superposition state collapses into another quantum state, affecting the configuration of the remaining possible states of the network. Moreover, by making some observation to the network, we are reducing the total amount of uncertainty and, consequently, the reduction of the waves crossing the network (Table 1).

Table 1. Probabilities obtained when performing inference on the Bayesian Network of Fig. 1.

	Evidences	Pr(Alarm = t)	Pr(Earthquake = t)	Pr(Burglar = t)	Pr(JohnCalls = t)	Pr(MaryCalls = t)
CLASSIC	JohnCalls = t	0.2277	0.0949	0.1333	1.0000	0.1671
	MaryCalls = t	0.5341	0.2033	0.3119	0.5040	1.0000
	Earthquake = t	0.2966	1.0000	0.0100	0.3021	0.2147
	Burglar = t	0.9402	0.0200	1.0000	0.8492	0.6587
	Alarm = t	1.0000	0.3581	0.5835	0.9000	0.7000
QUANTUM	JohnCalls = t	0.3669	0.1484	0.2124	1.0000	0.2321
	MaryCalls = t	0.6598	0.2239	0.3474	0.6032	1.0000
	Earthquake = t	0.4389	1.0000	0.0124	0.4012	0.2403
	Burglar = t	0.9611	0.02	1.0000	0.8583	0.6337
	Alarm = t	1.0000	0.3431	0.5560	0.9000	0.7000

In Table 1 there are two pairs of synchronised variables: (Earthquake, Burglar) and (MaryCalls, JohnCalls). The quantum probability of $Pr(Earthquake = t|JohnCalls = t)$ has increased almost the same quantity as for the probability $Pr(Burglar = t|JohnCalls = t)$ (56.37 % for earthquake and 59.34 % for Burglar). In the same way, when we observe that $MaryCalls = t$, then the percentage of a Burglary increased 11.38 %, whereas Earthquake increased a percentage of 10.13 % towards its classical counterpart.

6   Conclusions

In this work, we analysed a quantum-like Bayesian Network that puts together cause/effect relationships and semantic similarities between events. These similarities constitute acausal connections according to the Synchronicity principle and provide new relationships to the graphical models. As a consequence, events can be represented in vector spaces, in which quantum parameters are determined by the similarities that these vectors share between them. In the realm of quantum cognition, quantum parameters might represent the correlation between events (beliefs) in a meaningful acausal relationship.

The proposed quantum-like Bayesian Network benefits from the same advantages of classical Bayesian Networks: (1) it enables a visual representation of all relationships between all random variables of a given decision scenario, (2) can perform inferences over unobserved variables, that is, can deal with uncertainty, (3) enables the detection of independent and dependent variables more easily. Moreover, the mapping to a quantum-like approach leads to a new mathematical formalism for computing inferences in Bayesian Networks that takes into account quantum interference effects. These effects can accommodate puzzling phenomena that could not be explained through a classical Bayesian Network. This is probably the biggest advantage of the proposed model. A network structure that can combine different sources of knowledge in order to model a more complex decision scenario and accommodate violations to the Sure Thing Principle.

With this work, we argue that, when presented with a problem, we perform a semantic categorisation of the symbols that we extract from the given problem through our thoughts Osherson (1995). Since our thoughts are abstract, cause/effect relationships might not be the most appropriate mechanisms to simulate interferences between them. The Synchronicity principle seems to fit more in this context, since our thoughts can relate to each other from meaningful connections, rather than cause/effect relationships (Jung and Pauli 2012).

We end this work with some reflections. Over the literature of quantum cognition, quantum models have been proposed in order to explain some paradoxical findings (Pothos and Busemeyer 2009; Haven 2013). These decision problems, however, are very small. They are modelled with at most two random variables. Decision problems with more random variables suffer from the problem of the exponential generation of quantum parameters (like in Burglar/Alarm Bayesian Network). For more complex problems, how can one model them, since the only apparent way to do so, is through the usage of heuristic functions that can assign values to the quantum θ parameters? But even through this method, given the lack of experimental data, how can one validate such functions? Is the usage of these functions a correct way to tackle this problem, or is it wrong to proceed in this direction? How can such experiment be conducted? Is it even possible to show violations on the laws of probability theory for more complex problem?

References

Aerts, D.: Quantum structures: an attempt to explain the origin of their appearance in nature. Int. J. Theor. Phys. **34**, 1–22 (1995)

Aerts, D.: Quantum theory and human perception of the macro-world. Front. Psychol. **5**, 1–19 (2014)

Aerts, D., Broekaert, J., Gabora, L.: A case for applying an abstracted quantum formalism to cognition. New Ideas Psychol. **29**, 136–146 (2011)

Bordley, R.: Quantum mechanical and human violations of compound probability principles: toward a generalized heisenberg uncertainty principle. Oper. Res. **46**, 923–926 (1998)

Busemeyer, J.: Cognitive science contributions to decision science. Cognition **135**, 43–46 (2015)

Busemeyer, J., Bruza, P.: Quantum Model of Cognition and Decision. Cambridge University Press, Cambridge (2012)

Busemeyer, J., Wang, Z.: Quantum cognition: key issues and discussion. Topics Cogn. Sci. **6**, 43–46 (2014)

Busemeyer, J., Wang, Z., Townsend, J.: Quantum dynamics of human decision making. J. Math. Psychol. **50**, 220–241 (2006)

Busemeyer, J.R., Wang, Z., Trueblood, J.S.: Hierarchical Bayesian estimation of quantum decision model parameters. In: Busemeyer, J.R., Dubois, F., Lambert-Mogiliansky, A., Melucci, M. (eds.) QI 2012. LNCS, vol. 7620, pp. 80–89. Springer, Heidelberg (2012)

Busemeyer, J., Wang, Z., Shiffrin, R.: Bayesian model comparison favours quantum over standard decision theory account of dynamic inconsistency. Decision **2**, 1–12 (2015)

Caves, C., Fuchs, C., Schack, R.: Quantum probabilities as Bayesian probabilities. Phys. Rev. A **65**, 022305 (2002)

Feynman, R., Leighton, R., Sands, M.: The Feynman Lectures on Physics: Quantum Mechanics. Addison-Wesley, Reading (1965)

Griffiths, T., Kemp, C., Tenenbaum, J.: Bayesian models of inductive learning. In: Proceedings of the Annual Conference of the Cognitive Science Society (2008)

Haven, E., Khrennikov, A.: Quantum Social Science. Cambridge University Press, Cambridge (2013)

Jung, C., Pauli, W.: The Interpretation of Nature and the Psyche. Ishi Press, USA (2012)

Koller, D., Friedman, N.: Probabilistic Graphical Models: Principles and Techniques. MIT Press, Cambridge (2009)

Lambert-Mogiliansky, A., Zamir, S., Zwirn, H.: Type indeterminacy: a model for the KT(Kahneman-Tversky)-man. J. Math. Psychol. **53**, 349–361 (2009)

Leifer, M., Poulin, D.: Quantum graphical models and belief propagation. Ann. Phys. J. **323**, 1899–1946 (2008)

Lindorff, D.: Pauli and Jung: The Meeting of Two Great Minds. Quest Books, Wheaton (2004)

Martin, F., Carminati, F., Carminati, G.: Synchronicity, quantum information and the psyche. J. Cosmol. **3**, 580–589 (2009)

Moreira, C., Wichert, A.: Interference effects in quantum belief networks. Appl. Soft Comput. **25**, 64–85 (2014)

Moreira, C., Wichert, A.: The synchronicity principle under quantum probabilistic inferences. NeuroQuantology **13**, 111–133 (2014)

Mura, P.L.: Projective expected utility. J. Math. Psychol. **53**, 408–414 (2009)

Murphy, K.: Machine Learning: A Probabilistic Perspectives. MIT Press, Cambridge (2012)

Nielsen, M.A., Chuang, I.L.: Quantum Computation and Quantum Information. Cambridge University Press, Cambridge (2000)

Osherson, D.: Thinking. MIT Press, Cambridge (1995)

Pearl, J.: Probabilistic Reasoning in Intelligent Systems: Networks of Plausible Inference. Morgan Kaufmann Publishers, San Francisco (1988)

Pothos, E., Busemeyer, J.: A quantum probability explanation for violations of rational decision theory. Proc. Roy. Soc. B **276**, 2171–2178 (2009)

Russel, S., Norvig, P.: Artificial Intelligence: A Modern Approach. Pearson Education, London (2010)

Spirtes, P., Glymour, C., Scheines, R.: Causation, Prediction and Search. MIT Press, Cambridge (2000)

Tucci, R.: Quantum Bayesian nets. Int. J. Mod. Phys. B **9**, 295–337 (1995)

Tversky, A., Kahneman, D.: Extension versus intuitive reasoning: the conjunction fallacy in probability judgment. Psychol. Rev. **90**, 293–315 (1983)

Tversky, A., Kahnenman, D.: Judgment under uncertainty: heuristics and biases. Science **185**, 1124–1131 (1974)

Tversky, A., Shafir, E.: The disjunction effect in choice under uncertainty. Psychol. Sci. **3**, 305–309 (1992)

Yukalov, V., Sornette, D.: Decision theory with prospect interference and entanglement. Theor. Decis. **70**, 283–328 (2011)

Do Preferences and Beliefs in Dilemma Games Exhibit Complementarity?

Ismael Martínez-Martínez[1], Jacob Denolf[2](✉), and Albert Barque-Duran[3]

[1] Düsseldorf Institute for Competition Economics (DICE),
Heinrich Heine Universität Düsseldorf,
Universitätsstraße 1, 40225 Düsseldorf, Germany
ismael@imartinez.eu
[2] Department of Data Analysis, Ghent University,
H. Dunantlaan 1, 9000 Ghent, Belgium
jacob.denolf@ugent.be
[3] Department of Psychology, City University London, London EC1V 0HB, UK
albert.barque-duran@city.ac.uk

Abstract. Blanco *et al.* (2014) show in a novel experiment the presence of intrinsic interactions between the preferences and the beliefs of participants in social dilemma games. They discuss the identification of three effects, and we claim that two of them are inherently of non-classical nature. Here, we discuss qualitatively how a model based on complementarity between preferences and beliefs in a Hilbert space can give an structural explanation to two of the three effects the authors observe, and the third one can be incorporated into the model as a classical correlation between the observations in two subspaces. Quantitative formalization of the model and proper fit to the experimental observation will be done in the near future, as we have been given recent access to the original dataset.

Keywords: Quantum-like preferences and beliefs · Consensus effect · Social projection · Complementarity · Sequential prisoner's dilemma

1 Introduction

Especially over the last decade, there has been a growing interest in decision-making and cognitive models using the quantum probabilistic (QP) framework. This development encompasses publications in major journals (see Deutsch 1999; Pothos and Busemeyer 2013; Wang *et al.* 2014; and Yearsley and Pothos 2014; among others), special issues,[1] and dedicated workshops,[2] as well as several

---

We would like to express our gratitude to the authors Mariana Blanco, Dirk Engelmann, Alexander K. Koch, and especially Hans-Theo Normann for providing access to their experimental dataset.

[1] Journal of Mathematical Psychology, 2009, volume 53, issue 5, and Topics in Cognitive Science, 2013, volume 5, issue 4.

[2] Contributions to the Quantum Interaction conferences 2007–2014 held at Stanford, Oxford, DFKI Saarbrücken, AAAI Washington DC, RGU Aberdeen, Paris School of Economics, Leicester, and Filtzbach are available in the series Lecture Notes in Computer Science by Springer.

© Springer International Publishing Switzerland 2016
H. Atmanspacher et al. (Eds.): QI 2015, LNCS 9535, pp. 142–153, 2016.
DOI: 10.1007/978-3-319-28675-4_11

comprehensive books (Busemeyer and Bruza 2012; Khrennikov 2010; and Haven and Khrennikov 2010).

The idea of using quantum-like ideas to describe human information processing exists for nearly a hundred years. Bohr (1950), one of the founding fathers of quantum theory, was known to believe that aspects of quantum theory could provide insight about cognitive processes. However, Bohr never made any attempt to provide a formal cognitive model based on QP theory, and these started to appear only fairly recently. Some relevant examples are: Aerts and Aerts (1995), Bordley (1998), Bruza et al. (2009), Busemeyer et al. (2006; 2011), beim Graben and Atmanspacher (2009), Gabora and Aerts (2002), Lambert-Mogiliansky et al. (2009), Pothos and Busemeyer (2009), and Yukalov and Sornette (2011).

The majority of models presented in the quantum cognition literature addresses standard aspects of decision-making processes: order effects in belief updating (Trueblood and Busemeyer 2011), the constructive role of articulating impressions (White et al. 2014), and similarity judgments (Yearsley et al. 2014), among others. Nevertheless, QP theory is potentially relevant in any behavioral situation that involves uncertainty, as formalized by Danilov and Lambert-Mogiliansky (2008, 2010).

Not much literature has focused on strategic decision-making or game theory. When two or more agents interact, one agent is not only reacting to the information that she receives, but she is also generating information to other players. These strategic environments are different from standard decision-making scenarios under uncertainty, because each agent has to reason over two aspects of the problem: her actions and her expectations on the opponents' actions. Only a couple of works have been published regarding this specific topic and making use of the QP tools to model the way agents process the information in the play: Pothos and Busemeyer (2009), Pothos et al. (2011), and Busemeyer and Pothos (2012). Other approaches in which the quantumness enters through an extension of the classical space of strategies and/or signals have also been discussed, e.g., by La Mura (2005), Brandenburger (2010), and Brunner and Linden (2013); as well as a model to analyze games with agents exhibiting contextual preferences (Lambert-Mogiliansky and Martínez-Martínez 2014).

This article is not about the application of quantum physics to brain physiology. This is a controversial issue (Litt et al. 2006; and Hameroff 2007) about which we are agnostic. Rather, we are interested in QP theory as a mathematical framework for cognitive modeling. In specific, this note is about the application from QP theory to modeling the mutual influence between preferences and beliefs in sequential social dilemmas.

We present the first steps towards a quantum-like preferences and beliefs (QP&B) model that mimics the experimental results from Blanco et al. (2014) and provides a novel theoretical approach regarding cognitive dynamics in strategic interactions. Our model takes full advantage of the notions of measurement used in quantum mechanics. We claim that the relationship between a player's beliefs and his preferences is inherently non-classical. We will redefine these two properties as complementary. As such, they cannot be measured at the same time, as the act of measuring one property alters the state of the other property. The non-classical nature of such a relationship and it's application in cognition has already been discussed in, *e.g.*, Denolf (2014).

2   New Insights from a Quantum-Like Perspective

2.1   Sequential-Move Prisoner's Dilemma Game Explained

The data the QP&B model wants to replicate comes from a one-shot sequential-move prisoner's dilemma experiment from Blanco *et al.* (2014), summarized in Fig. 1. They design a within-subject sequential social dilemma experiment to observe interactions between the beliefs and preferences of players, which could have implications for the interpretation of observed behavior.[3]

Subjects play two consecutive games, one in the first- and one in the second-mover role. If the first mover (FM) cooperates ($a^{FM} = c$), payoffs depend on the action of the second mover (SM). If $a^{SM} = c$, payoffs are 14 for both first and second mover; if $a^{SM} = d$, the payoff is 7 for the first mover and 17 for the second one. When $a^{FM} = d$, the game ends with a payoff of 10 for both first mover and second mover. Unconditional cooperation is precluded by design (this is motivated by the near absence of unconditional cooperation in sequential-move prisoner's dilemma experiments; see Bolle and Ockenfels 1990; Clark and Sefton 2001; and Blanco *et al.* 2011). Therefore, players in the second mover role are always confronted with a cooperating first mover.

The unique subgame-perfect Nash equilibrium of the game in Fig. 1 (for rational, selfish players) is ($a^{FM} = d$, $a^{SM} = d$). The second mover would always defect. Thus, in the first-mover role, if the player knows that the second mover is rational and selfish, she will defect as well. Given the possibility of second-mover cooperation, a selfish first mover will choose $a^{SM} = c$, if and only if her belief about the frequency of second-mover cooperation is at least $3/7 \approx 0.43$.

To investigate the influence of a player's beliefs on his or her actions, the beliefs were elicited during the course of the game by asking the player how many opponents she believed to be cooperating. The precise moment of this beliefs measurement varied across two different groups of players (Baseline group and Elicit_Beliefs group). A third group of players was provided with the exact frequency of cooperation on the second move (True_Distribution group). An overview of the treatments of these groups can be found in Table 1.

Blanco *et al.* (2014) conclude that when subjects play both roles (being the first or the second player to take an action) in such experiment, a positive

---

[3] For the small game analyzed in this paper, it is enough for the reader to understand a player's *belief* as the subjective distribution with which the agent judges the likelihood of realization of each possible state of the world that the player could face, and which in general, influences the type of payoffs to be received from the actions. Also, as an idealized object, we can consider the *preferences* as an individual's attitude towards a set of outcomes, typically reflected through the *actions* taken in an explicit decision-making process. For more details, see Lichtenstein and Slovic (2006).

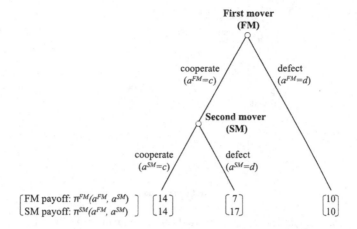

Fig. 1. Sequential-move prisoner's dilemma game (from Blanco *et al.* 2014).

Table 1. Treatments in the experiment by Blanco *et al.* (2014), also labeled as Table 1 in their original paper.

Treatment	Baseline	Elicit_Beliefs	True_Distribution
Task 1	2nd move	2nd move	2nd move
Feedback (a_{-i}^{SM})	No	No	Yes
Task 2	1st move	beliefs (a_{-i}^{SM})	1st move
Task 3	beliefs (a_{-i}^{FM})	1st move	beliefs (a_{-i}^{FM})
N. Participants	40	60	60

correlation between first and second-mover behavior was frequently reported. They attribute this observed correlation to be primarily originating through an indirect channel, where second-mover decisions influence beliefs through a consensus effect. The first-mover decision is a best response to these beliefs.

Specifically, beliefs about second-mover cooperation were biased toward own second-mover behavior, and most subjects then best respond to these stated beliefs. However, they also find evidence for a direct, preference-based channel. When first movers knew the true probability of second-mover cooperation, subjects' own second moves still had predictive power regarding their first moves.

2.2 About Beliefs and Judgments in Economics and Cognitive Science

By taking a fresh look at the data collected in Blanco *et al.* (2014), we will identify three distinct effects exhibited by the participants. We shall start out by defining these effects by looking at the observed outcomes of the beliefs and actions, without assuming any underlying mechanism. Focusing on the role of measurements will allow us to fully utilize the quantum paradigm. These three

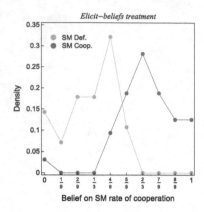

Fig. 2. *The consensus effect:* Second move defecting players (red line) believe that less opponents will cooperate. Second move cooperating players (blue line) believe more opponents will cooperate. Note that here the second move action was measured before the beliefs. As such, player's beliefs seem biased towards their actions (Color fiure online).

Table 2. Average cooperation rates by treatment in the experiment by Blanco *et al.* (2014), also labeled as Table 2 in their original paper.

Treatment	Baseline	Elicit_Beliefs	True_Distribution	Total
First mover (FM)	27.5 %	55.0 %	56.7 %	48.8 %
Second mover (SM)	55.0 %	53.3 %	55.0 %	54.4 %

effects all emerge as an influence of belief measurements and action measurements on each other or themselves.

Consensus Effect: Proof and an extensive commentary of the presence of this effect is presented in Blanco *et al.* (2014), where it is shown that players' beliefs are biased toward their own actions. As such, *e.g.*, a player who cooperates as second mover will expect a higher second-mover cooperation rate amongst the other players. A visualization of this effect can be found in Fig. 2. Viewing this in light of the performed measurements, the consensus effect denotes the influence of second mover action measurements on the beliefs of the same participant.

The Reasoned Player: The second effect is the influence belief measurements have on action measurements. As these actions are driven by one's preferences, this effect also encompasses the influence of the belief measurements on the preferences of the same player. We claim that the act of eliciting the beliefs of the player, fundamentally changes this player, even when disregarding the exact outcome of this belief measurement. When the player is asked to form an opinion about the cooperation rate of his opponents, he changes into a more reasoned state about the opponent, in opposition to a more intuitive state when not explicitly asked to form this opinion. This can be seen in Table 2. The average first move cooperation rate of players, after forming explicitly their beliefs about the cooperation of the opponent (Elicit_Belief), is twice the average first move cooperation rate of players, which beliefs were not elicited (Baseline) ($p = 0.00672$). This cooperation rate in the Elicit_Beliefs group is, however not differing significantly from the cooperation rate in the True_Distribution group. In this group, participants received full information about the cooperation rate of the opponents and are therefore assumed to make a more deliberate decision. Since these cooperation rates are similar, we can assume that players are in a similar reasoned state in the Elicit_Beliefs group.

Correlation Between First Move in the Second Round and Second Move in the First Round: The third effect we will discuss is the correlation between a player's first move and second move. This is observed in all three conditions, as noted in Result 1, 2 and 3 from Blanco *et al.* (2014) to be positive, meaning first move cooperators are likely to also cooperate on the second move and vice versa. We will differ our view on this effect slightly in comparison with the previously two described effects. We concur with Blanco *et al.* that this correlation is exhibited mostly through an indirect belief-based channel. This way, we attempt to include the observed correlation as a logical consequence of our previously described effects. The second move action measurement influences the first move action measurement through a player's beliefs. We assume this correlation to be classical in nature, as opposed to the two other effects.

It is our goal to build a model which incorporates these three effects in a natural and elegant way. To this, we will investigate and comment on the (quantum-like) nature of these effects, using these findings as building blocks for our QP&B model.

2.3 Complementarity of Preferences and Beliefs is Truly a Non-classical Effect

We argue that two of the above described effects have a fundamentally non-classical nature. With both the consensus effect and the players being in reasoned state after having their beliefs elicited, the act of measuring itself influences the system, regardless of its outcome. In this regard, the measurements of actions and the measurements of beliefs seem to be complementary in the vein defined by Bohr (1950). Two measurements are considered to be complementary if both cannot be performed at the same time. This is not a consequence of any practical or experimental difficulties, but an inherent property of the system itself.

In our case, this complementarity can be seen clearly, when the order in which measurements are performed, influences their outcomes. As can be seen in Fig. 2, an order effect clearly takes place when starting with measuring a player second move action and then measuring a player beliefs about the opponent second move action, as this specific order of measurements leads to players exhibiting the consensus effect. We refer to Busemeyer and Pothos (2012) for a more thorough commentary of the quantum-like nature of the consensus effect, as a form of social projection.

Reversing this order, first a belief measurement, then an action measurement, leads to the agent being in a reasoned state, changing his actions. Here the order effect is even more clear. The difference in the order of measurements (see Table 1), alters the first move action cooperation rate significantly (see Table 2), as the treatment sequence is the only difference between the Baseline group and Elicit_Beliefs group.

As such, two out of our three noted effects can be (at least partly) attributed to order in which the measurements are performed and are therefore considered to be consequences of the complementarity of the action and beliefs measurements. These order effect are hard to model using classical probabilities, leading to overly complex models. However, order effects are a naturally modeled within a quantum model, therefore, the presence of order effects can be seen as an indicator that a quantum model might be a fitting approach.

As player's first and second moves are driven by his/her preferences, we claim that a player's preferences and beliefs are complementary properties, which cannot be measured and/or exhibited at the same. We therefore propose to utilize the quantum statistical framework, based in a Hilbert Space to model these properties, as this type of models was originally devised to deal with similar complementary properties in a Physics setting. This idea will result in a model with few parameters, giving a clear view of the non-classical nature of the relationship between a player's beliefs and his preferences. Note that we consider the correlation between a player's first move and second classical in nature.

3   A Tentative Approach Towards a QP&B Model

We use this section to introduce some basics for the development of the proper QP&B model in the close future.[4] From a psychological point of view one may consider that we should define a two dimensional space of actions (either cooperation or defection), for both the first move ($\mathcal{H}_{FM}$) and second move ($\mathcal{H}_{SM}$) actions.

Let us consider a game-theoretical approach from the point of view of the players who can be active in the game. Then, it comes natural to define a four dimensional space of the mind for describing this game, $\mathcal{H} \equiv \mathbb{R}^4$ which can be decomposed as the tensor product of two subspaces of equal dimensions ($\mathbb{R}^2 = \mathcal{H}_{FM} = \mathcal{H}_{SM}$) associated to the space of the first-move and the space of the second-move in the sequential dilemma, respectively. As a consequence, $\mathcal{H} = \mathcal{H}_{FM} \otimes \mathcal{H}_{SM}$. This space, having a classical equivalent, allows us to incorporate the (considered classical) positive correlation between a player's first move and second move, one of our three described effects.

To model the assumed complementarity between the actions and beliefs, a belief base would have to be defined within $\mathcal{H}_{FM}$ and within $\mathcal{H}_{SM}$. This would model the reasoned player and consensus effect respectively. The tensor product of $\mathcal{H}_{FM}$ and $\mathcal{H}_{FM}$, would then define a belief base in $\mathcal{H}$ and model our three

---

[4] Please note that this is a preliminary proposal and the model may change substantially after proper fitting to the data set.

discussed effects in one Hilbert Space. However, using the same reasoning as with the action space, this would lead to a ten-dimensional space of beliefs: since there are ten players per session, then the question "how many opponents do you think will cooperate?" can lead to a finite spectrum of 10 outcomes $N \in \{0, ..., 9\}$. Since this would overparametrize our model, we propose the following solution: We see the belief measurement as an estimation of the likelihood a player thinks his current opponent will cooperate or defect. When, e.g., a player answers "7" to the belief question, the player thinks his opponent will cooperate with a probability of 7/9. This is the information that is vital to the game the player is currently playing, as he is assessing the behavior of his opponent. This will make our belief base 2 dimensional: the opponent is assumed to either cooperate (b_C) or defect (b_D). In this 2 dimensional belief space, the belief measurement is associated with a rotation, giving us the respective probability. So, the player answering "n" to the belief question, is associated with the state vector being projected on $(\sin\left(\frac{n}{9}.\frac{\pi}{2}\right), \cos\left(\frac{n}{9}.\frac{\pi}{2}\right))$, in terms of the base (b_C, b_D). Figure 3 illustrates the player answering "7" to the belief question.

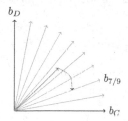

Fig. 3. The state vector rotates to $b_{7/9}$ when the player thinks 7 out of 9 opponents will cooperate.

Note that the here defined vectors $b_{i/9}$, associated with the outcomes of the belief measurement, are not orthogonal (which would be required in orthodox quantum mechanics). This will lead to, e.g., violations of the law of total probability.

As we see in Table 1, the treatments Baseline and True_Distribution operate on two types of observables in the space of first-moves: actions a^{FM} (either a_C or a_D) in Task 2 and beliefs (either b_C or b_D) in Task 3. Following from the above, we postulate the space $\mathcal{H}_{FM}$ admits two basis: one of actions and one of beliefs, and if both basis were meaningful (this means one is a non-trivial rotation of the other one) then the two observables would not commute, and therefore this would show complementarity in a quantitative estimation. We expect $\mathcal{H}_{FM}$ to be spanned both by $\{a_C^{FM}, a_D^{FM}\}$ and $\{b_C^{FM}, b_D^{FM}\}$. The first basis refers to the eigenvectors of the player taking action C or D, while the second basis is given in terms of the eigenstates of the two possible actions the rival is assumed to eventually take.

These two basis are related through a rotation of angle β_{FM}, and one state vector S_A given in terms of the action-basis can be converted into coordinates

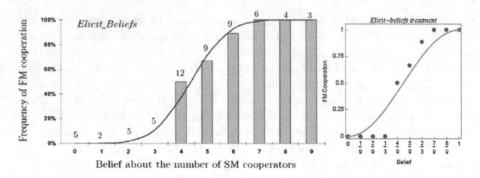

Fig. 4. Left: Experimental data (FM cooperation and Elicited beliefs) from Blanco et.al., with their fitted probit-regression. Right: Experimental points in blue color, with red solid theoretical curve $P(a^{SM} = c) = \sin^2 \theta$, with $\theta = n\frac{\pi}{2}$ (so $\beta_{FM} = 0$), where $n = N/9$ is the fraction of opponents believed to be cooperating.

with respect to the belief-basis through the operation $S_B = P_S A P^T$. We write

$$P = \begin{pmatrix} \cos \beta_{FM} & -\sin \beta_{FM} \\ \sin \beta_{FM} & \cos \beta_{FM} \end{pmatrix}. \tag{1}$$

This means that choosing the canonical basis $a_C^{FM} = (1,0)^T$ and $a_D^{FM} = (0,1)^T$ then the belief-basis is directly given as

$$b_C^{FM} = \begin{pmatrix} \cos \beta_{FM} \\ \sin \beta_{FM} \end{pmatrix}, b_D^{FM} = \begin{pmatrix} -\sin \beta_{FM} \\ \cos \beta_{FM} \end{pmatrix}. \tag{2}$$

An analogous description of two basis holds for the space $\mathcal{H}_{SM}$, therefore introducing a second angular parameter β_{SM} relating the outcomes in Task 1 and Task 2 of treatment Elicit_Beliefs.

Finally, we recall the fact that we have a correlation expected to be of classical nature between the components of the vector describing the cognitive state associated to the FM subspace and those of the SM. The authors Blanco *et al.* analyze this effect in terms of a Probit regression (see Fig. 4–Left panel) but we believe their data set can be perfectly explained if we consider that the connection between the agent's expected rate of cooperation for the SM (elicited in Elicit_beliefs condition, given in the True_Distribution group) and her own propensity to cooperate in the FM action. This relationship is represented by the angle between the FM basis and belief basis and leads naturally to a simple dependency $P(a^{FM} = c) = \sin^2 \left(n\frac{\pi}{2} + \beta_{FM}\right)$, where $n = N/9$ is the expectation on rivals' cooperation. We can assume that β_{FM} will be close to 0, as players thinking that the opponent will defect, will be likely to defect as well. As a first visual exploration, we plotted the function $P(a^{FM} = c) = \sin^2 \left(n\frac{\pi}{2}\right)$ to the data. See in Fig. 4–Right panel how this very simple model gives an equally successful (visual) explanation of their dataset, and requires no parameter since $N/9$ is endogenous to the play.

For the final model we just need to span $\mathcal{H} \equiv \mathcal{H}_{FM} \otimes \mathcal{H}_{SM}$ with the tensor combinations of the two bi-dimensional basis and work on the dataset to track down which subjects experience which sequence of measurements, in order to regress for the pair (β_{FM}, β_{SM}) after introducing the proper projectors. As β_{FM} and β_{SM} are the parameters which define the relationships between our action bases and measurement base, these two parameters will represent the consensus effect and the player collapsing into a reasoned state. The resulting Hilbert space will be 4 dimensional with 2 orthogonal planes associated with FM action, 2 orthogonal planes associated with SM action and 2 orthogonal planes, spanning a bundle of 8 non-orthogonal planes between them, associated with the beliefs. This will effectively incorporate the remaining two of three described effects into our model. Because of our dependency for $P(a^{FM} = c) = f(n)$, we do not introduce extra parameters or degrees of freedom for the classical correlation, and therefore we expect our model can explain the same effects as the discussion in Blanco et al. (2014) with less parameters, and scoring better in the quantitative estimations.

4   Discussion, Conclusion and Future Plans

We believe the relationship between a player's beliefs and his preferences is a prime candidate to receive a quantum treatment. It seems that our three discussed effects naturally lead to our proposed Hilbert Space, projectors and resulting probabilities. Next to this mathematical elegance, the use of complementary measurements seems to fit the complex relationship of beliefs and preferences on an interpretational level, as suggested in Dusenmeyer and Pothos (2012). Firstly, it explains the consensus effect as a form of social projection by making players beliefs aligning with their own actions, by assuming the action measurements influence the belief measurements. Secondly, players switching from an intuitive state to a reasoned state, explains the order effect occurring when players are asked to form an opinion about the opponents cooperation rates. By tensoring both Hilbert spaces modeling the previous described two effects, we also incorporate the correlation between players first moves and second moves, hereby making one space in which we model all three described effects.

However, as we present these preliminary results as a starting idea to discuss, not all work is done yet and some questions remain unanswered. Firstly, there has not been a formal fit established. Our presented proof so far are mostly interpretational and only indicative on a mathematical level. We plan a formal fit of the here proposed model to the available data in the near future, hereby also checking if our claim of the reduced dimensionality of the belief measurement holds up.

Next to this need of a formal fit we also wish to note another open question that needs further investigation. To fully investigate the quantum nature of the paradigm, expressed in order effect, we are actually one condition short in the used experiment. For a complete view of the complementarity we would need a new experimental condition with the last possible order of treatments.

Next to the Baseline group (action-action-beliefs) and Elicit_Beliefs group (action-belief-action), an extension of the original experiment with a new treatment (belief-action-action) is required. This should make the order effects even more apparent and eliminate other possible, more classical, models which also account for the consensus effect.

References

Aerts, D., Aerts, S.: Applications of quantum statistics in psychological studies of decision processes. Found. Sci. **1**, 85–97 (1995)

Blanco, M., Engelmann, D., Koch, A.K., Normann, H.-T.: Preferences and beliefs in a sequential social dilemma: a within-subjects analysis. Games Econ. Behav. **87**, 122–135 (2014)

Blanco, M., Engelmann, D., Normann, H.-T.: A within-subject analysis of other-regarding preferences. Games Econ. Behav. **72**(2), 321–338 (2014)

Bohr, N.: On the notions of causality and complementarity. Science **111**(2973), 51–54 (1950)

Bolle, F., Ockenfels, P.: Prisoner's dilemma as a game with incomplete information. J. Econ. Psychol. **11**(1), 69–84 (1990)

Bordley, R.F.: Quantum mechanical and human violations of compound probability principles: toward a generalized Heisenberg uncertainty principle. Oper. Res. **46**, 923–926 (1998)

Brandenburger, A.: The relationship between quantum and classical correlation in games. Games Econ. Behav. **69**(1), 175–183 (2010)

Brunner, N., Linden, N.: Connection between Bell nonlocality and Bayesian game theory. Nat. Commun. **4**(2057), 1–6 (2013)

Bruza, P., Busemeyer, J.R., Gabora, L.: Introduction to the special issue on quantum cognition. J. Math. Psychol. **53**(5), 303–305 (2009)

Busemeyer, J.R., Bruza, P.: Quantum Models of Cognition and Decision. Cambridge University Press, Cambridge (2012)

Busemeyer, J.R., Pothos, E.M.: Social projection and a quantum approach for behavior in Prisoner's Dilemma. Psychol. Inq. **23**(1), 28–34 (2012)

Busemeyer, J.R., Pothos, E.M., Franco, R., Trueblood, J.S.: A quantum theoretical explanation for probability judgment errors. Physchol. Rev. **118**(2), 193–218 (2011)

Busemeyer, J.R., Wang, Z., Townsend, J.T.: Quantum dynamics of human decision-making. J. Math. Psychol. **50**, 220–241 (2006)

Clark, K., Sefton, M.: The sequential prisoner's dilemma: evidence on reciprocation. Econ. J. **11**(468), 51–68 (2001)

Danilov, V.I., Lambert-Mogiliansky, A.: Measurable systems and social sciences. Math. Soc. Sci. **55**, 315–340 (2008)

Danilov, V.I., Lambert-Mogiliansky, A.: Expected utility theory under non-classical uncertainty. Theor. Decis. **68**(1–2), 25–47 (2010)

Denolf, J.: Subadditivity of episodic memory states: a complementarity approach. In: Atmanspacher, H., Bergomi, C., Filk, T., Kitto, K. (eds.) QI 2014. LNCS, vol. 8951, pp. 67–77. Springer, Heidelberg (2015)

Deutsch, D.: Quantum theory of probability and decisions. Proc. Roy. Soc.A **455**(1988), 3129–3137 (1999)

Gabora, L., Aerts, D.: Contextualizing concepts using a mathematical generalization of the quantum formalism. J. Exper. Theor. Artif. Intell. **14**(4), 327–358 (2002) beim Graben, P., Atmanspacher, H.: Extending the philosophical significance of the idea of complementarity. In: Atmanspacher, H., Primas, H. (eds.) Recasting Reality-Wolfgang Pauli's Philosophical Ideas and Contemporary Science, pp. 99–113. Springer-Verlag, Heidelberg (2009)

Hameroff, S.R.: The brain is both neurocomputer and quantum computer. Cogn. Sci. **31**, 1035–1045 (2007)

Haven, E., Khrennikov, A.: Quantum Social Science. Cambridge University Press, Cambridge (2012)

Khrennikov, A.: Ubiquitous Quantum Structure: From Psychology to Finance. Springer, Berlin (2010)

La Mura, P.: Correlated equilibria of classical strategic games with quantum signals. Int. J. Quan. Inf. **3**(1), 183–188 (2005)

Lambert-Mogiliansky, A., Zamir, S., Zwirn, H.: Type indeterminacy: a model for the KT(Kahneman-Tversky)-man. J. Math. Psychol. **53**, 349–361 (2009)

Lambert-Mogiliansky, A., Martínez-Martínez, I.: Games with type indeterminate players: a Hilbert space approach to uncertainty and strategic manipulation of preferences. In: Proceedings of the Quantum Interaction Conference (2014, in press)

Lichtenstein, S., Slovic, P.: The Construction of Preference. Cambridge University Press, Cambridge (2006)

Litt, A., Eliasmith, C., Kroon, F.W., Weinstein, S., Thagard, P.: Is the brain a quantum computer? Cogn. Sci. **30**, 593–603 (2006)

Pothos, E.M., Busemeyer, J.R.: A quantum probability explanation for violations of 'rational' decision theory. Proc. Roy. Soc. B **276**, 2171–2178 (2009)

Pothos, E.M., Busemeyer, J.R.: Can quantum probability provide a new direction for cognitive modeling? Behav. Brain Sci. **36**, 255–327 (2013)

Pothos, E.M., Perry, G., Corr, P.J., Matthew, M.R., Busemeyer, J.R.: Understanding cooperation in the Prisoners Dilemma game. Pers. Individ. Differ. **51**(3), 210–215 (2011)

Trueblood, J.S., Busemeyer, J.R.: A quantum probability account of order effects in inference. Cogn. Sci. **35**, 1518–1552 (2011)

Wang, Z., Solloway, T., Shiffrin, R.M., Busemeyer, J.R.: Context effects produced by question orders reveal quantum nature of human judgments. Proc. Natl. Acad. Sci. USA **111**(26), 9431–9436 (2014)

White, L.C., Pothos, E.M., Busemeyer, J.R.: Sometimes it does hurt to ask: the constructive role of articulating impressions. Cognition **133**(1), 48–64 (2014)

Yearsley, J.M., Pothos, E.M.: Challenging the classical notion of time in cognition: a quantum perspective. Proc. Roy. Soc. B **281**, 20133056 (2014)

Yearsley, J.M., Pothos, E.M., Hampton, J.A., Barque Duran, A.: Towards a quantum probability theory of similarity judgments. In: Proceedings of the Quantum Interaction Conference (2014, in press)

Yukalov, V.I., Sornette, D.: Decision theory with prospect interference and entanglement. Theor. Decis. **70**, 283–328 (2011)

Complementarity

Generalized Quantum Theory, Contextual Emergence and Non-Hierarchic Alternatives

Hartmann Römer$^{(\boxtimes)}$

Institute of Physics, University of Freiburg, Freiburg im Breisgau, Germany
hartmann.roemer@physik.uni-freiburg.de

Abstract. The concept of emergence is critically analyzed in particular with respect to the assumed emergence of mental properties from a neuronal basis. We argue that so-called contextual emergence is needed to avoid an eliminatory reductionism. Quantum-like features of the emergent qualities are to be expected. As a consequence, non-causal relations like entanglement correlations have to be considered as full fledged elements of reality. "Observable extension" is proposed as a contextual alternative to emergence avoiding the asymmetry between purportedly basic and emergent properties.

1 Introduction

By convention sweet, by convention bitter, by convention hot, by convention cold, by convention color: but in reality atoms and void. This is the first and for all times prototypal formulation of a reductionist world view given in the fifth century B.C. by Democritus from Abdera. The endeavor is understanding the world in terms of a limited number of "primary qualities" of a basic layer of reality like positions and velocities of atoms and reducing "secondary qualities" of a somehow subordinate ontological status like color and smell to the primary ones. For good reasons, some version of physical reductionism is a widespread if not dominant attitude in contemporary science. It offers an attractive reduction of complexity in understanding large parts of our world and it takes profit from the impressive success of physics in exactness, certainty, coherence and applicability. The reduction of thermodynamics to mechanics is often considered as paradigmatic for the success of a reductionist program. (But see our discussion in Sect. 3.) *Neuronal reductionism* as a strategy of understanding mental phenomena in terms of neuronal activities has many vigorous proponents. This is another example of a physical reductionism, because the possibility to understand neuronal activity in physical terms is generally accepted.

Eliminative reductionism is an extreme form of reductionism attributing reality only to the basic layer. For instance, eliminative neural reductionism [1] attributes to the "popular psychology" terminology only the meaning of an incomplete shorthand notation for the true and exact neuronal description. This radical view is rarely adopted and will not be discussed further. Much more widespread is *emergentism*, an attitude granting to notions of the secondary,

© Springer International Publishing Switzerland 2016
H. Atmanspacher et al. (Eds.): QI 2015, LNCS 9535, pp. 157–167, 2016.
DOI: 10.1007/978-3-319-28675-4_12

"higher", "emergent layer" its own although ontologically somehow subordinate status. The claim is that systems described in terms of the basic layer will develop new and surprising features once a certain threshold of complexity is passed. Many versions of emergentism are advocated reaching from a milder form of reductionism up to a decidedly anti-reductionist attitude. In more formal terms, the question of the interpretation of emergentism becomes a problem of the specification of the relationship between two different descriptions or modelisations of a part of reality, one of them considered "basic" and one considered "emergent". Three questions are of particular interest in this context. (1) What is the ontological status of the emergent layer? (2) What is the novelty status of the emergent layer? (3) What about the possibility of "downward causation" from the emergent to the basic layer. Approaching these questions we shall proceed as follows: (More material can be found in [2].)

First we shall present a very general formal scheme for describing and modelling systems of most general type. It has been developed under the name of "Weak" or *Generalized Quantum Theory*(GQT) [3–5] arising from physical quantum theory by shedding off all formal features pertaining to physics in the narrow sense and thus widening the range of applicability beyond physics still keeping salient quantum notions like complementarity and entanglement. GQT can be seen to be in direct accordance with basic categorial fundamentals of the human cognitive system. GQT strongly suggests that quantum-like features of systems are generic and that the ontological constitution of systems in classical physics should be considered exceptional. This message is noteworthy, because neuronal emergentism is normally inspired by a classical or even mechanistic world model. Next we shall critically analyze the standard example of the emergence of thermodynamics and arrive at the notion of *Contextual Emergence* [6,7]. Then we shall investigate to what extent neuronal emergence fulfills the criteria of Contextual Emergence.

Finally, we propose *observable extension* as a more symmetric alternative to the hierarchical concept of emergence and give tentative answers to the three questions raised above.

2   Generalized Quantum Theory

World is never given to us directly but primarily only as it appears on our internal stage. Naive realism assumes that the world, at least in essence, really is like it appears to us. This is a very strong assumption underrating the active role of the human cognitive system and the human activity as a "model builder". The preferred world model of contemporary physical and neuronal reductionism exhibits the influence of classical mechanics and is in danger to confuse a world model with the world itself.

In fact the appearance of the world is bound to fundamental *existentials*, constitutive features of our human mode of existence and thereby also categorial elements of human cognition, similar to Kant's categories. Four of them are of particular importance for us: (For more details see [8]).

1. *Excentricity/oppositeness*: Every perception or cognition of the form accessible to us is irrevocably bound to the figure of oppositeness by always being the perception or cognition of something by someone. The *epistemic cut* separating the "observer" from the "observed object" may be movable but it is never completely removable.
2. *Temporality*: The world is not given to us in the mode of a timeless panoramic picture but rather like a movie or a temporal sequence of events which occur in the running window of a distinguished "now".
3. *Facticity*: We do not so much live in a world of potentialities but rather in a world of facts, which hit on us and occur to us. The "now" is of prototypal facticity.
4. *Freedom and causality* are not in contradiction but offshoots from the same root of temporality differentiated into past, present and future. They rely on each other: Causality is required for freely chosen actions to have predictable effects and causal regularities are detected by freely creating causes and observing their effects.

Weak or *Generalized Quantum Theory* (GQT) [3–5] is a conceptual core of quantum theory, which arose from an axiomatic formulation of physical quantum theory by leaving out all features which seemed to be special to physical systems. As we shall see, it takes into account the above existential universals right in the heart of its structure. GQT is not physics but a very general theory of the structure of observed systems. For the purposes of this note, it suffices to give a short account of the vital structural features of GQT. For recent developments and applications see [5, 9].

The following notions are taken over from quantum physics:

System: A system is anything which can be (imagined to be) isolated from the rest of the world and be subject to an investigation. A system can be as general as "impressionism", a school of art together with all persons involved in production and interpretation. Unlike the situation in, e.g., classical mechanics the identification of a system is not always a trivial procedure but sometimes a creative act. In many cases it is possible to define *subsystems* inside a system.

State: A system must have the capacity to reside in different states without losing its identity as a system. One may differentiate between *pure states*, which correspond to maximal possible knowledge of the system and *mixed states* corresponding to incomplete knowledge.

Observable: An observable corresponds to a feature of a system, which can be investigated in a more or less meaningful way. *Global observables* pertain to the system as a whole, *local observables* pertain to subsystems. In the above-mentioned example, observables may, for instance, correspond to esthetic investigations.

Measurement: Doing a measurement of an observable A means performing the investigation which belongs to the observable A and arriving at a result a, which can claim *factual validity*. What factual validity means depends on the system:

Validity of a measurement result for a system of physics, internal conviction for self observation, consensus for groups of human beings. The result of the measurement of A will in general depend on the state z of the system before the measurement but will not be completely determined by it.

Immediately after a measurement of an observable A with result a, the system will be in an *eigenstate* z_a of the observable A with *eigenvalue* a. The eigenstate z_a is a state, for which an immediate repetition of the measurement of the same observable A will again yield the same result a with certainty, and after this repeated measurement the system will still be in the same state z_a. This property, which is also crucial in quantum physics justifies the terminology "eigenstate of an observable A" for z_a and "eigenvalue" for the result a. We emphasize that this is an idealized description of a measurement process abstracting from its detailed temporal structure.

Two observables A and B are called *complementary*, if the corresponding measurements are not interchangeable. This means that the state of the system depends on the order in which the measurement results, say a and b, were obtained. If the last measurement was a measurement of A, the system will end up in an eigenstate z_a of A, and if the last measurement was a measurement of B, an eigenstate z_b will result eventually. For complementary observables A and B there will be at least some eigenvalue, say a, of one of the observables for which no common eigenstate z_{ab} of both observables exists. This means that it is not generally possible to ascribe sharp values to the complementary observables A and B, although both of them may be equally important for the description of the system. This is the essence of quantum theoretical complementarity which is well defined also for GQT. Some people prefer to apply the term "complementarity" to what we call "maximal complementarity": Knowledge of the value od A implies complete indeterminacy of the value of B and vice versa. This holds for the position and momentum observables Q and P of quantum mechanics. But according to this definition already oblique components of angular momentum would not be complementary.

Notice, that a measurement will in general change the state of a system by production of an eigenstate of the last-measured observable. This generic quantum feature is realized in a paradigmatic way for the human mind under the first person perspective of self-observation. It will also hold for human thought in general and for all kinds of discourse, belief or decision systems. Quantum features like complementarity and indeterminacy should be common there. Detailed empirical investigations of quantum features in psychological systems have been performed for bistable perception [10–12], human thought and the formation of concepts [13,14], apparent irrationality and non-classical logic in decision processes [15,16], semantic networks, learning and order effects in questionnaires [9,17]. For further information see [18] There are striking similarities of the measurement process with creative processes [19].

Non-complementary observables, for which the order of measurement does not matter, are called *compatible*. After the measurement of compatible observables A and B with results a and b, the system will be in the same common eigenstate z_{ab} of A and B irrespective of the order in which the measurements were performed. In classical systems all observables are compatible and possess simultaneous eigenstates, and the phenomenon of complementarity does not occur. It should be clear from our general structural consideration and from the examples given, that this is a strong additional assumption. For general reasons, quantum-like behavior of systems should be the rule rather than the exception. We also see, how the above-mentioned categorial universals are built into the structure of GQT [8]:

Excentricity is taken into account by the pivotal position of measurement in GQT. In physical quantum theory the epistemic cut is known under the name of Heisenberg cut. Moreover, observables, right by definition, assume the existence of an epistemic cut. They are sitting right astride on it with a footing both on the side of the observer and the observed. Temporality is present in the relevance of the (temporal) ordering of measurements. In addition, quantum systems in general have temporal dynamics. Facticity resides in the factual character of measurement results. Freedom and causality show up in GQT in the strange interplay of freedom in the choice of the observable to be measured and the causal dynamics of the system.

Entanglement can also be defined in the framework of Generalized Quantum Theory [3–5, 20]. It may and will show up under the following conditions:

1. Subsystems can be identified within the system such that local observables pertaining to different subsystems are compatible.
2. There is a global observable of the total system, which is complementary to local observables of the subsystems.
3. The system is in an *entangled state* for instance in an eigenstate of the above-mentioned global observable and not an eigenstate of the local observables.

Given these conditions, the measured values of the local observables will be uncertain because of the complementarity of the global and the local observables. However, so-called *entanglement correlations* will be observed between the measured values of the local observables pertaining to different subsystems. These correlations are non-local and instantaneous. They are not usable for signals or causal influences. They are non-causal order structures resulting from the holistic structure of quantum systems. The crucial importance of non-causal ordering structures is a fundamental message of quantum theory. The explanatory monopole of causal relations, often tacitly assumed under the influence of a mechanical paradigm cannot be held up.

Comparing Generalized with full physical quantum theory the following vital differences are worth noticing:

– In its minimal version and in contrast to other approaches [21], GQT does not ascribe quantified probabilities to the outcomes of measurements of an observable A in a given state z. Indeed, to give just one example, for esthetic observables quantified probabilities seem to be inappropriate from the outset. What rather remains are modal logical qualifications like "impossible", "possible" and "certain". Related to the absence of quantified probabilities, the set of states in GQT is in general not modeled by a linear Hilbert space.

– Related to this, GQT in its minimal form provides no basis for the derivation of inequalities of Bell's type for measurement probabilities, which allow for the conclusion that the indeterminacies of measurement values are of an intrinsic ontic nature. In many (but not all) applications of GQT indeterminacies may be epistemic and due to incomplete knowledge of the full state or uncontrollable perturbations by outside influences or by the process of measurement. Notice that complementarity in the sense of GQT may even occur as a consequence of different partitions in coarse grained classical dynamical systems [22,23]. In this sense, GQT is a phenomenological framework theory allowing to leave the question of the ontic or epistemic character of indeterminacies open.

For some applications (see, e.g., [9–12,17],) one may want to enrich the above-described minimal scheme of GQT by adding further structure, e.g., an underlying Hilbert space structure for the states.

3   Contextual Emergence

The statistical theory of thermodynamics is often considered to be the classic example of a successful reduction and a well-understood emergence relationship. We already mentioned that emergence concerns the relationship between two descriptions of a part of the world, one of them primary and basic, one secondary and emergent. In this exemplary case the basic level is a system of (many) particles described microscopically by classical or quantum mechanics with the positions, momenta and spins of the particles as fundamental observables. The emergent macroscopic level is described as a system of classical constitution with different macroscopic observables like volume, pressure, temperature and entropy. The macroscopic state is determined by the values of a sufficient number of macroscopic observables. The macroscopic observables *supervene* [24] the microscopic observables because a change in the macroscopic ones is necessarily accompanied by a change in the microscopic ones but nut necessarily vice versa. Both the macroscopic and the microscopic description are formally well developed complete theories making emergence and supervenience exemplarily clear issues in this case.

On closer inspection the reduction of thermodynamics to microphysics proceeds in two steps:

First, the detailed microscopic description of states, which is neither feasible nor even desirable for a large system is replaced by a statistical description. This is done by first introducing *mixed states*, i.e. ensembles or sets of pure microscopic states with an attribution of a probability to each of them. In a second step, *macrostates*, defined by the values of macroscopic thermodynamical observable are identified with appropriate mixed states. There are many mixed states without thermodynamic interpretation.

Notice, that the reduction of thermodynamics to microphysics is not to be understood such that in complex microphysical systems after passing a complexity threshold completely new concepts of a thermodynamic description arise automatically by themselves and from nothing. The concept of probability, applied in the first step is not newly born but pre-existent. It is also applicable to small microscopic systems for which, as opposed to large systems, a detailed microscopic description is still feasible.

Some observables like the total energy are common to the microscopic and macroscopic description. In general, the identification of macroscopic observables like volume and temperature is neither enforced by the microscopic description nor by the concept of mixed states. It comes about by applying different contexts to a section of reality in addition to its microphysical description. For this reason, Atmanspacher, Bishop and beim Graben [6,7] talk about *Contextual Emergence*. For a successful Contextual Emergence relationship a further condition must be fulfilled: The mixed states corresponding to thermodynamic macrostates must have a sufficient degree of stability under the microscopic dynamics. Otherwise, these mixed states would quickly develop into mixed states without thermodynamic interpretation. A change of the topology of the states may be necessary to achieve stability.

Thermodynamics is a particularly clear case of Contextual Emergence. There is a widespread hope, that other emergence situations conform with this example. This amounts to demanding a lot: Both the basic and the emergent layer must be well formalized and endowed with dynamics which meet the above-mentioned stability requirement.

As for the emergence of a mental from a neuronal description the situation seems to be as follows: For the neuronal layer, a satisfactory formal description is largely available. States and observables are essentially under control, perhaps with some restrictions for the dynamics of larger neuronal assemblies. The situation is much more problematic on the mental level. First of all, we expect it to be organized in a quantum-like rather than a classical manner [18,25], making reduction to neuronal properties much more difficult. Moreover, there is no comprehensive description and classification of mental states and observables. The dynamics on the mental level can in no way considered to be understood. Exactness is sometimes attempted by restriction to a small set of mental observable, which are, however, so much devised with an eye on the neuronal substrate that reduction becomes almost tautological. The status of the stability requirement is also unclear. Mental dynamics is largely unknown, and one has the impression that on the one hand quite different neuronal states frequently correspond to similar mental states and on the other hand sometimes a small change of the neuronal state often leads to a large change of the mental state. Mental and neuronal properties will correspond to very different topologies and partitions of states. It is just this difference, which makes the "emergence" of a quantum-like mental from a classical neuronal domain possible.

In any case, contextuality will be decisive for neuronal emergentism at least as much as for thermodynamics. The hope for completely reductionist emergentism for the mental domain deriving all mental features in an automatic and cogent way from neuronal ones seems to be futile.

4   Alternatives to Emergence

Emergence and supervenience are genuinely asymmetric concepts distinguishing between a basic, lower, ontologically primary and an emergent, higher, ontologically secondary level. The vision of physical reductionism is a hierarchic structure of the world with a basic physical layer given, for instance, by elementary particle physics and above it a tower of higher stepwise emergent levels like chemistry, life and mind. One may ask oneself, whether such a hierarchic ordering of the world really has an ontological status reflecting a real feature of the world or whether it is epistemic and arises only from a particular description of the world such that in a different description the layers and/or their ordering might be different.

A frequently invoked argument in favor of an ontological hierarchy is concerned with complexity. Emergence arises, when the complexity on the basic layer exceeds a certain threshold. However, one should keep in mind that complexity is an epistemic notion referring to a mode of description. What is complex in one description may be simple in another description. Consider the exemplary case of the emergence of thermodynamics from microscopic mechanics. Experience shows that for thermodynamical systems far from equilibrium the treatment of the fluctuating behavior of the thermodynamic observables becomes complicated to the verge of intractability. In this situation, a microscopic atomic description suggests itself and, indeed, molecular dynamics is the method of choice here. In this case, the direction of emergence seems to be reversed. As a matter of fact, thermodynamic fluctuations were historically one important reason for the acceptance of atomism.

Contextuality of emergence and the high degree of autonomy of the emergent level are further arguments against an ontological hierarchy. As an example, the function of a software is largely independent of its underlying hardware substrate realization and could be achieved in many different ways. It is also conceivable that mental properties could rest on a basis quite different from neurons. As far as physics is concerned, it is quite uncertain, whether a really fundamental level has already been reached and whether it exists at all. In addition, recent developments seem to indicate that elementary particle theory is not understandable without and closely interwoven with cosmology, which according to the traditional view should emerge from particle theory.

From the preceding considerations we see, that the ontological status of the emerging layer is quite strong and independent and not strictly subordinate. Moreover, an ontologically hierarchical order of the world is disputable. In this situation it is suggestive to question the asymmetry inherent in the concept of emergence with the distinction between basic and emergent layer. Emergence is a relationship between two formal systems with different sets of states and observables both of them describing a certain sector of reality. Neural emergence with a basic neuronal and an emergent mental layer is the example of central interest for us. A more symmetric alternative to emergence in general and neural emergence in particular would be *extension of the set of observables* or more briefly *Observable Extension*. This amounts to describing a sector of reality by just one formal system with one large set of observables corresponding to both layers of emergence. For example, rather than neuronal emergence, one considers just one large comprehensive system "man" or even "man plus physical and social environment" which contains both neuronal and mental observables. This is in accordance with a standpoint of neutral dual aspect monism with respect to the matter-mind problem. We already saw that complementarity should occur between mental observables of the comprehensive system. One can also argue that complementarity between neuronal observables on one side and mental observables on the other side should be common [25]. So, in any case, the comprehensive matter-mind system should be quantum-like in the sense of GQT.

For "Observable Extension" contextuality is at least as vital as for Contextual Emergence. The identification of additional observables is not automatically enforced by the other observables but corresponds to the introduction of new concepts and contexts into the investigation of the comprehensive system.

For complementary observables different values for one of them will in general change expectations for the measured values of the other one. So, the basic dictum of supervenience "Change on the emergent layer leads to change on the basic layer" also holds for complementary observables in an appropriately symmetrized form.

5   Conclusions

We are now in the position to attempt answers to the three questions raised in the Introduction.

The first two questions concerned the ontological status and the novelty of "emergent" properties. It should be abundantly clear from the preceding considerations, in particular from the analysis of the paradigmatic case of the emergence of thermodynamics, that contextuality is a vital element in the discussion of emergence. It is even more central in the symmetric alternative concept of "Observable Extension". Unless one is willing to adopt a radical eliminatory reductionism, the "emergent" properties are not automatically generated by the "basic" layer beyond a certain threshold of complexity. Rather they come from different contexts becoming applicable or useful. Finding such contexts and detecting their applicability is a subtle achievement of creativity whose origin is a deep and difficult question [19]. As for the novelty of the "emergent" features: They are not suddenly born from the basic layer like Athena from the head of Zeus but they correspond to preexistent notions and the novelty consists in their applicability or usefulness with increasing complexity on the basic level. To give a very simple example: If the complexity of a system of points in a plain is increased from two to three points the concept of angles becomes applicable and useful, but it was already existent and not newly born with the appearance of the third point.

The third question raised in the Introduction was about "downward causation" from the emergent to the basic level. It is formulated in a slightly provocative way as *Kim's Dilemma* [26]. For the status of the emergent mental level in relation to its neuronal basic the following dire alternative seems to hold: Either mental properties are just abbreviations for neural properties in the sense of an eliminative reductionism or else, due to the assumed causal closure of the physical world, they are impotent and causally decoupled from the physical world. This leads Kim to the assertion that emergence and supervenience are formulations rather than solutions of a problem.

The assumption of causal closure of the physical world is questionable [2]. But even taking it for granted, a smooth resolution of the dilemma comes from the concept of contextuality both in the form of Contextual Emergence and of "Observable Extension". There is no causal interaction between the neuronal and the mental level and, in fact, no such interaction is needed. The relationship of the different layers is not causal in its nature but a correspondence and order structure, which is due to the fact that the same part of reality is observed from different perspectives. From the example of the emergence of thermodynamics we easily see that the relationship between the microscopic and thermodynamical description is not a causal one. Of course, the microstate changes when the values of thermodynamic variables change, but this simultaneity in change only reflects the fact, that both descriptions are different sides of the same medal. This becomes even clearer if we consider complementary observbles in one and the same system. Nobody would interpret the subtle relationship between position and momentum distributions as causal effects.

Kim's dilemma just results from an unjustified monopolization of causal relationships as explanatory structures. Quantum theory with its inevitable non-causal entanglement correlations lends yet another disproof of such a one-sided claim.

References

1. Churchland, P.M.: The Engine of Reason, the Seat of the Soul. Cambridge University Press, Cambridge (1995)
2. Römer, H.: Emergenz und Evolution. Talk Offenburg, October 2013 (2013, to be published)
3. Atmanspacher, H., Römer, H., Walach, H.: Weak quantum theory: complementarity and entanglement in physics and beyond. Found. Phys. **32**, 379–406 (2002)
4. Atmanspacher, H., Filk, T., Römer, H.: Weak quantum theory: formal framework and selected applications. In: Adenier, G., Khrennikov, A.Y., Nieuwenhuizen, T.M. (eds.) Quantum Theory: Reconsiderations and Foundations-American Institute of Physics, pp. 34–46, New York (2006)
5. Filk, T., Römer, H.: Generalized quantum theory: overview and latest developments. Axiomathes **21**(2), 211–220 (2011). doi:10.1007/s10516-010-9136-6. http://www.springerlink.com/content/547247hn62jw7645/fulltext.pdf
6. Bishop, R., Atmanspacher, H.: Contextual emergence in the description of properties. Found. Phys. **36**, 1753–1777 (2006)
7. Atmanspacher, H., beim Graben, P.: Contextual emergence of mental states from neurodynamics. Chaos Compl. Lett. **2**, 151–168 (2007). (see also Scholarpedia-article www.scholarpedia.org/article/contextual_emergence)

8. Römer, H.: Why do we see a classical world? Travaux Mathématiques XX, 167–186 (2012). http://arxiv.org/abs/1112.6271
9. Atmanspacher, H., Römer, H.: Order effects in sequential measurements of noncommutative psychological observables. J. Math. Psychol. **56**, 274–280 (2012). http://arxiv.org/abs/1201.4685
10. Atmanspacher, H., Filk, T., Römer, H.: Quantum Zeno features of bistable perception. Biol. Cybern. **90**, 33–40 (2004)
11. Atmanspacher, H., Bach, M., Filk, T., Kornmeier, J., Römer, H.: Cognitive time scales in a Necker-Zeno model of bistable perception. Open Cybern. Syst. J. **2**, 234–251 (2008)
12. Atmanspacher, H., Filk, T., Römer, H.: Complementarity in bistable perception. In: Atmanspacher, H., Primas, H. (eds.) Recasting Reality: Wolfgang Pauli's Philosophical Ideas and Contemporary Science, pp. 135–150. Springer-Verlag, Berlin (2008)
13. Aerts, D., Gabora, L., Sozzo, S.: Concepts and their dynamics: a quantum-theoretic modelling of human thought. Topics Cogn. Sci. **5**, 737–772 (2013)
14. Aerts, D., Sozzo, S., Veloz, T.: Quantum structure in cognition and in the foundations of human reasoning (2015). arXiv:1412.8704
15. Aerts, D., D'Hooghe, B.: Classical logical versus quantum conceptual thought: examples in economics, decision theory and concept theory. In: Bruza, P., Sofge, D., Lawless, W., Rijsbergen, K., Klusch, Matthias (eds.) QI 2009. LNCS, vol. 5494, pp. 128–142. Springer, Heidelberg (2009)
16. Pothos, E.M., Busemeyer, J.D.: A quantum probability model explanation for violations of rational decision theory. Proc. Roy. Soc. **B276**, 2171–2178 (2009)
17. Wang, Z., Busemeyer, J.D.: A quantum question order model supported by empirical tests of an a priori and precise prediction. Topics Cogn. Sci. **5**, 689–1710 (2013)
18. Atmanspacher, H.: Quantum approaches to consciousness. In: Zalta, E. (ed.) Stanford Encyclopedia of Philosophy (2011)
19. Römer, H., Jacoby, G.E.: Schöpfer, Schöpfung, Schöpfertum, Talk Offenburg (2011, to appear)
20. Römer, H.: Verschränkung (2008). In: Knaup, M., Müller, T., Spät, P. (eds.) Post-Physikalismus, pp. 87–121. Verlag Karl Alber, Freiburg im Breisgau (2011)
21. Aerts, D., Durt, T., Grib, T., Van Bogaert, B., Zapatrin, A.: Quantum structures in macroscopic reality. Int. J. Theor. Phys. **32**, 489–498 (1993)
22. beim Graben, P., Atmanspacher, H.: Complementarity in classical dynamical systems. Found. Phys. **36**, 291–306 (2006)
23. beim Graben, P., Filk, T., Atmanspacher, H.: Epistemic entanglement due to non-generating partitions of classical dynamical systems. Int. J. Theor. Phys. **52**, 723–734 (2013)
24. Kim, J.: Supervenience and Mind. Cambridge University Press, Cambridge (1993)
25. Römer, H., Walach, H.: Complementarity between phenomenal and physiological observables, October 2008. In: Walach, H., Schmidt, S., Jonas, W.B. (eds.) Neuroscience, Consciousness and Spirituality, pp. 97–107. Springer Publishing Company (2011). doi:10.1007/978-94-007-2079-4, ISBN 978-94-007-2078-7
26. Kim, J.: Blocking causal drainage and other maintainance chores with mental causation. Philos. Phenomenological Res. **67**, 151–176 (2003)

Complementarity in Psychophysics

Pierre Uzan[(✉)]

CNRS, Laboratory SPHERE, History and Philosophy of Science,
University Paris-Diderot, Paris, France
pierre.uzan@paris7.jussieu.fr

Abstract. Besides the application of the notion of complementarity to psychological and physical descriptions of the individual, this paper explores the possibility of defining complementary observables in the same phenomenal domain. Complementary emotional observables are defined from experimental data on experienced emotions reported by subjects who have been prepared in a state of induced emotion. Complementary physiological observables are defined in correspondence with conjugate, physiological quantities that can be measured.

Keywords: Complementarity · Psychophysics · Emotional observables · Induced emotion · Physiological observables · Conjugate physiological quantities

1 Introduction

The notion of complementarity has been implemented according to different ways in quantum mechanics [1–3]. In a first sense, it applies to the *descriptions* of a same quantum system that exclude each other but are nevertheless required together to give a complete information on it. Mathematically speaking, a "description" can be defined as an algebra of experimental propositions and two Boolean descriptions, which are governed by classical logic, can be said "complementary" if they cannot be embedded into a single Boolean description. It is the case of the wave/corpuscle descriptions of particules which are associated with exclusive phenomena in the double-slit experiment. However, the notion of complementarity is also used to indicate the *non-commutativity of physical observables,* which relies on the fact that the order in which are measured the corresponding physical quantities is not indifferent. It is for example the case for the position and moment observables whose degree of complementarity is evaluated by the Planck constant.

On the other hand, the recent propositions for generalizing quantum theory have shown that its key-concepts can apply beyond the strict quantum domain, and even beyond the material realm [4]. Diverse non-physical phenomena, such as bistable perception, combination of concepts in a sentence or decision making in uncertain situation have been successfully modeled within this generalized framework, by taking into account the quantum-like effects that are involved–like order effects or interference effects [5–7]. Along this line of thought, this paper will discuss the possibility of successfully applying the notion of complementarity to psychophysics.

© Springer International Publishing Switzerland 2016
H. Atmanspacher et al. (Eds.): QI 2015, LNCS 9535, pp. 168–178, 2016.
DOI: 10.1007/978-3-319-28675-4_13

The idea of complementarity of mental and bodily *descriptions* of the individual can indeed be traced back to Spinoza's double-aspect monism. According to Spinoza, Extension and Mind are (among an infinite number of attributes) two intelligible and non-interacting aspects of the neutral substance, which is God or Nature. Spinoza's parallelism of aspects has been re-interpreted by Pauli in terms of complementarity of descriptions, which then, in agreement with Bohr's project to apply the notion of complementarity beyond physics, generalizes the notion of complementary descriptions in quantum mechanics. The latter application of the notion of complementary descriptions to the mind-matter relationship has been explored in details by Primas with a special focus on the notion of time [8]: Mc Taggart's A-time and B-time are conceived of as *complementary representations* of time, which can then be used to parametrize both causal chains of mental and physical events. Let us also mention the suggestion of Walach and Römer [9, 10] to apply the notion of complementarity of mental and bodily *descriptions* of the individual to single *observables*, defined across domains, and not (only) to algebras of propositions. The underlying idea is that the measurement of a psychological observable generally changes the state of the subject and then the possible results of the measurement of a physiological observable –and reciprocally.

We shall here focus on the possibility of defining complementary observables *in the same phenomenal domain* and not across domains. The reason of this choice is that such an approach to complementarity in psychophysics can be very useful for tackling the long-standing question of the nature of the psychophysical correlations *on experimental basis*, by appealing to Bell-type inequalities [11]. In addition, if the complementarity of mental observables has been successfully explored in the domain of cognition and decision making [7], it seems that it is not yet the case for observables relative to the *subjective experience*, that is, observables that evaluate the *emotional content* of the mental states of a subject in a life situation. Likewise, it seems that the complementarity of *physiological observables*, which are defined from the macroscopic physiological quantities (such as the heart rate, the blood pressure or the skin conductance), has not yet been explored.

In Sect. 2, complementary emotional observables will be defined from experimental data on the intensity of the emotions experienced by subjects prepared in a state of induced emotion, which then defines an emotional context. In contrast, a theoretical method for defining complementary physiological observables from couples of conjugate physical variables will be presented in Sect. 3. This method will be applied to cardiovascular quantities (systolic blood pressure and stroke volume) that can be easily measured. The conclusion and the scope of this study will be briefly discussed in the final Sect. 4.

2 Complementary Emotional Observables

Emotional observables measure the degree of specified emotions experienced by a subject, such as anger, sadness, happiness, or fear. The complementarity of emotional observables will be shown by computing their commutator from the relevant experimental data. This can be done if we can compute from these data the conditional probabilities that an individual be "observed" (through a questionnaire or other means) in an emotional state if she/he has been conditioned or "prepared" in some specified emotional state by a reliable method. This is actually the case for the data provided by several recent papers, like that of Prkachin et al. [12] that will be analysed hereafter.

These authors have reported data about the measurement of cardiovascular variables of subjects experiencing emotional states induced by particular stimuli constructed according to Lang's theory [13]. These stimuli are capable of triggering relatively "pure" emotions by referring to specific incidents in their lives. In the present case, the experimenter tells the subjects stories that are directly related to these specific incidents, but other methods based on the projection of films have also been shown reliable [14]. The five considered emotional contents are here "happiness" (noted as H), "sadness" (S), "anger" (A), "fear" (F) and "disgust" (D). In order to show the reliability of the method of conditioning, Prkachin and his colleagues have measured the average reported intensity (average on a population of 31 individuals, 23 females and 8 males) of the five basic emotions experienced on the six possible trials (the five trials of induced specific emotions and a trial where no specific emotion is induced). We shall here be exclusively interested in the latter part of the data. This intensity of the experienced emotions is measured on a scale of 0 (no emotion experienced) to 7 (extremely intense emotional experience). The results, which are presented in Prkachin's paper (p. 259), are reported hereafter (Table 1).

Table 1. Average intensity of each of five emotions experienced on six trials

Target	Emotional rating				
	Happiness	Anger	Fear	Sadness	Disgust
Neu	0.24	0.03	0.09	0.15	0.03
	(0.66)	(0.17)	(0.38)	(0.57)	(0.17)
Hap	**5.30**	0.03	0.24	0.21	0.15
	(1.36)	(0.17)	(0.71)	(0.49)	(0.87)
Ang	0.00	**5.15**	0.39	0.81	1.21
	(0.00)	(1.15)	(1.12)	(1.36)	(1.62)
Fea	0.21	0.73	**4.61**	1.09	0.36
	(0.74)	(0.31)	(1.50)	(1.59)	(1.08)
Sad	0.06	1.27	0.79	**5.15**	0.36
	(0.24)	(1.81)	(1.50)	(1.62)	(1.06)
Dis	0.06	1.58	0.58	0.85	**4.97**
	(0.24)	(1.94)	(0.97)	(1.46)	(1.40)

For example, we can read on the fourth line (target emotion = fear), that a subject submitted to a fear-induced stimulus will, on average, report an intensity of fear of 4.61 (with a standard deviation SD of 1.50) and an intensity of happiness of 0.21 (with SD = 0.31). All the data of this table show that among the reported emotions, the target emotion, induced by the trial, obtains a much higher rating than all other emotions[1], which shows the reliability of the method. Nevertheless, note that the target emotion is never reported with its maximal intensity (that is, with a rating of 7), which shows that the emotional state of a subject is not totally determined by the conditioning. We will then write a state of induced emotion B as W_B (and not as B) to distinguish this state from the state of "pure" emotion B (which would give rise to a rating of 7).

Now, for each reported emotion, these data do not provide the number of subjects that report each of the 8 possible ratings, from 0 to 7, but an only number, its average intensity on the population. We cannot then work, as is usually the case for the quantum models of cognition and decision making [7], in an 8-dimensional state space corresponding to the 8 possible weightings of each reported emotion. Nevertheless, the average intensity of each reported emotion can be used to estimate the conditional probability to report this emotion for a subject prepared in a given state of induced emotion. From Table 1, the conditional probability to report the emotion A for a subject "prepared" in a state of induced emotion W_B will be defined as the rate of the reported average intensity of A with respect to the sum of all the reported average intensities of emotions for subjects prepared in W_B. For example, the probability to report an emotion of disgust for a subject prepared in an emotional state of anger can be computed from the third line of Table 1 as $p(D/W_A) = 1.21 / 7.56 = 0.160$.

In order to interpret geometrically these conditional probabilities, the emotional states and the emotional observables will be represented within a 2-dimensional state space where each emotion E defines the orthonormal E-basis $\{ |E>, |\daleth E> \}$, the vector $|E>$ (written in Dirac notation) representing a state of extreme emotion E (with a rating of 7) and the vector $|\daleth E >$ a state where no emotion E is felt (rating 0). This 2-dimensional state space is a complex Hilbert space capable of representing incompatible emotions (see hereafter). In this state space, an emotional state is represented by a unit vector, while emotional observables will be defined as projectors. For example, the Fear observable and the Sadness observable are respectively defined by the projectors $F_{op} = |F> < F|$ and $S_{op} = |S> < S|$. As shown in the following diagram, the probability *amplitude* that a subject reports the emotion S if he/she has been conditioned in a state W_F of induced fear, which can be computed from the data by taking the square root of the corresponding conditional probability, will be interpreted as the magnitude of the projection of $|W_F >$ onto $|S >$:

$$< S|W_F > =_{df} (P (S/W_F))^{1/2} \equiv \text{length OH.}$$

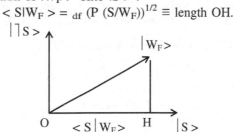

---

[1] Note that the authors interpret the latter result ontologically, by saying that the subjects *are* in a "mixed" emotional state even if the target emotion is nevertheless predominant. However, it seems that from a purely phenomenological approach it cannot be rigorously asserted on the basis of reports that the subject *was* in the same emotional states *before* questioning her/him. This point of view is strengthened by some recent results that show that the fact of reporting one's emotion changes the values of one's physiological variables and then of the correlated emotional variables [14].

To show the complementarity of two emotional observables, we have first to represent their associated basis in the same 2-dimensional Hilbert space, then to define the corresponding emotional observables and compute their commutator. For example, let us consider the emotions Anger (A) and Disgust (D), whose associated observables are, respectively, the projectors $A_{op} = |A><A|$ and $D_{op} = |D><D|$.

The following diagram shows in the 2-dimensional emotional state space the basis $\{|A>, |\exists A>\}$ and $\{|D>, |\exists D>\}$ respectively associated to these emotions and the angles between these vectors and the state of induced anger $|W_A>$ that will be used to compute the components of the vector $|D>$ in the basis $\{|A>, |\exists A>\}$:

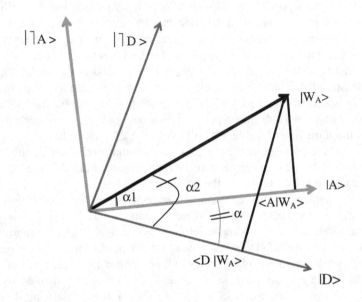

The probability amplitude $< D|A >$ of the transition from the state of pure anger to the state of pure disgust can be computed as follows:

$\cos \alpha 1 = < A|W_A > = (5.15/7.56)^{1/2} = 0.825$ (see line 3), hence $\alpha 1 = 38.2°$
$\cos \alpha 2 = < D| W_A > = (p(D/W_A))^{1/2} = 0.4$ (see above), hence $\alpha 2 = 73.8°$
$\alpha = \alpha 2 - \alpha 1 = 35.6°$, and then $< A|D > = \cos \alpha = 0.847$.

Now, the state $|D>$ can be written in the A-basis as:

$$|D> = <A|D> |A> + <\exists A|D> |\exists A>,$$

where the probability amplitude $< \exists A|D >$ can be computed from $< A|D >$ as follows:

$$<\exists A|D> = \left(1 - |<A|D>|^2\right)^{1/2} = 0.531.$$

Consequently, $|D> = 0.847 |A> + 0.531 |\exists A>$.

To compute the commutator of the observables A_{op} and D_{op}, we will express their associated matrix in the same orthonormal basis $\{|A >, |\exists A >\}$ of the two-dimensional state space. In this basis, the projector $A_{op} = |A > < A|$ is associated with the matrix:

$$M(A_{op}) = \begin{bmatrix} 1 & 0 \\ 0 & 0 \end{bmatrix}.$$

To find the matrix associated with the observable D_{op} in the basis $\{|A >, |\exists A >\}$ we use the aforementioned decomposition of $|D >$ in the basis $\{|A >, |\exists A >\}$ to compute the outer product $D_{op} = |D > < D|$ in this basis:

$$M(D_{op}) = (0.847; 0.531) \otimes (0.847; 0.531) = \begin{bmatrix} 0.717 & 0.449 \\ 0.449 & 0.282 \end{bmatrix}$$

The commutator of the observables A_{op}, D_{op} can then be computed as:

$$[A_{op}, D_{op}] = \begin{bmatrix} 1 & 0 \\ 0 & 0 \end{bmatrix} \begin{bmatrix} 0.717 & 0.449 \\ 0.449 & 0.282 \end{bmatrix} - \begin{bmatrix} 0.717 & 0.449 \\ 0.449 & 0.282 \end{bmatrix} \begin{bmatrix} 1 & 0 \\ 0 & 0 \end{bmatrix}$$
$$= (0.449) \begin{bmatrix} 0 & 1 \\ -1 & 0 \end{bmatrix}.$$

This result shows the *complementarity of the observables* A_{op} *and* D_{op} that, respectively, measure the average intensity of anger and disgust experienced by a subject conditioned in a state of induced anger. Their degree of incompatibility can be estimated by the norm of this commutator:

$$\| [A_{op}, D_{op}] \| = 0.449.$$

It can be shown that all couples of emotions involved in these data are complementary. Moreover, many other examples of complementary emotional observables can be provided from the relevant experimental data reported in the literature (for example, from the papers by Kassam and Mendes [14], Pauls and Stemmler [15] and by Sinha et al. [16]).

3 Complementary Physiological Observables

In the physiological domain, it seems that no data about successive measurements of quantities or measurements of quantities in different specified contexts (as is the case in Sect. 2) has been systematically reported. We will then use a theoretical method to define couples of complementary observables that generalizes the one which is used for defining conjugate observables in standard quantum theory (like position and momentum). The underlying idea is that conjugate *variables* of classical physics (like pressure and volume, pulsation and time,...) can be used to define complementary physiological *observables* because, as it can be shown, their measurements are *inter-dependent*. This method can be applied to several couples of cardiovascular observables that are involved in the relevant data.

Let us first give an example of conjugate variables that will be used hereafter to define complementary physiological observables. To say that the variables p (pressure) and v (volume) are conjugate variables in the thermodynamic description of any fluid means that they are always associated to each other, as a product of a generalized "force" (intensive variable) and a generalized "displacement" (extensive variable), in the calculation of the change of the internal energy of this system - as is also the case for the couples temperature/entropy and chemical potential/number of molecules:

$$d \, U \, = \, -p \, dv \, + \, T \, ds \, + \, \Sigma_i \mu_i dn_i \, + \ldots$$

Now, the couple of conjugate variables p, v can be used for defining conjugate cardiovascular observables in as much as they are involved in the definitions of the blood pressure and the stroke volume, which is the volume of blood pumped the heart in a cycle. These cardiovascular variables can be easily measured as shown by the relevant physiological studies and, particularly for our purpose, in many psychophysical studies (for example, see [12, 14–16]). The interdependency of the measurements of the blood pressure and the stroke volume in a cardiac cycle can be described as follows: To measure the volume of blood in a ventricle of the heart, we send ultrasounds on it (echography), which exert a pressure on this cavity and then change the blood pressure. Reciprocally, to measure the blood pressure, we change the blood flow by exerting a pressure on the arm's artery (by using a cuff filled with air and progressively emptied), which changes the volume of blood pumped by the heart.

This idea of interdependency of the measurement of physiological quantities can be implemented by defining complementary physiological observables acting on the physiological state space. Due to the fact that physiological quantities are continuous, this state space is here an infinite-dimensional complex Hilbert space H spanned by the vectors associated to the possible values (which are supposed non-degenerated) of all physiological quantities. The physiological state of a subject is represented by a unit vector of the state space H.

To implement the previous example, let us first define a *pressure observable*, which computes the blood pressure of the left ventricle of the heart of a subject in state |W > of H. This observable can be defined as:

$$< p \, | \mathbf{P}_{op} | \, W \, > \, =_{df} \, p < p \, | \, W \, >$$

in the "p-representation", that is, in the continuous basis $\{|p >\}$ of the eigenvectors of $\mathbf{P}_{op}$ associated with its possible values. A straightforward correspondence can be established between the expectation value of the pressure observable $\mathbf{P}_{op}$ and the systolic blood pressure (SBP), which is the maximal blood pressure that can be measured:

$$SBP = <\mathbf{P}_{op}>_{ED}$$

where ED, the end of diastole state, specifies the moment of the cardiac cycle when the blood pressure is at its maximum value.

Let us now consider a volume observable, defined as:

$$< v \,|\Delta\mathbf{V}_{op}\,|\, W > =_{df} (v - v_{ES}) < v \,|\, W >,$$

where v_{ES} is the end-systolic volume of the left ventricle of the heart (which is the minimal volume of blood in this ventricle). This observable measures the increasing in the volume of blood contained in this ventricle of the heart with respect to its minimal value v_{ES}. The interest of this definition is that the stroke volume (SV), which is the difference $(v_{ED} - v_{ES})$, is equal to the expectation value $< \Delta\mathbf{V}_{op} >$ of the observable $\Delta\mathbf{V}_{op}$ at the same end of diastole state:

$$SV = < \Delta\mathbf{V}_{op}>_{ED}.$$

To show the complementarity of $\mathbf{P}_{op}$ and $\Delta\mathbf{V}_{op}$, the pressure and volume observables, we have first to show that the p-representation $< p\,|W>$ and the v-representation $< v\,|W>$ of *any* physiological state $|W>$ are Fourier transforms. This can be done by noting that $< p\,|W>$ and $< v\,|W>$ are square-summable functions that admit (by Plancherel theorem) a Fourier decomposition. The phase of the harmonic functions evolved in these Fourier decompositions can be estimated, for a couple of blood pressure p and an additional volume Δv of the left ventricle of the heart, as the rate of p. Δv to its maximal value ΔU. The latter quantity ΔU is the mechanical work of the heart in a cycle when the temperature remains constant and no chemical reactions take place (which is indeed the case here). Due to homeostasis, ΔU can be considered as a constant for a given subject [17] and, taking into account that the right ventricle pressure is about seven time smaller than the systolic pressure SBP, it can be calculated as [18]:

$$\Delta U = 1.14\, SBP \times SV.$$

Consequently, one can write $< v\,|\,W>$ and $< p\,|\,W>$ as Fourier transforms:

$$< v\,|\,W> = (\varepsilon)^{-1/2} \int_p < p\,|\,W > \exp 2\pi i/\varepsilon\,(p.\,\Delta v)\,d\,p$$

$$< p\,|\,W> = (\varepsilon)^{-1/2} \int_v < v\,|\,W > \exp - 2\pi i/\varepsilon\,(p.\,\Delta v)\,dv,$$

where $\varepsilon = \Delta U\,/1.14$.

Taking now into account, from the expression of $< v\,|\,W>$ above, that $< v|p >$ can be computed as:

$$< v \mid p > \ = \ (\varepsilon)^{-1/2} \exp 2\pi i/\varepsilon \, (p. \, \varDelta v),$$

the action of the observable P_{op} in the v-representation can be computed as:

$$< v \mid P_{op} \mid W > \ = \ \int_p < v \mid p > \ < p \mid P_{op} \mid W > dp$$

$$= \ (\varepsilon)^{-1/2} \int_p p < p \mid W > \exp 2\pi i/\varepsilon \, (p. \, \varDelta v) \, dp.$$

In the right member of this equation one can recognize (to within a constant factor) the Fourier transform of $p < p \mid W >$, which is the derivative of $< v \mid W >$ regarding the variable v. Consequently:

$$< v \mid P_{op} \mid W > \ = \ -i \, \varepsilon \, \partial/\partial v \, < v \mid W >,$$

and then ΔV_{op} and P_{op} are conjugate observable:

$$[\varDelta V_{op}, \ P_{op}] \ = \ i \, \varepsilon \, \mathbf{Id},$$

their degree of incompatibility ε characterizing the cardiovascular cycle of the subject under consideration.

This method can of course be applied to other couples of conjugate physical variables that refer to complementary descriptions of a same physiological phenomenon, as is the case for the temporal and the spectral descriptions of the heart beat.

4   Conclusion and Prospects

This meta-analysis shows that the notion of complementarity can be implemented in psychophysics, regarding the subjective experience and regarding the physical description of the individual. Emotional, complementary observables have been defined by referring to experimental data on measurements of experienced emotions reported by subjects prepared in a given state of induced emotion. In the physiological domain, complementary observables corresponding to cardiovascular quantities can be defined by generalising the notion of conjugate observables in quantum mechanics. As has been mentioned, the few examples presented in this paper can be easily completed by considering several couples of psychological and physiological observables defined from other independent data, for example from those provided by Kassam and Mendes [14], Kriebig et al. [19], Paul and Stemmler [15] or Sinha et al. [16].

Beyond this conclusion, the possibility of defining couples of complementary psychological observables and complementary physiological observables paves the way for moving forward the difficult question of the nature of psychophysical correlations *on experimental grounds,* when the metaphysically-based strategies seem to lead to a dead end (see, for example, the analysis of Kim [20] or Esfeld [21]). This experimental test appeals to a statistical approach based on inequalities that generalize both Bell and Tsirelson inequalities. As explained by Uzan [11] from an idea originally suggested by Primas and Atmanspacher [22], the nature of the psychophysical correlations can be decided by comparing the CHSH correlation factor between couples of complementary psychological observables and complementary bodily observables with a signalling bound (which is a function of the commutators of the emotional and physiological observables) and with the Bell bound. This work can be achieved by referring to data such as those provided in the previously quoted articles, which report the change scores of cardiovascular variables of subjects experiencing emotional states. In particular, this approach could justify on experimental grounds that the psychophysical correlations are to be conceived of as relations of generalized entanglement. The work presented in this paper is then a first step for tackling the mind-body problem according to an approach which has never been applied in the field of psychophysics and can prove very fruitful.

References

1. Bohr, N.: Complementarity: bedrock of the quantal description. In: Kalckar, J. (ed.) Foundations of Quantum Physics II (1933–1958), Collected Works 7, pp. 284–285. Elsevier, Amsterdam (1996)
2. Bernays, P.: Uber die Ausdehnung des Begriffes der Komplementarit¨at auf ¨ die Philosophie. Synthese **7**, 66–70 (1948)
3. Atmanspacher, H.: Dual-aspect monism à la Pauli and Jung. J. Conscious. Stud. **19**(9–10), 96–120 (2012)
4. Atmanspacher, H., Römer, H., Walach, H.: Weak quantum theory: complementarity and entanglement in physics and beyond. Found. Phys. **32**, 379–406 (2002)
5. Atmanspacher, H., Filk, T.: The Necker-Zeno Model for Bistable Perception. Top. Cogn. Sci. **5**(4), 800–817 (2013)
6. Aerts, D., Gabora, L., Sozzo, S., Veloz, T.: Quantum structure in cognition. Fundam. Appl. arXiv:1104.3344v1 [cs.AI] (2011)
7. Busemeyer, J.R., Bruza, P.: Quantum Models of Cognition and Decision. Cambridge University Press, Cambridge (2012)
8. Primas, H.: Time-entanglement between mind and matter. Mind Matter **1**, 81–119 (2003)
9. Walach, H.: The complementarity model of brain-body relationship. Med. Hypothesis **65**, 380–388 (2005)
10. Walach, H., Römer, H.: Complementarity of phenomenal and physiological observables: a primer on generalised quantum theory and its scope for neuroscience and consciousness studies. In: Walach, H., Schmidt, S., Jonas, W.B. (eds.) Neuroscience, Consciousness and Spirituality. Studies in Neuroscience, Consciousness and Spirituality, vol. 1, pp. 97–107. Springer, Netherlands (2011)
11. Uzan, P.: On the nature of psychophysical correlations. Mind Matter **12**(1), 7–36 (2014)
12. Prkachin, K.M., Williams-Avery, R.M., Zwa, C., Mills, D.E.: Cardiovascular changes during induced emotion: an application of lang's theory of imagery. J. Psychosom. Res. **47**(3), 255–267 (1999)
13. Lang, P.J.: A bio-informational theory of emotional imagery. Psychophysiology **16**, 495–512 (1979)
14. Kassam, K.S., Mendes, W.B.: The effects of measuring emotion: physiological reactions to emotional situations depend on wether someone is asking. Plos One **8**(6), e64959 (2005)
15. Paul, C.A., Stemmler, G.: Repressive and defensive coping during fear and anger. Emotion **3**(3), 284–302 (2003)

16. Sinha, R., Lovallo, W.R., Parsons, O.A.: Cardiovascular differentiation of emotions. Psychosom. Med. **54**, 422–435 (1992)
17. Balaban, R.S.: Metabolic homeostasis of the heart. In: Perspectives on SGP Symposium on Mitochondrial Physiology and Medicine, 28 May 2012
18. Uehara, M., Koibuchi, S.K.: Thermodynamics of the Heart. In: Tadashi, M. (ed.) Application of Thermodynamics to Biological and Materials Science, InTech (2011)
19. Kreibig, S.D., Wilhelm, F.H., Roth, W., Gross, J.J.: Cardiovascular, electrodermal, and respiratory response patterns to fear- and sadness-induced films. Psychophysiology **44**, 787–806 (2007)
20. Kim, J.: Physicalism, or Something Near Enough. Princeton University Press, Princeton (2005)
21. Esfeld, M.: La philosophie de l'esprit. Armand Colin, Paris (2005)
22. Atmanspacher, H.: Mind and matter as asymptotically disjoint, inequivalent representations with broken time-reversal symmetry. BioSystems **68**, 19–30 (2003)

A Compositional Explanation of the 'Pet Fish' Phenomenon

Bob Coecke and Martha Lewis[✉]

Department of Computer Science, University of Oxford,
Parks Rd, Oxford OX1 3QD, UK
martha.lewis@cs.ox.ac.uk

Abstract. The 'pet fish' phenomenon is often cited as a paradigm example of the 'non-compositionality' of human concept use. We show here how this phenomenon is naturally accommodated within a compositional distributional model of meaning. This model describes the meaning of a composite concept by accounting for interaction between its constituents via their grammatical roles. We give two illustrative examples to show how the qualitative phenomena are exhibited. We go on to apply the model to experimental data, and finally discuss extensions of the formalism.

1 Introduction

A question in cognitive science is to characterise how humans understand expressions involving the composition of many concepts. The principle of semantic compositionality is often attributed to Frege, and is summarized by Kamp and Partee (1995) as follows:

> The meaning of a complex expression is a function of the meaning of its parts and of their syntactic mode of combination.

One approach to understanding the meaning of a complex expression is to model concepts as sets, and the meaning of a complex expression as determined by various operations on its parts. Some combinations of concepts such as 'red car' can be understood in this way, by taking the intersection of things that are red and things that are cars, whereas others such as 'red wine' cannot be characterised as a straightforward intersection, because red wine is not a standard red colour. This failure of concepts to behave conjunctively is showcased via the 'pet fish' problem, given in Osherson and Smith (1981) as a counterexample to a fuzzy set model of concepts. The problem is as follows. Concepts, as used by humans, are characterised as fuzzy sets, with the typicality of an item x to the concept L given by a membership function $m_L(x)$. A goldfish is considered not to be a very typical pet, nor a very typical fish, say $m_{pet}(goldfish) = m_{fish}(goldfish) = 0.5$. However the goldfish is a typical pet fish, say $m_{pet\ fish}(goldfish) = 0.9$. This contradicts rules of conjunction in fuzzy set theory, in which the membership

© Springer International Publishing Switzerland 2016
H. Atmanspacher et al. (Eds.): QI 2015, LNCS 9535, pp. 179–192, 2016.
DOI: 10.1007/978-3-319-28675-4_14

of an item in the intersection of two fuzzy sets is given by the minimum of its membership in either one. The phenomenon

$$m_{A \wedge B}(x) > \min(m_A(x), m_B(x))$$

is called *overextension* and

$$m_{A \vee B}(x) < \max(m_A(x), m_B(x))$$

underextension.

This and similar phenomena have been experimentally verified in Hampton (1988a; 1988b). The data collected is a series of typicality ratings for concepts and their combinations. Further evidence is reported in Hampton (1987), in which the importance of attributes in conjunctions of concepts is dependent on the importance of the same attributes in the conjuncts. In addition to the phenomena of over- and underextension, non-commutativity of membership in conjunctions is exhibited, together with attributes becoming more or less important depending on the order of combination. These phenomena are very puzzling if concepts are conceived of as fuzzy sets. Kamp and Partee (1995) themselves provide a thorough analysis of these phenomena, and propose a model which circumvents some of these problems. However, it is not able to account for the 'pet fish' phenomenon.

In order to solve the problems encountered by the fuzzy set theoretic view of concepts, quantum theory inspired models of concepts are developed in, amongst others, Aerts and Gabora (2005a; 2005b), Aerts et al. (2013), Pothos and Busemeyer (2012). These models view concepts as subspaces of a vector space. Similarity of one concept to another is measured by the projection of one concept onto another. The combination of two concepts is modelled as a tensor product. The 'pet fish' phenomenon then arises when the representation of the combined concept is entangled. The combination of more than two concepts may also be effected simply by taking the tensor product of the constituent concept spaces. These approaches, however, require that the representational space for a concept grows in size as more elements are added to the compound. This means that compounds will become unwieldy, and more importantly that compound concepts cannot be directly compared with their constituents.

It is then possible to investigate how well these models characterise human concept combination by examining the probability of agreeing with certain statements, or rating similarity between concepts. A review of such phenomena is given in Pothos and Busemeyer (2012). Data such as that collected by Hampton (1988a; 1988b) is argued to provide evidence for quantum structure in human thought (Aerts 2009), since the similarity ratings do not adhere to classical probability theory. This failure to adhere to classical probability theory is then termed 'non-compositionality'. However, whilst these approaches can provide a modelling of the data, they do not give an explanation of the fact that humans *do* successfully combine concepts. Further, the role of syntax is ignored. We will argue that the compositional nature of human thought can be explained, in a way that retains the qualitative phenomena discussed, and in a way that maps meanings to one shared space.

Clark and Pulman (2007) represent the meaning of words as vectors, and use the tensor product to combine words and their grammatical roles into sentences, using ideas developed in Smolensky and Legendre (2006). However, this again has the limitation, explicitly recognised, that sentences and words of different compositional types may not be compared. Coecke et al. (2010) in part inspired by the high-level description of quantum information flow introduced in Abramsky and Coecke (2004), utilise grammar in order to use composite spaces without increase in size of the resulting meaning space. This is the model that we will use to explain these compositional phenomena. The meaning of a composite concept, or a sentence, arises from the meaning of its constituents, mediated by grammar. This allows composite concepts to be directly compared with their constituents, and the meaning of sentences of varying length and type to be compared. In this paper we will apply this compositional distributional model of meaning to the 'pet fish' problem, and show how the qualitative phenomena of overextension and non-commutativity naturally arise - i.e., we show how a goldfish can be a good 'pet fish', even though it is neither a typical pet, nor a typical fish, and within this we also explain why a 'pet fish' is different to a 'fishy pet'. We provide a modelling of experimental data, and go on to discuss how a fuller account of human concept use will be developed.

The remainder of the paper is organised as follows. In Sect. 2, we describe the compositional distributional model of semantics. In Sect. 3 we describe how the 'pet fish' phenomenon may be modelled and give two illustrative examples. We go on to model experimental data in Sect. 4, and discuss the results and further work in Sect. 5

2   A Compositional Distributional Approach to Meaning

The account of meaning of Coecke et al. (2010), unifies compositional accounts of meaning, where the meaning of a sentence is seen as a function of the meanings of the individual words in the sentence, and distributional accounts of meaning, where the meaning of individual words are characterised as vectors. The main source of word meanings in distributional semantics is to derive word meanings from text corpora via word co-occurrence statistics and a review of techniques. Other methods for deriving such meanings may be carried out. In particular, we can view the dimensions of the vector space as attributes of the concept, and experimentally determined attribute importance as the weighting on that dimension. The compositional account and the distributional account are linked by the fact that they share the common structure of a *compact closed category*. This allows the compositional rules of the grammar to be applied in the vector space model to map syntactically well-formed strings of words into one shared meaning space.

In the remainder of this section, we firstly describe pregroup grammar, used for the compositional rules. We then how the reductions of the grammar may be mapped to finite dimensional vector spaces, and go on to give an example sentence reduction. We then describe a further type of structure, Frobenius algebras. These have been used to model information flow in sentences using relative pronouns such as 'which'. We may therefore use these structures to model the sentence 'pet which is a fish'.

2.1 Pregroup Grammars

In order to characterise the composition of concepts, the model uses Lambek's pregroup grammar (Lambek 1999). A pregroup $(P, \leq, \cdot, 1, (-)^l, (-)^r)$ is a partially ordered monoid $(P, \leq, \cdot, 1)$ where each element $p \in P$ has a left adjoint p^l and a right adjoint p^r, that is, the following inequalities hold:

$$p^l \cdot p \leq 1 \leq p \cdot p^l \quad \text{and} \quad p \cdot p^r \leq 1 \leq p^r \cdot p$$

The pregroup grammar then uses atomic types, such as n, s, their adjoints n^l, s^r..., and composite types which are forming by concatenating atomic types and their adjoints. We use the type s to denote a declarative sentence and n to denote a noun. A transitive verb can then be denoted $n^r s n^l$. If a string of words and their types reduces to the type s, the sentence is judged grammatical. The sentence 'James shoots pigeons' is typed $n \, (n^r s n^l) \, n$, and can be reduced to s as follows:

$$n \, (n^r s n^l) \, n \leq 1 \cdot s n^l n \leq 1 \cdot s \cdot 1 \leq s$$

However, this symbolic reduction can also be expressed graphically as follows:

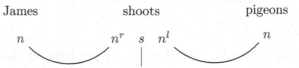

In this graphical representation, the elimination of types by means of the inequalities $n \cdot n^r \leq 1$ and $n^l \cdot n \leq 1$ is represented by a 'cup' while the fact that the type s is retained is represented by a straight wire.

2.2 Grammatical Reductions in Vector Spaces

We give here a brief description of how the reductions of the pregroup grammar may be mapped into the category of vector spaces. For full details, see Coecke et al. (2010).

The mapping uses the fact that both pregroups and vector spaces are instances of compact closed categories. We map the atomic types n, s of the pregroup grammar to vector spaces N, S. In the category of vector spaces over $\mathbb{R}$, only one adjoint N^* of N exists and it is isomorphic to N, and hence n^r and n^l also both map to V. Similarly s^r, s^l map to S.

The concatenation of types to form composites is mapped to the tensor product $\otimes$. So the sentence 'James shoots pigeons', is typed $nn^r s n^l n$ in the pregroup grammar, and is represented in the tensor product of vector space $N \otimes N \otimes S \otimes N \otimes N$.

The reductions $\epsilon^r : nn^r \leq 1$, $\epsilon^l : n^l n \leq 1$ are mapped to the linear extension to the tensor product of the inner product:

$$\epsilon : N \otimes N \to \mathbb{R} :: \sum_{ij} c_{ij} \overrightarrow{v}_i \otimes \overrightarrow{w}_j \mapsto \sum_{ij} c_{ij} \langle \overrightarrow{v}_i | \overrightarrow{w}_j \rangle$$

and type introductions $\eta^r : 1 \leq n^r n$, $\eta^l : 1 \leq nn^l$ are implemented as

$$\eta : \mathbb{R} \to N \otimes N :: 1 \mapsto \sum_i \overrightarrow{e}_i \otimes \overrightarrow{e}_i$$

These are all presented mathematically rigorously in Coecke et al. (2010) and an introduction to relevant category theory given in Coecke and Paquette (2011).

Now, individual words are assigned meanings within the vector space. This might be implemented via statistical analysis of text corpora, or attribute weightings elicited in an experiment. Nouns are represented as vectors in a single space N, whereas other word types are represented in larger spaces. For example, transitive verbs are typed $n^r s n^l$ and are therefore represented in the rank 3 space $N \otimes S \otimes N$. The reductions of the pregroup are implemented as inner products, and if the sentence is grammatical, one sentence vector $\overrightarrow{s} \in S$ should result. Meanings of sentences may then be compared by computing the cosine of the angle between their vector representations. So, if sentence A has vector representation $\overrightarrow{s}_A$ and sentence B has representation $\overrightarrow{s}_B$, their degree of synonymy is given by:

$$\text{sim}(A, B) = \frac{\overrightarrow{s}_A \cdot \overrightarrow{s}_B}{||\overrightarrow{s}_A|| ||\overrightarrow{s}_B||} \tag{1}$$

We now give an example sentence reduction.

An Example Sentence. To express the sentence 'James shoots pigeons', we firstly give types to the words in the sentence, so as before we have $n(n^r s n^l)n$. The reduction of the sentence is $\epsilon^r \otimes 1_s \otimes \epsilon^l$. Moving to the vector space, we represent nouns within a vector space N, sentences within a vector space S. A transitive verb is then represented in the tensor product space $N \otimes S \otimes N$.

So if we represent $\overrightarrow{shoots}$ by:

$$\overrightarrow{shoots} = \sum_{ijk} c_{ijk} \overrightarrow{e}_i \otimes \overrightarrow{s}_j \otimes \overrightarrow{e}_k$$

then we have:

$$\overrightarrow{\text{James shoots pigeons}} = \epsilon_N \otimes 1_S \otimes \epsilon_N (\overrightarrow{James} \otimes \overrightarrow{shoots} \otimes \overrightarrow{pigeons})$$

$$= \sum_{ijk} c_{ijk} \langle \overrightarrow{James} | \overrightarrow{e}_i \rangle \otimes \overrightarrow{s}_j \otimes \langle \overrightarrow{e}_k | \overrightarrow{pigeons} \rangle$$

$$= \sum_j \sum_{ik} c_{ijk} \langle \overrightarrow{James} | \overrightarrow{e}_i \rangle \langle \overrightarrow{e}_k | \overrightarrow{pigeons} \rangle \overrightarrow{s}_j$$

Strings of words may also reduce to other types, such as nouns. An adjective can be given the type nn^l, and then a phrase such as 'red car' is typed $nn^l n \leq n$. Another type of word that has been well studied is the possessive pronoun. In Sadrzadeh et al. (2013), the authors analyse the possessive pronoun as utilising a Frobenius algebra.

2.3   Frobenius Algebras

We state here how a Frobenius algebra is implemented within a vector space over $\mathbb{R}$. For a mathematically rigorous presentation see Sadrzadeh et al. (2013). A vector space V over $\mathbb{R}$ with a fixed basis $\{\vec{v}_i\}_i$ has a Frobenius algebra given by:

$$\Delta :: \vec{v}_i \mapsto \vec{v}_i \otimes \vec{v}_i \quad \iota :: \vec{v}_i \mapsto 1 \quad \mu :: \vec{v}_i \otimes \vec{v}_i \mapsto \delta_{ij} \vec{v}_i \quad \zeta :: 1 \mapsto \sum_i \vec{v}_i$$

This algebra is commutative, so for the swap map $\sigma : X \otimes Y \to Y \otimes X$, we have $\sigma \circ \Delta = \Delta$ and $\mu \circ \sigma = \mu$. It is also special so that $\mu \circ \Delta = 1$. Essentially, the μ morphism amounts to taking the diagonal of a matrix, and Δ to embedding a vector within a diagonal matrix. This algebra may be used to model the flow of information in noun phrases with relative pronouns.

An Example Noun Phrase. In Sadrzadeh et al. (2013), the authors describe how the subject and object relative pronouns may be analysed. We describe here the subject relative pronoun. The phrase 'James who shoots pigeons' is a noun phrase; it describes James. The meaning of the phrase should therefore be James, modified somehow. The word 'who' is typed $n^r n s^l n$, so the sentence 'James who shoots pigeons' may be reduced as follows:

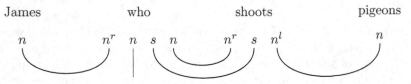

Sadrzadeh et al. (2013) go on to show that this may be reduced to

$$(\mu_N \otimes \iota_S \otimes \epsilon_N)(\overrightarrow{James} \otimes \overrightarrow{shoots} \otimes \overrightarrow{pigeons})$$

This gives the result:

$$\overrightarrow{James\ who\ shoots\ pigeons} = \overrightarrow{James} \odot (\underline{shoots} \times \overrightarrow{pigeons}) \qquad (2)$$

where $\underline{shoots}$ is a matrix representing the verb 'shoot', $\times$ refers to matrix multiplication and $\odot$ refers to elementwise multiplication.

We have given a brief overview of the key aspects of the model of meaning. These ideas will now be used to give an account of the 'pet fish' phenomenon, firstly by recognising that 'pet' in 'pet fish' functions as an adjective, and secondly by analysing the expression 'pet which is a fish'.

3   A Compositional Distributional Account of the 'Pet Fish' Phenomenon

We will use the compositional distributional model of meaning to give an account of the 'pet fish' problem. The fuzzy-set theoretical view of the problem sees the types of the words 'pet' and 'fish' as the same, namely that both should be viewed as nouns and the word 'pet fish' formed from their intersection. However, the word 'pet' in this context is undeniably an adjective. Within pregroup grammar, it is typed as nn^l, and therefore within the model, this is viewed as a matrix $\underline{pet} = \sum_{ij} p_{ij} \overrightarrow{e}_i \otimes \overrightarrow{e}_j$. The meaning of 'pet fish' is therefore

$$\overrightarrow{pet\ fish} = \sum_{ij} p_{ij} \overrightarrow{e}_i \langle \overrightarrow{e}_j | \overrightarrow{fish} \rangle$$

The problem is essentially that an item such as a goldfish may not be a typical 'fish', nor a typical 'pet', but a very typical 'pet fish'. To measure this within our model, we use the cosine similarity of meaning vectors $sim(\overrightarrow{A}, \overrightarrow{B})$ given in Eq. (1) as a proxy for typicality. We may justify this by remarking that typicality may be characterised as a function of similarity. Given two word vectors, e.g. $\overrightarrow{dog}$ and $\overrightarrow{pet}$, the vector representing 'dog' should have a higher similarity to the concept 'pet' than, for example 'spider' should, i.e. we should have:

$$sim(\overrightarrow{dog}, \overrightarrow{pet}) = \frac{\overrightarrow{dog} \cdot \overrightarrow{pet}}{||\overrightarrow{dog}|| ||\overrightarrow{pet}||}$$
$$> \frac{\overrightarrow{spider} \cdot \overrightarrow{pet}}{||\overrightarrow{spider}|| ||\overrightarrow{pet}||}$$
$$= sim(\overrightarrow{spider}, \overrightarrow{pet})$$

We now examine the effect of concept combination on cosine similarity, and see that the 'pet fish' phenomenon is reproduced.

3.1   Creating Adjectives

Adjectives, verbs, adverbs and various other grammatical types may be viewed as operators. An adjective, in particular, is a matrix in $N \otimes N$, and the application of an adjective to a noun within the framework is matrix multiplication of the noun by the adjective. It is simple to craft a matrix $\underline{pet}$ that transforms the vector $\overrightarrow{fish}$ such that:

$$sim(\underline{pet} \times \overrightarrow{fish}, \overrightarrow{goldfish}) > sim(\overrightarrow{fish}, \overrightarrow{goldfish})$$

where $\times$ refers to matrix multiplication.

However, this process may be simplified even further. Kartsaklis et al. (2013) characterise an n-ary operator by the sum of the words it takes as arguments.

For example 'pet' is $\sum_i \vec{n_i}$ where the $\vec{n_i}$ are words that co-occur with 'pet' such as 'dog', 'cat', 'spider' and so forth. Each word may occur more than once in this sum to give a frequency calculation. This gives a tensor whose rank is one less than the desired rank. Therefore, Kartsaklis et al. (2013) suggest expanding the rank using the Frobenius copy operator Δ. The meaning of an adjective-noun combination such as 'pet fish' may then be calculated as

$$\overrightarrow{\text{pet fish}} = \sum_{ij} p_{ij}\, \vec{e}_i \langle \vec{e}_j | \overrightarrow{fish} \rangle$$

If the Frobenius copy operation and the inner product are both carried out with respect to the same basis, we obtain

$$\overrightarrow{\text{pet fish}} = \overrightarrow{pet_{adj}} \odot \overrightarrow{fish_{noun}}$$

Although the vectors $\overrightarrow{pet_{adj}}$ and $\overrightarrow{pet_{noun}}$ are likely to be similar, they will not be identical. This allows the combinations 'pet fish' and 'fishy pet' to be different. We will see that this method of forming adjectives can reproduce the qualitative phenomena required, and it is notable that we can do this without expanding the rank of the data space.

Another way of expressing the combination of the two concepts 'pet' and 'fish' is by the extended 'fish which is a pet', or 'pet which is a fish'. In the experiments from Hampton (1987; 1988a; 1988b), this is how the two combinations are phrased. One of the key findings from these experiments was typicality of an item to each ordering is not identical. In order to express 'fish which is a pet', we use the verb 'to be' as a transitive verb. These are typed as $N \otimes S \otimes N$ and can also be expressed as a sum of their arguments, i.e. as $\sum_{ij} \vec{n}_i \otimes \vec{n}_j$ where $\vec{n}_i$ is the subject of the verb and $\vec{n}_j$ the object. Here we have discarded the sentence type S. In the treatment of the relative pronoun 'which', the sentence type is also discarded, and therefore the verb matrix can be used directly. We can express the combination 'fish which is a pet' analogously to the expression given in Eq. 2:

$$\overrightarrow{\text{fish which is a pet}} = \overrightarrow{fish} \odot (\underline{is} \times \overrightarrow{pet})$$

where $\underline{is}$ is the matrix of the verb 'to be'.

In the next section we show that these two methods of combination give us some of the qualitative properties we need for the 'pet fish' phenomenon.

3.2   Toy Model Using Adjective Vectors

This toy model applies the way of forming an adjective as a sum of noun vectors. Suppose that the nouns 'dog', 'cat', 'goldfish', 'shark', 'pet' and 'fish' have attribute weights as presented in Table 1. Each attribute is weighted as given by the entries in the table. These weights are hypothetical weights, but could be elicited from humans in an experiment, or from text corpora. We can form the adjective 'pet' by forming a superposition of 'dog', 'cat', and 'goldfish':

$$\overrightarrow{pet_{adj}} = \overrightarrow{dog} + \overrightarrow{cat} + \overrightarrow{goldfish} = [2.5, 0.6, 1, 1, 2.7]^\top$$

Table 1. List of concepts and attributes for adjective vector model

	Pet	Fish	Goldfish	Cat	Dog	Shark
Cared-for	1	0.2	0.7	0.9	0.9	0
Vicious	0.2	0.8	0	0.2	0.4	1
Fluffy	0.7	0	0	0.9	0.7	0
Scaly	0.2	1	1	0	0	1
Lives in the sea	0	0.8	0	0	0	1
Lives in house	0.9	0.3	0.9	0.9	0.9	0

Table 2. Cosine similarity for adjective vector model

	Goldfish	Cat	Dog	Shark
Pet (noun)	0.7309	0.9816	0.9809	0.1497
Fish	0.5989	0.2500	0.3292	0.9670
Pet (adj) fish	0.9377	0.5524	0.6197	0.5861

The cosine similarity of each animal to the nouns 'pet', 'fish', and 'pet fish' are shown in Table 2. The qualitative phenomenon that a goldfish is a better example of a pet fish than of either a pet or a fish is exhibited.

3.3   Toy Model Using Relative Pronouns

We give here a toy model for the composition of two concepts using Frobenius multiplication, and show that the qualitative attributes we require are exhibited. Suppose we again have attributes as listed in the rows of Table 1 for the concepts as given in the columns.

Weights for the matrix for the verb 'to be' are given in Table 3 below. These weights express the extent to which the attributes co-occur. For example, the extent to which something is vicious is also cared-for is given weight 0.02. We assume that the extent to which an attribute is itself, for example, the extent to which a vicious thing is vicious, is greater than the extent to which it is anything else. Hence the diagonal is emphasised. Ideally, the verb 'to be' would interact directly with the attribute space as does the relative pronoun, as this will form a future line of enquiry.

Using this representation of the verb 'to be' and the grammatical structure of relative pronouns, we have the following:

$$\overrightarrow{\text{pet which is a fish}} = \overrightarrow{pet} \odot (\underline{is} \times \overrightarrow{fish}) = [0.29, 0.18, 0.06, 0.22, 0.22, 0.35]^\top$$

and

$$\overrightarrow{\text{fish which is a pet}} = \overrightarrow{fish} \odot (\underline{is} \times \overrightarrow{pet}) = [0.23, 0.24, 0, 0.27, 0.27, 0.32]^\top$$

Table 3. Matrix of weights for the verb 'to be'

	Cared-for	Vicious	Fluffy	Scaly	Water	House
Cared-for	1	0.02	0.08	0.03	0.02	0.09
Vicious	0.02	1	0.05	0.06	0.05	0.02
Fluffy	0.08	0.05	1	0	0	0.09
Scaly	0.03	0.06	0	1	0.05	0.02
Lives in the sea	0.02	0.05	0	0.05	1	0
Lives in house	0.09	0.02	0.09	0.02	0	1

The similarity of each of the vectors for 'goldfish', 'cat', and 'shark' to the concepts 'pet', 'fish', 'pet which is a fish' and 'fish which is a pet' is given in Table 4. We see that the similarity of 'goldfish' to 'pet which is a fish' and 'fish which is a pet' is higher than its similarity to either 'pet' or 'fish'. In addition, similarity of each animal to 'pet which is a fish' is not identical to its similarity to 'fish which is a pet'.

Table 4. Cosine similarity for relative pronoun model

	Goldfish	Cat	Shark
Pet	0.7309	0.9816	0.1497
Fish	0.5989	0.2500	0.9670
Pet which is a fish	0.8999	0.7783	0.4467
Fish which is a pet	0.8898	0.6540	0.5730

4   Modelling Attribute Combination

In Hampton (1987), Hampton collects data on the importance of attributes in concepts and their combination. Concepts are considered in pairs that are related to some degree, for example 'Pets', and 'Birds'. Six pairs are considered in total, detailed below. Participants are asked to generate attributes for each concept and for their conjunctions, where conjunction in this case is rendered as 'Pets which are also Birds', or 'Birds which are also Pets'. For example, attributes such as: 'lives in the house', 'is an animal', 'has two legs', are generated for 'Pets', 'Birds'. For each pair of concepts and their conjunction, attributes that had been generated by at least 3 out of the 10 participants were collated. Participants were then asked to rate the importance of each attribute to each concept and to each conjunction. Importance ratings were made on a 7 point verbal scale ranging from 'Necessarily true of all examples of the concept' to 'Necessarily false of all examples of the concept'. Numerical ratings were subsequently imposed ranging from 4 to −2 respectively.

The question then arises of how the importance of attributes in the conjunction of the concepts is related to the importance of attributes in the constituent concepts. Key phenomena are that conjunction is not commutative, that inheritance failure can occur (i.e., an attribute that is important in one of the concepts is not transferred to the conjunction), that attribute emergence can occur, where an attribute that is important in neither of the conjuncts becomes important in the conjunction, and further, that necessity and impossibility are preserved. In order to model this data, Hampton uses a multilinear regression.

We use the importance values for each attribute and their conjunction to determine a set of weights for the verb 'to be', which, when substituted in to the phrase 'A which is a B', or 'B which is an A', provides the appropriate attribute weights. We require a matrix $\underline{is}$ such that:

$$\vec{A} \odot (\underline{is} \times \vec{B}) = \vec{AB}$$

and

$$\vec{B} \odot (\underline{is} \times \vec{A}) = \vec{BA}$$

where $\vec{AB}$ stands for the combination 'A which is a B' and vice versa. The importance values are rated on a scale $4, 3, 2, 1, -1, -2$. We map these into a $[0, 1]$ interval by $r \mapsto (r + 2)/6$, where r is the relevant rating.

To fit parameters, we use MATLAB's fmincon with the active-set algorithm and constraint that verb entries must be greater than 0. Results are reported in Tables 5 and 6. F-HA stands for 'Furniture and Household Appliances', F-P 'Foods and Plants', W-T 'Weapons and Tools', B-D 'Buildings and Dwellings', M-V 'Machines and Vehicles', B-P 'Birds and Pets'.

Table 5. Cosine similarity measure for multilinear regression (MLR) and for the compositional distributional (CD) model, for the ordering 'A which is a B'

Cosine similarity	F-HA	F-P	W-T	B-D	M-V	B-P
MLR	0.9905	0.9944	0.9791	0.9839	0.9948	0.9727
CD	0.9996	1.0000	0.9997	0.9996	1.0000	0.9999

Table 6. Cosine similarity measure for multilinear regression (MLR) and for the compositional distributional (CD) model, for the ordering 'B which is a A'

Cosine similarity	F-HA	F-P	W-T	B-D	M-V	B-P
MLR	0.9898	0.9965	0.9930	0.9945	0.9948	0.9673
CD	0.9997	1.0000	0.9996	0.9997	1.0000	0.9999

Modelling the combination of the pairs of concepts using the grammatical attributes of the phrase 'A which is a B' allows for a greater accuracy in modelling the conjunction. In the tables above, we have used the same matrix for the verb 'is' in each ordering. It is unsurprising that we are able to obtain a good fit to the data, since we are using k^2 weights in the verb 'to be' for $2k$ datapoints, and the results we show here are therefore not of any statistical significance. However, by using the verb 'to be' in this way, we are able to take account of how attributes interact with one another. Further work will examine how the matrices thus obtained reflect Hampton's findings regarding the necessity and impossibility of attributes, attribute emergence and inheritance failure.

5   Discussion

We have described a compositional distributional model of meaning (Coecke et al. 2010), which utilises grammar to describe how the meaning of a compound arises from the meaning of its parts. This account of meaning is inherently compositional, and importantly, the meanings of composites inhabit the same space as their constituents, so that the inner product may be used to compare concepts directly. We apply this model to the 'pet fish' problem, describing how the phrases 'pet fish' and 'pet which is a fish' may be modelled within the formalism, and giving two illustrative models which show how the qualitative phenomena are naturally produced. We go on to model a set of data from Hampton (1987). This highlights how attributes in concepts interact, via the verb 'to be'.

The approach we have outlined contrasts with approaches in the quantum cognition literature departing from an assumption of non-compositionality. The claim of non-compositionality in the literature refers to the fact that human concept combination and judgements cannot be modelled using classical probability. Instead, we take a semantic approach. Within the model of meaning that we describe, the meaning of a sentence is rendered as a vector. The meaning of individual words in the sentence or noun phrase are given by vectors or tensors, and a method for combining them is specified. We therefore view the meaning of a complex expression as being exactly specified by the meaning of its parts and of how they are combined. The 'non-compositional' phenomena described may well have a description that is compositional when both meaning and grammar are taken into account, and in particular we have argued that the 'pet fish' example may be viewed as compositional.

Further work will extend the account to other cognitive phenomena. We can straightforwardly apply the modelling of 'pet fish' to account for the conjunction fallacy Tversky and Kahneman (1983), since this is an example of overextension. Another oft-cited phenomenon is the asymmetry of similarity judgements (Tversky 1977), in which, for example, Korea is judged more similar to China than China is to Korea. There are two approaches we might take to modelling this. Firstly, as detailed in Coecke et al. (2010), we can choose a graded truth-theoretic space as the sentence space. Then, the sentence 'Korea is similar to China' can be modelled as mapping to a higher value than 'China is similar to Korea'.

Alternatively, a fuller account of the ways in which concepts interact can be developed. Whilst synonymy is useful as a proxy for membership, and of course in comparing meaning, we must develop measures that allow the description of various relationships between concepts. Balkır (2014) uses the non-symmetric measure of relative entropy to characterise hyponymy, which is related to the idea of membership in a concept. Hyponymy is a stricter notion than membership, however, and therefore we need to generalise this model. Other relationships are typicality and meronymy, where a concept forms part of another concept, such as 'finger' to 'hand'.

We will further investigate evidence for these type of phenomena in text corpora, and different ways of modelling adjectives. Given a large enough number of dimensions, it is possible to create a matrix for an adjective that can exactly recreate the meaning vector for an adjective-noun combination. It would be interesting to look at the existence of this type of phenomena when the context, as expressed by a choice of basis vectors, is specified, rather than being, for example, the most commonly used words in the corpus.

Another area for research is the interaction of ambiguous concepts. These ideas are investigated in Bruza et al. (2013), in which the authors elicit similarity judgements on novel combinations of ambiguous words such as 'apple chip' - here, 'apple' could be interpreted as either a fruit or a computer brand, and 'chip' as either food or hardware. The authors define non-compositionality as the failure of the interpretation of the combination of two concepts such as 'apple chip' to be modelled as a joint probability distribution over the interpretations of the two constituent concepts. Within the compositional distributional model of meaning that we have described, ambiguity in word meanings can be modelled by the use of density matrices, and this ambiguity interacts with other words in the sentence which may serve to disambiguate the word (Piedeleu et al. 2015) It would be interesting to model the phenomena found in Bruza et al. (2013) within this framework.

Finally, the role of the verb 'to be' should be investigated. This verb should have a functional role, as do relative pronouns, as well as a distributionally determined meaning.

Acknowledgements. Martha Lewis gratefully acknowledges support from EPSRC (grant EP/I03808X/1) and AFOSR grant Algorithmic and Logical Aspects when Composing Meanings. Many thanks to James Hampton for use of datasets.

References

Abramsky, S., Coecke, B.: A categorical semantics of quantum protocols. In: Proceedings of the 19th Annual IEEE Symposium on Logic in Computer Science (2004). ISSN 1043-6871. doi:10.1109/LICS.2004.1319636

Aerts, D., Gabora, L.: A theory of concepts and their combinations i: The structure of the sets of contexts and properties. Kybernetes **34**(1/2), 167–191 (2005a)

Aerts, D.: Quantum structure in cognition. J. Math. Psychol. **53**(5), 314–348 (2009)

Aerts, D., Gabora, L.: A theory of concepts and their combinations ii: a hilbert space representation. Kybernetes **34**(1/2), 192–221 (2005b)

Aerts, D., Gabora, L., Sozzo, S.: Concepts and their dynamics: a quantum-theoretic modeling of human thought. Top. Cogn. Sci. **5**(4), 737–772 (2013)

Balkır, E.: Unsing density matrices in a compositional distributional model ofmeaning. Master's thesis, University of Oxford (2014). URL http://www.cs.ox.ac.uk/people/bob.coecke/Esma.pdf

Bruza, P.D., Kitto, K., Ramm, B.J., Sitbon, L.: A probabilistic framework for analysing the compositionality of conceptual combinations (2013). arXiv preprint arXiv:1305.5753

Clark, S., Pulman, S.: Combining symbolic and distributional models of meaning. In: AAAI Spring Symposium: Quantum Interaction, pp. 52–55 (2007)

Coecke, B., Paquette, É.O.: Categories for the practising physicist. In: Matiyasevich, Y.V., Nerode, A. (eds.) LFCS 1994. LNCS, vol. 813, pp. 173–286. Springer, Heidelberg (1994)

Coecke, B., Sadrzadeh, M., Clark, S.: Mathematical foundations for a compositional distributional model ofmeaning (2010). arXiv preprint arXiv:1003.4394

Hampton, J.: Inheritance of attributes in natural concept conjunctions. Mem. Cogn. **15**(1), 55–71 (1987)

Hampton, J.: Overextension of conjunctive concepts: evidence for a unitary model of concept typicality and class inclusion. J. Exp. Psychol. Learn. Mem. Cogn. **14**(1), 12 (1988a)

Hampton, J.: Disjunction of natural concepts. Mem. Cogn. **16**(6), 579–591 (1988b)

Kamp, H., Partee, B.: Prototype theory and compositionality. Cognition **57**(2), 129–191 (1995)

Kartsaklis, D., Sadrzadeh, M., Pulman, S., Coecke, B.: Reasoning about meaning in natural language with compact closed categories and frobenius algebras. In: Chubb, A., Eskandarian, J., Harizanov, V. (eds.) Logic and Algebraic Structures in Quantum Computing and Information, Association for Symbolic Logic Lecture Notes in Logic. Cambridge University Press, New York (2013)

Lambek, J.: Type grammar revisited. In: Lecomte, A., Perrier, G., Lamarche, F. (eds.) LACL 1997. LNCS (LNAI), vol. 1582, pp. 1–27. Springer, Heidelberg (1999)

Osherson, D.N., Smith, E.E.: On the adequacy of prototype theory as a theory of concepts. Cognition **9**(1), 35–58 (1981)

Piedeleu, R., Kartsaklis, D., Coecke, B., Sadrzadeh, M.: Open system categorical quantum semantics in natural languageprocessing. In: CALCO 2015 (2015). arXiv:1502.00831

Pothos, E.M., Busemeyer, J.R.: Can quantum probability provide a new direction for cognitive modeling. Behav. Brain Sci. **36**(03), 255–274 (2012)

Sadrzadeh, M., Clark, S., Coecke, B.: The Frobenius anatomy of word meanings i: subject and objectrelative pronouns. J. Log. Comput. **23**(6), 1293–1317 (2013)

Smolensky, P., Legendre, G.: The Harmonic Mind: From Neural Computation To Optimality-theoretic Grammar (vol. 1 Cognitive Architecture). MIT Press, Cambridge (2006)

Tversky, A.: Features of similarity. Psychol. Rev. **84**(4), 327–352 (1977)

Tversky, A., Kahneman, D.: Extensional versus intuitive reasoning: the conjunction fallacy in probability judgment. Psychol. Rev. **90**(4), 293 (1983)

Social and Cultural Applications

Conceptual Machinery of the Mythopoetic Mind: Attis, A Case Study

Sándor Darányi[1]([⊠]) and Peter Wittek[1,2]

[1] University of Borås, Borås, Sweden
sandor.daranyi@hb.se
[2] ICFO-The Institute of Photonic Sciences, Barcelona, Spain

Abstract. In search for the right interpretation regarding a body of related content, we screened a small corpus of myths about Attis, a minor deity from the Hellenistic period in Asia Minor to identify the non-commutativity of key concepts used in storytelling. Looking at the protagonist's typical features, our experiment showed incompatibility with regard to his gender and downfall. A crosscheck for entanglement found no violation of a Bell inequality, its best approximation being on the border of the local polytope.

1 Introduction

With Ref. [1] now presenting "quantum information science" to the public, reporting on work in progress, below we look at two of the key phenomena of quantum mechanics (QM), noncommutativity and entanglement.

To contrast Refs. [2–4], Refs. [5] or [6]'s methodological claims, we are interested to find out if conceptual entanglement may be shown outside of a cognitively typical questionnaire or polling scenario, in our case, in classical narratives populating mythologies, with text variants considered as repeated measurements of the same experiment. One of the aforementioned pioneering efforts, Ref. [7] employed four concepts (horse, bear, tiger, cat) in the *Animal* category vs. four vocal reactions (growl, whinny, snort, meow) from the *Act* category to create examples of *The Animal Acts* predicate and have users rank the typicality of the resulting combinations. On the other hand, in the literary analysis we depart from, below we describe our subject matter, *The Protagonist Acts*, by means of a pair of logical oppositions, one pertaining to the gender of the hero, the other to his downfall. We will use a measurement apparatus akin to the Clauser-Horne-Shimony-Holt (CHSH) inequality as a decision criterion for detecting nonlocality.

The Protagonist Acts is a popular module used by several narrative genres for plot generation, from classical mythology over heroic legends to fairy tales, cartoons and beyond. The two major ways to formalize narration in the structuralist tradition are Refs. [8] and [9], with a possible middle-of-the-road approach provided by Ref. [10]'s monomyth theory, aided by a comprehensive motif inventory by Ref. [11], and a canonical tale type catalog by Ref. [12]. Taken together, these preliminaries necessitate a modelling approach which may or may not fall back on genomics [13].

© Springer International Publishing Switzerland 2016
H. Atmanspacher et al. (Eds.): QI 2015, LNCS 9535, pp. 195–206, 2016.
DOI: 10.1007/978-3-319-28675-4_15

In the current paper, we will focus on a different question though, looking at the type of the "conceptual glue" holding related content together, admittedly trying to go beyond standard statistical concepts, and will screen a small corpus of Hellenistic myths for order-dependent observations and possibly entangled concepts related to gender and destiny. We aim to demonstrate the following:

- Incompatibility of measurements, leading to noncommuting observations;
- As not all measurements are incompatible, we can partition them into commuting fractions. In the terminology of information theory, we can label the resulting two partitions as Alice and Bob. The measurements within a party do not commute, but they do so between the parties;
- In this setup, we try to demonstrate the violation of a Bell inequality, which would be a curious instance of superclassical correlations in the context of folklore research.

Below we are able to argue the noncommutativity of observations on the gender and destiny of Attis, but a Bell violation remains elusive.

2   Background

Mythology is a universal phenomenon in old cultures worldwide. For this paper, we define it as the first systematic attempt of thinking about the origins of the world and its beings, their existence and fate, told by series of stories in first oral, then written tradition. Typically, such considerations address creation in primordial times vs. legendary or prehistoric times from the vantage point of the storyteller, the first phase dealing with the divine aspect of things becoming, the second with their semidivine unfolding, due to heroes, tricksters and other kinds of mediators between heaven and earth.

Classical mythology refers to the often syncretic plethora of Greek and Roman stories about the gods, heroes and humans, including the origins of social institutions and moral conduct. As difficult as it is to assign a starting date to classical myths, with regard to the selected type of deity below, the so-called dying god, the concept could span a long period, e.g. from 3000 B.C. up to Hellenistic times, and cover an area much beyond classical Greece and the Mediterranean, including the Ancient Near East.

In this enormously big cultural space, over the millennia different interpretation attempts tried to come up with coherent explanations of mythic content. Their overview is the subject of many books, so let it suffice here to mention only a few prominent schools and their representatives in chronological order. We can distinguish between the allegorical theory from the ancient, in a sense leading to the symbolic theory through the Middle Ages and up till the 19th century; then again, rationalism and euhemerism in classical antiquity, to be followed by a theory of nature myths in the 19th century, itself based in then new comparative philology, leading to a spectrum of competing modern methods. These include e.g. the ritual school (e.g. Frazer, Harrison), the social study of myth (Durkheim, Mauss), the philosophy of symbolic forms and the myth of the state (Cassirer), psychological analysis (Jung, Hillmann), different directions in anthropology (Malinowski, Leach, Lévi-Strauss, Maranda), or the combination of structural anthropology with multivariate content analytics [14].

From our perspective, in what follows mythology will be a classification tool for the savage mind [15], using an attenuating series of logical oppositions to compromise between normative extremes by mediation, so that the process manifests itself as a chronological sequence of text variants of related but different content by different communities or authors. Thus whereas such variants are expected to "somehow" belong together and manifest a gradually progressing pattern of mythological text cycles organized between highly complex conceptual poles [16], the very nature of this "somehow" is a matter of investigation. Here, conceptual correlations are being considered as one particular type of intellectual linkage among text variants about the same gross topic, fertility, and discussing the same hero, Attis.

Once widespread in the Mediterranean and the Ancient Near East, the fertility myth is a symbolic prescription of how to restore individual and community welfare. Briefly, proper moral conduct being the key, disaster strikes due to ill behaviour or violation of social norms, whereas the role of the regulator (a male or female deity or a human, such as a sacred king or queen) is to remedy the insult to the supernatural, and thereby bring back fertility, an indicator if things are on the right track.

Lately we have shown how to insert narrative elements manifesting specific grammatical categories into the term and function slots of the canonical formula of myth proposed by Ref. [17], demonstrating its workings on a set of myths about flower heroes and minor deities from Ancient Greece and Asia Minor in the Hellenistic period [14]. These mythic actors belong to the family of *dying gods*, a category in comparitive religion whose presence and absence relates to the virulence and decay of e.g. vegetation, and in the broadest sense, fertility [18]. Our prime example for this treatise, the Phrygian Attis is one of them, being the consort of Cybele, the Magna Mater, a variant of the Mediterranean Great Goddess whose cult was imported to Rome in 205-204 BCE. The plot in shorthand is close to the Adonis myth: a youth either sacrifices his virility to the goddess or is punished by her to the same end, both outcomes leading to the restoration of natural and/or social well-being[1].

With Attis as our actor in *The Protagonist Acts* statement, we depart from the working assumption that this predicate contains the following mutually exclusive elements encoded in its state: [gender group: male, androgynous (= of double gender, bisexual), asexual] x [action modifier group: (indirect vs. direct)

---

[1] Stories about the fate of Attis, Adonis and other minor deities explain the origins of certain flowers and trees. However, the violet, the anemone, the hyacinth, the daffodil, or the pine tree have no agricultural significance, so one has to consider them as efforts to restore fertility on a more abstract level, such as invoking the arrival of spring or addressing the annual solar cycle. Social welfare as a concern is attested by the fact that Attis has an explicit cult, passed on between regional communities, finally imported to the capital of the empire.

vs. (self vs. not self)]. To wit, in the majority of available text variants, in the final chapter of his story Attis emasculates himself (direct self-mutilation [DS]); or they mutually castrate each other with his partner (not-direct self-mutilation [NDS]); alternatively he is killed by a spear or an unspecified wound on boar hunting (not-direct not-self-mutilation [NDNS], i.e. killing by accident or similar); and in some cases, it is the goddess who mutilates him (direct not-self-mutilation [DNS]).

Below we will focus on gender and downfall as measurements made by Alice and Bob, our two pieces of independent recording apparatus, so that their interpretation of the running text will play the role of the recorded values. The reason why interpretation matters is that these texts, considered as our corpus, are contradictory with regard to the outcome and therefore the general impression about the protagonist is that of ambiguity. In other words, with interpretation in the eye of the beholder, we do not expect individuals to come to the same conclusions. More detail about this is given below.

2.1 The Ambiguity About Attis

A typical plot of a flower aetiology myth, from Pausanias' *Description of Greece*, helps one understand the context where ambiguity regarding the protagonist's gender on corpus level renders his canonical interpretation difficult. The story originally seems to have followed a cyclic pattern, probably both symbolizing and reinforcing the annual cycle of the vegetation, starting with an androgynous or purely male donor who passed on the male principle to a female receiver, who in turn gave birth to, or became the origin of, another androgynous or male offspring, itself or himself the next donor. In Pausanias' reporting, respective subject-verb-object (SVO) propositions in active or passive voice for narration (i.e. for building concatenated statements) are as follows: Papas *drops* semen; semen is dropped (= falls) to earth = earth *absorbs* semen; semen *impregnates* Agdos; Agdos becomes = *bears* Agdistis; Agdistis *drops* virility; virility *impregnates* earth; earth *bears* tree; tree *drops* fruit; fruit *impregnates* Nana; Nana *bears* Attis; Attis *drops* virility; virility *impregnates* earth; earth *bears* flower. Here, Papas is the sky-god; earth is the Great Goddess, personified by the mountain Agdos; Agdistis is their androgynous offspring with an uncontrollable, devastating nature which needs to be "regulated"; and Nana is a sacred princess or a priestess, i.e. the personification of the Goddess with a penchant for unusual conception, at least from a human perspective. Tree, fruit and flower are variables that can take different values as the plot thickens.

With the number of surviving text variants somewhere between 20–25, of which we used 20 in the current attempt, given the above small cycle of myths about violating social norms and mending them by mutilation as a compensation for the crime, the first and strongest impression one is left with after having read them is that of confusion. Namely, in spite of the dramatic peak of the narrative culminating in his castration, the gender of the hero is sort of unstable, and seems to be oscillating between three alternatives out of four. The presentation of Attis as a male (in most of the sources), or an eunuch ("neither male nor female" in Hermesianax), is easy to document. Further, clearly, he cannot be a female, although implicit in the situation, the act of mutilation brings the state of the quasi-female dangerously close. But the missing link to understand the big picture in its complexity is the fourth alternative, the concept of divine androgyny, of Semitic origins [19, p. 218], which – in support of Rapp on Kybele in [20] – Hepding identifies with the tendencies of the Phrygian variant, and refers to the Neoplatonic speculations of Iulian for a parallel [19, p.212]. The other source who describes Attis as a hermaphrodite, i.e. a being of both genders, is Hippolytus.

In this androgynous context, castration or emasculation have several interpretations, one of them being a positive move toward the perfection of the Great Mother – a man who cannot become a woman can still go halfway by rendering himself a non-male. Another one is the punishment for abandoning chastity sworn to the deity, inducing some sort of an artificial replacement state by getting rid of sin. More importantly, this latter explanation has a second layer of meaning: losing one's virility is a prevention of creative excess aiming at male dominance, a kind of *hybris*. This perspective is familiar from the story of Aphrodite whose birth was a result from Ouranos' castration, caused by his unruly behaviour toward Gaia, i.e. his non-diminishing urge to procreate, apparently upsetting world order to that extent that Kronos had to intervene and tame the sky-god, or risk increasing disorder.

On the other hand, Gaia – another name for the Great Goddess – has the archaic capability of procreating "without sweet union of love" (i.e., by parthenogenesis), thus giving birth to Ouranos the sky, Pontos the sea and Ourea the mountains as the firstborn of the ancient deities (Hesiod *Theogony* 129–132). This capacity is also passed down to the dominant goddesses of the next two generations, first to Rhea, then to Hera[2]. However, such creative acts without male intervention imply another interpretation too, namely that the primordial goddess inherently possesses the male principle as well, hence her husband's or partner's redundancy, a rendering that brings us back to androgyny.

As we will see, these fragments are pieces of a puzzle that will become important below when we recognize in them the key to e.g. Iulian the Apostate's Gnostic explanation of Attis' role in the universe, one of our androgynous examples. The same holds for Hippolytus' account who refuted Gnostic heresies and thereby preserved for us a comparable story in shorthand. But before we proceed, it's time to explain how we want to check if conceptual entanglement or its components are present in our sample.

---

[2] Hera, queen of the gods, was outraged by Zeus' ability to procreate Athene by himself and, in revenge, she conceived the dragon Typhaon by hitting on the ground (*Homeric hymn to Apollon* 309). Flora, here Rhea's Latin equivalent, helped Juno, i.e. Hera, fall pregnant by touching her either with a magic herb (Festus Grammaticus 97), or a flower (Ovidius *Fasti* 5, 229), both being parallels to Nana's miraculous pregnancy by an almond. Out of this fatherless conception resulted the monstruous Ares, i.e. Mars, the god of war.

3   Measurements in the Context of Mythological Texts

If we aspire to study classical and potentially nonlocal correlations in myths, we must consider the act of text interpretation – a.k.a. hermeneutics – as measurement. Just like no incompatibility or entanglement has ever been detected without measuring some system properties beforehand, no interpretation can result without having read the text first.

3.1   Material and Method

The following sources were consulted: Pausanias *Description of Greece* VII, 17; Hermesianax in Pausanias VII, 17, 9; Herodotus *History* I, 34–45; Lucianus *De Dea Syria* c. 15; Arnobius *Adversus Nationes* V, 5; Diodorus *Bibliotheca Historica* III, 58; Ovidius *Fasti* IV, 221; Fulgentius *Mitologiarum Libri* III, 5; Minucius Felix *Octavius* 22; Servius *Scholia ad Aeneidem* IX, 115; Arnobius' Source 2 (Valerius Pontifex in Hepding 1903:118); Iulianus *Orationes* V; Sallustius *De Diis et Mundo* 4; Hippolytus *Refutation of All Heresies* 5; Theophilus of Antioch *To Autolycus* 8; Eusebius of Caesarea *Praeparatio Evangelica* II, 43; Clemens Alexandrinus *Exhortation to the Heathen* 2; Tatian *Address to the Greeks* 8; Augustine *City of God* 6, 7; and Catullus 63. Tertullianus and Valerius Flaccus were left out this comparison because they have information about the gender of Attis only but not his downfall.

To decide if incompatibility can affect such feature-based measurements, we designed a limited set of scenarios for texts with multiple possible interpretations in our sample. These texts were Servius, Herodotus, Iulianus and Hippolytus. After preliminary screening, we focused on the scenario where Attis' gender was androgynous in heaven and male on earth, as in the Gnostic accounts[3], whereas the type of downfall was concurrently DNS (antagonist harms protagonist) and NDS (antagonist and protagonist mutually harm each other).

Based on the sample, we shall be working toward a Bell scenario which means that one party will have two two-output measurements, whereas the other party has two three-outcome measurements. In doing so, for transparency reasons, we recall the following line of thought in our experiment design:

– Texts which contain conflicting information about gender and downfall seem to suggest that incompatibility is to be associated with the reader and not the text. However, on one hand, with the number of available variants strictly limited, one cannot exclude such sources without weakening the statistical basis of findings. On the other hand, incompatibility – just like any conceptual content – is in the eye of the beholder, as texts do not contain concepts, only their written imprint which resonates in the reader in unspecified ways.

---

[3] The underlying assumption here is that two text variants with contradictory content may have merged into a syncretic new one from a historically more complex perspective. This is why, in spite of the mutually exclusive gender features, we did not decompose such texts into shorter hypothetic fragments but retained them as they were for analysis, thereby violating the exclusiveness assumption.

Incompatibility as we base it on the act of interpretation is the sum total of respective decisions of the observer, i.e. the result of measurement, but this interpretation depends on the occurrence of certain concepts in the text;
- In experimental tests of the Bell inequalities a key issue concerns the "fair sampling" assumption. Essentially this presupposes that the detected events constitute an unbiased sample of the particles emitted. For the analysis of text variants one would need to assume firstly that writers are no more likely to record versions of the myth that contain certain features, and that texts containing certain features are no more likely to have survived, because if e.g. authors preferred to record versions of the myth where Attis was male, or these versions were somehow more likely to have survived, this would change the analysis.

But what does an unbiased sample mean with respect to mythology? For one thing, the size of the set is constant because those who could have penned down new conceptual variants are all dead. Also, we can assume that no new versions will surface (unless a new Nag Hammadi library will be found etc.). On the other hand, one cannot make sure whether any of the recorded variants had preferences for gender or downfall at the time of being written up, although it's fair to suspect that authors had certain belief systems they contrasted with the by then recorded beliefs to take a stance. But this is a situation one cannot help, not even on the level of speculation. So one could suggest that this could be a potential problem of sampling *after* one had proven that the bias was there at the time of recording, which is absolutely impossible, a limitation of the method we must be aware of.

3.2   Incompatibility

Interpretation is always a matter of preconception. In our case, stories about Attis are contradictory as a corpus because of uncertainties about his gender, leaving room for speculations. And nowhere else more so than in Iulian's text which now placates him as probably androgynous, then elsewhere as predominantly male. Which communication shall we believe? What we hope to show is that it depends on the different impressions one gains by looking for one or the other alternative in the first place. This assumes ambiguous episodes in the narratives, hence we depart from Ref. [21].

Our first aim will be to demonstrate that these two measurements do not commute. In the language of information theory, let us now focus on one party first, Alice. As said, she has two two-output measurements, so one measurement means a pair of oppositions. A simple setup, for instance, is the following (Table 1):

- Alice's first measurement ($x = 0$): male ($a = 0$) or not male ($a = 1$);
- Alice's second measurement ($x = 1$): androgynous ($a = 0$) or not androgynous ($a = 1$).

Since female never occurs in any of the text variants, we can regard the not male as meaning eunuch.

Table 1. Distribution of measurements.

	Alice's measurements				Bob's measurements					
	Measurement 1 ($x = 0$)		Measurement 2 ($x = 1$)		Measurement 1 ($y = 0$)			Measurement 2 ($y = 1$)		
	Male	Not male	Androgynous	Not androgynous	DS	DNS	Neither	NDS	NDNS	Neither
	$a = 0$	$a = 1$	$a = 0$	$a = 1$	$b = 0$	$b = 1$	$b = 2$	$b = 0$	$b = 1$	$b = 2$
a = Hermesianax in Pausanias VII, 17,	0	1	0	1	0	0	1	0	1	0
b = Herodotus I, 34-45	1	0	0	1	0	1	0	1	0	0
c = Lucianus De Dea Syria c.15	1	0	0	1	0	1	0	0	0	1
d1 = Pausanias VII, 17	1	0	0	1	1	0	0	0	0	1
d2 = Arnobius Adversus V, 5	1	0	0	1	1	0	0	0	0	1
e = Diodorus Biblioth. Histor. III, 58	1	0	0	1	0	1	0	0	0	1
f = Ovidius Fasti IV, 221	1	0	0	1	1	0	0	0	0	1
g1 = Fulgentius Mitol. III, 5	1	0	0	1	0	1	0	0	0	1
g2 = Minucius Felix Octav. 22	1	0	0	1	0	1	0	0	0	1
h = Servius Schol. ad Aen. IX, 115	1	0	0	1	1	0	0	1	0	0
i = Arnobius' Source 2 (Valerius Pontif.)	1	0	0	1	1	0	0	0	0	1
j1 = Iulianus Orat. V	1	0	1	0	1	0	0	0	0	1
j2 = Sallustius De Diis et Mundo c.4	1	0	0	1	1	0	0	0	0	1
k = Hyppolitus Refutation of all Heresies	1	0	1	0	0	1	0	0	0	1
l = Theophilus of Antioch to Autolycus	1	0	0	1	1	0	0	0	0	1
m = Eusebius Praeparatio Evangelica	1	0	0	1	0	1	0	0	0	1
n = Clemens Alexandrinus Exhortation	1	0	0	1	0	1	0	0	0	1
o = Tatian Address to the Greeks 8	1	0	0	1	0	1	0	0	0	1
p = Augustine City of God 6, 7	1	0	0	1	0	1	0	0	0	1
r = Catullus 63	1	0	0	1	1	0	0	0	0	1

Starting with clues which present Attis as a man will reinforce this impression by a number of references in the text, and somehow downplay the other option. Likewise, looking for androgyny will result in an impression of the same structure, i.e. belief vs. disbelief. However, our point is that the proportions of the two downplayed alternatives will be different, and this difference cannot be traced back anywhere else but to the context, i.e. the sequence of measurements invoking non-commutativity. In this sense, we postulate that conceptual incompatibility comes with the coexistence of conflicting interpretations pertaining to the same source, and the dominant impression is proportional to the respective occurrences of the rival concepts – if we focus on the androgynous features first, and find e.g. 2 of them, whereas for a next step Attis' male nature is recorded e.g. 19 times, then 2/19 expresses something about this impression. In reverse order, 19/2 would state our confidence about Attis being a man rather than someone of a double nature.

Demise of the hero is another aspect of the narrative where incompatibility seems to be at work. To show this, we define two three-output measurements as follows:

– Bob's first measurement ($y = 0$): direct self ($b = 0$), direct not-self ($b = 1$), or neither ($b = 2$).
– Bob's second measurement ($y = 1$): not-direct self ($b = 0$), not-direct not-self ($b = 1$), or neither ($b = 2$).

E.g. in Herodotus, Attis is killed by Adrastos' spear in a hunting accident, who in turn kills himself on his grave. Depending on where we want to lay stress, one can read this as mutual downfall of an accidental protagonist and his like antagonist where the other and the self are just aspects by which death arrives; or one can focus on the self in the suicide and the other in the accident as key aspects, rendering both involuntary downfalls as secondary. Hence both, contradictory readings must be recorded for measurements. Not much different is the text of Servius: there, Attis is a youth who flees his king, the antagonist willing to rape him, but they end up in castrating each other. To commemorate her hero, the Magna Mater orders his priests to ritually mutilate themselves. Without this rite as the conclusion of the story, the protagonist and antagonist mutually harming each other is the single outcome; however, with the rite, an alternative is to stress the voluntary self-punishment aspect repeated annually at the summer solstice. Again, we have to record both contradictory interpretation options.

4 Studying Correlations

Our argument for the availability of a Bell test is that given a single narrative (or a set of narratives) with two typical elements, e.g. gender and downfall, in a time-like separation scenario, their correlation can be detected, i.e. we realize that these elements co-occur in the same story or corpus, alongside the same plot. Space-like separation here means that we assume two single concept queries, Alice and Bob, with no feedback between them. This, of course, has no physical

204   S. Darányi and P. Wittek

meaning. It simply means that the information about gender has no influence on information about downfall. A retrieved concept is represented by a group of two logical oppositions, each of which are manifest by a set of related terms. Alice and Bob's measurements on their separated concepts will reveal by their joint probabilities if the concepts are linked in a way beyond simple term-level co-occurrence.

Therefore to study correlations between Attis' gender and his demise, we treat the two-party measurements as a Bell scenario. Alice has a pair of two-output measurements, whereas Bob has a pair of three-output measurements, so we can briefly write this as a $[(2\ 2)\ (3\ 3)]$ scenario. This is clearly different from the CHSH test, which is $[(2\ 2)\ (2\ 2)]$. As Ref. [22] proved, the two correspond to the same polytope, the $[(2\ 2)\ (3\ 3)]$ scenario is a lifting of the CHSH case. With the measurement distribution given in Table 1, we perform an analysis of the CHSH inequality.

Since in the Collins-Gisin notation we can ignore one output, we have a certain degree of freedom in choosing which outputs we include in the Bell test. We choose $a = 0$ from $x = 0$, $a = 1$ from $x = 1$, $b = 1$ from $y = 0$ and $b = 1$ from $y = 1$. While this choice is arbitrary, a Bell violation would show in any choice of outputs from the measurements. The joint probabilities $p(ab|xy)$ are given in Table 2.

With this configuration, we find a value of 2.0 for the inequality, which indicates no violation, but the observed correlations are on the margin of the local polytope.

Table 2. Joint probabilities of the measurements

		$x = 0$	$x = 1$
	1	0.95	0.05
$y = 0$	0.5	0.5	0
$y = 1$	0.05	0	0.05

5   Conclusion and Future Research

On a collective level, myths are classificatory structures, using a system of logical oppositions. The prevalence of opposites indicates the possibility for conceptual entanglement in general. The current case study has shown the noncommutativity of observations on the gender and destiny of Attis, but a Bell violation remained elusive. This may go back to an incomplete working hypothesis, the sample size, the odd nature of the current data – some options e.g. "not male" or "NDNS" almost never appear –, or a combination thereof. In spite of its expected increase in complexity, the results presented here pave the way for an extended case study with more actors and types of action where we plan to compare more sophisticated interpretation scenarios.

Further, a challenging implication of Ref. [23] adds a new perspective to looking for entanglement in myths as follows:

- Classical mythology stopped to evolve, so for an external observer with an external measurement device, two concepts inside the system may appear as dislocated yet the same, with no metric differences a.k.a. change between them, being entangled;
- For a parallel observer inside the system, who measures evolution in terms of two entangled concepts with regard to the rest of the universe, the same two concepts are perceived as dislocated, with metric differences, change and chronology separating them;
- Occasionally both observation modes may be available to the mind, perhaps related to subjective vs. objective experience.

Acknowledgement. This project has received funding from the European Union's Seventh Framework Programme for research, technological development and demonstration under grant agreement no FP7-601138 PERICLES. PW would like to thank Alexia Salavrakos for the discussions on Bell inequalities. The authors are grateful to two unknown reviewers plus Roger Pearse's blogs on antiquity and his links to translations. http://www.roger-pearse.com/weblog/ Other classical sources were used from the Perseus Digital Library. http://www.perseus.tufts.edu/hopper/.

Dedicated to the memory of Hugo Hepding (1878–1959), classical philologist, ethnographer and librarian.

References

1. Bawden, D., Robinson, L., Siddiqui, T.: "Potentialities or possibilities": towards quantum information science? J. Assoc. Inf. Sci. Technol. **66**(3), 437–449 (2015)
2. Aerts, D., Aerts, S., Broekaert, J., Gabora, L.: The violation of Bell inequalities in the macroworld. Found. Phys. **30**(9), 1387–1414 (2000)
3. Aerts, D., Gabora, L.: A theory of concepts and their combinations I: the structure of the sets of contexts and properties. Kybernetes **34**(1/2), 151–175 (2005)
4. Aerts, D., Gabora, L.: A theory of concepts and their combinations II: a Hilbert space representation. Kybernetes **34**(1–2), 192–221 (2005)
5. Aerts, D., Broekaert, J., Sozzo, S., Veloz, T.: Meaning – focused and quantum – inspired information retrieval. In: Atmanspacher, H., Haven, E., Kitto, K., Raine, D. (eds.) QI 2013. LNCS, vol. 8369, pp. 71–83. Springer, Heidelberg (2014)
6. Aerts, D., Sozzo, S.: Entanglement zoo I: foundational and structural aspects. In: Atmanspacher, H., Haven, E., Kitto, K., Raine, D. (eds.) QI 2013. LNCS, vol. 8369, pp. 84–96. Springer, Heidelberg (2014)
7. Aerts, D., Sozzo, S.: Entanglement zoo II: examples in physics and cognition. In: Atmanspacher, H., Haven, E., Kitto, K., Raine, D. (eds.) QI 2013. LNCS, vol. 8369, pp. 97–109. Springer, Heidelberg (2014)
8. Propp, V.: Morphology of the Folktale. University of Texas Press, Austin, TX, USA (1968)
9. Lévi-Strauss, C.: Structural Anthropology. University of Chicago Press, Chicago, IL, USA (1983)

10. Campbell, J.: The Hero With a Thousand Faces, vol. 17. New World Library, Novato (2008)
11. Thompson, S.: Motif-Index of Folk-Literature, pp. 1–6. Indiana University Press, Bloomington (1958)
12. Uther, H.: The Types of International Folktales: A Classification and Bibliography Based on The System Of Antti Aarne and Stith Thompson. Academia Scientiarum Fennica, Helsinki, Finland (2004)
13. Ofek, N., Darányi, S., Rokach, L.: Linking motif sequences to tale type families by machine learning. In: 4th Workshop on Computational Models of Narrative Proceedings of CMN-13 (2013)
14. Darányi, S., Wittek, P., Kitto, K.: The Sphynx's new riddle: how to relate the canonical formula of myth to quantum interaction. In: 7th International Quantum Interaction Symposium Proceedings of QI-13, pp. 47–58 (2013)
15. Lévi-Strauss, C.: Mythologiques I-IV. Plon, Paris, France (1964–1971)
16. Darányi, S.: Formal aspects of natural belief systems, their modelling and evolution: a semiotic analysis. Semiotica 108(1), 45–63 (1996)
17. LéviStrauss, C.: The structural study of myth. In: Sebeok, T.A. (ed.) Myth: A Symposium, pp. 50–66. Indiana University Press, Bloomington (1965)
18. Frazer, J.: The Golden Bough: A Study in Magic and Religion. A Touchstone Book. Simon & Schuster, New York (1995)
19. Hepding, H.: Attis: seine Mythen und sein Kult.J. Ricker'sche Verlagsbuchhandlung (Alfred Töpelmann) Gieszen (1903)
20. Roscher, W.: Ausführliches Lexikon der griechischen und römischen Mythologie: Laas - Myton. Number 2. k. Teubner (1993)
21. Bruza, P., Woods, J.: Quantum collapse in semantic space: interpreting natural language argumentation. In: 2nd International Symposium on Quantum Interaction Proceedings of QI-08, Oxford, UK (2008)
22. Pironio, S.: All clauser-home-shimony-holt polytopes. J. Phys. A Math. Theoret. 47(42), 424020 (2014)
23. Moreva, E., Brida, G., Gramegna, M., Giovannetti, V., Maccone, L., Genovese, M.: Time from quantum entanglement: an experimental illustration. Phys. Rev. A 89(5), 052122 (2014)

Preventing (Another) Lubitz:
The Thermodynamics of Teams and Emotion

W.F. Lawless[(⊠)]

Augusta, GA 30901, USA
w.lawless@icloud.com

Abstract. We propose a series of metrics enacted with Artificial Intelligence (AI) based on quantum mechanics (e.g., the substitution of interdependence for entanglement), entropy (e.g., the maximum random exploration of solution spaces for maximum entropy production, or MEP) and biology (e.g., in Hilbert space, counting neutral voters as entangled agents that produce limit cycles). Once humans teach a team of machines to perform at a level that meets human expectations, the computational team will also know how its human supervisors are supposed to perform. What happens once the machines discover that their human counterparts can make human mistakes is becoming an area of research. Most accidents are caused by human error, including malfeasance, incompetence and, as in the case of Lubitz, murder. The idea for our application is built around a computational model of emotion. Assuming the lowest state for a well-performing team is its ground state, elevated states can be labeled as emotional states to serve as a team metric. For co-pilot Lubitz who purposively flew his Germanwings aircraft into the Alps to murder his passengers, contradicting the prevailing view that little can be done to prevent other pilots with malevolent aims, an opportunity for an intelligent AI system to take temporary command of a distressed crew aboard an aircraft, overseen perhaps by air controllers on the ground, might be able to prevent similar tragedies. But the case of Lubitz is more general and widespread than addressing a miscreant; e.g., inattentive submarine commanders; human error with automobiles; overloaded crews at sea.

1 Introduction

A great puzzle in social science is the failure of rational models of teamwork, a rising concern for AI researchers. Social learning theory (i.e., rewards and punishments; associations; modelling) works partially with individuals, but not with teams. These theories of methodological individualism, including game theory, have also failed to advance the field of economics. To address interdependence, the phenomenon central to teamwork, we offer an alternative theory composed of: quantum mathematics for interdependence (e.g., interference); biology for population effects (e.g., N counts); and min-max entropy production for a metric of team performance (with minimum entropy production as LEP, and maximum entropy production as MEP). Based on interdependence, we report on three mathematical breakthrough applications: First, that the interdependence between an individual's observations and actions, once measured,

H. Atmanspacher et al. (Eds.): QI 2015, LNCS 9535, pp. 207–215, 2016.
DOI: 10.1007/978-3-319-28675-4_16

breaks intuition, leading to the measurement problem of incompleteness, accounting for the failure of survey instruments to predict human action; second, that at the team and larger levels of analyses, the ill-effects on min-max entropy production from consensus-seeking rules and authoritarian leadership suppress the search for solutions to the problems that teams seek to solve; and third, that with LEP as a team's ground state, as a team's entropy production elevates from internal conflict, intelligent decisions are precluded, an opening for AI.

To achieve robust intelligence [26], earlier we concluded that two teams competing against each other are required to best determine the reality of a situation (i.e., situational awareness). But we also concluded that mobile neutrals are necessary to determine the ultimate decisions, power and outcomes of teams, firms and organizations. We review both conclusions herein.

To offset the entropy produced as a byproduct of their activities, teams and firms require free energy [34]; teamwork can husband or squander free energy resources, but when successful, can multiply them. If searches of social reality were rational, a model of team thermodynamics would have been discovered long ago. However, teams are interdependent systems [10], interdependence creates observational uncertainty [26], and its measurement collapses it to create belief incompleteness.

Multitasking (MT) is the function of individuals willing to pool their skills to accomplish the goals they are unable to accomplish as individuals (e.g., [3]). MT invokes an interdependence among the members of a team, until now a hindrance [21] or too difficult to conceptualize [2]. In information theory [10], interdependence detracts from organizational performance. And unable to resolve the persistent gap he had found among preferences and choices in games, Kelley [20] abandoned game theory in experimental social psychology. For Big data, interdependence increases uncertainty and measurement generates incompleteness ([27], p. 6). Theoretically, MT is usually considered to be an individual skill; however, individuals multitask poorly [22]. Teams have traditionally been organized around a division of labor. But this overlooks the large benefits that can be derived from multitasking [4]. Talented humans will always be able to intuit most of the organizational decisions necessary to self-organize multitasking for a business. We attribute the "division of labor" approach to a simpler era; in contrast, MT remains an unsolved theoretical problem. But unless scientists can construct valid mathematical models of teams governed by interdependence to produce predictable results, computational teams of multi-agents will always be ineffective, inefficient, conceptually incomplete, or all three.

Assuming that interpretations of reality are generally stable and accessible (i.e., two tribes agree that a waterfall exists at coordinate x,y), [32] extended Conant's ideas on interdependence from information theory into a model of "Team Efficiency". But interdependence means that social reality is unstable. Interdependence creates alternate perspectives; free speech encourages adherents to compete for their beliefs [17] or policies; e.g., per Justice Ginsburg [14], "… as with other questions of national or international policy, informed assessment of competing interests is required".

Game theory does not support the value of competing interests for social welfare (e.g., competition is devalued in the Prisoners Dilemma Game [38]), precluding validation likely because these models do not model social reality, conceded by its strongest adherents [35]. Despite this disconnect with reality, Rand and Nowak ([35], p. 413) concluded that cooperation produces the superior social good, a conclusion widely accepted by social scientists, a conclusion contradicted by the non-experimental evidence.

For example, by comparing night-time satellite photos to see the social well-being in competitive South Korea compared to its lack under the cooperation brutally enforced by the leaders of North Korea [26], our theory has led us to conclude that, rather than a hindrance, interdependence is a resource that societies facing competitive pressures exploit with MT to self-organize teams to solve intractable problems, reduce corruption and make better decisions. The key to exploiting interdependence is to construct centers of competition, like Google and Apple, Democrats and Republicans, or Einstein and Bohr. These centers generate the information that societies exploit to better organize themselves, be it for competition among politicians, sports teams, businesses, or entertainment. As proof, often the first action by authoritarians or gangs is to suppress opposing conflict centers on the way towards the suppression of many forms of expression and activity among its people (e.g., China; Russia; and Cuba).

The belief in the ubiquitous value of cooperation has led to strange bedfellows. Consensus-rules (CR) govern many of the decision processes used by the ruling levels of the Communist Chinese party [33]; gangs [26]; and the National Academy of Sciences (NAS; e.g., dels.nas.edu/global/Consensus-Report). CRs attempt to increase information by reducing the barriers to participation in a discussion among the parties to a decision [12], but at the expense of failing to compete for the best available argument [25]. There are several weaknesses with CR decisions: they place weaker arguments on an equal footing with stronger ones, negating tests of the strength of the ideas in play; they increase the likelihood of mistakes; and they allow minorities to block progress on reaching decisions. The EU rejected the pernicious nature of CR [28]. Borrowed from James Madison [29], we have relabeled CRs as "minority" rules. Nonetheless, cooperation internal to teams is vital when faced with well-defined problems (e.g., sports); but when faced with ill-defined problems like politics or science, the conflict from competition can produce more creative solutions [16].

We go much deeper to understand why game theorists take strong exception to competition by rejecting its value to free societies. We believe the reason that most scientists are unable to readily "see" the root of the MT problem and its solution is that human behavior operates in a physical reality socially reconstructed as an illusion of a rational world [1]. That is, the brain has a sensorimotor system independent of vision ([36]; we use independent to mean a correlation of zero), the two working interdependently to create what appears to be a "rational" world, but is actually bistable [26], meaning that as an individual focuses on improving one aspect of, say action (e.g., skills), its observational uncertainty increases. A meta-analysis [18] supports our hypothesis that the relationship between self-reported scales of ability with actual ability is poor. Similarly, [5] found only a poor association between the views of the managers of businesses and the actual performance of their businesses.

The interdependence between team members allows us to sketch mathematically how the tools of entropy production may be deployed in a model of teams and firms to construct metrics of performance.

2   Mathematical Model

2.1   Mathematical Model of Behavior and Beliefs

From [3], teams form to solve the problems that the same collection of individuals performing the identical actions cannot solve. Firms form to produce a profit [7]; but stabilized once they produce more social benefits than costs [8].

But the mathematics that follow are counterintuitive for individuals because thinking rationally is a convergence process. We combine quantum mathematics (matrix algebra of two community operators that convert into Fourier pairs to account for the incompleteness of situational awareness; from [9]); uncertainty relations (information flow in orthogonal models of teams; from [13]); and biology (the movement of individuals between different teams can be tracked with limit cycles in Lotka-Volterra type equations; from [31]). The results are metrics that, in the limit, represent LEP [34] and MEP [30].

Given that observation and motor activities are controlled in the brain by independent systems (i.e., zero correlations), assume that human behavior occurs in physical reality, while observations are reconstructed as interpretations (e.g., beliefs; from [2]; or mistakes; from [15]). Assume that the beliefs of human agents when challenged cause oscillations (Fig. 1).

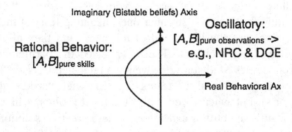

Fig. 1. The x axis displays real behavior while the imaginary axis displays the social reconstruction of reality. Agreement among opposing teams produces no oscillation. The two end points for imaginary beliefs reflect oscillatory dynamics (e.g., rules in 2005 to govern the Nuclear Regulatory Commission's oversight of the Department of Energy's High-Level radioactive Waste tank closures led to endless debates from about 2007-2011 until citizens recommended that the tanks be closed; in [25]).

2.2   Mathematical Model of Bistability

Bistable interdependence occurs between action and observation, and between competing claims. Socially reconstructed reality is challenged by those with competing interests, causing social dynamics [26].

We model bistability with Fourier pairs applied to two operators, A and B, to represent competing tribes. When two erstwhile competitors agree, no oscillations exist (the goal of an autocracy), and their operators commute:

$$[A, B] = AB - BA = 0 \tag{1}$$

But with disagreement between two competitors, the operators do not commute (i.e., their eigenvalues are not equal), indicating orthogonality, causing oscillations:

$$[A, B] = iC \tag{2}$$

where C measures the "gap" with rotational distance in reality between A and B. As MT improves, the tradeoffs internal to each group's focus on tasks interferes with the bistable interpretation of how best to further improve performance, motivating tradeoffs. From [9], Eq. (2) becomes (3):

$$\sigma_{A(skills)} \sigma_{B(interpretations)} \geq \frac{1}{2} \tag{3}$$

Where $\sigma_{A(skills)s}$ is the standard deviation of variable A over time, $\sigma_{B(interpretations)}$ is the standard deviation of its Fourier transform, the two forming a Fourier pair that reflects tradeoffs between the physical reality of skills and the social interpretation of situations. For example, from Eq. (3), as uncertainty in a team's or firm's skills decrease (e.g., improved MT skills), uncertainty in its interpretations increase (i.e., poorer situational awareness), requiring that a team engage a relatively dispassionate observer as a coach to address its problems.

Equation (2) captures social disagreement (e.g., political, judicial, scientific), but insufficiently for social dynamics. If all individuals are committed to one side or the other, conflict ensues [23]. We claim that neutrals can enter into a state of interdependence with both sides, akin to quantum entanglement, allowing neutrals to process both sides of an issue. Neutrals not only moderate conflict, they often decide elections [26]. If true, the competition for them generates limit cycles modeled with Lotka-Volterra-type equations (see Fig. 2).

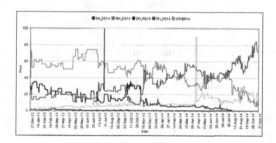

Fig. 2. Results of the recently complete race to control both Houses of Congress. Notice the primary limit cycles (red and green curves) from about mid-November 2013 to mid-July 2014. We claim that predictions made during this time when interdependence governs were unrealistic. Once neutrals have made a decision, here post mid-July 2014, predictions became credible [19] (Color figure online).

2.3   Mathematical Model of Social Uncertainty

Today, well-known in the engineering community, ([9], p. 45) proposed the following uncertainty principle for signal detection that a (see Fig. 3): ... narrow waveform [time] yields a wide [frequency] spectrum, and a wide waveform [time] yields a narrow [frequency] spectrum and that both the time waveform and frequency spectrum cannot be made arbitrarily small simultaneously.

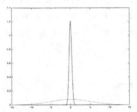

Fig. 3. The wide Gaussian is Fourier transformed from the narrow one. While the Standard deviation for the latter is 0.33, that for the wide one has increased to about 5.0; the two multiplied together roughly constitute a constant value greater than 1/2.

As an example of skills coupled to a lack of awareness that supports bistability, firms like Arthur Anderson, the auditor of Enron in 2000, missed the collapse of a business they were auditing; KPMG has been accused of having repeated this mistake [26].

3   Entropy Production and Multitasking

Like entanglement at the quantum level, interdependence reduces the degrees of freedom (dof) in a social group (Kenny et al., 1998). Given ρ, for interdependence (Eq. 4, below):

$$\rho = \frac{(\text{MS}_{GT} - \text{MS}_{SGT})}{\text{MS}_{GT} + (N - 1)\text{MS}_{SGT}} \tag{4}$$

MS_{GT} is the sum of the mean squares on a measurement of a factor, T, that is a group's focus as it assigns roles to produce MT; MS_{SGT} is the aggregated contribution from the individuals on a measurement of factor T; and N represents the number of members in a group being measured (from [21], p. 235). At one extreme, ρ ranges to -1 as MT goes to zero when the group is replaced by a collection of independent individuals; or to +1 as MT replaces the individuals with subservience to a team, like groupthink.

Less degrees of freedom (*dof*) reduces entropy; if a team reduces the *dof* among its members, setting Boltzman's constant k to 1 gives

$$\log(dof_{Teammates}) \leq \log(dof_{\sum Individuals}) \tag{5}$$

Assuming that when a set of tasks performed by the least number of individuals forms a complete circuit (or complete network graph) to MT (for a restaurant, assume this means five individuals: a waiter, cook, dish washer, cashier and manager; similar arguments can be made for autonomous multi-UAVs), then a group is converted into a team with the least entropy (LEP).

Balch (in [26]) used low information entropy as a principle for multi-agent teams. But he overlooked the interdependence involved in MT. Guided by Balch that three slaves make a unit group, log 3/3 = 0; from him, three independent individuals give an entropy of 3*1/3 log 1/3 = 1.584. In contrast, using graph theory [37], we calculate that a team of independent individuals interdependently completing a circuit to allow the team to MT, like the different roles played by the independent members of a baseball team, gives LEP [34].

Returning to Eq. (3), we revise it to give us the standard deviation of LEP times the standard deviation of MEP. Taking limits, as σ_{LEP}- > 0, we find in the limit that lim $(\sigma_{MEP}) = \infty$. This result means that as teamwork improves to a maximum, i.e., as entropy for a structure to support teamwork goes to zero, MEP reaches a maximum. In other words, at MEP, the best teams are able to perform a maximum search of the environment for solutions to difficult problems, our second novel application.

Moreover, as σ_{LEP}- > ∞ in reverse, σ_{MEP}- > 0, unexpectedly reinforcing our second novel technique. It means that as teamwork becomes dysfunctional, possibly due to the zealous enforcement of consensus rules or authoritarianism, problem solving tasks cease. This accounts for the Department of Energy's use of ordinary cardboard boxes as its primary disposal container of solid radioactive wastes until the whistle was blown on it in 1983 ([24]; see Fig. 3); it accounts for the environmental problems in China [26]; and it accounts for the inability of youth in gang controlled areas to flourish in school. For example, using patent applications over the last thirteen years (the data is from USTPO, in [26]), we looked at Israel's applications filed in the US with whether or not it was experiencing an Intifada (-1), peace (0) or hostilities (+1), finding a significant correlation (r = 0.53, p <.05, two-tailed test), suggesting that internal conflict (Intifada) reduces MEP (Fig. 4).

Fig. 4. As an example of the suppression of the practice of science, a picture from DOE of its disposal of most of its solid radioactive weapons wastes in cardboard boxes, a daily practice until about 1985 [24].

4 Conclusions

For future research, if the minimum state for an optimal team forming a circuit is LEP, then LEP is a team's ground state, allowing it to generate MEP as a result. On the other hand, if, for example, in a conflict between a pilot and the co-pilot, both partners are placed into an elevated or "excited state" that can be measured by the entropy produced, MEP reduces to zero. Working backwards from this answer means that the team's LEP goes to a maximum as internal conflict forces a team to splinter. In business, the result is like the 300 stores that Sears plans to spinoff (Kapner & Dulaney, in [26]); in city government, it's a bankrupt Detroit [11]; in Palestine, it's an internal battle for control (e.g., [6]); and in the recent air crash by Libutz, it was a case of murder that AI may have been able to avoid or moderate. Should a case similar to that of Libutz re-occur and if an AI system can place an airplane into a safe mode, possibly overseen by human controllers on the ground, then the AI system should be allowed to takeover the aircraft at least temporarily.

If our model is successful, we expect that AI can be used to model the satisfactory performance of human and artificial teams, giving society a significant tool to intercede when the human operators of machines, automobiles, submarines or even airliners are out of control.

References

1. Adelson, E.H.: Lightness perceptions and lightness illusions. In: Gazzaniga, M. (ed.) The New Cognitive Sciences, 2nd edn, pp. 339–351. MIT Press, Cambridge (2000)
2. Ahdieh, R.G.: Beyond individualism and economics. Accessed 12 May 2009 ssrn.com/abstract = 1518836
3. Ambrose, S.H.: Paleolithic technology and human evolution. Science **291**, 1748–1853 (2001)
4. Bartel, A., Cardiff-Hicks, B., Shaw, K.: Compensation Matters: Incentives for Multitasking in a Law Firm, NBER Working Paper No. 19412 (2013)
5. Bloom, N., Dorgan, S., Dowdy, J., Van Reenen, J.: Management practice and productivity. Quart. J. Econ. **122**(4), 1351–1408 (2007)
6. Casey, N.: Gaza Explosions Hit Senior Fatah Members Homes. Blasts Rekindle Tensions Between Two Main Palestinian Political Factions Wall Street Journal. (2014, 11/7) http://online.wsj.com/articles/gaza-explosions-hit-senior-fatah-members-homes-1415356232?mod=WSJ_hps_sections_world
7. Coase, R.: The nature of the firm. Economica **4**, 386 (1937)
8. Coase, R.: The problem of social costs. J. Law Econ. **3**, 1–44 (1960)
9. Cohen, L.: Time Frequency Analysis. Prentice Hall, Upper Saddle River (1995)
10. Conant, R.C.: Laws of information which govern systems. IEEE Trans. Sys. Man Cybern. **6**, 240–255 (1976)
11. Editorial Board (EB) Detroit's Fight Against Blight. New York Times (2014, 6/7). http://www.nytimes.com/2014/06/08/opinion/sunday/detroits-fight-against-blight.html?_r=0
12. Fiore, S.: Why the Science of Team Science Matters: The Evidence and a Path Forward, Science of Teams Science (SciTS), Austin (2014, 8/6)

13. Gershenfeld, N.: The Physics of Information Technology. Cambridge University Press, Cambridge (2000)
14. Ginsburg, R.B.: Justice High court throws out states climate lawsuit, Wash. Post (2011, 6/20)
15. Graziano, M.S.A.: Consciousness and the Social Brain. Oxford University Press, Oxford (2013)
16. Hackman, J.R.: Six common misperceptions about teamwork. Harvard Business Review (2011). blogs.hbr.org/cs/
17. Holmes, O.W.: Dissent: Abrams v. United States (1919)
18. Zell, E., Krizan, Z.: Do people have insight into their abilities? a metasynthesis? Perspect. Psychol. Sci. 9(2), 111–125 (2014)
19. IEM chart (2014). https://iemweb.biz.uiowa.edu/graphs/graph_Congress14.cfm)
20. Kelley, H.H.: Lewin, situations, and interdependence. J. Soc. Issues 47, 211–233 (1992)
21. Kenny, D.A., Kashy, D.A., Bolger, N.: Data analyses in social psychology. In: Gilbert, D.T., Fiske, S.T., Lindzey, G. (eds.) Handbook of Social Psychology, 4th edn, pp. 233–265. McGraw-Hill, Boston (1998)
22. Wickens, C.D.: Engineering Psychology and Human Performance, 2nd edn. Merrill, New York (1992)
23. Kirk, R.: More terrible than death. Massacres, drugs & America's war in Columbia, Public Affairs (2003)
24. Lawless, W.F.: Problems with military nuclear wastes. Bull. At. Scientists 41, 38–42 (1985)
25. Lawless, W.F., Akiyoshi, M., Angjellari-Dajcic, F., Whitton, J.: Public consent for the geologic disposal of highly radioactive wastes and spent nuclear fuel. Int. J. Environ. Stud. 71(1), 41–62 (2014)
26. Lawless, W.F., Moskowitz, I.S., Mittu, R., Sofge, D.A.: Thermodynamics of teams: towards a robust computational model of autonomous teams. In: Proceedings AAAI Spring 2015, Stanford University (2015)
27. Llinas, J.: Reexamining information fusion–decision making inter-dependencies. In: Presented at the IEEE CogSIMA Conference, TX (2014)
28. WP.: White Paper. European governance (COM (2001) 428 final; Brussels, 25.7.2001). Brussels, Commission of the European Community (2001)
29. Madison, J.: Federalist paper No. 58 (1787–1978) http://thomas.loc.gov/home/histdox/fed_58.html
30. Martyushev, L.M.: Entropy and entropy production: old misconceptions and new breakthroughs. Entropy 15, 1152–1170 (2013)
31. May, R.M.: Stability and Complexity in Model Ecosystems. Princeton University Press, Princeton (1973/2001)
32. Moskowitz, I.S., Lawless, W.F., Mittu, R.M., Russell, S., Hyden, P.: A network science approach to entropy and training, foundations of autonomy, stanford. In: Proceedings AAAI Spring 2015 (2014)
33. White, L.T.:. Unstately power. Local causes of China's intellectual, legal, and government reforms. Sharpe, NY (1998)
34. Nicolis, G., Prigogine, I.: Exploring C Complexity. Freeman, Newyork (1989)
35. Rand, D.G., Nowak, M.A.: Human cooperation. Cogn. Sci. 17(8), 413–425 (2013)
36. Rees, G., Frackowiak, R., Frith, C.: Two modulatory effects of attention that mediate object categorization in human cortex. Science 275, 835–838 (1997)
37. Smith, J.: Personal communication. July 2014
38. Schweitzer, F., Fagiolo, G., Sornette, D., Vega-Redondo, F., Vespignani, A., White, D.R.: Economic networks: the new challenges. Science 325, 422–425 (2009)

Ideologies and Their Points of View

Kirsty Kitto[1](✉) and Dominic Widdows[2]

[1] Queensland University of Technology, Brisbane, Australia
kirsty.kitto@qut.edu.au
[2] Microsoft Bing, Bellevue, USA

Abstract. It is well known that different arguments appeal to different people. We all process information in ways that are adapted to be consistent with our underlying ideologies. These ideologies can sometimes be framed in terms of particular axes or dimensions, which makes it possible to represent some aspects of an ideology as a region in the kind of vector space that is typical of many generalised quantum models. Such models can then be used to explain and predict, in broad strokes, whether a particular argument or proposal is likely to appeal to an individual with a particular ideology. The choice of suitable arguments to bring about desired actions is traditionally part of the art or science of rhetoric, and today's highly polarised society means that this skill is becoming more important than ever. This paper presents a basic model for understanding how different goals will appeal to people with different ideologies, and thus how different rhetorical positions can be adopted to promote the same desired outcome. As an example, we consider different narratives and hence actions with respect to the environment and climate change, an important but currently highly controversial topic.

1 A Clash of Ideologies

Climate change is a hotly debated and disputed topic in the United States, Australia, and several other countries. For example, at the beginning of April 2015, the President of the USA gave a speech connecting climate change to personal health [7], while on the other hand, the Treasurer of the state of Wisconsin [14] led an initiative to ban employees of the Board of Commissioners of Public Lands from discussing climate change. Taken out of context, such headlines might be quite surprising: for example, if the purpose of the Wisconsin ban is really (as claimed by its supporters) to prevent employees from wasting time on non-work-related activities, one would expect other topics to be explicitly banned in a similar manner, or at least, one would expect a quantitative demonstration that discussing climate change was an especially large drain on the resources of the Board in question.

In context, however, such speeches and decisions make much more sense. Politics generally tends to bundle issues together into platforms, and these are often associated with political parties: that is, issues become partisan. The US provides a particularly extreme example right now. There are a great range of divisive political issues currently under debate, including climate change, gun control, abortion, foreign relations, even the legality or otherwise of refusing to

© Springer International Publishing Switzerland 2016
H. Atmanspacher et al. (Eds.): QI 2015, LNCS 9535, pp. 216–227, 2016.
DOI: 10.1007/978-3-319-28675-4_17

sell a wedding cake, and whether the actions of an elected official are scandalous or business-as-usual. The surprising thing is that on most or all of these issues, it is expected that knowing whether someone is 'liberal or conservative', or 'Democrat or Republican' will predict their position with considerable accuracy. Not all issues are polarised in this fashion: for example, some anti-vaccination advocates take their stance because they believe the government should not be able to coerce parents (a belief associated more with some Republicans), whereas some anti-vaccination advocates take their stance because they believe that vaccines are chemicals and chemicals are typically harmful (a belief associated more with some Democrats). However, on many if not most issues, party-political polarisation has become normal.

Of course, two-party political systems are especially prone to such rivalry, so in this case they are particularly obvious. However, identity and ideology guide many other decisions and actions in our daily lives, often in a much more subtle fashion. The purpose of this paper is partly to analyze some of these phenomena, and partly to propose ways forward, or recognize the ways others have already proposed. In broad strokes, successfully persuading someone to believe something to which they are ideologically opposed is usually futile. If a theist or an atheist tries to persuade (respectively) an atheist or theist to believe something different, this usually results not in any change of mind, but in a reinforced belief that theists/atheists are typically intolerant and won't leave others in peace.

Instead, a more useful alternative is often to propose actions that are entirely consistent with an individual's current ideology, and also work towards a common objective. In many walks of life this is already obvious. Businesses want to increase revenue, but will not try to convince their customers that giving them money is a good thing: instead, they will try to assure customers that their products are desirable and money-well-spent. There is no ideological disagreement here, the participants simply have different roles and interests. However, as issues become more ideological, people often want to 'win the argument', even as (ironically) the chances of this become smaller and smaller. These are precisely the sort of situations where seeking common-ground which is *away from* the theatre of conflict can be most effective.

In the rest of this paper, we will describe some of the current scientific literature around the framing of ideologies and how these affect which new information is accepted and which decisions are taken. Some of this literature already uses spatial models with different conceptual axes. This lends itself naturally to a representation of the "common ground" idea, as new axes are introduced. This method follows the same pattern as the Purposeful Choice model of Widdows [19], but as well as adding objective axes to represent desired states or goals, we also add rhetorical positions to suggest arguments that may be persuasive to different individuals in reaching these goals.

2   Framings in Society

In society, ideologies often arise as a product of group-membership. The benefits of gathering together in groups are well-known, for example, in the *Descent of Man*, Darwin wrote:

All animals living in a body, which defend themselves or attack their enemies in concert, must indeed be in some degree faithful to one another; and those that follow a leader must be in some degree obedient. [4, Ch. 4]

Darwin goes on to describe many of the animal and human behaviors that arise from this principle, including various forms of empathy, conscience, remorse, avoiding shame and seeking praise. Most of Darwin's examples pertain to action rather than belief, but others have applied such rules of group membership to study beliefs as well, for example, Braman et al. state that:

Given how much the ordinary individual depends on peers for support — material and emotional — and how little impact his beliefs have on the physical environment, he would likely be best off if he formed risk perceptions that minimized any danger of estrangement from his community [12].

This connection between belief and belonging is already ancient. A particularly strong example is found in some western monotheist religions, where belonging to a religious group is identified with 'sharing a faith'. Such shared understandings are particularly powerful, the group is a hard thing to leave.

Psychology has adopted these notions using two key concepts: framings and ideologies. A *frame* is a perspective or context within which a concept is understood. One of the best understood examples of framing stems from the work of Tversky and Kahneman [17], who showed that asking the same question can lead to significantly different responses when it is framed in a positive or negative light. Stronger still, an *ideology* could be thought of a frame that a person acquires as they grow up. Ideologies are generally thought of as fixed, meaning that they do not change very much once they are acquired, through inheritance, culture, and experience. In what follows we shall focus upon one conceptualisation of an ideology, the grid group framework that was proposed by Douglas [5] and Wildavsky [20].

3   A Case in Point: Skepticism About Climate Change

While much of the work in QDT considers idealised or simple cases, it could have very real relevance in our understanding of many modern global problems, a number of which have become highly polarising [12]. Scientific facts are being re-framed according to the preferences of individuals in specific ideological groups, and this can result in vastly different understandings about the risks associated with issues like climate change, vaccinations, drugs, and environmental damage. These debates have led to a cynicism about whether it is possible to shift attitudes and opinions towards a public consensus about how we should act in the face of increasing societal challenges. Is a shared understanding of the risks associated with these problems even possible?

Some recent studies have started to create hope that a re-framing of these social debates could be achieved, and lead to outcomes that are more consistent with the findings of science about "what needs to be done". For example, Bain et al. [3] provide an example where the long running debate surrounding climate change belief or disbelief is reframed. They show that when asking a person about their intention to act in a way that might mitigate the climate change problem, framing it in three different ways can have a significant effect. Thus, climate change deniers stated that they intended to act in a manner that was more environmentally friendly when they were asked about this intended action within the context of two alternative frames that centred around forming a society that was: (i) more considerate and caring; or (ii) more economically and technologically developed. These results were demonstrated over two different studies, with N = 155 and N = 347 climate change skeptics.

Another study by Kahan et al. [10] tested a two-channel communication strategy where scientific information (channel 1) was combined with cultural meanings (channel 2) in a two-nation (United States, n = 1,500; England, n = 1,500) study. While the scientific information was held constant, the cultural meaning of it was manipulated. This led to a finding that the standard cultural polarisation about climate change science could be decreased by exposing subjects to information about geoengineering. Interestingly, this study found that subjects exposed to information about geoengineering were more concerned about climate change risks than a control group.

Finally, Kitto et al. [13] have reported an order effect, where re-framing a question about climate change belief by asking questions about scientific and political belief first appears to decrease the likelihood of people denying that climate change is happening, and increase the likelihood of people claiming that it is happening (admittedly with a small sample of climate change skeptics).

These are highly interesting effects. Much of the literature to date has tended to demonstrate that climate change belief is driven by underlying cognitive ideologies, and is not amenable to change. Thus, Kahan et al. [12] demonstrates the manner in which increasing science literacy actually serves to polarise a nationally representative population from the United States, along what are basically progressive and conservative lines. Of particular note, this study demonstrates that those who deny that human-induced climate change is occurring become even stronger in their disbelief as they become more educated (similarly, believers become stronger in their belief as they become more educated). Such an observation contradicts the ongoing assumption that "if we only had more data people would believe us". In fact, more data is likely to induce a greater level of disbelief for someone who has an ideology that is hostile to climate change science.

4   A Subspace Model of Ideologies and Points of View

The work discussed above [6, 13, 15] suggests that multiple factors lead to skepticism about climate change. However, when coupled with the work of Bain et al. [3] we see that the understanding an individual expresses about an issue can perhaps be shifted when the point of view from which they are considering

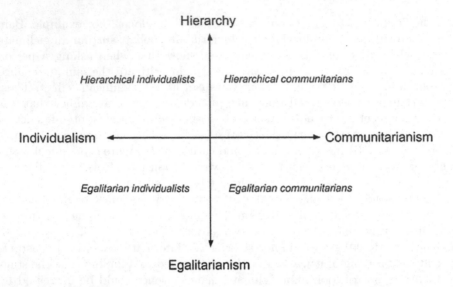

Fig. 1. The grid-group framework proposed by Douglas [5] and Wildavsky [20], and used to explain much ideologically driven behaviour. Hierarchical Individualists are strongly correlated with discounting the risks associated with climate change.

the issue is shifted. Here, we attempt to understand these results using the Purposeful Point of View model proposed by Widdows [19].

One of the underlying cognitive factors most predictive of climate change skepticism is that provided by the grid group framework [20]. In stark contrast to the common conservative-liberal spectrum, this schema makes use of two dimensions to represent the commitment of a person, broadly to (a) the strength of group boundaries (Individualism → Communitarianism), and (b) the number and variety of prescriptions that a society should make (Egalitarianism → Hierarchy). In Fig. 1. we see these relationships mapped out on a two dimensional grid. A person falls somewhere on each of the two scales to end up categorised into one of four cultural worldview quadrants, or ideologies: Hierarchy-individualism (HI); Hierarchy-communitarianism (HC); Egalitarianindividualism (EI); and Egalitarian-communitarianism (EC). Surveys are traditionally used to find out where people fit on this two dimensional spectrum. While the grid group framework is most often sketched out as an orthogonal set of axes, there is no a priori reason why this would be the case in reality. Of particular interest to our current argument, people who are denoted as hierarchical individualists tend to be those most likely to express views corresponding to climate change skepticism [9].

While a large amount of work has been completed in the area of climate change denial, the grid group model is general, and it has been used to explain many different attitudes to risk and social norms (see e.g. [8,11] for some examples). Climate change denialism is just one of the most intensely studied. What we are interested in for the purposes of our current argument is the idea that *cultural worldviews* (along with many other factors, some of which are probably yet to be discovered) are key drivers when it comes to the acceptance or rejection of a rhetorical position. We also note that all categories on the grid group framework show evidence of being affected by their underlying ideology. For example, one recent paper [11] shows that people from all ideologies are more likely to get basic mathematical problems wrong when they are framed in terms of a competing ideology. None of us are immune to the ideologies that we inherit, acquire, and grow as we develop. Once formed they can have a significant effect upon our capacity for logical reasoning.

5 Scaling Up: A General Model of Skepticism and Rhetoric

For the sake of clarity, we shall consider two subsets of the population; hierarchical individualists and egalitarian communitarians. These two highly polarised ideologies, lie at opposite corners of Fig. 1, and are responsible for some of the most interesting behaviours that have so far shown up in the literature in this field. In traditional understandings, these ideologies are considered very static, they do not change, and drive most of the behaviour that we see surrounding attitudes towards climate change, immunisation etc.

We can represent these ideologies using a standard basis in a 2-dimensional Hilbert space: $|HE\rangle, |CI\rangle$. For the sake of simplicity, these axes are considered to be perpendicular to each other. Semantically, this means they can vary independently: in terms of information retrieval, they may even be considered to be irrelevant to one another [18, Ch. 8]. By contrast, the positions HI and EC in this model are genuinely opposite or mutually exclusive. This is an important intuitive difference between quantum and Boolean logics: *north* and *south* are opposites, but the *north-south* and *east-west* directions are orthogonal complements, and so the operation that corresponds algebraically to 'logical NOT' is orthogonal projection, not scalar multiplication by -1. This assumption of orthogonality simplifies the modelling that follows, but we note that it is possible to make use of the formalism of Positive Operator Valued Measures (POVM) to relax it [2], which would lead to a more realistic (if somewhat more complex) model.

In practice, people are highly unlikely to align completely with one or the other ideology, they will lie somewhere in between, and we represent the cognitive state $|\psi\rangle$ of this type of more complex individual using the standard superposition relationship:

$$|\psi\rangle = a|HI\rangle + b|EC\rangle. \tag{1}$$

How will this cognitive state affect the propensity of a person to act upon climate change? It depends upon the context that they find themselves in, and their resulting point of view.

5.1 Scenario 1: Different Results of an Action

If the discussion is framed around the question "Do you believe in climate change?" then the states are already quite fixed. For adherents of HI, the notion

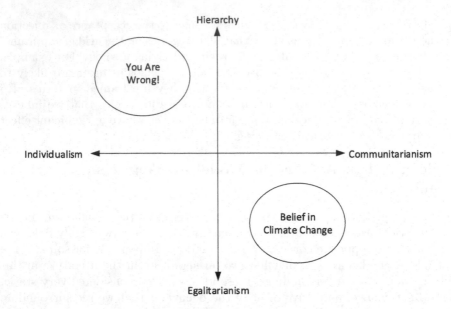

Fig. 2. How the idea of *belief in climate change* might appear to an observer who already identifies with groups that reject this belief.

of belief in climate change is already framed as belonging to a different group that is identified with opposition to their way of life and worldview. If they are approached from a belief/disbelief framing then they will almost certainly fall back into a situation where they state that anthropogenic climate change is not occurring. Similarly, the EC is highly likely to express belief in climate change as a way of identifying with their group. This situation is outlined in Fig. 2.

5.2 Scenario 2: Aligning Incompatible Ideologies Using Different Points of View

Based upon the results discussed above [3,8], we know that reframing the issue of climate belief (or more importantly here, disbelief), can lead to a higher probability that a person who is skeptical about climate change might nonetheless become more likely to act to mitigate its effects. In the case of Bain et al. the reframing was towards a nicer, more caring, or more technologically advanced society [3], a result which suggests a way forwards. Instead of insisting that skeptics *should* believe in climate change, an alternative is to propose actions that they can agree on, *whether or not* belief in climate change is accepted beforehand.

This scenario can be straightforwardly represented in the Point Of View (POV) model. All that we require is a POV state that is directed in such a manner that people closely aligned with the hierarchical individualist ideology will become more likely to consider climate change worth acting upon (than they did in the belief state). The crucial addition here is that we need *more dimensions* to describe the beliefs and objectives.

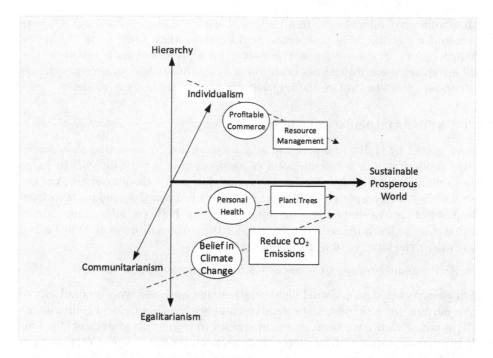

Fig. 3. Objectives and actions that may appeal to individuals with various ideologies

Such a model is depicted in Fig. 3. In this model we have introduced a third dimension, which is an objective axis in the sense of [19], labelled Sustainable Prosperous World. Naturally this is an objective that all participants are likely to consider reasonable, in spite of ideological differences about how is might be achieved. Three different POVs are represented in Fig. 3, each projecting out from an initial underlying grid group worldview:

Hierarchical Individualist: This POV is a vector that sees a sustainable prosperous world as arising through appropriate resource management.

Egalitarian Communitarian: This POV moves towards the same outcome but from the perspective of climate change belief.

Egalitarian Individualist: This POV takes personal health and wellness as the driving reason for trying to achieve a sustainable prosperous world.

Note that despite these ideological differences, all parties are converging towards the same endpoint in Fig. 3. This is a markedly different outcome to that which we currently witness in the world media as it covers contentious issues (where it is highly polarised). However, there is some fit in this scenario with our lived experience; when two people from opposing ideologies meet and connect before they start to discuss climate change, they often have a far more sensible (i.e. convergent) discussion. Such anecdotes pervade society, and are supported by the data from [3], but until now they have been difficult to consistently model. However, with our new POV based understanding of this situation, we can now talk about what might occur in a rhetorical situation that primed our subjects to consider a sustainable prosperous world (rather than their state of climate change belief). Statements can themselves be represented as a vector in our Hilbert space (perhaps with the addition of extra dimensions as necessary), and we can now start to explore the implications of this using a toy model.

5.3   A Toy Mathematical Model

As suggested by [1,19], this scenario may be modelled by assuming that people judge similarity from a specific point of view, making it very difficult to judge the similarity of two concepts, say *moon* and *ball* in an absolute sense. On the surface they are completely dissimilar, but if we are asked to judge them from the point of view of shape then they quickly become highly similar in our minds. Such a concept holds immediate relevance for the current discussion. When asked to consider the validity of a statement such as

   A: *We should reduce CO$_2$ emissions by burning less fossil fuels.*

then we expect that people will judge this statement by considering its similarity to their current point of view. In particular, those with a Hierarchical Individualist (HI) point of view have been shown in studies to reject this statement [9]. This likely rejection is modelled by a large angle between *HI* and *Reduce CO2 emissions* in Fig. 3. We could however consider a different statement, such as

   B: *We should carefully manage natural resources and avoid excessive pollution.*

A person with a Hierarchical Individualist point of view might be more inclined to agree with this statement. This greater likelihood of agreement is modelled by a much smaller angle between *HI* and *Resource Management* in Fig. 3. These angles are explicitly highlighted in Fig. 4, where clearly $\cos(HI, B) > \cos(HI, A)$. (Here we assume the standard procedure in information retrieval of using the cosine of the angle between two vectors as a measure of similarity, which we interpret as making agreement more likely.) The greater appeal of statement B becomes even more apparent when viewed from the point of view of an *HI* observer whose goals are aligned with the Sustainable Prosperous World objective axis marked *SPW* in Fig. 5. Here the comparison between similarities is given by the inequality $\cos(SPW - HI, SPW - B) > \cos(SPW - HI, SPW - A)$. From the perspective of *HI*, B and *SPW* are closely aligned, whereas A is much less relevant.

   This toy model thus considers two rhetorical devices: one to introduce the *SPW* objective axis, and another to introduce the statement B as an alternative to A that is less jarring to the *HI* point of view. Between these, the angle between *HI* and the statement proposing a given action has been much reduced, and thus the similarity or agreement between the purposes and actions has been significantly increased.

   It is important to note that the *HI* point of view has *not* been changed in this discussion. Instead of trying to change someone's ideology or point of view,

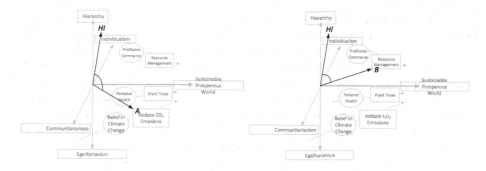

Fig. 4. Smaller angles indicate actions that may appeal more to a particular POV.

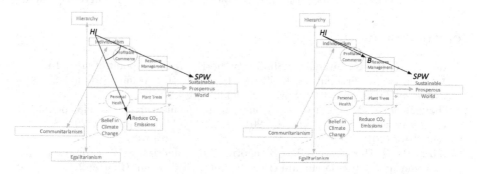

Fig. 5. Smaller angles indicate actions that may appeal more to a particular POV.

the discussion has introduced objectives and actions that make sense from their pre-existing point of view.

There are immediate mathematical problems for this model. For example, since the H and E axes are opposite, their cosine similarity would be -1. This makes an immediate description in terms of (say) quantum probabilities challenging. Also, the angles themselves may be misleading, and only the relative comparisons between angles may make sense. (For example, both the angles in Fig. 5 are smaller than the angles in Fig. 4.) Recently, a more complete quantum model of similarity has been developed [16], and it will be interesting to see if that model provides any more insight into the way in which such a scenario might play out. We note also that while we have made heavy use of the grid-group framework in deriving this model, there is no *a priori* reason why this must be so. Other well-accepted descriptions of ideologies could well provide suitable ground-spaces for such a model. Nonetheless, the formalism presented here appears to capture some of the effects discussed above.

6   Conclusions

Ideologies and worldviews are a key factor that drive the acceptance or rejection of many issues that are well understood by science (e.g. the acceptance of human induced climate change). While ideologies appear to be immutable and unchanging, some recent results give us reason to believe that reframing highly polarized debates might be possible, but this is a different phenomenon to mathematically model. In this paper we have proposed a Point of View model, which allows us to show how a statement will be interpreted according to a person's underlying worldview, according to a grid group framework. The model shows that there is a natural way in which to model the difference that a subject perceives to lie between some statement and their underlying worldview, and we have linked this to the possible acceptance or rejection of that statement. If one can be generated that aligns key social questions with the ideology of the subject, then it may be possible to generate a consensual approach towards solving key socio-environmental and technological problems that society is currently facing.

References

1. Aerts, S., Kitto, K., Sitbon, L.: Similarity metrics within a point of view. In: Song, D., Melucci, M., Frommholz, I., Zhang, P., Wang, L., Arafat, S. (eds.) QI 2011. LNCS, vol. 7052, pp. 13–24. Springer, Heidelberg (2011)
2. Aliakbarzadeh, M., Kitto, K.: Non-orthogonal measurements via povm. In: Atmanspacher, H., et al. (eds.) QI 2015. LNCS, vol. 9535, pp. 284–293. Springer, Heidelberg (2016)
3. Bain, P.G., Hornsey, M.J., Bongiorno, R., Jeffries, C.: Promoting pro-environmental action in climate change deniers. Nat. Clim. Change **2**(8), 600–603 (2012). doi:10.1038/nclimate1532
4. Darwin, C.: The Descent of Man. Penguin, London (1871). Reprint 2004
5. Douglas, M.: Risk Acceptability According to the Social Sciences. Russell Sage Foundation, New York (1985)
6. Heath, Y., Gifford, R.: Free-market ideology and environmental degradation the case of belief in global climate change. Environ. Behav. **38**(1), 48–71 (2006)
7. Jackson, D.: Obama: climate change impact on health is personal. http://www.usatoday.com/story/theoval/2015/04/08/obama-climate-change-public-health-abc-news/25450489/
8. Kahan, D.M., Braman, D., Gastil, J., Slovic, P., Mertz, C.K.: Culture and identity-protective cognition: explaining the white-male effect in risk perception. J. Empir. Leg. Stud. **4**(3), 465–505 (2007)
9. Kahan, D.M., Braman, D., Slovic, P., Gastil, J., Cohen, G.L.: The second national risk and culture study: Making sense of - and making progress in - the american culture war of fact. Technical report, Yale Law School, Public Law Working Paper No. 154; GWU Law School Public Law Research Paper No. 370; Harvard Law School Program on Risk Regulation Research Paper No. 08–26 (2007). SSRN: http://ssrn.com/abstract=1017189 or doi:10.2139/ssrn.1017189
10. Kahan, D.M., Jenkins-Smith, H., Tarantola, T., Silva, C.L., Braman, D.: Geoengineering and climate change polarization: testing a two-channel model of science communication. The Ann. Amer. Acad. Polit. Soc. Sci. **658**(1), 192–222 (2015)
11. Kahan, D.M., Peters, E., Dawson, E.C., Slovic, P.: Motivated numeracy and enlightened self-government (2013)
12. Kahan, D.M., Peters, E., Wittlin, M., Slovic, P., Ouellette, L.L., Braman, D., Mandel, G.: The polarizing impact of science literacy and numeracy on perceived climate change risks. Nat. Clim. Change **2**, 732–735 (2012)

13. Kitto, K., Sonnenburg, L., Boschetti, F., Walker, I.: Modelling attitudes to climate change — an order effect and a test between alternatives. In: Atmanspacher, H., Bergomi, C., Filk, T., Kitto, K. (eds.) QI 2014. LNCS, vol. 8951, pp. 119–131. Springer, Heidelberg (2015)

14. Lehmann, E.: ClimateWire: wisconsin agency bans talk of climate change. http://www.scientificamerican.com/article/wisconsin-agency-bans-talk-of-climate-change/

15. Lewandowsky, S., Gignac, G.E., Oberauer, K.: The role of conspiracist ideation and worldviews in predicting rejection of science. PLOS ONE **8**, e75637 (2013)

16. Pothos, E.M., Busemeyer, J.R., Trueblood, J.S.: A quantum geometric model of similarity. Psychol. Rev. **120**(3), 679–696 (2013)

17. Tversky, A., Kahneman, D.: The framing of decisions and the psychology of choice. Science **211**(4481), 453–458 (1981)

18. Widdows, D.: Geometry and Meaning. CSLI Publications, Stanford (2004)

19. Widdows, D.: Purposeful choice and point-of-view: a generalized quantum approach. In: Atmanspacher, H., Haven, E., Kitto, K., Raine, D. (eds.) QI 2013. LNCS, vol. 8369, pp. 244–256. Springer, Heidelberg (2014)

20. Wildavsky, A.: Choosing preferences by constructing institutions: a cultural theory of preference formation. Am. Polit. Sci. Rev. **81**(1), 3–22 (1987)

Semantic Representations

Graded Semantic Vectors: An Approach to Representing Graded Quantities in Generalized Quantum Models

Dominic Widdows[1]([✉]) and Trevor Cohen[2]

[1] Microsoft Bing, Redmond, USA
dwiddows@microsoft.com
[2] University of Texas School of Biomedical Informatics at Houston,
Houston, USA

Abstract. Semantic vector models are traditionally used to model concepts derived from discrete input such as tokenized text. This paper describes a technique to address continuous and graded quantities using such models. The method presented here grows out of earlier work on modelling orthography, or letter-by-letter word encoding, in which a graded vector is used to model character-positions within a word. We extend this idea to use a graded vector for a position along any scale. The technique is applied to modelling time-periods in an example dataset of Presidents of the United States. Initial examples demonstrate that encoding the time-periods using graded semantic vectors gives an improvement over modelling the dates in question as distinct strings. This work is significant because it fills a surprising technical gap: though vector spaces over a continuous ground-field seem a natural choice for representing graded quantities, this capability has been hitherto lacking, and is a necessary step towards a more complete vector space model of conceptualization and cognition.

1 Introduction and Outline

This paper proposes and demonstrates a general approach for encoding naturally graded quantities within semantic vector models. This is important in theory for understanding how discrete relationships (such as "a cheetah is a land animal") and graded quantities (such as "a cheetah can reach speeds of 70 miles-per-hour") might be combined in a single cognitive model. It's important in practice for the engineering of rich search and navigation systems (for example, for finding books-for-sale on a particular topic within a given price-range). These motivations are discussed more thoroughly in Sect. 2.

The paper describes one approach to solving this problem. Section 3 introduces the method with a first example case, the challenge of modelling orthography. That is, instead of treating each word as atomic, it is modelled as a collection of characters bound to different positions. Vectors representing the positions of letters within a written word are thus a first example of graded semantic vectors. Section 4, at the heart of the paper, describes how the technique used to model

© Springer International Publishing Switzerland 2016
H. Atmanspacher et al. (Eds.): QI 2015, LNCS 9535, pp. 231–244, 2016.
DOI: 10.1007/978-3-319-28675-4_18

orthography can be generalized to cover any number of other graded scales, and concepts with attributes that take values along these scales. This section also describes some of the mathematical properties of this model which make it quantum-like: some of these are well-known, some are relatively novel, and some are proposed for further investigation.

The rest of the paper is devoted to worked examples demonstrating the potential of the method. Section 5 explains how this can be extended to temporal concepts in modelling a table of information about Presidents of the USA. Section 6 shows how properties of particular items can be recovered, compared, and inferred from the semantic vector model. Finally, Sect. 7 proposes further work expanding these developments.

2 The Problem of Graded Representation

Any attempt at a complete account of cognition must sooner or later address the challenge of comparing graded quantities. Such notions include larger and smaller, higher and lower, before and after, nearer and farther, faster and slower, and so on. It is not enough to classify items into discrete buckets such as 'small, medium and large', or 'ancient, medieval, and modern', because while these may work for some original purpose, situations inevitably arise wherein a coarser classification must become more fine-grained to serve some new situation.

Our typical approach to this challenge is to introduce numerical scales with some agreed units, such as seconds for time, meters for distance, degrees for temperature, currency units for money, and so on. Given suitable measuring equipment, real world situations can be described using these numerical scales and compared appropriately: for example, the question of whether the temperature in a room is above or below a given target temperature can be transformed to a question of comparing numbers. This comparison can be carried out in a computing machine, for example by comparing the corresponding digits in binary representations of the measured ambient temperature and the desired target temperature. Such a system would typically not be thought of as intelligent: it can compare graded quantities that are usefully related to the concepts *too hot*, *too cold*, and the desired state of *just right*, but in a closed way that is quite removed from the way humans communicate about these concepts and that does not learn or generalize without external help.

On the other hand, recent decades have established firmly systems that do learn and generalize directly from the way humans communicate, but not in a way that supports the representation of graded quantities. Here we are referring to semantic vector models, a family of models that build representations from large corpora of natural language [1]. Models of this sort have usually been constructed from discrete data, such as tokenized text: canonical early examples of this methodology include the vector space model for search [2] and Latent Semantic Analysis [3]. The connection with generalized quantum models arises from the key observation that the Hilbert spaces and projections used quantum mechanics are from the same family as the vector spaces and similarity measurements used in semantic vector models [4,5], albeit with some customary differences such as the use of complex coordinates in quantum mechanics and real coordinates in natural language applications [6].

In natural language processing, these methods can be used to learn quite successfully that (for example) *hot* and *cold* are related to one another, possibly even that they are antonyms, and that they are also related to *temperature*. But this is typically done by mapping *hot* and *cold* to individual points in a vector space, without any notion that there is a scale of physical temperature values, that *hot* and *cold* describe regions in this value space (subject to context and vagueness), and that other terms such as *warm, cool, frigid*, etc. also describe regions on this scale.

Many corpus-based techniques deliberately neglect this challenge, for example, by replacing all strings of digits with a single token such as NUMBER in preprocessing (see e.g., [7], though the practice is widespread and standard). Obviously this throws away a lot of information with intended meaning. This raises the challenge of combining such text-based similarity models with information from graded and continuous observations. Given that the vector space models used in distributional semantics are naturally continuous, combining such modalities should in theory not be too difficult.

In the rest of this paper we demonstrate one such combined model. The example applications include string similarity, exploring tabular data, and finding nearby terms in document search. Each of these application areas already has a well-developed scientific literature and engineering practices, and the goal of this paper is not to claim that graded vector techniques are superior to these established practices. Instead we show that graded vector techniques can at least be applied to a wide range of areas with interesting results.

3 First Example: Encoding of Orthography in Semantic Vectors

This section introduces graded semantic vectors using a motivating example. Our first application of vector representations to model graded quantities and relationships was in encoding orthography, that is, in modelling a word as an ordered list of characters in given positions. This work was presented at an earlier Quantum Interaction conference [8]. This paper also discusses previous work in this area, including alternative encoding and similarity measurement techniques such as Levenshtein distance.

Orthographic representation involves various challenges. It is motivated psychologically (trying to reproduce human behavior when reading strings of alphabetic characters) and technologically (for example for spelling correction). Such a system should recognize that *line* and *link* are written similarly, it should see similarities between *nile* and *line* but should still distinguish them, and so on. The system should have a way to give a lower weight to internal differences, because humans are particularly robust to word-internal character changes.

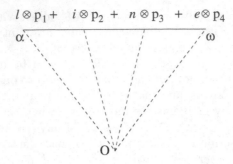

$$l \otimes p_1 + \quad i \otimes p_2 + \quad n \otimes p_3 + \quad e \otimes p_4$$

Fig. 1. Interpolation to generate four demarcator vectors and encode the string *line*.

Table 1. Pairwise similarities between orthographic vectors for *line* and other words.

line	line	1.0	line	lint	0.73
line	lime	0.73	line	nile	0.76
line	file	0.62	line	curve	0.32
line	lie	0.82	line	of	−0.02

The solution technique presented in [8] is outlined in Fig. 1, and illustrates much of the machinery that will be used more generally in this paper. We start with distinct vectors for each character in the alphabet to be used. One approach is to select these randomly. (Note that throughout this paper the notation for a concept and the vector representing that concept will often be conflated, so in vector equations w will often refer to the vector representing the character w.)

The simplest way to build a word vector out of the vectors for its constituent characters is to add these character vectors together to make word vectors, for example, given vectors for the characters l, i, n and e, the vector for the word *line* would be $l+i+n+e$. However, due to the commutativity of vector addition, this process leads to exactly the same result for the word *nile*.

This directional encoding problem is often addressed by introducing another pairwise operator on vectors, known as a "binding" operator, such as the convolution product. That is, for two vectors a and b, there is a product $a \otimes b$ defined in such a way that it is naturally dissimilar to both a and b, but if a and a' are similar then $a \otimes b$ and $a' \otimes b$ are also similar. Binding operators have a natural inverse, which we shall refer to as a "release" operator.

Now suppose we define vectors for each of the positions in a word: for example, for a word with four letters, these might be written p_1, p_2, p_3, and p_4. Then the string *line* will become represented as $l \otimes p_1 + i \otimes p_2 + n \otimes p_3 + e \otimes p_4$. This leaves the question of how to define the vectors p_i. This is done by interpolation between a pair of *demarcator* vectors which we will call α and ω. These can be selected at random (which in high dimensions means they will be roughly orthogonal), or using some other method. Then $p_1 = \alpha$, $p_2 = \frac{2}{3}\alpha + \frac{1}{3}\omega$, $p_3 = \frac{1}{3}\alpha + \frac{2}{3}\omega$, and $p_4 = \omega$. This whole setup is depicted in Fig. 1.

Some examples of the similarities between pairs of words obtained using this method are shown in Table 1. These pairwise similarities were obtained using 200-dimensional complex vectors, with random vectors for the vector for each letter and the α and ω vectors, circular convolution for the binding operation (which for complex vectors is conveniently given by the pairwise addition of complex arguments [9]), and cosine similarity as the similarity measure.[1]

These results were computed using the Semantic Vectors package, a freely-available open-source software package described in [6]. It's easy to see that words that 'look' similar to one another have higher similarity scores. Moving letters around reduces similarity, as does substituting one letter for another. Vectors for words with different numbers of letters are produced in the obvious way by dividing the distance between α and ω vectors appropriately. Examples and results from using this method are presented in [8], which also reviews some of the observed cognitive features of lexical encoding in human word recognition experiments, and shows that the orthographic encoding technique described here parallels many of these features.

4   A General Approach to Encoding Graded Attributes

The method for orthographic encoding summarized in the previous section can readily be adapted to model all kinds of other graded concepts. The basic idea is the same throughout. Let C be a set of concepts we wish to model, and let $f : C \to \mathbb{R}$ be a mapping from C to the real numbers that describes a property of the concepts in C. For example, f may be a function that takes a data record for a particular vehicle, and returns its weight or fuel efficiency.

Our goal is to create a semantic vector model for these concepts, so that more similar concepts are closer to one another in this space, and other properties and behaviors can ideally be recovered and predicted. This is done using a Vector Symbolic Architecture or VSA [11], which is a vector space V equipped with a binding operator $\otimes : V \times V \to V$, such as the convolution product of complex vectors introduced in Sect. 3. The symbol $\otimes$ is adapted from the tensor product symbol used in linear algebra. Many applications of vector composition, including quantum mechanics, and more recently artificial intelligence (e.g., [9,10]) have been explored. Throughout this paper, the result of binding is a vector in the original space rather than a higher order tensor or any other object. The algebraic properties of VSAs in general, the computational properties of several example implementations, and related work in this rapidly developing area is discussed in several papers including [10,12].

To encode tabular data, demarcator vectors α and ω are selected just as in Sect. 3. The, for each function f, its range over the whole of C is computed, giving the minimum value $f_{\min} \in \mathbb{R}$ and maximum value $f_{\max} \in \mathbb{R}$ of f over C. A value $f(c) \in \mathbb{R}$ is then modelled by interpolation just as in the orthographic example, by the vector

---

[1] For more on the use of complex and binary vectors in such representations, see [6,10].

$$D(f(c)) = \frac{f_{\max} - f(c)}{f_{\max} - f_{\min}}\alpha + \frac{f(c) - f_{\min}}{f_{\max} - f_{\min}}\omega.$$

The subtractions in this equation are merely shorthand for distances when we know that one quantity is larger than another: the equation can perhaps be most easily understood as "a vector between α and ω representing $f(c)$ in proportion to its distance from $f_{\min}$ and $f_{\max}$". Global information about the range of f over the whole of C is necessary for $f(c)$ to be computed, which has so far been accomplished by preprocessing the entire dataset before indexing the individual concepts.

Since each concept may have multiple attributes (there are potentially many functions f), it is important to record which attribute took which value. The binding operation features here also. An elemental vector $E(f)$ is generated for each function f. Elemental vectors are described in [10] and earlier works: they are used as building blocks for learning semantic vectors, and can be obtained in many ways. Thanks to the near-orthogonality of most vectors in high-dimensional spaces, even random allocation guarantees near-orthogonality of elemental vectors, which is enough to provide good results in many applications.

Now we can easily define a semantic vector $S(c)$ for each concept in C, using the definition

$$S(c) = \sum E(f) \otimes D(f(c)), \tag{1}$$

where the sum is taken over all the available functions f and uses the standard vector sum operator $+$.

4.1   Generalized Quantum or Quantum-Like Properties

The Quantum Interaction audience will be particularly interested to know what properties make this a generalized quantum or quantum-like representation. These include properties of semantic vector models in general:

- The use of Hilbert spaces to model concepts and the scalar product and projection operators to measure similarity.
- The geometric foundation this gives for logical and probabilistic interpretations.

These properties are well-known to the community and have been emphasized in the literature for at least a decade [4,5]. A more explicit analysis and evaluation of the probabilistic interpretation is also in-progress in another paper by the authors (in press). Quantum-like properties of the graded representation defined in Eq. 1 include:

- For discrete graded properties such as character positions in a word, the technique of quantizing a space of continuous values is similar to that used for modelling angular momentum in quantum mechanics [13].

- The superposition of bound products leads to an *entangled* representation, in the sense that the sum of these products cannot be factorized into the product of two individual vectors. This is related to the description of such systems as fully distributed or holographic [9], meaning that each concept and its contributing factors is represented over several dimensions, and each dimension is used as a feature in the representation of several different concepts and semantic properties.
- The representation can be quantized, in the sense that it can be used to categorize concepts using vague predicates such as "Which items are old?" or "Which items are heavy?"

This said, there is still much to investigate in this area. The quantization of concepts using vague predicates has yet to be implemented and tested effectively. Also, the relationship between various binding operations and quantum models should be explored further: for example, in which VSA's is the operation "binding with a" self-adjoint, and in which cases is it part of a more general family or operators? Similar questions are currently being asked in cognitive science [14], and we anticipate that this will remain an active topic for research and discussion.

The rest of this paper is devoted to example models, which the authors hope will illustrate the practical usefulness of graded semantic vectors, and encourage deeper theoretical research with technological use-cases directly in mind.

5   Tabular Data and Continuous Quantities

Tabular datasets are a very common case where rows refer to concepts and columns refer to attributes or properties of those concepts, and which often contain graded values. The example presented in this section is a summary of the case-study in [10, Sect. 6.5], which explores different methods for building a semantic vector model to represent a tabular dataset listing the Presidents of the USA (columns including name, party, state of birth, religion, years of birth, death, taking and leaving office, and age at these times).

Using random elemental vectors for data values (approximating the standard approach of treating numbers as unique terms), the combined vectors for the rows tend to share features only if they have an exactly equal value in at least one column. Example results for the queries *J. Adams* and *T. Roosevelt* are shown in Table 2. The nearest neighbors tend to come from exact matches: for example, Adams and Jefferson both died in the same year (1824), and Roosevelt and Coolidge both died at the same age (60). There are several erroneous similarities and these are generally poor results.

The indexing method was then improved in two ways. Firstly, orthographic vectors (in the sense of Sect. 3) were used for the textual columns. Secondly, for the columns involving time, graded vectors were used. Results using this method are shown in Table 3. Note that several spurious results have disappeared, and historically closer presidents are now preferred.

This technique of generating vectors to represent numeric quantities can also be used to create queries for particular columns. For example, we can now search

Table 2. Nearest neighbors in a model built from tabular data, with each distinct value treated as a random elemental vector.

J. Adams		T. Roosevelt	
J. Adams	1.00	T. Roosevelt	1.00
Jefferson	0.063	Coolidge	0.072
G.H.W. Bush	0.061	Van Buren	0.067
Washington	0.050	Fillmore	0.059
G.H.W. Bush	0.056	J.Q. Adams	0.046
G.W. Bush	0.048	Taft	0.044

Table 3. Nearest neighbors with values treated as orthographic or graded numeric vectors.

J. Adams		T. Roosevelt	
J. Adams	1.00	T. Roosevelt	1.00
J.Q. Adams	0.266	Coolidge	0.340
Jackson	0.198	L.B. Johnson	0.314
Washington	0.197	Eisenhower	0.314
Buchanan	0.196	Hoover	0.309
Jefferson	0.196	Wilson	0.307

for items whose year of taking office or whose year of birth are close to a particular value, by generating the vector $E(\text{column}) \otimes D(year)$, where D again refers to a demarcator vector. Note the way the column is important, because it gives both the property to be searched for, and the appropriate endpoints. Results for year of birth and year of taking office near to 1800 are given in Table 4. The method using raw elemental vectors is more or less random, whereas the use of numeric vectors gives results that are all in the right periods.

This technique can be extended to sort rows with respect to the magnitude of the entry in a particular column by measuring the similarity between the vector representation of each row and $E(\text{column}) \otimes D(\alpha)$ and/or $E(\text{column}) \otimes D(\omega)$. Figure 2 shows the correlation between the age at inauguration of each of the presidents in the data set and scores produced by two methods of estimating their relative ages at inauguration from their row vector representations directly. For these experiments, binary vector representations generated using the Binary Spatter Code [15] were used to represent the data set. In the first method (labeled α), the similarity between the vector product $E(\text{aie\_column}) \otimes D(\alpha)$ (where aie_column is the age at inauguration column header) and $S(\text{president})$, the row vector representation of each president, was used as an estimate of relative age at inauguration, with younger ages receiving higher scores. The metric of similarity $(\text{sim}(x, y))$ in this case is $1 - \frac{2}{n}\text{HammingDistance}(x, y)$, where n is the dimensionality of the binary vectors concerned. In the second method $(\alpha - \omega)$, the similarity to the vector product $E(\text{column}) \otimes D(\omega)$ was also taken into

Table 4. Nearest neighbors for date-specific searches.

Random Elemental Vectors				Numeric Vectors			
Took office	1800	Born	1800	Took office	1800	Born	1800
Taylor	0.030	Fillmore	0.17	Jefferson	0.216	Taylor	0.261
Eisenhower	0.022	F.D. Roosevelt	0.040	J. Adams	0.198	Buchanan	0.247
Jefferson	0.019	Taft	0.023	J.Q. Adams	0.190	Hayes	0.243
Carter	0.019	G.H.W. Bush	0.018	Madison	0.185	B. Harrison	0.238
Reagan	0.018	Van Buren	0.016	Monroe	0.182	Harding	0.237

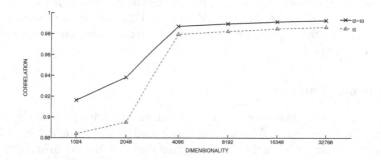

Fig. 2. Pearsons's r correlation at various dimensions between age at inauguration (aie) and: Label α: Similarity of the president vector to $E(\text{aie\_col}) \otimes D(\alpha)$ Label $\alpha - \omega$: Similarity of the president vector to $E(\text{aie\_col}) \otimes D(\alpha)$ minus similarity to $E(\text{aie\_col}) \otimes D(\omega)$.

account, such that the score used to estimate relative age was sim $\big(S(\text{president}),$ $E(\text{aie\_column}) \otimes D(\alpha)\big) -$ sim $\big(S(\text{president}), E(\text{aie\_column}) \otimes D(\omega)\big)$. As illustrated in Fig. 2, both approaches correlate well with the encoded age at inauguration, with the $\alpha - \omega$ method obtaining Pearson correlations above 0.9 even at relatively low dimensionalities.

6   Inferring Proximity

Binding to graded vectors permits a novel mode of inference — proximity can be inferred by comparing the results of "release" operations using different elemental vectors if a common set of demarcator vectors is applied across columns. For example, if $S(\text{washington}) = E(\text{took\_office}) \otimes D(1789) + E(\text{left\_office}) \otimes D(1797)$ and $S(\text{harding}) = E(\text{took\_office}) \otimes D(1921) + E(\text{left\_office}) \otimes D(1923)$, we should be able to infer that Harding had a shorter term of office as we would anticipate

$$\text{sim}\big(S(\text{harding}) \oslash E(\text{took\_office}), S(\text{harding}) \oslash E(\text{left\_office})\big) >$$

$$\text{sim}\big(S(\text{washington}) \oslash E(\text{took\_office}), S(\text{washington}) \oslash E(\text{left\_office})\big).$$

In practice, however, it is necessary to project the results of the "release" operation onto the two-dimensional plane spanned by the α and ω vectors used to construct the graded vectors of interest[2]. Proximity between two vector products $\big($e.g. $V1 = S(\text{washington}) \oslash E(\text{took\_office})$ and $V2 = S(\text{washington}) \oslash E(\text{left\_office})\big)$ can then be calculated by applying distance metrics to their projections on the $\alpha\omega$ plane:

$$ed(V1, V2) = \sqrt{(\langle V1|\alpha\rangle - \langle V2|\alpha\rangle)^2 + (\langle V1|\omega\rangle - \langle V2|\omega\rangle)^2}$$
$$sp(V1, V2) = \quad \langle V1|\alpha\rangle \times \langle V2|\alpha\rangle + \langle V1|\omega\rangle \times \langle V2|\omega\rangle$$

The first of these metrics, $ed(V1, V2)$, estimates the euclidean distance between projections on the $\alpha\omega$ plane. The second, $sp(V1, V2)$, estimates the scalar product of these projections, providing a similarity metric. We now present evaluations of these metrics.

6.1 Proximal Dates

For $ed(V1, V2)$, we evaluate the extent to which this metric can infer the relative age at which a candidate took office (this information was explicitly encoded for the evaluation illustrated in Fig. 2) from the encoded demarcator vector representations of their birth and inauguration years. Binary vector representations of the data set were again generated using the Binary Spatter Code [15], and the correlation between actual age at inauguration and age as estimated by $ed\big(S(\text{president}) \oslash E(\text{birth\_year}), S(\text{president}) \oslash E(\text{inauguration\_year})\big)$. The results of these experiments are shown in Fig. 3, which plots Pearson's correlation between inferred age and actual age at different dimensionalities. These results suggest that though strong correlation can be obtained, the dimensionality required to achieve this is orders of magnitude higher than that required when searching for explicitly encoded values.

6.2 Proximal Terms

Another application for this sort of inference involves identifying documents within which two terms occur in proximity. This can be accomplished by creating document vectors as the superposition of bound products between vectors representing terms and graded vectors representing their positions within the document. If a common α and ω vector are used throughout, $sp(V1, V2)$ can be used to find documents in which the terms of interest occur in proximity. Table 5 shows the highest-ranked documents in response to a search for the phrase "chronic pain" in two 1024-dimensional Inverse Document Frequency weighted binary vector space models of the OHSUMED corpus of biomedical abstracts [16] (terms occurring more than 100,000 times were excluded from the

---

[2] With binary vectors this is accomplished by comparing $S(\text{president}) \oslash E(\text{column\_header})$ to $D(\alpha)$ and $D(\omega)$ using $1 - \frac{2}{n}\text{HammingDistance}(x, y)$. This corresponds to the scalar product if binary vectors are viewed as bipolar vectors $\{1, -1\}$.

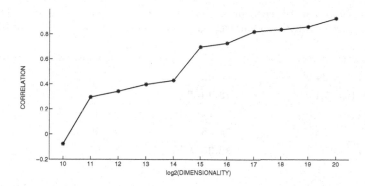

Fig. 3. Inferred correlation between age at inauguration and proximity between projections of $S(\text{president}) \oslash D(\text{year\_birth\_column})$ and $S(\text{president}) \oslash D(\text{year\_inauguration\_column})$ on the $\alpha\text{-}\omega$ plane. Y axis = Pearson's r. X axis = $\log_2(\text{dimensionality in bits})$.

Table 5. Comparison between proximity-based and conventional search for phrase "chronic pain". Score gives the number of standard deviations above the mean score across all documents in the corpus.

Proximity-based search	Conventional search
80.39: Chronic pain [letter] [comment].	13.53: Pain.
70.32: Management chronic pain.	13.53: Pain control.
69.35: Chronic pain depression.	13.53: No pain, no pain.
65.12: Pain chronic pancreatitis.	13.42: Chronic pelvic pain.
61.61: Chronic pain search.	12.90: Management of chronic pain [letter]

indexing process). The first of these models (proximity-based search) estimates proximity as $sp\big(S(\text{document}) \oslash E(\text{term1}), S(\text{document}) \oslash E(\text{term2})\big)$. The second (conventional search) uses a simple Random Indexing approach, in which document vectors are constructed as weighted superpositions of elemental term vectors.

These results suggest that the proximity-based approach is more likely to retrieve documents containing the phrase in its entirety. To test this hypothesis, we extracted all two-word terms ($n = 176{,}246$) from the Specialist Lexicon [17] provided by the National Library of Medicine, and searched for them in the OHSUMED set using both conventional and proximity-based procedures, retrieving the top 50 nearest neighboring documents in each case, and evaluating whether or not each of these contained an exact match (with both terms and documents converted to lowercase) for the two-word term in question. As one might anticipate, many of the phrases did not occur in the OHSUMED corpus, so we report results for those phrases that were identified by at least one of the procedures only ($n = 24{,}290$). The results are shown in Table 6 which gives the mean and *median* precision at $k = 50$ across models, stratified in accordance with the number of instances of the term retrieved by at least one of the models.

Table 6. Comparison between proximity-based and conventional search. The mean and *median* precision at k = 50 are shown, with best results at each level in boldface.

Instances of term in results	Proximity-based search		Conventional search	
≥ 1 (n = 24,290)	**13.02**	*4*	9.42	*4*
≥ 10 (n = 5,116)	**43.44**	*36*	31.18	*24*
≥ 20 (n = 2,519)	**62.14**	*60*	44.98	*40*
≥ 30 (n = 1,407)	**75.58**	*80*	56.44	*56*
≥ 40 (n = 801)	**83.36**	*92*	65.66	*70*

Results are stratified in this way so as to reveal more pronounced differences in performance for examples in which documents containing the term are relatively frequent, which is where we would anticipate proximity search having an advantage (as if only a few documents contain the term, both proximity-based and conventional search would be expected to retrieve these within the top 50 results).

Interestingly, the applicability of these metrics is task-specific, and each of the metrics was abandoned early as an approach to the task for which it was not formally evaluated. The first metric evaluated, $ed(V1, V2)$, is not productive as a means to retrieve documents containing terms in proximity, and tends to retrieve documents containing only one of the two words in the term of interest. This may occur because it will reward instances in which only one word occurs if this word occurs close to the end of a document, as in this case the projections of the vector representations of both terms on the α axis of the $\alpha\omega$ plane will be small, leading to a small euclidean distance (suggesting close proximity). In contrast the scalar product $(sp(V1, V2))$, which multiplies the magnitudes of these projections, will be low (suggesting great distance). As such $(sp(V1, V2))$ rewards the presence of both words and is a better fit for the "proximal terms" task. However, this metric was not productive in the "proximal dates" task, where the absence of one of the elements of comparison is not an issue, and the distances of interest are small in comparison with the range that were represented.

7   Summary and Technology Potential

This paper has demonstrated that graded data can be represented in a distributional model along with discrete and relational data. This can be done by reusing the VSA operations and demarcator vector techniques introduced already: no special new mathematical operators need to be used. The representation stays holistic throughout: we do not have to attach any special semantics to particular dimensions. The potential for such combined semantic models is considerable. For example, inference in the biomedical domain often involves a combination of information derived from textual sources and quantitative measurements. As further work, we intend to apply the techniques developed in this paper to combine the narrative text and structured data (such as lab values) to generate more comprehensive representations of clinical and biomedical data sets. Similarly, the orthographic encoding technique can clearly be applied to practical language engineering tasks such as spelling correction: this work would involve comparing and evaluation the orthographic encoding method described here with other established textual similarity measures for accuracy and computational cost, to establish the relative strengths of different methods and key integration opportunities.

Acknowledgments. This research was supported by NIH/BD2K supplement R01LM011563-02S1.

References

1. Cohen, T., Widdows, D.: Empirical distributional semantics: methods and biomedical applications. J. Biomed. Inform. **42**(2), 390–405 (2009)
2. Salton, G., McGill, M.: Introduction to Modern Information Retrieval. McGraw-Hill, New York (1983)
3. Landauer, T., Dumais, S.: A solution to Plato's problem: the latent semantic analysis theory of acquisition. Psychol. Rev. **104**(2), 211–240 (1997)
4. van Rijsbergen, K.: The Geometry of Information Retrieval. Cambridge University Press, Cambridge (2004)
5. Widdows, D.: Geometry and Meaning. CSLI Publications, Stanford (2004)
6. Widdows, D., Cohen, T.: Real, complex, and binary semantic vectors. In: Busemeyer, J.R., Dubois, F., Lambert-Mogiliansky, A., Melucci, M. (eds.) QI 2012. LNCS, vol. 7620, pp. 24–35. Springer, Heidelberg (2012)
7. Lebret, R., Collobert, R.: Word emdeddings through Hellinger PCA (2013). arXiv:1312.5542
8. Cohen, T., Widdows, D., Wahle, M., Schvaneveldt, R.: Orthogonality and orthography: introducing measured distance into semantic space. In: 2013 Proceedings of the Seventh International Conference on Quantum Interaction, Leicester, UK (2013)
9. Plate, T.A.: Holographic Reduced Representations: Distributed Representation for Cognitive Structures. CSLI Publications, Stanford (2003)
10. Widdows, D., Cohen, T.: Reasoning with vectors: a continuous model for fast robust inference. Logic J. IGPL **23**(2), 141–173 (2015)
11. Gayler, R.W.: Vector symbolic architectures answer Jackendoff's challenges for cognitive neuroscience. In: Peter Slezak (ed.) ICCS/ASCS International Conference on Cognitive Science, pp. 133–138. University of New South Wales, Sydney (2004)
12. Kelly, M.A., Blostein, D., Mewhort, D.: Encoding structure in holographic reduced representations. Can. J. Exper. Psychol. **67**(2), 79 (2013). Revue canadienne de psychologie expérimentale
13. Bohm, D.: Quantum Theory. Prentice-Hall, New York (1951). Republished by Dover (1989)
14. Khrennikov, A., Basieva, I., Dzhafarov, E.N., Busemeyer, J.R.: Quantum models for psychological measurements: an unsolved problem. PloS one **9**(10), e110909 (2014)
15. Kanerva, P.: Binary spatter-coding of ordered k-tuples. In: Vorbrüggen, J.C., von Seelen, W., Sendhoff, B. (eds.) ICANN 1996. LNCS, vol. 1112, pp. 869–873. Springer, Heidelberg (1996)

16. Hersh, W., Buckley, C., Leone, T.J., Hickam, D.: OHSUMED: an interactive retrieval evaluation and new large test collection for research. In: Proceedings of the 17th ACM SIGIR Conference on Research and Development in Information Retrieval, pp. 192–201 (1994)
17. N. C. f. B. Information, U. S. N. L. o. M. R. Pike, B. MD, USA, SPECIALIST Lexicon and Lexical Tools, September 2009

Embedding Probabilities in Predication Space with Hermitian Holographic Reduced Representations

Trevor Cohen[1](✉) and Dominic Widdows[2]

[1] University of Texas School of Biomedical Informatics at Houston, Houston, USA
trevor.cohen@uth.tmc.edu
[2] Microsoft Bing, Redmond, USA

Abstract. Predication-based Semantic Indexing (PSI) is an approach to generating high-dimensional vector representations of concept-relation-concept triplets. In this paper, we develop a variant of PSI that accommodates estimation of the probability of encountering a particular predication (such as fluoxetine TREATS major_depressive_disorder) in a collection of predications concerning a concept of interest (such as major depressive disorder). PSI leverages reversible vector transformations provided by representational approaches known as Vector Symbolic Architectures (VSA). To embed probabilities we develop a novel VSA variant, Hermitian Holographic Reduced Representations, with improvements in predictive modeling experiments. The probabilistic interpretation this facilitates reveals previously unrecognized connections between PSI and quantum theory - perhaps most notably that PSI's estimation of relatedness across multiple reasoning pathways corresponds to the estimation of the probability of traversing indistinguishable pathways in accordance with the rules of quantum probability.

Keywords: Distributional semantics · Vector symbolic architectures · Holographic reduced representations · Quantum interactions

1 Introduction

The increasing availability of electronic text presents opportunities for automated acquisition of computer-interpretable knowledge. Two fundamental issues related to the application of such automatically extracted knowledge are how best to represent and reason with it. It differs from knowledge in manually curated resources in several respects, the most obvious being in scale, indicating a need for reduced-dimensional representations and scalable inference methods. In addition, it contains distributional information, as the same assertion may be extracted from multiple contexts, and is unlikely to be perfectly accurate. This suggests a need for a continuous-valued alternative to the discrete estimates of truth or falsehood provided by symbolic logical inference. Previously, we have addressed these issues using a geometric approach to representation known as

© Springer International Publishing Switzerland 2016
H. Atmanspacher et al. (Eds.): QI 2015, LNCS 9535, pp. 245–257, 2016.
DOI: 10.1007/978-3-319-28675-4_19

Predication-based Semantic Indexing (PSI) [1] that mediates a scalable form of approximate inference [2]. However, the association strengths estimated by PSI cannot be interpreted probabilistically, which is desirable from a theoretical perspective, as well as for practical purposes such as their integration with probabilities from other sources. Consequently in this paper, we develop a probabilistic interpretation of PSI and the operators that it mediates, revealing a deeper relationship to the probabilistic calculus of quantum mechanics than had been elucidated previously.

2   Background

2.1   Distributional Semantics and Predication-Based Semantic Indexing

Methods of distributional semantics learn the relatedness between terms from their distribution across large electronic text collections [3]. A commonly used methodological approach involves generating vector space models of corpora in which terms are represented as vectors derived from the contexts in which they occur, such that terms occurring in similar contexts will have similar representations. Such models have shown remarkable successes in simulating human behavior on certain cognitive tasks (see for example [4]). However, they do not encode the nature of the relationship between terms, and therefore are limited in their utility as a means to model analogical reasoning, or support logical operations. Predication-based Semantic Indexing (PSI) [1] was developed to model sets of concept-relation-concept triplets, known as *semantic predications*, extracted from the biomedical literature by a natural language processing system known as SemRep [5]. PSI concept vectors encode both the nature and the distribution of the predications in which a concept occurs. Consequently, a PSI space can provide answers to questions such as "what TREATS schizophrenia?". Later iterations of PSI used reversible vector transformations to mediate analogical inference, used for predictive modeling in drug repurposing and other applications (for a review, see [2]).

2.2   Quantum-Inspired Operations and Interpretations

Several authors have provided interpretations of vector space models of distributional semantics that relate to quantum theory. Widdows and Peters develop distributional models of negation and disjunction, using the connectives of quantum logic [6]. Aerts and Czachor draw parallels between the application of the Singular Value Decomposition in Latent Semantic Analysis [4] and spectral decomposition in quantum physics, and show how the relatedness between terms within a set of sentences can be represented as a density matrix [7]. Bruza and his colleagues draw an analogy between word vectors in distributional models and state vectors in quantum mechanics, from which it follows that context-specific associations of a term might be revealed by a process analogous to collapse of a state vector upon measurement [8].

Regarding PSI, the utility of quantum-logical operators has been clearly demonstrated across several experiments, and aspects of the model have been interpreted with respect to their relationship to quantum mechanics. Vector space equivalents of disjunction and negation, described as quantum logic by Birkhoff and von Neumann [9], and applied previously in information retrieval experiments [6], have been applied to PSI spaces to direct search toward concepts of interest [10], and evaluate the relatedness between concepts across multiple predicate paths with improved performance in predictive modeling experiments [11]. In analogical retrieval experiments, performance was improved with compound cue vectors generated by superposing cue vectors derived from several pairs of cue concepts [12]. This phenomenon was interpreted with respect to its relationship to entanglement. Implicit in this interpretation is the notion that the semantic concept vectors generated by PSI are analogous to the state vectors used in quantum mechanics to estimate the probabilities of different outcomes. In addition, we have developed a complex vector based implementation of PSI [11], which bears some relation to quantum mechanics also. However, PSI was not conceived with quantum mechanics in mind, and to date our adoption of quantum-related mathematics has been primarily pragmatically motivated, and arguably somewhat ad-hoc.

In this paper we aim to provide a more extensive account of the relationships between PSI and quantum mechanics. To do so, we develop a probabilistic interpretation of PSI, through which the semantic distance metrics derived by the method can be interpreted with respect to the probabilities of encountering particular predications in the collection from which the space was derived. In the vector space model for information retrieval, the cosine similarity $q \cdot d$ between a query q and a document d can naturally be interpreted as the probability that d is relevant to q, and the correspondence between this interpretation and Born's rule in quantum mechanics has been recognized for some years [13]. This paper takes this parallel further with the key mathematical observation that when searching over multiple relationships at once in a vector representation, the superposition operation used naturally in vector spaces gives rise to a probabilistic interpretation based on squared amplitudes, and so the way probabilities are combined follows the rules of quantum rather than classical probability.

The remainder of the paper proceeds as follows. First, we describe the complex vector based implementation of PSI, and the modifications required to facilitate a probabilistic interpretation. We then provide probabilistic interpretations of PSI-based methods of retrieval and inference, present an evaluation of our modified implementation, and conclude with a discussion of the implications of this work.

3   Mathematical Structure and Methods

3.1   Circular Holographic Reduced Representations (CHRR)

PSI derives vector representations of concepts by superposing vector products representing concept-predicate pairs, such as "ISA fluoxetine". These vector products are composed using reversible vector transformations provided by a family of representational approaches known as Vector Symbolic Architectures or VSAs [14], and are commonly referred to as "binding", represented with the symbol $\otimes$, and the inverse of binding (or "release") represented with the symbol $\oslash$. A range of VSAs with suitable binding and superposition operations can be implemented over various number fields including the real numbers $\mathbb{R}$, complex numbers $\mathbb{C}$, and binary numbers $\mathbb{Z}_2$. As we have argued previously, the use of complex vectors is standard in quantum theory, but comparatively unexplored in information retrieval and distributional semantics [15].

The longest-established VSA using complex numbers is Plate's Circular Holographic Reduced Representation (CHRR) [16,17]. CHRR uses complex vectors each of whose coordinates is a number on the unit circle $U(1)$ in the complex plane, thus the space of available vectors in n dimensions is $U(1)^n \subset \mathbb{C}^n$. We will refer to such a complex vector as a *circular vector*. For our present purposes, this architecture provides both a binding operator with an exact inverse such that $A \otimes B \oslash A = B$ (which is not the case for Holographic Reduced Representations in general), and a continuous-valued vector space representation conducive to a probabilistic interpretation (this is more difficult with the Binary Spatter Code (BSC) [18], another influential VSA).

Binding ($\otimes$) in CHRR is accomplished by pairwise multiplication, the natural group operation on $U(1)^n$, so that $X \otimes Y = \{X_1Y_1, X_2Y_2, ...X_{n-1}Y_{n-1}, X_nY_n\}$. This is equivalent to addition of the phase angles of the unit length circular vectors concerned. Release ($\oslash$) is accomplished by binding to the inverse of a circular vector, where the inverse of a vector is its complex conjugate. PSI also requires a superposition operator ($+$). In CHRR this is accomplished by pairwise addition of unit circle vectors, with subsequent normalization of each circular component back to unit length. In practice, for pairwise addition, this is just the average of the phase angles, which as a group addition operation suffers from the obvious objection that it is not associative, so that the elements added later have more significance than those added earlier. In some cases, this preference for more recent items may be desirable, for example, in modelling short-term memory [19]. Where it is not desirable, its effects can be mitigated by storing several vectors and superposing them in a batch: for example, in the case of PSI, normalization occurs after training concludes, so the sequence in which superposition occurs is not relevant. The benefits of CHRR in this form are partly computational: only one number needs to be stored for each complex dimension, binding and superposition are fast and simple operations, and sparse representations can be supported without undue difficulty [15,17]. However, the restriction from $\mathbb{C}^n$ to $U(1)^n$ has been found unsuitable for a fuller probabilistic interpretation, and as described later in the paper, we have extended the CHRR model by relaxing the requirement that coordinates lie on the unit circle.

3.2   Predication-Based Semantic Indexing (PSI))

PSI is based upon the random indexing paradigm [20], in which basic *elemental vectors* representing terms, concepts or documents are superposed to generate *semantic vector* representations. In high dimensions, randomly-chosen vectors make suitable elemental vectors thanks to their high probability of being mutually almost orthogonal. With CHRR, elemental vectors are initialized by randomly assigning a phase angle to each of a user-defined number of dimensions which determine the dimensionality of the resulting PSI space. Elemental vectors are generated for each concept $E(\text{concept})$, and each relation type $E(\text{PREDICATE})$ and its inverse $E(\text{PREDICATE-INV})$. Semantic vectors are learned gradually by superposing the bound products of elemental vectors representing predicate-argument pairs. For example, encoding a single instance of the predication "prozac ISA fluoxetine" is accomplished as follows:

$$S(\text{prozac}) \mathrel{+}= E(\text{ISA}) \otimes E(\text{fluoxetine})$$
$$S(\text{fluoxetine}) \mathrel{+}= E(\text{ISA-INV}) \otimes E(\text{prozac})$$

Thus, the semantic vector for prozac encodes the assertion that it is (the brand name of) fluoxetine, and the semantic vector for fluoxetine encodes the assertion that it has the hyponym prozac. As the same predication may be extracted from many documents, the generated vectors encode distributional information. So statistical weighting metrics are often applied such that the extent to which a predication contributes to a semantic vector is some function of its frequency and the global frequency of the other concept and/or predicate concerned. After training is complete, the net result is a set of semantic concept vectors derived from the predications each concept occurs in. Elemental predicate vectors for each concept and predicate (and its inverse) are also retained.

4   Embedding Probabilities in Predication Space

This section describes how the CHRR model using vectors in $U(1)^n$ was extended to use more general vectors in $\mathbb{C}^n$. This supports the probabilistic operations we depend on, and also makes the architecture much more similar to the Hilbert space models used standardly in quantum mechanics.

Scaling: In accordance with Plate's original description of CHRR [16], in previous work we have normalized semantic vectors at the component level after training. This ensures that the vectors produced during training consist of numbers on the unit circle in the complex plane. To accommodate a probabilistic interpretation, we instead apply normalization to the vector as a whole, such that $\|S(\text{C})\| = 1$ after training. A consequence of this modification is that the components of our vectors do not necessarily fall on the unit circle of the complex plane.

Binding: Binding and release are still conducted by adding the phase angles of the components concerned (as though they were unit circle vectors). However, with semantic vectors the radii of the circular components are likely to differ on account of the training process, and are retained. During binding and release, the magnitudes of corresponding circular components are multiplied. As elemental

Table 1. "mdd" = Major Depressive Disorder. "ssri" = Selective Serotonin Reuptake Inhibitor.

Predication	Frequency	Predication	Frequency
ssri TREATS mdd	64	prozac ISA ssri	16
fluoxetine TREATS mdd	36	prozac ISA antidepressive_agents	4
prozac ISA fluoxetine	25	prozac TREATS anxiety_disorders	4

Table 2. Non-zero entries of mdd vector in unreduced concept-concept-predicate matrix.

	TREATS-INV ssri	TREATS-INV fluoxetine
mdd	$\sqrt{\frac{64}{100}} = 0.8$	$\sqrt{\frac{36}{100}} = 0.6$

vectors are constructed with unit length circular components, this particularly affects operations involving pairs of semantic vectors, or their superpositions.

Vector Comparison: In Plate's original model, and in our previous work, comparison between vectors is conducted at the component level, such that for two k-dimensional vectors V_1 and V_2, $\text{sim}(V_1, V_2) = \frac{1}{k} \sum_i^k \cos(V_1^i, V_2^i)$, the mean pairwise cosine distance between components. For our current purposes, we instead employ the hermitian inner product between normalized circular vectors.

Weighting: Instead of the heuristically-motivated approaches we have utilized previously, such as predication-level TF-IDF weighting, the square root of the number of times a predication occurs is used as a weighting metric. As we will subsequently illustrate, this step is a prerequisite to the recovery of the probabilities of events of interest using quantum mechanical operators. The training operations for a predication C_1 PRED C_2 with pf instances in the knowledge base then becomes:

$$S(C_1) \mathrel{+}= E(\text{PRED}) \otimes E(C_2) \times \sqrt{pf}$$
$$S(C_2) \mathrel{+}= E(\text{PRED-INV}) \otimes E(C_1) \times \sqrt{pf}$$

For the remainder of the paper we will refer to CHRR with these modifications as Hermitian Holographic Reduced Representations (HHRR), and refer to HHRR-based PSI with the modified weighting metric we have described as probabilistic PSI (pPSI).

Table 3. Simulations in 1000-dimensional Complex PSI Space. "mdd" = Major Depressive Disorder. "ssri" = Selective Serotonin Reuptake Inhibitor.

Vector	Bound product	$\bar{x}$ similarity	$\bar{x}$ probability
$S(\text{mdd})$	$E(\text{TREATS}_{\text{INV}}) \otimes S(\text{ssri})$	0.8001 ± 0.0049	0.6402 ± 0.0078
$S(\text{mdd})$	$E(\text{TREATS}_{\text{INV}}) \otimes S(\text{fluoxetine})$	0.6002 ± 0.0116	0.3603 ± 0.0139

4.1   Estimating Probabilities

A pPSI space can be considered as a reduced-dimensional approximation of a weighted and normalized term-by-term-by-predicate matrix, which we will refer to directly for illustrative purposes. Consider the small collection of predications in Table 1. In the case of this collection and $S(\text{mdd})$, the non-zero values of the matrix that is being approximated after normalization of the semantic vectors are shown in Table 2. The probability of drawing the predication "ssri TREATS mdd" from the pool of predications concerning "mdd" is then equal to the squared length of the projection of $S(\text{mdd})$ on the "TREATS-INV ssri" axis. In symbols, the correspondence between this probability, $|S\rangle = S(\text{mdd})$, and the basis vectors $|X\rangle$ representing TREATS-INV ssri and $|Y\rangle$ representing TREATS-INV fluoxetine can be expressed as follows:

$$|S\rangle = (\sqrt{\tfrac{64}{100}}) \cdot |X\rangle + (\sqrt{\tfrac{36}{100}}) \cdot |Y\rangle$$
$$P(\text{ssri TREATS mdd}) = \quad \| \, |X\rangle\langle X|S\rangle \, \|^2 = \tfrac{64}{100}$$

To derive a pPSI space from the collection of predications in Table 1, $S(\text{mdd})$ is generated by superposing the bound products of high-dimensional elemental circular vectors representing TREATS-INV ssri and TREATS-INV fluoxetine. Unlike $|X\rangle$ and $|Y\rangle$, these bound products may only be approximately orthogonal to one another. Nonetheless, the dimensionality of the space concerned ensures that random elemental vectors, and hence their bound products, are mutually orthogonal or close-to-orthogonal with high probability [2]. So, for example, over 1,000 simulations with different random initializations of a 1,000-dimensional pPSI space the squared length of the projection of $S(\text{mdd})$ onto the vector product $E(\text{TREATS-INV}) \otimes E(\text{ssri})$ approximates $\tfrac{64}{100}$, as illustrated in Table 3. This is, of course, the probability of drawing "ssri TREATS mdd" from the collection of 100 mdd-related predications in Table 1.

4.2   Disjunction and Negation

Similarly, the probability of drawing one of a specified set of predications can be determined by the squared length of the projection of a semantic (cf. state) vector onto the subspace spanned by the vectors representing the component predicate-argument pairs of interest. If $|S\rangle$ represents $S(\text{prozac})$ and the basis vectors $|W\rangle$, $|X\rangle$, $|Y\rangle$ and $|Z\rangle$ represent predicate-argument pairs ISA fluoxetine; ISA ssri; ISA antidepressive agents and TREATS anxiety disorders respectively, then:

$$|S\rangle = (0.7143) \cdot |W\rangle + (0.5714) \cdot |X\rangle + (0.2857) \cdot |Y\rangle + (0.2857) \cdot |Z\rangle$$

The probability of drawing either ISA fluoxetine or ISA ssri is the square of the length of the projection of $|S\rangle$ onto the subspace spanned by $|W\rangle$ and $|X\rangle$. This projection can be expressed as $(|W\rangle \langle W| + |X\rangle \langle X|) |S\rangle = |W\rangle\langle W|S\rangle + |X\rangle\langle X|S\rangle = (0.7143) \cdot |W\rangle + (0.5714) \cdot |X\rangle$, with a squared length of $0.7143^2 + 0.5714^2 = 0.8367 = \frac{(25+16)}{49}$, the probability of drawing either "prozac ISA fluoxetine" OR

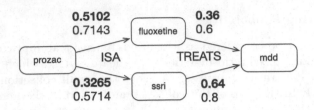

Fig. 1. Transition **Probabilities** and Amplitudes

"prozac ISA ssri" from the collection of 49 prozac-related predications in Table 1. This probability can also be estimated from a pPSI space derived from the predications in Table 1 as the squared length of the projection of S(prozac) onto an orthonormal subspace constructed by applying the Gram-Schmidt procedure to bound products $E(\text{ISA}) \otimes E(\text{fluoxetine})$ and $E(\text{ISA}) \otimes E(\text{prozac})$. Over 1,000 simulations with different random initializations the mean squared length of this projection was 0.8370 ± 0.0048.

It follows that the probability of drawing something other than ISA fluoxetine or ISA ssri is the squared length of the vector $|S\rangle - (|W\rangle \langle W| + |X\rangle \langle X|) |S\rangle$, the projection of $|S\rangle$ onto a subspace orthogonal to that spanned by $|W\rangle$ and $|X\rangle$. The squared length in this case is $\|(0.2857).|Y\rangle + (0.2857).|Z\rangle\|^2 = 2 \times 0.2857^2 = 0.1632 = \frac{8}{49}$.

4.3   Logical Leaps

An appealing feature of PSI is the capacity for efficient yet approximate inference across multiple reasoning pathways simultaneously. This is accomplished by transforming the task of exploring these pathways into the task of comparing the similarity between concept vector representations. Consider once again the collection of predications in Table 1, and the task of estimating the strength of the indirect relationship between the concepts "prozac" and "mdd" across the predicate path ISA:TREATS. One way to think of this task is as the estimation of the probabilities of a set of transitions, shown in Fig. 1. Though this is a schematic representation, it is worth noting that any vector in the PSI space can be interpreted as a position, and so the notion of a journey from concept to concept is arguably more literal than analogical.

One way of estimating the probability of "getting from" prozac "to" mdd along this pathway would be to use a Markovian approach in accordance with the laws of classical probability. Specifically, we assume the probability of reaching a destination reachable by two disjoint alternative paths is the sum of the probabilities of each of the paths, where the probability of a path is the product of the probabilities of the transitions along this path.[1] The probability of

---

[1] We consider paths to be disjoint if they do not share any points along the path except for the beginning and end. Combining the probabilities of paths with intersections is more difficult, but in the case of 2-step paths, distinct paths are always disjoint in this sense.

our semantic journey would then be $(0.5102 \times 0.36) + (0.3265 \times 0.64) = 0.3926$. Alternately, we could utilize Feynman's rules for calculating probabilities across multiple indistinguishable paths [21], applied to model cognitive phenomena in [22]. In contrast to the Markov approach, probability would then be estimated as the square of the sum of the path *amplitudes*, which are the products of the component amplitudes in each path - the lengths of the projections of the (semantic) state vectors onto the relevant (elemental) basis vectors. With $|S_p\rangle$ representing the vector product $S(\text{prozac}) \oslash E(\text{ISA})$ and $|S_m\rangle$ representing the vector product $S(\text{mdd}) \oslash E(\text{TREATS} - \text{INV})$, and the basis vectors $|E\rangle, |F\rangle$ representing elemental vectors $E(\text{ssri})$ and $E(\text{fluoxetine})$ respectively, the component amplitudes are $\| |E\rangle\langle E|S_p\rangle \| = 0.5714$; $\| |E\rangle\langle E|S_m\rangle \| = 0.8$; $\| |F\rangle\langle F|S_p\rangle \| = 0.7143$; and $\| |F\rangle\langle F|S_m\rangle \| = 0.6$. The combined probability of our semantic journey would then be $\big((0.5714 \times 0.8) + (0.7143 \times 0.6)\big)^2 = 0.7845$.

Which, if any, of these probabilities correspond to the estimation of distance in pPSI? Distance across a specified predicate path in PSI is measured by binding the semantic concept vector for one concept to the inverse of the product of the "release" operation on elemental vectors representing the predicates concerned, and comparing the result to the other semantic concept vector. With pPSI, for our example this would be accomplished by measuring the inner product of the semantic vector $|S_m\rangle = S(\text{mdd})$ and the vector $|S_{pit}\rangle = S(\text{prozac}) \oslash E(\text{ISA}) \otimes E(\text{TREATS-INV})$. This gives the length of the projection of one vector onto the other, $\langle S_{pit}|S_m\rangle = \langle S_m|S_{pit}\rangle$, and squaring this length gives an estimate of the probability of the journey from one concept to another across this path, $\langle S_{pit}|S_m\rangle^2$. Over 1,000 simulations with different random initializations, the mean squared length of this projection was 0.7843 ± 0.0075, corresponding to the probability estimated using rules of quantum probability.

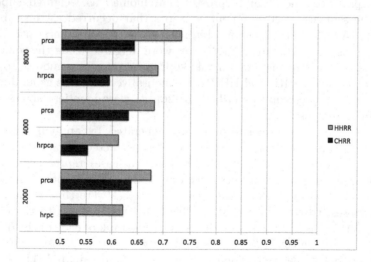

Fig. 2. Predictive modeling experiments. X axis = AUROC (≈ 0.5 with random selection). Y axis = dimensionality. prca = "prostate carcinoma". hrpca = "hormone-refractory_prostate_cancer".

5   Evaluating HHRR

That HHRR more accurately preserves probability amplitudes during encoding suggests it may offer advantages over CHRR in predictive modeling experiments. To evaluate this hypothesis, we repeated part of the experiments documented in [23] in which the length of the projection of a drug's semantic vector into a subspace derived from vector representations of ten PSI reasoning pathways was used to rank order a set of 1398 pharmaceutical agents with respect to their likely activity against prostate cancer cells in high-throughput screening experiments. In the original experiments, which used the BSC [18] as a VSA, reasoning pathways were inferred from known therapeutic relationships. We re-used the pathways from the "Knowledge Withheld" condition, in which predications directly linking a pharmaceutical agent and a type of cancer were withheld from the model. Unlike HRR, the binding operator in the BSC is its own inverse, so directionality of a predicate pathway is not encoded. Consequently, we used the pathway directionalities suggested in Fig. 2 of the original paper. We generated 2000, 4000 and 8000-dimensional CHRR and HHRR spaces from version 24.2 of the publicly available SemMedDB database of semantic predications [24], containing 70,364,020 predications extracted from 23,921,088 MEDLINE citations. Concepts occurring 500,000 times or more in the set were excluded from the analysis, and only predications involving predicates in the set {AFFECTS, ASSOCIATED_WITH, AUGMENTS, CAUSES, COEX-ISTS_WITH, DISRUPTS, INHIBITS, INTERACTS_WITH, ISA, PRE-DISPOSES, PREVENTS, SAME_AS, STIMULATES, TREATS} were encoded. To accommodate inference across triple-predicate pathways, we also created *second-degree semantic vectors* [25] for the cue concepts "hormone-refractory_prostate_cancer" and "prostate_carcinoma" as weighted superpositions of the semantic vectors for all concepts that occurred as the subject of an ASSOCIATED_WITH relationship with them. These superposition operations, and those occurring during training, were weighted using the square root of the predication frequency, which was kept constant across models to isolate differences between CHRR and HHRR. Elemental vectors were generated using the deterministic procedure described in [26], so were identical across models with common dimensionality.

For each cue concept, a subspace was generated by applying the Gram-Schmidt procedure to a set of ten vectors, each constructed following the pattern $S(\text{disease}) \oslash E(\text{PRED1}) \otimes E(\text{PRED2})$, where $S(\text{disease})$ represents either the first- or second-order semantic vector for one of the cue concepts. The semantic vectors of the 1398 pharmaceutical agents in the set were then projected into these subspaces, to measure the strength of their relatedness to the cue concepts across the reasoning pathways from [23]. The rank of each of the 68 agents that were active against PC3 cells with a growth rate of 1.5 standard deviations or more below the average across agents was then evaluated. The results of these experiments are shown in Table 2, which gives the area under the receiver operator characteristic curve (AUROC) for each model, with an AUROC of 0.5 anticipated with a random ordering of the agents. HHRR outperforms CHRR across both cue concepts and at all dimensionalities, supporting the hypothesis that the additional representational power it provides offers advantages for predictive modeling.

6 Discussion

In this paper, we developed a method through which the probabilities of encountering particular predications in a collection are embedded in a reduced-dimensional geometric space. This reveals a new perspective on PSI, in which the logical operations it mediates can be interpreted probabilistically, providing a principled way to combine PSI's estimates with estimates of probability derived from other sources. It also provides the means to define the meaning of the measures of association that PSI produces. Predicate-specific strength of association between concepts that are directly related (e.g. between $S(\text{mdd})$ and $E(\text{fluoxetine}) \otimes E(\text{TREATS})$ can now be defined as the magnitude of the probability amplitude of drawing a particular predication from the set of predications involving a concept. Disjunction and negation operators applied to PSI spaces can now also be interpreted probabilistically, providing a closer correspondence to Birkhoff and von Neumann's quantum logic of "experimental propositions" [9] than when these operators yield abstract similarity metrics that permit a geometric interpretation only. In addition, the association strengths measured using "logical leaps" across dual-predicate paths that subsume multiple relationships can be interpreted probabilistically based on squared amplitudes, in accordance with the rules of quantum probability. Of note, these measurements are conducted without recourse to the elemental vectors representing the middle terms that lie along a predicate path. Consequently, the possible pathways are indistinguishable at the time the estimation is made, a prerequisite to the application of squared sum of amplitudes to estimate path probabilities [21].

To mediate this interpretation, we developed a novel VSA variant, HHRR. HHRR is a modification of CHRR, and shows advantages over it in predictive modeling experiments. These advantages may be attributed to additional representational power provided by relaxing the constraint that semantic vector coordinates lie on the unit circle of the complex plane. As elemental vector coordinates still maintain this constraint, this results in a delegation of representational duties in which semantic and distributional information are encoded by the phase angles and magnitudes of circular vectors respectively. This raises implementation issues, such as the extent to which the discretized representation of phase angles (described in [17]) affects the resolution with which semantic information is encoded, which we will explore in future work. As noted by De Vine, superposition in CHRR suggests an interpretation involving interference effects [17] - superposing circular components with similar phase angles will result in positive interference, while components with dissimilar phase angles will exhibit negative interference. The effects of these interference effects on the relative magnitudes of the circular components are preserved by HHRR, but not by CHRR, after normalization. Our empirical results suggest HHRR is better positioned to encode distributional information. This was not the primary concern of Plate's original work, which focused on the encoding and retrieval of representations of combinations of discrete symbols [16], but is important for applications in distributional informatics and information retrieval. Predictive modeling may be further improved through application of supervised machine learning approaches to pPSI vectors, which we will explore in future work.

7   Conclusion

We developed a probabilistic interpretation of PSI, revealing previously unrecognized connections to quantum theory. This development required generation of a novel VSA variant, with improved performance in predictive modeling experiments.

Acknowledgments. This research was supported by US National Library of Medicine grant R01 LM011563. We would like to acknowledge Lance De Vine, for contributing the CHRR implementation that was adapted in the current research.

References

1. Cohen, T., Schvaneveldt, R., Rindflesch, T.: Predication-based semantic indexing: permutations as a means to encode predications in semantic space. In: AMIA Annual Symposium Proceedings, pp. 114–118 (2009)
2. Widdows, D., Cohen, T.: Reasoning with vectors: a continuous model for fast robust inference. Logic Journal of IGPL (2014). p. jzu028
3. Cohen, T., Widdows, D.: Empirical distributional semantics: methods and biomedical applications. J. Biomed. Inform. **42**, 390–405 (2009)
4. Landauer, T.K., Dumais, S.T.: A solution to Plato's problem: the latent semantic analysis theory of acquisition, induction, and representation of knowledge. Psychol. Rev. **104**, 211–240 (1997)
5. Rindflesch, T.C., Fiszman, M.: The interaction of domain knowledge and linguistic structure in natural language processing: interpreting hypernymic propositions in biomedical text. J. Biomed. Inform. **36**, 462–477 (2003)
6. Widdows, D., Peters, S.: Word vectors and quantum logic experiments with negation and disjunction. In: Oehrle, R.T., Rogers, J. (eds.) Proceedings of Mathematics of Language, vol. 8 (2003)
7. Aerts, D., Czachor, M.: Quantum aspects of semantic analysis and symbolic artificial intelligence. J. Phys. A Math. Gen. **37**, L123–L132 (2004)
8. Bruza, P.D., Cole, R.J.: Quantum logic of semantic space: an exploratory investigation of context effects in practical reasoning. In: Artemov, S., Barringer, H., d'Avila Garcez, A.S., Woods, J.H. (eds.) We Will Show Them: Essays in Honour of Dov Gabbay, pp. 339–361. College Publications, London (2005)
9. Birkhoff, G., von Neumann, J.: The logic of quantum mechanics. Ann. Math. **37**, 823–843 (1936)
10. Cohen, T., Widdows, D., Schvaneveldt, R., Rindflesch, T.: Logical leaps, quantum connectives: forging paths through predication space. In: Proceedings of the AAAI Fall Symposium on Quantum Informatics for Cognitive, Social, and Semantic Processes (QI 2010) (2010)

11. Cohen, T., Widdows, D., De Vine, L., Schvaneveldt, R., Rindflesch, T.C.: Many paths lead to discovery: analogical retrieval of cancer therapies. In: Busemeyer, J.R., Dubois, F., Lambert-Mogiliansky, A., Melucci, M. (eds.) QI 2012. LNCS, vol. 7620, pp. 90–101. Springer, Heidelberg (2012)
12. Cohen, T., Widdows, D., Schvaneveldt, R., Rindflesch, T.C.: Finding Schizophrenia's Prozac emergent relational similarity in predication space. In: Song, D., Melucci, M., Frommholz, I., Zhang, P., Wang, L., Arafat, S. (eds.) QI 2011. LNCS, vol. 7052, pp. 48–59. Springer, Heidelberg (2011)
13. van Rijsbergen, K.: The Geometry of Information Retrieval. Cambridge University Press, Cambridge (2004)
14. Gayler, R.W.: Vector symbolic architectures answer Jackendoff's challenges for cognitive neuroscience. In: Slezak, P. (ed.) ICCS/ASCS International Conference on Cognitive Science, pp. 133–138. University of New South Wales, Sydney (2004)
15. Widdows, D., Cohen, T.: Real, complex, and binary semantic vectors. In: Busemeyer, J.R., Dubois, F., Lambert-Mogiliansky, A., Melucci, M. (eds.) QI 2012. LNCS, vol. 7620, pp. 24–35. Springer, Heidelberg (2012)
16. Plate, T.A.: Holographic Reduced Representation: Distributed Representation for Cognitive Structures. CSLI Publications, Stanford (2003)
17. De Vine, L., Bruza, P.: Semantic oscillations: encoding context and structure in complex valued holographic vectors. In: Quantum Informatics for Cognitive, Social, and Semantic Processes (QI 2010) (2010)
18. Kanerva, P.: The spatter code for encoding concepts at many levels. In: Marinaro, M., Morasso, P.G. (eds.) ICANN, pp. 226–229. Springer, London (1994)
19. Kanerva, P.: Hyperdimensional computing: an introduction to computing in distributed representation with high-dimensional random vectors. Cogn. Comput. 1(2), 139–159 (2009)
20. Kanerva, P., Kristofersson, J., Holst, A.: Random indexing of text samples for latent semantic analysis. In: Proceedings of the 22nd Annual Conference of the Cognitive Science Society, vol. 1036 (2000)
21. Feynman, R., Hibbs, A.: Quantum Mechanics and Path Integrals. MacGraw Hill, New York (1965)
22. Busemeyer, J.R., Wang, Z., Lambert-Mogiliansky, A.: Empirical comparison of Markov and quantum models of decision making. J. Math. Psychol. 53(5), 423–433 (2009)
23. Cohen, T., Widdows, D., Stephan, C., Zinner, R., Kim, J., Rindflesch, T., Davies, P.: Predicting high-throughput screening results with scalable literature-based discovery methods. CPT Pharmacometrics Syst. Pharmacol. 3(10), e140 (2014)
24. Kilicoglu, H., Shin, D., Fiszman, M., Rosemblat, G., Rindflesch, T.C.: Semmeddb: a pubmed-scale repository of biomedical semantic predications. Bioinformatics 28(23), 3158–3160 (2012)
25. Cohen, T., Widdows, D., Schvaneveldt, R., Rindflesch, T.: Discovery at a distance: farther journeys in predication space. In: Proceedings of the First International Workshop on the role of Semantic Web in Literature-Based Discovery (SWLBD 2012), Philadelphia, PA, October 2012
26. Wahle, M., Widdows, D., Herskovic, J.R., Bernstam, E.V., Cohen, T.: Deterministic binary vectors for efficient automated indexing of MEDLINE/PubMed abstracts. In: AMIA Annual Symposium Proceedings 2012, pp. 940–949 (2012)

Modelling Cued-Target Recall Using Quantum Inspired Models of Target Activation

David Galea(✉) and Peter Bruza(✉)

Queensland University of Technology, Brisbane, Australia
dp_galea@hotmail.com, p.bruza@qut.edu.au

Abstract. This article presents and evaluates Quantum Inspired models of Target Activation using Cued-Target Recall Memory Modelling over multiple sources of Free Association data. Two components were evaluated: Whether Quantum Inspired models of Target Activation would provide a better framework than their classical psychological counterparts and how robust these models are across the different sources of Free Association data.

In previous work, a formal model of cued-target recall did not exist and as such Target Activation was unable to be assessed directly. Further to that, the data source used was suspected of suffering from temporal and geographical bias. As a consequence, Target Activation was measured against cued-target recall data as an approximation of performance. Since then, a formal model of cued-target recall (PIER3) has been developed [10] with alternative sources of data also becoming available. This allowed us to directly model target activation in cued-target recall with human cued-target recall pairs and use multiply sources of Free Association Data. Featural Characteristics known to be important to Target Activation were measured for each of the data sources to identify any major differences that may explain variations in performance for each of the models.

Each of the activation models were used in the PIER3 memory model for each of the data sources and was benchmarked against cued-target recall pairs provided by the University of South Florida (USF). Two methods where used to evaluate performance. The first involved measuring the divergence between the sets of results using the Kullback Leibler (KL) divergence with the second utilizing a previous statistical analysis of the errors [9]. Of the three sources of data, two were sourced from human subjects being the USF Free Association Norms and the University of Leuven (UL) Free Association Networks. The third was sourced from a new method put forward by Galea and Bruza, 2015 in which pseudo Free Association Networks (Corpus Based Association Networks - CANs) are built using co-occurrence statistics on large text corpus.

It was found that the Quantum Inspired Models of Target Activation not only outperformed the classical psychological model but was more robust across a variety of data sources.

© Springer International Publishing Switzerland 2016
H. Atmanspacher et al. (Eds.): QI 2015, LNCS 9535, pp. 258–271, 2016.
DOI: 10.1007/978-3-319-28675-4_20

1   Introduction

A crucial aspect of producing models that predict the probability of recall is modeling the activation of a target word in memory prior to cuing. Much evidence shows that for any individual, seeing or hearing a word activates words related to it through prior learning. Seeing "planet"activates the associates "earth", "moon", and so on, because "planet-earth", "planet-moon", "moon-space" and other associations have been acquired in the past. This activation aids comprehension, is implicit, and provides rapid, synchronous access to associated words. Therefore, some models of activation fundamentally rely on the probabilities of such associations.

Conventionally, the way in which words are represented in memory is modelled using a network comprising the target word and its most common associates in a directed weighted graph called a Free Association Network (FAN). See Fig. 1 for an example. However, the notion of relational weighting has been challenged with an alternative viewpoint which suggests only the existence of a relationship between the words in the graph is required in the model (i.e., a 1 or 0 representing the presence or absence of a link) [10]. This $\{1, 0\}$ measure often seems to provide a better practical predictor of activation level than the weighted probability measure. Theoretically the use of the $\{1, 0\}$ measure implies that, when a link is activated, it is activated regardless of how strong its weight in the FAN (i.e., strength of activation is not important). Therefore, this paper will focus on binary FANs as the basis of activation models.

Our previous work examined three models of activation inspired by quantum entanglement [9]. Within this work, the performance of the models was based on two components; firstly the model's behaviour was compared to a baseline psychological model (i.e. Spooky-Action-At-A-Distance Activation, Spreading Activation [6]) and secondly an error analysis was performed in which the activations were compared to a set of human derived cued-target probabilities of recall. This presented a problem as the activation process is one component of many that make up the cued-target probability of recall, however at the time, no model allowed us a direct evaluation of target activation against human derived target activations. Since then, a formal model of cued-target recall, the PIER3 model has been developed which incorporates target activation modelled by binary FANs [10]. As a result, we may now directly compare the cued-target recall calculated using the activation models to human derived cued-target recall data.

The purpose of this paper is to investigate whether the Quantum Inspired models of Target Activation provide a better method of approximating human cued-target recall data than classical models within psychology. No new Quantum Inspired models will be introduced, rather the three Binary Models presented in [9] will be tested alongside the PIER3 model of Target Activation. The second major addition to this work will be the use of multiple sources of FANs in testing the models. In previous work, the University of South Florida (USF) Norms where used as the sole source of FANs. Since then another major source of FANS has been developed by the University of Leuven (UL) and will be used in this article. Furthermore, a new set of pseudo FANs, known as Corpus Based

Association Networks (CANs) will also be used. These networks are artificially created by extracting networks from large text corpus. The choice to include multiple data sources was made to test the robustness of each model against FANs collected under varying conditions. Network features known to influence Target Activation will be explored for each of the three data sources to identify any featural differences within the data sources that may be influencing the performance of target activation models in predicting the probability of recall of a target word in response to a cue. In the proceeding section the models of Target Activation will be introduced.

2   Activation Models

In order to aid in understanding the models considered in this paper, the following situation of a hypothetical target with two associates, a single associate-to-target and associate-to-associate links, all of which can be represented using the Markov Chain Matrix as given in Table 1.

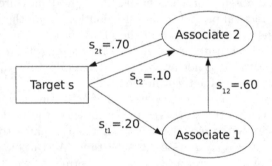

Fig. 1. A hypothetical target with two associates and single associate-to-target and associate-to-associate links [4].

Table 1. Matrix corresponding to hypothetical target shown in Fig. 1. Free association probabilities are obtained by finding the row of interest(the cue) and running across to the associate word obtained [2].

	Target (t)	Associate 1 (a_1)	Associate 2 (a_2)
Target (t)		0.2	0.1
Associate 1 (a_1)			0.6
Associate 2 (a_2)	0.7		

2.1   The PIER3 Memory Model

The PIER3 memory model is designed to model extra-list cuing. In extra-list cuing, participants typically study a list of to-be-recalled target words shown on a monitor for 3 seconds each (e.g., "planet"). The study instructions ask them to read each word aloud when it appears and to remember as many as possible, but participants are not told how they will be tested until the last word is shown. The test instructions indicate that new words, the test cues, will be shown and that each test cue (e.g.,"universe") is related to one of the target words just studied. These cues are not present during study (hence, the name "Extra-list cuing"). As each cue is shown, participants attempt to recall its associatively related word from the study list. The key component of the model is to compute the probability that a target word T is recalled in response to the cue word Q:

$$Pr\left(T|Q\right) = \frac{S\left(T,Q\right)}{S\left(T,Q\right) + S\left(Q,D\right)} \tag{1}$$

where

$$S\left(T,Q\right) = S\left(Q,T\right)_Q + S\left(T,Q\right)_T + S\left(T\right) \ , S\left(Q,D\right) = \frac{D_Q}{n_Q} \tag{2}$$

and $S\left(Q,T\right)_Q$ is the Cue (Q) to Target (T) strength, which is simply the free association probability of the cue producing the target, $S\left(T,Q\right)_T$ is the free association probability of the target producing the cue, and $S\left(T\right)$ is the activation strength of the Target's FAN. D_Q denotes the number of distractors in the cue's FAN and n_Q is the total number of words in the cue's FAN. We can seen from (1) that the PIER3 Memory Model is a signal to noise ratio, where the signal is $S\left(T,Q\right)$ and the noise is $S\left(D,Q\right)$. The formal definition of a cue's distractors is those cue's associates that are not shared with the target, nor are 2-Step Mediators ($a_i \rightarrow a_j \rightarrow T$ implies that a_i is a 2 Step Mediator). Except for FANs sourced from the USF data, pilot studies found that this definition resulted in strong over approximations of the probability of recall (i.e., when the FANs were sourced from the University of Leuven data, or artificial FANs derived from Wikipedia. Consequently, in the development to follow 2-Step Mediators are considered to be distractors in the cue's FAN. In the proceeding section, the PIER3 model of target activation will be introduced along with the three Binary Entanglement Models.

2.2   Modelling Target Activation in PIER3

The PIER3 model's Activation model is given by,

$$S\left(T\right) = \frac{m_T}{n\left(n-1\right)} \tag{3}$$

where m_T is the number of instantiated connections in the Target's network and n is the number of nodes (words) in the Target's network. Taking the example from Fig. 1, $m_T = 4$ and $n = 3$. The corresponding probability of target activation is given by,

$$S(T) = \frac{4}{3\left(3-1\right)} \approx 0.66 \tag{4}$$

A key component of this model is that the weighted strengths within the FAN are not considered, rather whether the connections exist or not.

In the following section, the Quantum Inspired Models of Activation will be introduced.

2.3 Entanglement Activation Model

One method used to model activation is to view a target's network as a composite quantum system as discussed by [6]. Using the example of Fig. 1 to view a target's association network, this would translate into a quantum system modelled by three qubits each corresponding to a column in Table 2. Figure 2 depicts this system, where each word is in a superposed state of being activated (denoted by the basis state $|1\rangle$) or not activated (denoted by the basis state $|0\rangle$). Thus the states of the words in the associative network are represented as,

$$|t\rangle = \bar{\pi}_t |0\rangle + \pi_t |1\rangle \ , \ |a_1\rangle = \bar{\pi}_{a_1} |0\rangle + \pi_{a_1} |1\rangle \ , \ |a_2\rangle = \bar{\pi}_{a_2} |0\rangle + \pi_{a_2} |1\rangle \qquad (5)$$

The amplitudes of the respective qubits can be derived from the matrix depicted in Table 1. Consider the column associate a_2. The two non-zero values in this column represent the level and the number of times associate a_2 is recalled in a free association experiment. Intuitively, the more non-zero entries and the higher the values, the more a_2 is activated. Galea et al. 2011 formalized this by taking the square root of the average of these values as being the amplitude [6]. For example $\pi_{a_2} = \sqrt{0.35}$. In the "all or none" approach, we no longer consider the strength of the relationships in ascribing the amplitudes, rather the existence (or non-existence) of a relationship. Consequently, the original semantic network depicted in Table 1 now takes the form in Table 2. The intuition behind entanglement activation is that the target t "activates its associative structure in synchrony" [2]. This intuition is modelled using an entangled state,

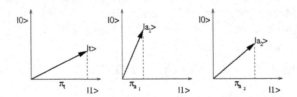

Fig. 2. Three bodied quantum system of words [1]

Table 2. Matrix corresponding to hypothetical target system shown in Fig. 1 where all of the link weightings not equal to zero have been set to 1.

	Target (t)	Associate 1 (a_1)	Associate 2 (a_2)
Target (t)	0	1	1
Associate 1 (a_1)	0	0	1
Associate 2 (a_2)	1	0	0

$$\psi'_t = \sqrt{p_0}\,|000\rangle + \sqrt{p_1}\,|111\rangle, \tag{6}$$

which represents a situation in which the entire associative structure is either completely activated ($|111\rangle$) or not activated at all ($|000\rangle$).

The question remains how to ascribe values to the probabilities p_0 and p_1. One approach is to assume the target is not activated. Given that p_1 refers to the probability of the target being activated, this reflects the strength of activation, namely $S(T)$ as proposed by Galea et al. 2011 [6]:

$$p_1 = S(T) = 1 - (1 - Pr(T)) \prod_i (1 - Pr(\text{Word}_i)). \tag{7}$$

Equation 7 is known to overestimate activation, particularly as the number of words in the semantic network increases [6].

In the proceeding section, we summarize the three existing entanglement models presented by Galea et al. 2012 [9]. Each is based on a different approach to re-scaling the activation, where the scale is intended to alleviate the overestimation problem. Observe that each model retains Eq. 7's structure, however the $Pr(\text{Word}_i)$ (the square of the amplitude) is redefined for each of the three models according to a different scaling factor.

2.4   Entanglement Binary V1

The Entanglement Binary V1 Activation Model assumes that the $Pr(\text{Word}_i)$'s strength is scaled by the ratio of the number of associate to word links to the number of words (n) within the network, namely:

$$S(T) = 1 - (1 - Pr(T)) \prod_i (1 - Pr(\text{Word}_i)). \tag{8}$$

$$Pr(\text{Word}_i) = \frac{\#\{Pr(\text{Word}_i | Pr(\text{Word}_j)) \neq 0; \forall j \neq i\}}{n}. \tag{9}$$

Taking the example from Fig. 1, the target's and associates' probabilities are

	Target (t)	Associate 1 (a_1)	Associate 2 (a_2)
$Pr(\text{Word})$	1/3	1/3	2/3

and the corresponding probability of target activation is given by,

$$S(T) = 1 - \left(1 - \frac{1}{3}\right)\left(1 - \frac{1}{3}\right)\left(1 - \frac{2}{3}\right) \approx 0.852. \tag{10}$$

2.5   Entanglement Binary V2

The Entanglement Binary V2 Activation Model assumes that the $Pr(\text{Word}_i)$'s strength is scaled by ratio of the number of associate to word links to the total number of possible links within the network (excluding self resonant links), i.e.,

$$S(T) = 1 - (1 - Pr(T)) \prod_i (1 - Pr(\text{Word}_i)). \tag{11}$$

$$Pr(\text{Word}_i) = \frac{\#\{Pr(\text{Word}_i|Pr(\text{Word}_j)) \neq 0; \forall j \neq i\}}{n(n-1)} \tag{12}$$

Taking the example from Fig. 1, the target's and associates' probabilities are:

	Target (t)	Associate 1 (a_1)	Associate 2 (a_2)
$Pr(\text{Word})$	$1/(3(3-1))$	$1/(3(3-1))$	$2/(3(3-1))$

and the corresponding probability of target activation is given by

$$S(T) = 1 - \left(1 - \frac{1}{6}\right)\left(1 - \frac{1}{6}\right)\left(1 - \frac{2}{6}\right) \approx 0.54. \tag{13}$$

2.6   Entanglement Binary V3

The Entanglement Binary V3 Activation Model assumes that the $Pr(\text{Word}_i)$'s strength is scaled by the ratio of the number of associate to word links with the number of actual links within the network m (excluding self resonant links),i.e.,

$$S(T) = 1 - (1 - Pr(T)) \prod_i (1 - Pr(\text{Word}_i)) \tag{14}$$

$$Pr(\text{Word}_i) = \frac{\#\{Pr(\text{Word}_i|Pr(\text{Word}_j)) \neq 0; i \neq j\}}{m} \tag{15}$$

$$m = \#\{Pr(\text{Word}_i|\text{Word}_j) \neq 0; \forall i,j; i \neq j\}. \tag{16}$$

Taking the example from Fig. 1, the target's and associates' probabilities are

	Target (t)	Associate 1 (a_1)	Associate 2 (a_2)
$Pr(\text{Word})$	$1/4$	$1/4$	$2/4$

and the corresponding probability of target activation is now given by

$$S(T) = 1 - \left(1 - \frac{1}{4}\right)\left(1 - \frac{1}{4}\right)\left(1 - \frac{2}{4}\right) \approx 0.72. \tag{17}$$

3   Emprirical Analysis of Activation Models

3.1   Data

The activation models were empirically analyzed using FANs from three different sources. The first two sources are human generated: The USF Free association norms and the UL free association data.

The University of South Florida (USF) data provided two components for this analysis, the first is comprised of 4068 individual target-cue pairs, and a probability of recall of the target with respect to the cue. The probability of recall was established by humans in extra-list cuing experiments [5]. The second component is the FANs for each of the 4068 cue and target words.

The University of Leuven (UL) provided the second source of FANs, in which crowd sourcing was used to collate free association data from human subjects. Each human subject was presented a set of target words and asked to produce the First, Second and Third Associates that came to mind. The results of these tests were provided for this analysis with the following procedure used to create the FANs. A global FAN between all targets and associates was firstly constructed and from which localized networks for individual targets were extracted. The localized target's network was found by only considering the target's associates that exceed a minimum threshold of 2 observed target to associate relationships. The probabilities for a given target to associate, associate to target and associate to associate pairs were formed as the ratio of the number of occurrences of the pair to the total occurrences for the target. The UL data comprises 10048 networks, however only those required for the 4068 cued-target pairs of the USF data were used. Each of the UL FANs can be broken into three different forms, the first is when only the target's first associates (when collected) are considered G_1, the second involves both the first and second Target Associates G_2, and lastly when the first, second and third target Associates are used G_3. Unfortunately, at this stage no further cued-target pairs could be sourced and consequently both the USF and UL results will be assessed on the USF data. The UL data was chosen as it is a recent collection of free association data. The data was collected using a web-based application thus perhaps eradicating issues of temporal and geographical bias present in the USF data. Lastly, the UL data was collected for multiple languages, however only the English data will be used in this report.

The final dataset of FANs was collected automatically using an algorithmic approach that we recently developed [13] The algorithms computes FANs from an underlying text corpus, in this case the Wikipedia 2008 collection. The process involves taking each word (w) in a defined vocabulary (V) and forming a vector based representation ($\underline{w}$) using a sliding window over the corpus to accumulate word co-occurrence statistics. Free association probabilities are simulated using an asymmetric measure based on vector projections. This approach was inspired by a quantum approach to similarity [11]. The resulting networks are referred to as Corpus-based association networks (CANs). Computing CANs involved a number of parameters: the maximum number of nodes, the minimum strength between two vectors to be identified as an association, the text corpus used, the set of stop words and the window size. For this analysis, the parameters used match those defined in Galea et al. 2015 [13], which were those derived to optimize the performance of CANs in approximating FANS. Lastly, as with the UL Free Association Data, only the 4068 cued-target pairs (of the USF data) were used in the analysis to follow.

As mentioned previously, as the underlying FANs are from various sources, it is important to compare their network characteristics. Two key structural features of FANs as outlined in Nelson et al. 2013 [10] being the set size and connectivity will be measured and compared. Set size corresponds to the network

Table 3. Comparison of network features (Mean, Standard Deviation)

	n	$\langle k \rangle$
USF	$(13.93, 4.56)$	$(5.64, 1.42)$
G_1	$(41.75, 10.83)$	$(3.59, 0.99)$
G_2	$(81.4, 17.06)$	$(4.3, 1.02)$
G_3	$(120.8, 22)$	$(4.86, 1.02)$
CAN	$(39.14, 16.62)$	$(35.04, 24.83)$

dimension of the FAN (n) with connectivity measured by the average number of connections per node ($\langle k \rangle$). The network dimension and average number of connections was computed for the 4068 cue-target pairs, the results of which are given in Table 3.

Here we observe a strong disparity in the mean and standard deviations of the set size and average number of connections for the differing data sources. For the set sizes, if we use the USF as a baseline, then the average increases substantially for three variants of the UL FANs with the CANs giving similar results to the first associate UL data (G_1). The same behaviour is exhibited by the standard deviations. The CAN data provided the greatest mean and standard deviation of the set size, however given this is a direct parameter of the CAN model it has not been explored in great detail for this report. For the average number of connections, we identify that the relationship between the USF and UL data is inverted than for the set size. Here the USF data provides the strongest average number of connections, and that this value decreases with the addition of the second and third associates in the UL FANs. As with the set size (network dimension), the CAN data provides the greatest average and standard deviation of the average number of connections. In contrast to set size, the connectivity is not a direct parameter of the model, but a result of the methods used to identify connections. Here we can conclude that the methods used to identify a connection in the CAN model, in general, do so at a greater rate than what is observed in the human collected data. In order to compare the combination of the mean with the standard deviation, a new statistical feature, the Coefficient of Variation was employed. The Coefficient of Variation (C.V.) is computed as the ratio of the standard deviation to the mean, and is interpreted as

Table 4. Coefficient of Variation (C.V.) of the set size and average number of connections

	C.V. of n	CV of $\langle k \rangle$
USF	0.327	0.251
G_1	0.259	0.275
G_2	0.209	0.237
G_3	0.182	0.209
CAN	0.424	0.708

the strength of variation of the data relative to it's mean. This was computed for the set size and average number of connections and is presented in Table 4. The results indicate that UL's free association data generates a considerable smaller C.V. for the set size than for both the USF and CAN data. Furthermore, we observe that as the second and third Associates ($G2$, $G3$) are considered in the UL data, the C.V. decreases indicating that variation of the set sizes decreases as the average set size increases. Interestingly, the CAN data provides the greatest set size C.V. indicating that it has the greatest dispersion of results. The same relationship between the USF, UL and CAN data is preserved in the C.V.'s for the average number of connections as for the set size. This is to be expected as computational methods produce more associations than humans can produce. In the following section, the procedure taken to analyze the target activation models will be discussed.

3.2   Procedure

In the proceeding analysis the probability of recall will be generated solely by the PIER3 Model, with the only variation being the activation term $S(T)$. The three entanglement models ($V1$, $V2$ and $V3$), along with the PIER3 Activation Model, will be used to compute the Probability of Recall. The three data sources discussed: the USF, UL (and it's three variants) and CAN will be used to test the performance of each of the models against the human probability of recall baseline that is part of the USF data.

In previous work, the statistical framework used was based on a mean, median and standard deviation comparison of the models presented to (a) a baseline model and (b) an error analysis of the model compared to the human collected data. In both, the distributions were analyzed to determine whether the data was normally distributed thus allowing the two primary factors, its mean and standard deviation to be used as a basis for comparison. This served well in previous research as the data used was, in most part, normally distributed. The preliminary analysis performed in this study show that this fundamental axiom was not satisfied in all cases, and consequently the use of the mean and standard deviation as a sole method of comparison was put into question. It was decided that a further method was required to allow for varying distribution types to be utilized and compared. One method that allows this to occur is the Kullback-Leibler (KL) Divergence [12], which for two discrete probability distributions U and V measures the amount of information lost when V is used to approximate U. It is calculated using the following,

$$KL(U||V) = \sum_i u_i \ln\left(\frac{u_i}{v_i}\right) \tag{18}$$

In our case, this can be used to model how much information we lose when we use the models of activation to form the probability of recall as opposed to using the actual probabilities collected from human subjects. The closer the models of activation are at approximating the human derived data will result in less information being lost. Hence in this case, identical distributions produce a 0 KL value, with a larger KL value indicating a greater difference between the two distributions. Unfortunately the KL Divergence isn't bounded, and thus can not provide a normalized method of comparison. We can however, rank models M based on increasing divergence $KL(H||M)$ from the human baseline H. The only remaining requirement is to convert the human and model derived cued-target probabilities into a discrete probability distribution. This was achieved by imposing that the cue-target pairs form the complete sample space and then normalizing by the respective probability aggregates.

3.3   Results

For the 4068 cue-target pairs, the probability of recall was computed for each model of activation for each data set. The results for each were evaluated against the human derived probabilities of recall using the KL Divergence, the results of which are presented in Table 5. Here we observe that for the UL data (G_1, G_2 and G_3), the closest model to the human data is the Entanglement Binary V3, followed closely by the Entanglement Binary V1 model. For the USF data, the PIER3 provides the best results, and for the CAN data the Entanglement Binary V1 ranks closest to the human baseline.

As given before, the KL divergence is not bounded and thus only a relative (ranked) comparison can be made between the respective models. To provide a standardized method of comparison, an an error analysis was performed by comparing the mean errors of the models in relation to the human baseline probabilities of recall. Two statistical features, the mean and standard deviation of the errors were calculated and are presented below in Table 6. Here using the mean error as a method of comparison, we observe that in all cases outside of the USF data, the Entanglement Binary V1 produced the smallest mean error. For the USF data, the Entanglement Binary V3 model produced the smallest mean error. This presents a difference to the results found using the KL Divergence in which the Entanglement Binary models were outperformed by the classical PIER3 model. Consequently, when using the mean error to compare we can infer that the Entanglement Binary Models (here focusing on V1) are robust against different sources of data, a feature we haven't observed to the same level in the PIER3 model. Further to that, we observe that for each data source the mean errors satisfied the inequality $V2 \leq V3 \leq V1$. As mentioned previously, not all distributions observed were normal in nature. The Entanglement Binary V3

Table 5. KL divergence comparison

	G_1	G_2	G_3	USF	CAN
Entanglement binary V1	0.12297	0.12626	0.12894	0.12217	0.14271
Entanglement binary V2	0.16332	0.15611	0.15599	0.1023	0.21791
Entanglement binary V3	0.1185	0.12144	0.12415	0.1163	0.15406
PIER3 activation	0.16237	0.15565	0.15568	0.10289	0.20751

Table 6. Comparison of the mean and standard deviation on the error

	G_1	G_2	G_3	USF	CAN
Entanglement binary V1	$(0.003, 0.228)$	$(0.008, 0.233)$	$(0.010, 0.235)$	$(0.095, 0.227)$	$(0.022, 0.267)$
Entanglement binary V2	$(-0.332, 0.221)$	$(-0.369, 0.222)$	$(-0.394, 0.225)$	$(-0.136, 0.214)$	$(-0.190, 0.297)$
Entanglement binary V3	$(-0.046, 0.227)$	$(-0.058, 0.230)$	$(-0.065, 0.233)$	$(0.029, 0.224)$	$(-0.069, 0.275)$
PIER3 activation	$(-0.331, 0.221)$	$(-0.369, 0.222)$	$(-0.394, 0.225)$	$(-0.123, 0.215)$	$(-0.151, 0.299)$

method provided loosely normal distributions, however given that $V1$ was the best performing method this did not influence the final conclusion made.

At this stage, the standard deviations in the model do not provide enough variance to make any conclusive remarks when comparing the different models of activation. What can be said is that having a standard deviation of ~ 0.22 is quite large (the range for the errors is $[-1, 1]$) and this variance needs to be addressed in future modeling.

We can conclude that in all cases bar the USF data, the classical model (PIER3) was strongly outperformed by it's Quantum Inspired counterparts. Within the Quantum Models, the Entanglement Binary V1 provided the best overall results both in terms of the KL Divergence and the Error Analysis and was robust against FANs from varying data sources. The PIER3 Model was shown to vary substantially for different sources of FANs, and only excelled in the ranked comparison of the KL Divergence using the USF data. This may suggest that the PIER3 model, which was built using the USF data as its testing framework, only performs well on the USF data, and that a modification to the model to allow for networks of varying network structures should be considered.

4   Discussion

An interesting relationship was observed in the error analysis in which the three Entanglement Models satisfied the inequality $V2 \leq V3 \leq V1$. The behaviour exhibited by the three Entanglement Binary models is not unexpected. Recall that the Probability for each word w in a given network for a target t using Entanglement Binary Version i is found using the formula,

$$Pr(w)_i = \frac{m_i}{s_i} \tag{19}$$

where $m_i = \#\{Pr(w_i|w_j) \neq 0; \forall j = 1 \ldots n; j \neq i\}$, s_i is the scaling parameter for the Binary Version i and n is the number of associates and target. For V1; $s_i = n$, for V2; $s_i = n(n-1)$ and for V3; $s_i = n_T$ where n_T is the total number of connections in the network. Clearly,

$$n \leq n_T \leq n(n-1) \Rightarrow \frac{1}{n(n-1)} \leq \frac{1}{n_T} \leq \frac{1}{n} \tag{20}$$

Hence,

$$\frac{m_i}{n(n-1)} \leq \frac{m_i}{n_T} \leq \frac{m_i}{n} \Rightarrow Pr(w)_2 \leq Pr(w)_3 \leq Pr(w)_1 \tag{21}$$

And from which we find that,

$$S(T)_2 \leq S(T)_3 \leq S(T)_1 \tag{22}$$

where $S(T)_i$ is the Entanglement Binary Version i. This inequality can be extended to allow for the PIER3 Model of Cue-Target Recall, i.e.

$$Pr(T|Q)_2 \leq Pr(T|Q)_3 \leq PR(T|Q)_1 \tag{23}$$

where $Pr(T|Q)_i$ represents the PIER3 Model of Cue-Target Recall when the Entanglement Binary Version i is used. This inequality also holds for the Mean Error Analysis, i.e.

$$Pr(T|Q)_2 - Pr(T|Q)_H \leq Pr(T|Q)_3 - Pr(T|Q)_H \leq Pr(T|Q)_1 - Pr(T|Q)_H \tag{24}$$

Which when applied to a finite set of Cue-Target pairs, we arrive at,

$$\mu(Pr(T|Q)_2 - Pr(T|Q)_H) \leq \mu(Pr(T|Q)_3 - Pr(T|Q)_H) \leq \mu(Pr(T|Q)_1 - Pr(T|Q)_H) \tag{25}$$

How the models compare with respect to KL divergence is unknown at this stage, however if we were to use the means as a sole measure, then based on the empirical evaluation performed here, future work should be centered on $V1$.

5   Summary and Outlook

This report was performed to identify whether models of Target Activation inspired by Quantum Entanglement provide a better platform in deriving cued-target recall than classical psychological models. A new approach to assessing performance, the KL Divergence, was added to the mean and standard deviation analysis of the errors. It was found that using both methods, the models of target activation inspired by Quantum Entanglement were superior to the classical PIER3 Target Activation Model. Of the three Quantum Entanglement models, the Entanglement Binary V1 provided not only the best performance but was robust against the three sources of data used.

Acknowledgements. The research presented in this paper would not have been achieved without the contributions of Prof Doug Nelson from the University of South Florida who provided the Human Free Association Networks [5]. The version of Wikipedia used was provided by Mr Lance Devine from the Queensland University of Technology. The University of Leuven Free Association data was provided by Mr Simon De Deyne from the University of Adelaide.

References

1. Bruza, P., Kitto, K., Nelson, D., McEvoy, C.: Extracting spooky-activation-at-a-distance from considerations of entanglement. In: Bruza, P., Sofge, D., Lawless, W., van Rijsbergen, K., Klusch, M. (eds.) QI 2009. LNCS, vol. 5494, pp. 71–83. Springer, Heidelberg (2009)
2. Bruza, P., Kitto, K., Nelson, D., McEvoy, C.: Is there something quantum-like about the human mental lexicon? J. Math. Psychol. **53**, 362–377 (2009)
3. Busemeyer, J., Bruza, P.: Quantum Cognition and Decision. Cambridge University Press, Cambridge (2012)
4. Nelson, D., McEvoy, C., Pointer, L.: Spreading activation or spooky activation at a distance? J. Exp. Psychol. Learn. Mem. Cogn. **29**(1), 42–52 (2003)
5. Nelson, D., McEvoy, C., Schreiber, T.: The University of South Florida, word association, rhyme and word fragment norms. Behav. Res. Meth. Instrum. Comput. **36**, 408–420 (2004)
6. Galea, D., Bruza, P., Kitto, K., Nelson, D., McEvoy, C.: Modelling the acitivation of words in human memory: the spreading activation, spooky-activation-at-a-distance and the entanglement models compared. In: Song, D., Melucci, M., Frommholz, I., Zhang, P., Wang, L., Arafat, S. (eds.) QI 2011. LNCS, vol. 7052, pp. 149–160. Springer, Heidelberg (2011)
7. Kintsch, W.: The role of knowledge in discourse comprehension construction-integration model. Psychol. Rev. **95**, 163–182 (1988)
8. Nelson, D., McEvoy, C.: Implicitly activated memories: The missing links of remembering. In: Izawa, C., Ohta, N. (eds.) Human Learning and Memory: Advances in Theory and Applications, pp. 177–198. Erlbaum, New Jersey (2005)
9. Galea, D., Bruza, P., Kitto, K., Nelson, D.: Modelling word activation in semantic networks. three scaled entanglement models compared. In: Busemeyer, J.R., Dubois, F., Lambert-Mogiliansky, A., Melucci, M. (eds.) QI 2012. LNCS, vol. 7620, pp. 172–183. Springer, Heidelberg (2012)
10. Nelson, D., Kitto, K., Galea, D., McEvoy, C., Bruza, P.: How activation, entanglement, and searching a semantic network contribute to event memory. Mem. Cogn. **41**(6), 797–819 (2013)
11. Trueblood, J., Pothos, E., Busemeyer, J.: Quantum probability theory as a common framework for reasoning and similarity. Front. Psychol. 5 (2015)
12. Kullback, S., Leibler, R.: On information and sufficiency. Ann. Math. Stat. **22**(1), 79–86 (1951)
13. Galea, D., Bruza, P.: Deriving word association networks from text corpora (2015). arXiv:1104.1322v1

Operators and Operator Valued Measures

Real-Orthogonal Projections as Quantum Pseudo-Logic

Marjan Matvejchuk[1]([⊠]) and Dominic Widdows[2]

[1] Kazan Technical University, Ul Karl Marks 3, Kazan 420008, Russia
Marjan.Matvejchuk@yandex.ru
[2] Microsoft Bing, Bellevue, WA, USA
dwiddows@microsoft.com

Abstract. In the paper, we study linear operators in complex Hilbert space $\mathbb{C}^n$ that are called real-orthogonal projections, which are a generalization of standard (complex) orthogonal projections but for which only the real part of the scalar product vanishes. We compare some partial order properties of orthogonal and of real-orthogonal projections. In particular, this leads to the observation that a natural analogue of the ordering relationship defined on standard orthogonal projections leads to a non-transitive relationship between real-orthogonal projections. We prove that the set of all real-orthogonal projections in a finite-dimensional complex space is a quantum pseudo-logic, and briefly consider some potential applications of such a structure.

Keywords: Hilbert space · Real-orthogonal · Idempotent · projection · Partial order · Logic

1 Introduction

Since its introduction by Birkhoff and von Neumann in the 1930's [1], many papers have been devoted to quantum logic.

Definition 1. *A quantum logic [2, 3] is a set L endowed with a partial order $\leq$ and unary operation $^\perp$ such that the following conditions are satisfied (the symbols $\vee$, $\wedge$ denote the lattice-theoretic operations induced by $\leq$):*

(i) L possesses a least and a greatest element, 0 and I, and $0 \neq I$.
(ii) $a \leq b$ implies $b^\perp \leq a^\perp$ for any a, $b \in L$.
(iii) $(a^\perp)^\perp = a$ for any $a \in L$.
(iv) If $\{a_i\}_{i \in X}$ is a finite subset of L such that $a_i \leq a_j^\perp$ for $i \neq j$, then supremum $\vee_{i \in X} a_i$ exists in L.
(v) If a, $b \in L$ and $a \leq b$, then $b = a \vee (b \wedge a^\perp)$.

AMS2000 subject classification. 15A57; 81P10.

H. Atmanspacher et al. (Eds.): QI 2015, LNCS 9535, pp. 275–283, 2016.
DOI: 10.1007/978-3-319-28675-4_21

Sometimes axioms (iv), (v) are replaced with:

(iv)′ If $a \leq b^{\perp}$ then there exists $a \vee b$.
(v)′ If a, $b \in L$ and $a \leq b$, then there exists $c \leq a^{\perp}$ such that $b = a \vee c$.

Algebraically, quantum logics are called orthomodular partially ordered sets (or, in short, orthomodular posets) [4]. A logic L does not have to be distributive nor a lattice. Two elements a, $b \in L$ are called orthogonal if $a \leq b^{\perp}$. We will denote the orthogonality of a, b by the symbol $a \perp b$.

An important interpretation of a quantum logic is the set of all orthogonal (=self-adjoint) projections (=idempotents) on a Hilbert space H. This is such a common example that it is sometimes called the *standard logic* on H [5], even though its failure to satisfy the distributive law makes it decidedly non-standard from the point of view of classical logic. Projections have been and are still extensively studied [6–9].

This paper concerns a generalization of the standard quantum logic on $\mathbb{C}^n$, which results from considering just the real part of the scalar product of two vectors. It will be shown that the ordering properties of such projections are somewhat different from those of standard orthogonal projections, resulting in an interesting and potentially useful algebraic structure. In the process we note a triviality of Theorem 5(d) of [10].

2 Some Definitions and Properties

Let $\mathbb{C}^n$ ($\mathbb{R}^n$) denote the complex (respectively real) Euclidean space with the Hermitian inner product

$$(x, y) = x_1\overline{y_1} + x_2\overline{y_2} + ... + x_n\overline{y_n}$$

for $x = (x_1, x_2, ..., x_n), y = (y_1, y_2, ..., y_n) \in \mathbb{C}^n$.

Two vectors x, y are called *orthogonal* if their Hermitian inner product is zero, i.e. $(x, y) = 0$.

One the real vector space $\mathbb{R}^n$, the Hermitian inner product is of course the same as the standard Euclidean scalar product. On the complex vector space $\mathbb{C}^n$ we can also consider pairs of vectors for which only the real part of the scalar product is zero.

Definition 2. *Two vectors $x, y \in \mathbb{C}^n$ are said to be real-orthogonal or $\mathbb{R}$-orthogonal if $Re(x, y) = 0$.*

Note that this property has been called *semi-orthogonal* [10]. We have chosen to use the term $\mathbb{R}$-orthogonal instead to avoid any confusion with the more recognised definition of semi-orthogonal matrices.[1]

Let $\mathbb{C}_{n,n}$ ($\mathbb{R}_{n,n}$) denote the set of complex (real, respectively) $n \times n$ matrices.

The symbol A^* will stand for the conjugate-transpose matrix of $A \in \mathbb{C}_{n,n}$, i.e. $A^*_{ij} = \bar{A}_{ji}$. It is well-known that $(Ax, y) = (x, A^*y)\ \forall x, y$.

By $H(A)$ we denote the Hermitian part of A, i.e. $H(A) = \frac{1}{2}(A + A^*)$. It is well known that $A \in \mathbb{C}_{n,n}$ is an orthogonal projection, i.e. an Hermitian idempotent, if and only if $(I_{n,n} - A)x$ and Ax are orthogonal for all $x \in \mathbb{C}^n$.

Definition 3. *A matrix $A \in \mathbb{C}_{n,n}$ is called a real-orthogonal projection or $\mathbb{R}$-orthogonal projection if the vectors $(I_{n,n} - A)x$, Ax are $\mathbb{R}$-orthogonal for all $x \in \mathbb{C}^n$.*

Definition 4. *Let us denote by $\mathcal{S}^{or}$ the set of all $\mathbb{R}$-orthogonal projections on $\mathbb{C}_{n,n}$.*

This is equivalent to the condition that $(I_{n,n} - A^*)A$ is skew-Hermitian, which is satisfied if and only if A^*A equals the Hermitian part of A, i.e.

$$A^*A = \frac{1}{2}(A + A^*) = H(A). \tag{1}$$

Note the following:

1. If A is an $\mathbb{R}$-orthogonal projection and $A = A^*$ then A is an orthogonal projection.
2. Any one-dimensional $\mathbb{R}$-orthogonal projection in $\mathbb{R}_{n,n}$ is an orthogonal projection.

Example 1. The matrix $A = \frac{1}{5}\begin{pmatrix} 4 & 2 \\ -2 & 4 \end{pmatrix}$ is neither Hermitian nor idempotent but satisfies Eq. 1, and thus is $\mathbb{R}$-orthogonal.

We wish to make clear that an $\mathbb{R}$-orthogonal projection need not be a projection in the usual sense, since it is not necessarily an idempotent.

3 Properties of Real-Orthogonal Projections

Property 1. A is an $\mathbb{R}$-orthogonal projection if and only if $I_{n,n} - A$ is an $\mathbb{R}$-orthogonal projection also.

---

[1] "In linear algebra, a semi-orthogonal matrix is a non-square matrix with real entries where: if the number of columns exceeds the number of rows, then the rows are orthonormal vectors; but if the number of rows exceeds the number of columns, then the columns are orthonormal vectors." Quoted directly from https://en.wikipedia.org/wiki/Semi-orthogonal_matrix.

Property 2. Any $\mathbb{R}$-orthogonal projection $A \in \mathbb{C}_{n,n}$ is a normal matrix with all eigenvalues on a circle about $\frac{1}{2}$ with radius $\frac{1}{2}$ in the complex plane, i.e. every eigenvalue λ of A satisfies $|\lambda|^2 = Re(\lambda)$ [10, Corollary 3(b)].

Thus for any $\mathbb{R}$-orthogonal projection A in $\mathbb{C}_{n,n}$ there exists a set of mutually orthogonal self-adjoint projections $\{p_j\}$ and a set of numbers $\{\lambda_j\}$, where $|\lambda_j|^2 = Re(\lambda_j)$ for any j, such that $A = \sum_j \lambda_j p_j$.

Theorem 1. *It has been demonstrated [10, Theorem 5] that:*

Let $A, B \in \mathbb{C}_{n,n}$ be $\mathbb{R}$-orthogonal projections. Let α be an arbitrary real scalar such that $0 < \alpha < 1$. Then the following statements hold:

(i) A^*B is an $\mathbb{R}$-orthogonal projection if and only if $H(A^*B) = H(A^*BA)$.
(ii) $A + B$ is an $\mathbb{R}$-orthogonal projection if and only if $H(A^*B) = 0$.
(iii) $A - B$ is an $\mathbb{R}$-orthogonal projection if and only if $H(A^*B) = H(B)$.
(iv) $\alpha A + (1 - \alpha)B$ is an $\mathbb{R}$-orthogonal projection if and only if $H(A^*B) = \frac{1}{2}[H(A) + H(B)]$.

Remark 1. Condition (iv) of Theorem 1 is fulfilled if and only if $A = B$.

Proof. Let condition (iv) of Theorem 1 be fulfilled: $H(A^*B) = \frac{1}{2}[H(A) + H(B)]$, i.e.

$$1/2(A^*B + B^*A) = 1/4[(A + A^*) + (B + B^*)] = 1/2(A^*A + B^*B).$$

Hence

$$0 = A^*A + B^*B - (A^*B + B^*A) = (A - B)^*(A - B).$$

Thus $A - B = 0$ and $A = B$.
The converse is trivial. ∎

4   A Partial Ordering on Real-Orthogonal Projections

Let us first present well-known facts about orthogonal projections. Let H be a Hilbert space and let p, q be orthogonal projections on H.

Property 3. The following conditions are equivalent:

(i) $p = pq (= qp)$.
(ii) $pH \subseteq qH$
(iii) $q - p$ is an orthogonal projection.

Definition 5. *Put $p \leq q$ if $p = pq$. Let the symbols $\vee, \wedge$ denote the lattice-theoretic operations induced by $\leq$.*

Note that $p \vee q$ is the orthogonal projection onto the subspace $\overline{pH + qH}$ and $p \wedge q$ is the orthogonal projection onto $pH \cap qH$.

Definition 6. *Let $p^{\perp} = I - p$.*

Property 4. The following conditions are equivalent:

(i) $pq = 0$.

(ii) $p + q$ is an orthogonal projection.

(iii) $p \vee q = p + q$.

(iv) $q \leq p^{\perp}$.

There are several ways to express ordering and conditionals between operators on vector spaces. Some are summarized in [11, Ch 5], which draws attention to the fact that some conditionals are only weakly transitive. In the paper [10] there is the (Löwner) partial ordering: $A \hat{\leq} B \Leftrightarrow B - A = G^*G$ for some matrix G with n rows.

The main contribution of this paper is to offer a new alternative to these approaches. First we offer a *pseudo* partial order and unary operation $^{\perp}$, with respect to which $\mathcal{S}^{or}$ becomes well-known structure.

Definition 7. *Let $A, B \in \mathcal{S}^{or}$. Put $A \leq_1 B$ if $B - A \in \mathcal{S}^{or}$, $A^{\perp} := I_{n,n} - A$, and $A \perp B$ if $B \leq_1 A^{\perp}$. Of course $A <_1 B$ if $A \leq_1 B$ and $B - A \neq 0$.*

Note that:

1. $A \leq_1 B$, and $B \leq_1 A$ then $A = B$.
2. If $A \perp B$ then $B \perp A$, and $A + B \in \mathcal{S}^{or}$.
3. The relation $\leq_1$ is an analogue of the partial order relation (see Properties 3, iii) on the set of standard orthogonal projections.
4. The relation $\leq_1$ does not possess the transitivity property.

Example 2. Let $p, q \in \mathbb{C}_{2,2}$, $q \neq p^{\perp}$, $q \neq p$ be one dimensional orthogonal projections. Let $\lambda \in \mathbb{C}$ be such that $|\lambda|^2 = Re(\lambda)$, $0 \neq \lambda \neq 1$. It is clear that $\lambda p^{\perp}$, $(1 - \lambda)q \in \mathcal{S}^{or}$. In addition, $\lambda p \leq_1 \lambda(p + p^{\perp}) = \lambda I_{2,2} \in \mathcal{S}^{or}$, $\lambda I_{2,2} \leq_1 (\lambda I_{2,2} + (1 - \lambda)q) \in \mathcal{S}^{or}$.

By $\lambda p^{\perp} + (1 - \lambda)q \notin \mathcal{S}^{or}$, we have $\lambda p \not\leq_1 \lambda I_{2,2} + (1 - \lambda)q = \lambda p + (\lambda p^{\perp} + (1 - \lambda)q)$.

Property 5. Note the unusual properties of $\leq_1$:

1. If $A <_1 B$ then $\dim(A\mathbb{C}^n) \leq \dim(B\mathbb{C}^n)$. Really, let B be an orthogonal projection and $A = \lambda B$, where $|\lambda|^2 = Re(\lambda)$ and $Im(\lambda) \neq 0$. Then $A <_1 B$ and $\dim(A\mathbb{C}^n) = \dim(B\mathbb{C}^n)$.
2. In $\mathbb{C}^n$ for any $\mathbb{R}$-orthogonal projection A, $\dim(A\mathbb{C}^n) > 1$ there exists one-dimension $\mathbb{R}$-orthogonal projection P, $\dim(P\mathbb{C}^n) = 1$ with $P <_1 A$. In real space $\mathbb{R}^n$ this is not true in general case. (It is sufficient to consider $\mathbb{R}$-orthogonal projection $A = \frac{1}{5}\begin{pmatrix} 4 & 2 \\ -2 & 4 \end{pmatrix}$ in $\mathbb{R}^2$. It is clear that $\dim(A\mathbb{R}^2) = 2$ and $P \not\leq_1 A$ for any one-dimensional orthogonal projection P.)

Remark 2. If $A, B \in \mathcal{S}^{or}$ and $A \leq_1 (I_{n,n} - B)$ then $AB \neq 0$, in general. For example, consider $A = \lambda P$, $B = (1 - \lambda)P$, where $|\lambda|^2 = Re(\lambda)$ and P is an orthogonal projection with $\dim P = 1$ (cf. Property 4, i).

Lemma 1. *Let $A, B \in \mathcal{S}^{or}$. The following conditions are equivalent:*

(a) $Re(Ax, Bx) = 0$, i.e. Ax and Bx are $\mathbb{R}$-orthogonal for all $x \in \mathbb{C}^n$.
(b) $A + B \in \mathcal{S}^{or}$.
(c) $B \leq_1 A^{\perp}$, i.e. $A \perp B$.

Proof

(a) $\Leftrightarrow$ (b). By [10, Theorem 1], $Re(Ax, Bx) = 0$ if and only if $H(A^*B) = 0$. By
[10, Theorem 5], $H(A^*B) = 0$ if and only if $A + B \in \mathcal{S}^{or}$.
(b) $\Rightarrow$ (c). Let $A + B \in \mathcal{S}^{or}$. By [10, Corollary 3(f)], $(I_{n,n} - (A + B)) \in \mathcal{S}^{or}$.
Hence $(I_{n,n} - A) = (I_{n,n} - (A+B)) + B \ (\in \mathcal{S}^{or})$. Thus $B \leq_1 I_{n,n} - A = A^{\perp}$.
(c) $\Rightarrow$ (b). Let $B \leq_1 I_{n,n} - A$. By the definition of $\leq_1$, $(I_{n,n} - A - B) \in \mathcal{S}^{or}$.
Then $(A + B) = (I_{n,n} - A - B)^{\perp} \in \mathcal{S}^{or}$. $\square$

Proposition 1. *Let* $A, B \in \mathcal{S}^{or}$. *Then* $A \leq_1 B$ *implies* $B^{\perp} \leq_1 A^{\perp}$ *for any* $A,$
$B \in \mathcal{S}^{or}$.

Proof. Let $A <_1 B$. Then $B - A \neq 0$, $B - A \in \mathcal{S}^{or}$. We have $(I_{n,n} - B) + (B - A) = I_{n,n} - A$. Hence $I_{n,n} - B <_1 I_{n,n} - A$, i.e. $B^{\perp} <_1 A^{\perp}$. $\square$

Let $A, B \in \mathcal{S}^{or}$. Let us suppose that there exists an $\mathbb{R}$-orthogonal projection C
such that: (1) $A \leq_1 C$, $B \leq_1 C$ and (2) $C \leq_1 D$ for any $D \in \mathcal{S}^{or}$ which $A \leq_1 C$,
$B \leq_1 C$. Let us denote C by $A \vee_1 B$.

Proposition 2. *Let* $A, B, C \in \mathcal{S}^{or}$. *Let* $A \leq_1 C$, $B \leq_1 C$ *and* $A \perp B$. *Then*
$A + B \leq_1 C$, *there exists* $A \vee_1 B$ *and* $A \vee_1 B = A + B$.

Proof

(i) By $A <_1 C$ and by $B <_1 C$, $H(C^*A) = H(A)$ and $H(C^*B) = H(B)$. Hence
$H(C^*(A+B)) = H(C^*A) + H(C^*B) = H(A) + H(B) = H(A+B)$. By [10,
Theorem 5(c)] $C - (A + B) \in \mathcal{S}^{or}$, i.e. $(A + B) \leq_1 C$.
(ii) It is clear that $A <_1 (A+B)$ and $B <_1 (A+B)$. Hence there exists $(A \vee_1 B)$
and $A \vee_1 B = A + B$. $\square$

Corollary 1. *If* $\{A_i\}_{1 \leq i \leq k}$ $(k \leq m)$ *is a subset of* $\mathcal{S}^{or}$ *such that* $A_i \leq_1 A_j^{\perp}$ *for*
$i \neq j$, *then supremum* $\vee_{1 \leq i \leq k} A_i$ *exists and* $= \sum_1^k A_i \ (\in \mathcal{S}^{or})$.

Proof. By Proposition 2, $A_1 + A_2 \leq_1 A_c^{\perp}$ if $c > 2$. By the induction, $\sum_1^{k-1} A_i \leq_1$
$A_k^{\perp}$. By Proposition 2 again, $\vee_{1 \leq i \leq k} A_i = \sum_1^k A_i \in \mathcal{S}^{or}$. $\square$

Proposition 3. *Let* $A, B \in \mathcal{S}^{or}$ *and let* $A \perp B$. *Then* $(A \vee_1 B)^{\perp}$ *is a maximal*
element from $\{F, F \in \mathcal{S}^{or} : F \leq_1 A^{\perp}, F \leq_1 B^{\perp}\}$.

Proof. By Proposition 2, $(A \vee_1 B)^{\perp} = (A+B)^{\perp} = I_{n,n} - (A+B) <_1 (I_{n,n} - A) = A^{\perp}$. By the analogy, $(A \vee_1 B)^{\perp} <_1 B^{\perp}$.

Let us assume for the moment that there exist $C \in \mathcal{S}^{or}$, $C \neq 0$, such that
$(A \vee_1 B)^{\perp} + C \leq_1 A^{\perp}$ and $(A \vee_1 B)^{\perp} + C \leq_1 B^{\perp}$. Then $I_{n,n} - A - B + C \leq_1 I_{n,n} - A$
and hence $A \leq_1 (A + B) - C$. By the analogy, $B \leq_1 (A + B) - C$. Now, by
Proposition 2 again, $(A + B) = A \vee_1 B \leq_1 (A + B) - C <_1 (A + B) = A \vee_1 B$.
This leads to a contradiction. $\square$

Remark 3. For orthogonal projections there is a known stronger result, which is that if P, Q are orthogonal projections then $(P \vee Q)^{\perp} = P^{\perp} \wedge Q^{\perp}$.

Theorem 2. *On the set $\mathcal{S}^{or}$ with $\leq_1$ and $\perp$ the conditions $(i) - (iv)$, (iv'), (v') of Definition 1 are fulfilled.*

Proof. Let us verify that $(i) - (iv)$, (iv'), (v') are fulfilled. Since 0, $I_{m,m} \in \mathcal{S}^{or}$, hence (i). By Proposition 1, we have (ii). The condition (iii) is obviously satisfied. By Corollary 1, we obtain (iv), (iv').

Let us prove (v'). Let A, $B \in \mathcal{S}^{or}$ and $A \leq_1 B$. Then $C := B - A \leq_1 A^{\perp}$ and by Proposition 2, $B = A + C = A \vee_1 C$. $\square$

Now, we offer a partial order on the set $\mathcal{S}^{or}$.

Definition 8. *Let A, $B \in \mathcal{S}^{or}$. Put $A \leq B$ if there exist finite subset $\{A_i\}_1^m \subset \mathcal{S}^{or}$ such that $(A + A_1 + ... + A_{k-1}) + A_k \in \mathcal{S}^{or}$ for all k, $1 \leq k \leq m$ and $A + \sum_{i=1}^m A_i = B$.*

Note that $A_1 + ... + A_{k-1} + A_k \notin \mathcal{S}^{or}$, in general (see Example 2). By the definition,

$$A \leq_1 A + A_1, \ A + A_1 \leq_1 (A + A_1) + A_2, \cdots ,$$

$$(A + A_1 + ... + A_{k-1}) + A_k \leq_1 (A + A_1 + ... + A_k) + A_{k+1} \ \text{for all } k.$$

Let us turn to Example 2. By the construction, $\lambda p < (\lambda I_{2,2} \mid (1 - \lambda)q)$.

It is clear that the relation $\leq$ is a transitive relation and $\leq_1$ entails $\leq$. But the converse is not true (Example 2). The relation $\leq$ is an analogue of the corresponding partial order relation on the set of all orthogonal projections, again.

5 An Interpretation of $\mathbb{R}$-orthogonality on $\mathbb{R}^{2n}$

It has been pointed out that the condition that two vectors in $\mathbb{C}^n$ be $\mathbb{R}$-orthogonal is just the same as the condition that they are orthogonal as vectors in $\mathbb{R}^{2n}$ using the euclidean scalar product.

This should lead to an identical version of the theory in strictly real vector spaces $\mathbb{R}^{2n}$, and a pseudo-logic based on a subgroup of operators $\mathcal{S}^{or} < GL(2n, \mathbb{R})$.

This approach has yet to be explored.

6 Potential Application Areas

Part of the motivation for studying pseudo-logical structures with non-transitive ordering relations is the potential to model non-monotonic reasoning.

In economics, a system of preference relations is required to satisfy the transitivity law to be considered rational, but there are many observed examples where people make choices that are not rational in this sense [12].

In physics, there is a relationship between transitivity and ergodic dynamical systems [13]. This leads to the suggestion that a non-transitive logic may help to model non-ergodic systems.

In information retrieval, various conditional operators on vectors have been investigated, with distinctions between strongly and weakly transitive conditionals [11, Ch 5]. As further work, we propose to investigate whether the relations on ℝ-orthogonal projections discussed in this paper satisfy any of these weaker logical conditions.

Finally, in linguistics, non-transitive or non-monotonic implications are reasonably common, particularly when the implication statement is an informal generalization (for example "penguins are birds", "birds fly", "penguins don't fly").

As future work, it is worth exploring the potential for using the logic of ℝ-orthogonal operators to model such situations.

7   Conclusion

This paper has explored a quantum pseudo-logical structure arising from a non-transitive ordering relation on real-orthogonal projections on complex vector spaces.

There is much work to do in exploring these structures further and understanding their algebraic implications, and related formalisms (for example, treating the vectors as real throughout). Given the variety of real-world application areas for non-monotonic reasoning, such exploration may be quite fruitful.

Acknowledgments. The authors would like to thank several attendees at the conference for valuable feedback, including Ismael Martinez-Martinez, Hans Römer and Thomas Filk.

References

1. Birkhoff, G., von Neumann, J.: The logic of quantum mechanics. Ann. Math. **37**, 823–843 (1936)
2. Pták, P., Pulmannová, S.: Orthomodular Structures as Quantum Logics. Kluwer Academic Publishers, Dordrecht (1991). INIS-m14676, p. 27
3. Cohen, D.: An introduction to Hilbert Spaces and Quantum Logic. Spriger, New York (1989)
4. Wilce, A.: Quantum logic and probability theory. In: Zalta, E.N. (ed.) The Stanford Encyclopedia of Philosophy (Spring 2003 Edition) Stanford University, Stanford (2003)
5. Varadarajan, V.S.: Geometry of Quantum Theory. Springer-Verlag, New York (1985)

6. Matvejchuk, M.: Unitary self-adjoint logics of projections. Int. J. Theor. Phys. **37**(1), 103–107 (1998)
7. Matvejchuk, M.: Probability measures in w^*j-algebras in hilbert spaces with conjugation. Proc. Am. Math. Soc. **126**(4), 1155–1164 (1998)
8. Ando, T.: Projections in Krein spaces. Linear Algebra Appl. **431**(12), 2346–2358 (2009)
9. Matvejchuk, M.: Idempotents in a space with conjugation. Linear Algebra Appl. **438**(1), 71–79 (2013)
10. Troschke, S.-O., et al.: On semi-orthogonality and a special class of matrices. Linear Algebra Appl. **289**(1), 169–182 (1999)
11. van Rijsbergen, K.: The Geometry of Information Retrieval. Cambridge University Press, Cambridge (2004)
12. Mas-Colell, A., Whinston, M., Green, J.: Microeconomic Theory. Oxford University Press, New York (1995)
13. Rebenshtok, A., Barkai, E.: Weakly non-ergodic statistical physics. J. Stat. Phys. **133**(3), 565–586 (2008)

Applying POVM to Model Non-orthogonality in Quantum Cognition

Mojtaba Aliakbarzadeh and Kirsty Kitto[✉]

Queensland University of Technology, Brisbane 4000, Australia
{m.aliakbarzadeh,kirsty.kitto}@qut.edu.au

Abstract. Much of the work currently occurring in the field of Quantum Interaction (QI) relies upon Projective Measurement. This is perhaps not optimal, cognitive states are not nearly as well behaved as standard quantum mechanical systems; they exhibit violations of repeatability, and the operators that we use to describe measurements do not appear to be naturally orthogonal in cognitive systems. Here we attempt to map the formalism of Positive Operator Valued Measure (POVM) theory into the domain of semantic memory, showing how it might be used to construct Bell-type inequalities.

Keywords: Semantic memory · Bell-type experiments · POVM

1 The Problem of Projective Measurements

Much of the work currently occurring in the field of Quantum Interaction (QI) relies upon the standard quantum measurement process as exemplified by Projective Measurement. This is by no means surprising, most introductory texts on Quantum Mechanics (QM) deal only with projective measurements as most physical systems are well represented using this formalism. However, projective measurements are highly restrictive. They are also not straightforward to construct for a cognitive system. For example, in the program of research that uses the quantum formalism to model word associations and recall [4,5,17] we consistently find that the assumption of an orthogonal relationship between meanings is difficult to justify, and models are easy to construct only for special scenarios. It would be useful to have new approaches that did not make such strict assumptions about orthogonality between operators, but still exhibited the power of the quantum approach.

Luckily, the quantum formalism has already been provided with this extension. A Positive Operator Valued Measure (POVM) makes no assumptions about the orthogonality of two operators P_i and P_j, i.e. $P_i, P_j \neq \delta_{ij} P_i$, which means that suddenly we no longer need to frame measurements in a simple {*yes, no*} basis. This simplification of structure gives rise to many useful properties, that could perhaps be the first step in constructing a more realistic quantum model of cognition.

© Springer International Publishing Switzerland 2016
H. Atmanspacher et al. (Eds.): QI 2015, LNCS 9535, pp. 284–293, 2016.
DOI: 10.1007/978-3-319-28675-4_22

With a few notable exceptions [11,12], the QI community has not made use of POVMs very much to date. It is the purpose of this paper to demonstrate some of the key features of the POVM approach, and to then show a potential application in the modelling of word association data. Starting with a careful consideration of what we mean by a quantum measurement, we shall build up an understanding of Projective vs POVM approaches to the modelling of semantic memory. We shall see that the POVM approach lends itself very naturally to the description of many of the phenomena that occur every day in the modelling of human memory and cognition, leading us to posit that the approach is perhaps better suited to the field of Quantum Cognition (QC) than that provided by projections.

We start with a consideration of what exactly we mean by a quantum measurement.

2   Quantum Measurement

What is a quantum measurement? Although clouded as a philosophical concept, the quantum axioms are very clear. A quantum measurement takes on two key roles mathematically:

1. It specifies the probabilities related to the different possible measurement outcomes, and then,
2. it projects the state onto a new post-measurement state, as per the observed measurement outcome.

Why, when, and where exactly the measurement occurred are all up for debate [15], but as noted by many before us [3,18,19] the recipe to follow is quite clear.

Quantum measurements are usually represented by a collection of measurement operators $\{M_m\}$, where the index m indicates a set of possible measurement outcomes for some experiment. If we apply the measurement on a quantum system in the state $|\psi\rangle$, the probability of obtaining a specific result m is

$$P(m) = \langle\psi|M_m^\dagger M_m|\psi\rangle, \tag{1}$$

and the state after measurement becomes

$$\frac{M_m|\psi\rangle}{\sqrt{\langle\psi|M_m^\dagger M_m|\psi\rangle}}. \tag{2}$$

These measurement operators satisfy the completeness equation

$$\sum_m M_m^\dagger M_m = I \tag{3}$$

which simply means that their probabilities sum to one. This is a version of the standard law of total probability that is frequently used in QI.

2.1 Projection-Valued Measure (PVM)

A special important class of the general measurement is known as projective measurement. It is represented by an observable M (a Hermitian operator) which has a spectral decomposition

$$M = \sum_m mP_m, \tag{4}$$

where P_m is the projector onto the eigenspace of M with eigenvalue m. The probability of obtaining result m, after applying the measurement to a quantum system in the state $|\psi\rangle$ is

$$P(m) = \langle\psi|P_m|\psi\rangle, \tag{5}$$

and the state after measurement becomes

$$\frac{P_m|\psi\rangle}{\sqrt{P(m)}}. \tag{6}$$

Unlike general measurements in QM, projective measurements are repeatable, which means that if we get state $|\psi_m\rangle$ after the first measurement, repeated measurements will give the same result.

2.2 Is Repeatability a Sensible Requirement?

Repeatability is a very strong assumption for quantum cognition. We can start to understand this problem through a consideration of the standard Stern Gerlach type of repeated measurement as it is normally revealed in physics. For example, if a particle with spin traverses through such a detector it will either go 'up' or 'down'. Now, if we take one of the resulting beams (say the particles that went 'up') and send it through another Stern Gerlach device that is oriented in precisely the same direction as the first one then we *know* that the particles will *all* emerge from the second measurement in an 'up' stream. However, this does not point to an underlying 'element of reality'. If we had placed a third analyser in between the first and the second ones then the final measurement would have resulted in a mixture; some particles would go 'up' and some 'down'. This experiment shows us that physical quantum measurements are inherently *repeatable*; we can reasonably expect the same result to occur if we repeat the same experiment directly after a first one.

The same scenario can be easily found in cognition. Consider an example that was raised by Jerome Busemeyer during the panel discussion that occurred during QI'14:

> *For example, ask me a question... say "what do I want to do on the weekend?" I know what I want to do, ask me again, yep I still want to do it, again, yep nothing has changed. Now ask me what my **wife** wants to do on the weekend. Yep I know what she wants to do. Now ask me what I want to do again: Oops! It just changed. [NB: not a verbatim quote — a recollection due to KK]*

However, a different form of scenario is also possible. For example, it is possible to perform two cueing measurements in a row, using the same word, and there is no guarantee that the subject will always respond in the same way. It might be possible that the following sequence occurs:

$$\vdots$$

$$cue = SPRING$$
$$response = COIL$$
$$cue = SPRING$$
$$response = LEAF$$

$$\vdots$$

A PVM used in the standard quantum formalism would not be suitable for modelling such a situation. The state has been prepared, and we know that with no intervening measurements to realign the basis states the probability of returning COIL to the cue SPRING is equal to 1. However, the subject will not always conform to this repeatability requirement; in this case they return LEAF instead of the response predicted by a projective measurement (COIL).

Here we see a key problem for projective measurements. They are too strict in their requirement for repeatability.

3   Positive Operator-Valued Measure (POVM)

In contrast to projective measurements, the POVM formalism provides a means for obtaining the probabilities of a set of measurement outcomes, but without the assumptions of orthogonality and projection. In Eq. (1), suppose we define

$$E_m = M_m^\dagger M_m, \qquad \sum_m E_m = I, \tag{7}$$

where E_m is a positive operator. In this scenario the probability of obtaining the result associated with E_m is given by

$$P(m) = \langle \psi | E_m | \psi \rangle. \tag{8}$$

The complete set of E_m that define the probability of each measurement outcome is known as a *POVM*. If we want to use a density matrix $\rho = \sum_i |\psi_i\rangle\langle\psi_i|$ (for pure or mixed state) then this probability is given by the trace: $tr(E_m\rho)$.

The violation of repeatability that arises in POVMs is a key feature which makes them potentially much more natural when it comes to the modelling of cognition. It is also easy to recover the notion of projective measurement with some extra assumptions. Those POVMs whose elements are idempotent (meaning that $E_m^2 = E_m$ for all m), are the subset of special measurements that we discussed above: PVM. We can look at the relation between PVM and POVM from the other side; if for our projective measurement we have $P_m P_{m'} = \delta_{mm'} P_m$ and $\sum_m P_m = I$ then $E_m = P_m^\dagger P_m = P_m$ [18].

In addition to not requiring repeatability, POVMs have many other interesting properties. For example, Naimark's dilation theorem [9] implies that any POVM can be *lifted* by an operator map to a projection valued measure, which allows us to re-generate the standard representation that has been used in QI until now. We note that Khrennikov et al. [11] interpreted the additional degree of freedom required in this theorem as the mental environment for a decision maker, an intriguing move that deserves more investigation. Similarly, quantum tomography provides us with another potential application of POVMs to the field of QC. Here, a series of known states are used to measure an unknown state (in the case of QC this would be the cognitive state of a subject). As measurement can always be characterised by a set of POVMs, it is possible to reconstruct these characterising POVMs as a representation of the cognitive state of a person. Finally, POVMs are not necessarily diagonal, as is the case for standard projective observables. This opens up the possibility of interference between different measuring devices, a phenomenon that occurs all to often when one is attempting to measure the cognitive state of a subject. For now we shall defer these interesting issues to future work, and instead turn to a consideration of how this formalism can be utilised in the construction of Bell-type inequalities as we return to the question of whether interesting non-compositional behaviour can be demonstrated for the case of conceptual combination.

4   Complementarity in Bell-Type Inequalities

A common practice in QI is to use Bell-type inequalities as a test for different types of contextuality in cognition. Starting with the seminal paper of Aerts et al. [1], which proposed a simple scenario where two concepts might combine in a subject's mind, many have attempted to make use of the formalism (see e.g. [2,4,5,8,13]). However, Dzhafarov [7] has called attention to the importance of demonstrating that marginal selectivity is satisfied in cognition, which calls much of this work into question. After all, while physics has an established set of reasons (stemming from Special Relativity) to believe that two systems should be considered separate once they are taken 'far enough away' from each other, psychology has no such embedded principles of separability. Indeed it is more often the opposite scenario that holds, and we now understand the importance of demonstrating that a system 'should' be considered separable before revealing a violation of a Bell-type inequality. Thus, it is important to begin collecting more datasets, but before we do this we have an opportunity to re-consider the notion of measurement in detail.

Let us start by carefully considering one of the data collection processes that have occurred in the above body of work.

Bruza et al. [4,5] model words in memory as states in a Hilbert space, where the tensor products of these states demonstrate interactions between words. They provide experimental structures to test the existence of non-local effects between concepts which would indicate that they exhibit non-compositional behaviour. In this model, context is considered as a particular choice of a measuring apparatus as in the quantum realm. Bruza et al. [4,5] applied the CHSH inequality to the analysis of compositionality between two concepts A and B as a specific example of a Bell-type inequality. Concepts with dominant and subordinate *senses* are chosen for A and B, and these are indicated by the numbers 1 and 2. Human recall of these concepts can then be described by the random variables $\{A_1, A_2\}$ and $\{B_1, B_2\}$ which take values over $\{+1, -1\}$. When the dominant sense of concept A is first primed, and A is interpreted in that sense by the human subject, then it is designated as $A_1 = +1$. If A is not interpreted in that sense after priming of the dominant sense then $A_1 = -1$. Similarly, $A_2 = 1$ relates to situations where the subordinate sense of concept A is primed and a result is returned that matches with that priming scenario etc.

It is worth making some observations about this approach. First note that it requires a very careful choice of primes. The primes must be biambiguous (i.e. having two possible interpretations which indicate two different underlying senses), which is a very strong requirement. Human language is *rarely* so strictly interpreted, and even if two clear senses exist, it is commonly the case that putting them in a novel context will lead to the emergence of new senses and meanings. Language is inherently a 'high end' complex phenomenon [14]. A similar problem comes in the choice of measurement settings. The experiment is structured with an equal choice of the different settings, but it would be possible to relax this assumption and still approach the modelling of the system in a formalised manner. Thus, if a subordinate sense is very unlikely to occur, then more experiments that prime a subject towards that sense will be necessary to reach significance.

The underlying motivation of this article to extend this experimental scenario to a more general case.

We note that different probabilities of occurrence for varyious measurement settings is a straightforward thing to model in the POVM formalism. We denote the probability that prime A_1 will be used in an experiment by γ, and use $1 - \gamma$ to represent the probability that we will select prime A_2. In the POVM approach A_1 and A_2 are considered *jointly non-ideally measurable*. To understand what this means we will require a little more formalism, which we find in a definition provided by De Muynck [6].

Definition 1 [6]: *A POVM $\{M_n\}$ represents a* nonideal *measurement of the observable (POVM) $\{N_k\}$ (which is not necessarily a PVM) if the POVMs are related according to*

$$M_n = \sum_k \lambda_{mk} N_k, \qquad \lambda_{mk} \geq 0, \qquad \sum_m \lambda_{mk} = 1. \tag{9}$$

Definition 2 [6]: *Two observables M_m and N_k are simultaneously, or jointly* measurable *if a bivariate POVM R_{mk} exists such that*

$$\sum_k R_{mk} = M_m, \sum_m R_{mk} = N_k. \tag{10}$$

*and there is a measurement procedure for measuring the observable represented
by the POVM R_{mk}. They are jointly non-idealy measurable if instead:*

$$\sum_k R_{mk} = \sum_n \lambda_{mn} M_n, \sum_m R_{mk} = \sum_l \lambda_{kl} N_l. \tag{11}$$

Definition 2 implies that two measurements are simultaneously measurable if
a POVM R_{mk} exists such that the marginals of R_{mk} are nonideal measurements
of $\{M_n\}$ and $\{N_k\}$. Thus, the POVM formalism gives us a natural way of quickly
asking if measurements can be carried out simultaneously or not.

In Bruza et al. [4,5] measurements are represented by PVMs e.g. ($A_1 =
0, A_1 = 1$) and ($A_2 = 0, A_2 = 1$). Allowing n and m to range over the values
$\{+1, -1\}$ we can represent this set of PVMs as (A_1^n, A_2^m). This gives a joint
nonideal measurement of PVMs (A_1^n, A_2^m) that can be interpreted by a bivariate
POVM (R_{mn}^γ) [16]:

$$R_{mn}^\gamma = \begin{pmatrix} 0 & \gamma(A_1 = 1) \\ (1 - \gamma)(A_2 = 1) & \gamma(A_1 = 0) + (1 - \gamma)(A_2 = 0) \end{pmatrix} \tag{12}$$

with a joint probability of $p_{mn} = Tr\rho R_{mn}^\gamma$. Note that the top left hand corner
of this matrix is equal to zero because the subject can not be primed with two
senses for a word at the same time.

The marginals R_{mn}^γ are:

$$R_{mn}^\gamma = \begin{pmatrix} \sum_n R_{1n}^\gamma \\ \sum_n R_{0n}^\gamma \end{pmatrix} = \begin{pmatrix} \gamma & 0 \\ 1 - \gamma & 1 \end{pmatrix} \begin{pmatrix} A_1 = 1 \\ A_1 = 0 \end{pmatrix} \tag{13}$$

$$R_{mn}^\gamma = \begin{pmatrix} \sum_n R_{m1}^\gamma \\ \sum_n R_{m0}^\gamma \end{pmatrix} = \begin{pmatrix} 1 - \gamma & 0 \\ \gamma & 1 \end{pmatrix} \begin{pmatrix} A_2 = 1 \\ A_2 = 0 \end{pmatrix} \tag{14}$$

We can now construct a generalized Bell experiment, which can be considered a
joint nonideal measurement of four PVMs ($A_1^n, A_2^m, B_1^n, B_2^m$); the direct product
of the bivariate POVMs (12) of each concept leads to quadrivariate POVM,
which can be written as

$$R_{m_A n_A m_B n_B}^{\gamma_A \gamma_B} = R_{m_A n_A}^{\gamma_A} R_{m_B n_B}^{\gamma_B}. \tag{15}$$

De Muynck [16] suggests that a mutual disturbance of measurement results
(complementarity) would occur for each concept separately. This implies that
there is no disturbing influence on the marginals of one concept which arises when
we change the measurement settings for another concept. This is precisely the
meaning of non-contextuality in physics. This raises a possibility for constructing
a POVM driven model of contextual behaviour without making use of a non-local
effect. Essentially this would imply that violations of some sort of a separability
assumption would be due to an effect that was more akin to incompatibility.
Thus, violation would imply a system where the choice of one cue was shown to
influence the results obtained for another one, a classic scenario of contextuality.

This has been done already. De Muynck [16] constructed the quadrivariate probability distribution of a generalized Bell experiment as:

$$p_{m_A n_A m_B n_B}^{\gamma_{AB}} = Tr\rho R_{m_A n_A}^{\gamma_A} R_{m_B n_B}^{\gamma_B} \tag{16}$$

and used this relationship to conclude that complimentarity provides us with a local explanation for violations of Bell-type inequalities.

Thus, we see that a small interpretative difference arises in the POVM approach that we are proposing for QI. Whereas a violation of a Bell-type inequality might occur due to an influence that behaves non-locally [15], this formalism aims to discuss a different form of contextual influence. Specifically, this approach is grounded in the principles of complimentarity, and so Eq. (16) is considering two measurement arrangements, and asking if they might be considered to influence one another or not.

5   Non-signalling in a Bell-Type Scenario

As discussed above in Sect. 4, many QI teams have constructed Bell-type inequalities and then attempted to demonstrate their violation for a variety of different systems that are not traditionally deemed quantum. The familiar game involves defining a pair of outputs (a, b), pair of inputs (A, B), and then deriving a joint probability distribution

$$p(a, b|A, B). \tag{17}$$

This joint probability distribution satisfies non-signaling, which in the case of QC is taken to be marginal selectivity if

$$\sum_b p(a, b|A, B) = \sum_b p(a, b|A, B') \tag{18}$$

$$\sum_a p(a, b|A, B) = \sum_a p(a, b|A', B). \tag{19}$$

How does a POVM approach cover the same scenario? As Vertesi [20] has shown, if M_a^A and M_b^B are POVMs applied locally for Alice and Bob, then the joint probability distribution can be calculated as:

$$p(a, b|A, B) = tr(\rho M_a^A \otimes M_b^B) \tag{20}$$

where

$$\sum_m M_a^x = \sum_m M_a^x = I. \tag{21}$$

The probability distribution (20) always satisfies non-signaling [10]:

$$p(a|A, B) = \sum_b p(a, b|A, B) \tag{22}$$

$$= \sum_b tr(\rho M_a^A \otimes M_b^B) \tag{23}$$

$$= tr(\sum_b M_a^A \otimes M_b^B \rho) \qquad (24)$$

$$= tr(M_a^A \otimes \sum_b M_b^B \rho) \qquad (25)$$

$$= tr(M_a^A \otimes I\rho) \qquad (26)$$

$$= p(a|A). \qquad (27)$$

6   Concluding Remarks

This paper is a very tentative first step towards a more coherent and well formed approach to the modelling of semantic memory using POVMs rather than assuming projective measurements. We discussed the reasons why such a generalisation is desirable: (i) there is no guarantee that cognitive operators are orthogonal, (ii) cognitive experiments do not always lead to repeatable outcomes, (iii) POVMs are unsharp and so allow for a straightforward weighting of probabilistic choices of experimental setting. We have sketched out the structure that we think a POVM approach to modelling semantic memory will require, and made some observations about the behaviour that we would expect from the POVMs themselves.

This contribution is just a first foray into our investigation of the potentially rich seam of POVMs in the field of QC. We anticipate that with a more coherent and well founded formalism we might come to understand the incredibly complex process that is human semantic recall.

References

1. Aerts, D., Aerts, S., Broekaert, J., Gabora, L.: The violation of bell inequalities in the macroworld. Found. Phys. **30**(9), 1387–1414 (2000)
2. Aerts, D., Sozzo, S.: Quantum entanglement in concept combinations. Int. J. Theor. Phys. **53**(10), 3587–3603 (2014)
3. Ballentine, L.: Quantum Mechanics: A Modern Development. World Scientific, Singapore (1998)
4. Bruza, P., Kitto, K., Ramm, B., Sitbon, L.: A probabilistic framework for analyzing the compositionality of conceptual combinations. J. Math. Psychol. **67**, 26–38 (2015)
5. Bruza, P., Kitto, K., Nelson, D., McEvoy, C.: Is there something quantum-like about the human mental lexicon? J. Math. Psychol. **53**, 362–377 (2009)
6. De Muynck, W.M., Martens, H.: Nonideal quantum measurements, simultaneous measurement of incompatible observables, and the Bell inequalities. In: Proceedings of the 3rd International Symposium Foundations of Quantum Mechanics in the Light of New Technology: Central Research Laboratory, Hitachi Ltd, Kokubunji, Tokyo, Japan, 28–31 August 1989, p. 171 (1990)
7. Dzhafarov, E.N., Kujala, J.V.: Probabilistic contextuality in EPR/Bohm-type systems with signaling allowed. (2014). http://arxiv.org/abs/1406.0243

8. Dzhafarov, E., Kujala, J.: Selectivity in probabilistic causality: where psychology runs into quantum physics. J. Math. Psychol. **56**, 54–63 (2012)
9. Gelfand, I., Neumark, M.: On the imbedding of normed rings into the ring of operators in Hilbert space. Rec. Math. [Mat. Sbornik] N.S. **12**(54), 197–217 (1943)
10. Hirsch, F.: Hidden Nonlocality. Ph.D. thesis, University of Geneva (2013). http://cms.unige.ch/sciences/physique/wp-content/uploads/Travail-de-Master.pdf
11. Khrennikov, A., Basieva, I.: Quantum model for psychological measurements: from the projection postulate to interference of mental observables represented as positive operator valued measures. NeuroQuantology **12**(3), 324–336 (2014). http://www.neuroquantology.com/index.php/journal/article/view/750
12. Khrennikov, A., Basieva, I., Dzhafarov, E.N., Busemeyer, J.R.: Quantum models for psychological measurements: an unsolved problem. Plos One **9**(10), e110909 (2014)
13. Kitto, K., Ramm, B., Sitbon, L., Bruza, P.D.: Quantum theory beyond the physical: information in context. Axiomathes **21**(2), 331–345 (2011)
14. Kitto, K.: High end complexity. Int. J. Gen. Syst. **37**(6), 689–714 (2008)
15. Maudlin, T.: Quantum Non-locality and Relativity: Metaphysical Intimations of Modern Physics, Aristotelian Society Series, vol. 13. Blackwell publishers limited, Oxford, UK (1994)
16. de Muynck, W.M.: POVMs: a small but important step beyond standard quantum mechanics (2006). http://arxiv.org/abs/quant-ph/0608087
17. Nelson, D.L., Kitto, K., Galea, D., McEvoy, C.L., Bruza, P.D.: How activation, entanglement, and search in semantic memory contribute to event memory. Mem. Cogn. **41**(6), 717–819 (2013)
18. Nielson, M.A., Chuang, I.L.: Quantum Computation and Quantum Information. Cambridge University Press, Cambridge (2000)
19. Peres, A.: Quantum Theory: Concepts and Methods, Fundamental Theories of Physics, vol. 57. Kluwer academic publishers, Dordrecht (1993)
20. Vértesi, T., Bene, E.: Two-qubit Bell inequality for which positive operator-valued measurements are relevant. Phys. Rev. A **82**(6), 062115 (2010)

Author Index

Printed in the United States
By Bookmasters